## Praise for
### *Twilight Warriors*

"In his book *Prodigal Soldiers*, James Kitfield masterfully told the tale of how the post-Vietnam generation of officers rebuilt the US military and marched to victory in the Persian Gulf War. Now with the insightful *Twilight Warriors*, he tells the story of the next generation of American warriors as they confront the challenges of the twenty-first century, battling ISIS, Al Qaeda, the Taliban and other shadowy groups that are determined to take the fight to our own shores, and pose the deadliest threat to the civilized world."

—MARK THOMPSON, *TIME* Magazine

ALSO BY JAMES KITFIELD

*War & Destiny: How the Bush Revolution in Foreign
and Military Affairs Redefined American Power*

*Prodigal Soldiers: How the Generation of Officers Born
of Vietnam Revolutionized the American Style of War*

# TWILIGHT WARRIORS

★ ★ ★

THE SOLDIERS, SPIES, AND SPECIAL AGENTS WHO ARE
REVOLUTIONIZING THE AMERICAN WAY OF WAR

James Kitfield

BASIC BOOKS
New York

Books published by Basic Books are available at special discounts for bulk purchases
in the United States by corporations, institutions, and other organizations. For more
information, please contact the Special Markets Department at Perseus Books,
2300 Chestnut Street, Suite 200, Philadelphia, PA 19103, or call (800) 810-4145,
ext. 5000, or e-mail special.markets@perseusbooks.com.

*Designed by Linda Mark*

Library of Congress Cataloging-in-Publication Data

Names: Kitfield, James, author.
Title: Twilight warriors : the soldiers, spies, and special agents who are
revolutionizing the American way of war / James Kitfield.
Other titles: Soldiers, spies, and special agents who are revolutionizing the American
way of war
Description: New York : Basic Books, [2016] | Includes bibliographical references
and index.
Identifiers: LCCN 2016019611 | ISBN 9780465064700 (hardcover)
Subjects: LCSH: Strategic culture—United States. | United States—History, Military—
    21st century. | Intelligence service–United States–History—21st century. | Terrorism—
    Prevention—United States. | Special operations (Military science)–United States—
    History—21st century. | Interagency coordination–United States. | United States—
    Armed Forces—Officers. | United States. Federal Bureau of Investigation—Officials
    and employees. | National security–United States. | Military art and science—United
    States–History–21st century.
Classification: LCC UA23 .K5263 2016 | DDC 355/.033573–dc23 LC record
available at https://lccn.loc.gov/2016019611

10 9 8 7 6 5 4 3 2 1

*To Bobbie and David Kitfield, Sr., for teaching me to admire the warrior spirit;*
*to Ruste Murray Kitfield for the love of literature and my Irish half;*
*and to Lydia, Charlie and Travis for making me whole.*

# Contents

## PART III

*This is another type of war, new in its intensity, ancient in its origin—war by guerrillas, subversives, insurgents, assassins, war by ambush instead of by combat; by infiltration, instead of aggression, seeking victory by eroding and exhausting the enemy instead of engaging him. . . . These are the kinds of challenges that will be before us . . . if freedom is to be saved, [and they require] a whole new kind of strategy, a wholly different kind of force.*

PRESIDENT JOHN F. KENNEDY
Speech to the West Point graduating class
June 6, 1962

# Prologue
## The Brotherhood

AN OLD F-105 FIGHTER JET CLIMBS EVER SKYWARD ON ITS PEDES-
tal just inside the security gate of Joint Base Anacostia-Bolling. On August 7, 2014, the long row of flags lining the wide thoroughfare on the other side fluttered in a breeze off the nearby Potomac River. The sprawling 900-acre base is home to an alphabet soup of assorted military and intelligence units that operate around the nation's capital. Satellite dishes near some of the buildings are as big around as ice-skating rinks. Yet just past a gas station and a grocery store, the streets of nearby neighborhoods are lined with tidy houses and carefully manicured lawns, seemingly a typical American suburb just coming to life on a summer morning. Only the denizens of this cloistered suburb were at war, had been for over a decade, while the nation beyond the gates of the base so clearly was not.

The gleaming metal and glass superstructure of the Defense Intelligence Agency (DIA) headquarters rises above the smaller structures on Anacostia-Bolling like an aircraft carrier at dock. Clusters of well-dressed men and women were filing into its entrance past a marble wall inscribed with the message "Committed to Excellence in Defense of the Nation."

The guests were handed a color program and ushered into an atrium containing hundreds of seats. The retirement ceremony of Lieutenant General Michael T. Flynn, the director of the agency, was soon to begin. The program identified the masters of ceremony as James Clapper, the nation's top intelligence official and director of national intelligence; Admiral Michael Rogers, head of the surveillance behemoth the National Security Agency (NSA); and General Martin Dempsey, chairman of the Joint Chiefs of Staff (JCS).

The mandarins of the vast US national security apparatus were in attendance, its top soldiers, spies, and federal agents gathered under one roof to send one of their own into retirement, a man who without fear of contradiction would be extolled during the ceremony as the "best intelligence officer of the past twenty years." Many of them had come of age together as field commanders in America's post-9/11 wars, and had risen to the top of their various agencies and professions as secret sharers of the truths revealed there. They had all lost friends and innocence in roughly equal measure, and had sworn never again to let the magnetic pull of Washington bureaucracies or careerism divide them to the benefit of a relentless enemy. Given the nature of the intelligence business that united them, quite a few also knew that Mike Flynn's premature retirement wasn't entirely of his own choosing, and that his cogent and frank intelligence assessments hadn't always been warmly received down certain corridors of power in Washington. In that sense there was an undercurrent of tension in the festivities not evident to the casual observer.

As the longtime national security correspondent for *National Journal* magazine, I was familiar with Mike Flynn's backstory, and had wrangled an invitation to his retirement to look for some answers. Flynn had recently granted me his final on-the-record interview before leaving office. In it, he warned that the United States was actually less safe from the threat of terrorism in 2014 than it was prior to the 9/11 attacks, even after more than a decade of war, or what the George W. Bush administration had termed a "global war on terrorism." The latest and most blunt of a series of public warnings Flynn had issued over the past year, it was not embraced across the river at the White House, nor welcomed in certain offices in the Pentagon where steep budget cuts were justified. I strongly suspected this was another reason that Flynn would not serve out his full, anticipated three-year term at the helm of the Defense Intelligence Agency.

Some of the other major topics competing in a crowded news cycle in August 2014 included continued revelations about the National Security Agency's massive surveillance programs disclosed by former NSA contractor Edward Snowden, and a fight between the CIA and the Senate Intelligence Committee over the latter's upcoming report on the agency's alleged torture of terrorist suspects in the aftermath of 9/11. The day before, at least five suspected Islamist extremists associated with the deadly Haqqani terrorist network were reported killed by a CIA drone strike in Pakistan's North Waziristan region. In the Middle East, the Islamic State of Iraq and Syria (ISIS) was continuing the surprise offensive it had launched earlier in the summer, capturing roughly a third of Iraq after carving an Islamist caliphate out of war-torn Syria. US general John Campbell had recently been designated as the next top commander in Afghanistan, and tasked with bringing US troops home by the end of 2016 at the latest, ending the United States' post-9/11 wars. On Capitol Hill, hardline Republican insurgents were once again threatening to shut down the US government in response to the Obama administration's policy regarding tens of thousands of immigrants seeking asylum from cartel and gang violence in Latin America.

In short, the world looked like a chaotic and increasingly dangerous place in the summer of 2014, and the US government's response seemed feckless and distracted. As I took my seat in the DIA atrium and looked at the men and women seated around me, I knew that many of them were at the hidden center of those stories and events, and that the world illuminated in the headlines was in large measure one of their making. And I was curious what they thought about it all.

Some of those present I knew mainly by reputation, many I had interviewed before or covered in war zones, a few I socialized with on occasion. Theirs was largely a secret society, but if you put in the work, respected the ground rules, and shared some of the hardships, even a journalist was sometimes allowed inside the inner sanctum.

I had interviewed James Clapper, the intelligence czar, for an article on the unprecedented level of intelligence fusion that now routinely occurred across an intelligence community of sixteen agencies that included more than 200,000 operators, including 30,000 private contractors, stationed in more than 165 countries at a reported annual cost of more than $76 billion. The revolution in intelligence gathering that Clapper represented wouldn't have been possible if the 9/11 terrorist attacks hadn't broken down the walls that once separated foreign and domestic intelligence, as well as civilian and military intelligence agencies and operations. The post-9/11 intelligence reforms proposed by the 9/11 Commission and adopted by the George W. Bush administration had created Clapper's job of intelligence director, the single point man responsible for coordinating all intelligence. Those reforms and more than a decade of war had pulled the armed forces into a counterterrorism realm once dominated by intelligence and law-enforcement agencies, just as they had drawn the CIA increasingly into paramilitary operations. To grasp how intermingled US military and intelligence operations had become, you only had to consider that two defense secretaries in that timeframe were former CIA directors, and that retired general David Petraeus, who devised the counterinsurgency campaigns in Iraq and Afghanistan, had served as CIA director. Clapper himself was a retired US Air Force lieutenant general.

Overseeing that massive intelligence gathering enterprise, Clapper often seemed harried and grumpy, like the obstreperous uncle at holiday gatherings who insists the world is going to hell. Yet he was accessible and a straight shooter, which I found ironic considering that a sizeable group of lawmakers had recently written to the president demanding that Clapper be fired for lying to Congress, the result of a clever senator's needling him about classified intelligence during open testimony. The director had denied that the NSA wittingly collected any type of data on hundreds of millions of Americans, an assertion he was later forced to admit was "erroneous" after NSA leaker Snowden revealed the agency's collection of telephone metadata.

When I talked to him, Clapper insisted that the unusually close relationships at the top of the US national security apparatus reflected bonds forged in wartime and were essential to the new model of intelligence-driven, multiagency counterterrorism operations. "Over a decade of conflict, the merits and virtues of that model—working jointly to combine the capabilities of all of these discrete intelligence and military organizations into a whole that is greater than the sum of its parts—have gained traction with a new generation of operators who don't know anything else," he told me. "That's why I don't think we will ever walk it back, not that anyone would want to."

Another scheduled presenter at Mike Flynn's retirement was JCS chairman Martin Dempsey. Remarkably, Dempsey was the first chairman of the Joint Chiefs of Staff to actually have served and fought as a field commander during this longest period of war in the nation's history. I was embedded with his commands for extended periods a number of times during the Iraq War, and had witnessed the generalship and unflappable temperament that paved the way to the military's top job. I once watched Dempsey sing "New York, New York" to a room packed with officers and their spouses; he had both a fine tenor and a common touch with the troops. I had also stood beside him on the ridgeline of Little Round Top at Gettysburg battlefield, listening as he admitted to his staff that the same kind of fundamental disagreements on strategy that ultimately spelled defeat for the Confederate Army in the decisive battle of the Civil War had also divided the US Army's leadership during the Iraq War.

Dempsey was part of a select group of US division and task force commanders who had stared into the abyss in the early days in Iraq, returned later in 2007–2008 during the surge in a last, desperate attempt to snatch an acceptable outcome from the jaws of almost certain defeat, and then rose to attain four-star status where those lessons from Iraq could be disseminated and institutionalized. Other members of that unique class included Dempsey's West Point classmate David Petraeus and former Afghanistan commander and counterterrorism pioneer Stanley McChrystal. Another West Point classmate and four-star officer, General Keith Alexander, had played an outsize role in the post-9/11 wars as the director of the National Security Agency. Alexander had retired the previous year after a long tenure but under considerable public fire as a result of the Snowden controversy. The experience left him noticeably bitter. From his office in downtown Washington, Alexander recently told me that the counterterrorism threat indicators at the major intelligence agencies were starting to go dark as a result of the Snowden revelations, a warning that Clapper seconded.

In the front row sat General John Campbell, vice chief of staff of the US Army. Another West Pointer, Campbell had recently received his marching orders to bring the last US troops home. America was closing the chapters on its post-9/11 wars, and Washington and the public had in many ways already moved on. Yet Campbell's own son was still fighting in Afghanistan, a point he took pains to stress when I interviewed him about the army's postwar drawdown already well under way. Democracies are not suited to long wars, and it took a certain generosity of spirit to risk your own flesh and blood in a war that had become little more than background noise to the vast majority of your fellow citizens.

I also spotted Brian McCauley, the FBI's deputy assistant director for international operations, in the audience. Affable and always ready with a wisecrack, McCauley had spent so much time in Afghanistan networking with other law enforcement and intelligence agencies and military officials that some of his colleagues had dubbed him the "mayor of Kabul." Beneath his friendly exterior beat the heart of a hard-core field agent, one who had become adept at playing the deadly game of cat-and-mouse and double- and triple-cross that was central to counterterrorism operations.

Flynn's civilian boss, Michael Vickers, the undersecretary of defense for intelligence, was likewise at the retirement ceremony. Vickers was the one who pushed him out without letting Flynn complete the typical third year in command at DIA, having decided that in a Washington that was standing down from a wartime footing, Flynn's constant "shaking things up" had become too disruptive. The always turf-conscious CIA didn't care for Flynn's expansion of DIA's Clandestine Service, seeing it as an encroachment on its spying domain. The DIA bureaucracy didn't appreciate reforms that would upend comfortable lives in Washington. Flynn figured a little disruption was the cost of trying to institutionalize lessons from wars that the bureaucrats in Washington were already trying to forget. Still, one of the great unanswered questions of the past decade was whether the bottom-up revolution in warfighting that these combat veterans led, based on relationships and habits of intelligence-sharing forged in wartime, could survive as those wars ended and the bureaucracies reasserted themselves in a competition for scarce dollars. The shoddy treatment of Mike Flynn was not a promising harbinger.

LIEUTENANT GENERAL MIKE Flynn finally took the stage. A noted maverick and combat veteran who distinguished himself as the intelligence chief for Joint Special Operations Command (JSOC) during its seminal fight with al-Qaeda in Iraq, and later in Afghanistan, Flynn had taken the helm of the seventeen-thousand-member Defense Intelligence Agency with the mandate of Defense Secretary Leon Panetta to "shake things up." He wasted no time in applying the hard lessons of combat in reorganizing the agency, creating five intelligence fusion centers to support the war fighters in the field who were ever foremost in his thoughts. The centers would become major new nodes in the globe-spanning intelligence network, a direct outgrowth of the intelligence-driven, network-centric style of counterterrorism operations that he had helped pioneer under former JSOC commander General McChrystal. Flynn also significantly increased the size of DIA's Clandestine Service of spies collecting "human intelligence," pushing more of its operators and analysts out into the field where they could work alongside combatant commanders and develop relationships that facilitated cross-agency intelligence sharing, another key takeaway from Iraq and Afghanistan.

From the podium Flynn waved to his many family members in the crowd, sitting gathered around his wife and high school sweetheart, Lori. Dark-haired, with an aquiline face and a surfer's wiry build, Mike is a proud Irish American, one of nine children of Francis and Helen Flynn, the latter ailing but watching the ceremony via a video teleconference screen. Helen Flynn possessed an irreverent Irish wit and a salty mouth, and she raised her children with an immigrant's devotion to hard work, faith, and education. By way of example, she had gone back to school after all the kids were grown and earned a law degree at the age of sixty. Most of what you needed to know about the upbringing of the Flynn clan was that they all wore white socks in working-class Middletown, Rhode Island, kept in a "Flynn family sock basket," because honestly, with nine kids who in the hell had the time to sort socks?

His late father had been a career army sergeant, fighting in both World War II and Korea. Francis Flynn taught his sons by example that being a good leader was not about how tough or smart you were; rather, about whether you cared enough for your troops to show them kindness and grace when they inevitably needed it. When Michael and later his brother Charlie told their father they, too, were joining the army, he didn't hide his pleasure at the news. As Mike Flynn recounted at his retirement ceremony, Francis Flynn told his sons, both of whom would improbably rise to the rank of general, "the name of 'soldier' is the proudest name anyone can bear."

Mike Flynn thanked the military commanders in the audience, including former Eighteenth Airborne Corps commander Dan McNeill, a mentor to both himself and McChrystal. He choked up addressing the families who had lost loved ones in the war, promising to honor and never forget their sacrifices. At a recent private retirement dinner I had seen Flynn deliver a similar message: We are here for a reason, and have laid down our lives for the cause of protecting this country and preserving what is good in it for our children and grandchildren. We are duty bound to keep America safe from an evil that would take away the freedoms we hold dear.

In his call-out to colleagues in attendance, Flynn made special note of Stanley McChrystal: "If there was any one individual in this country who changed the way America fights its wars, it was Stan," he told the capacity crowd. As JSOC's former commander and chief intelligence officer, respectively, McChrystal and Flynn really had pioneered a new style of warfare. At JSOC, the war-fighting subcomponent of the larger US Special Operations Command, they incubated a new model of military operations that relied on an unprecedented synergy that developed in the war zones between the Special Operations forces, intelligence and law enforcement agencies, and conventional military forces.

AFTER THE OFFICIAL ceremony, I saw Stanley McChrystal at the end of the reception line. He was tall and quiet and thin to the point of looking drawn, but there was something about him that always made him seem like the adult in any room he entered. Many in the public knew McChrystal best from the controversy prompted by a *Rolling Stone* article entitled "The Runaway General." The article quoted unnamed staff as making disrespectful comments about Vice President Joe Biden, and led

President Barack Obama to publicly relieve McChrystal of command in Afghanistan at a critical moment in the war. He was replaced by General Petraeus, the hero of the Iraq surge, who himself was later forced to step down as the director of the CIA because of revelations concerning an extramarital affair and the unauthorized release of classified information to his biographer and lover. Inside military and intelligence circles it was understood that Petraeus and McChrystal were the preeminent generals and wartime field commanders of their generation of officers, and the manner of their dismissal stuck in many a craw. As did the treatment of Mike Flynn.

The model of operations that McChrystal and Flynn helped pioneer was most closely associated in the public mind with drone strikes and the publicity surrounding Operation Neptune Spear and the killing of Osama bin Laden. Certainly it had little to do with the nation-building the United States conducted to help steer Iraq and Afghanistan on the road to democracy, and it was only one element of the manpower-intensive counterinsurgency operations that came to define those conflicts. Nor did McChrystal and Flynn see it as a war-winning model at the strategic level of conflict between nation-states and armies, or even against terrorist groups entrenched in failing societies. Rather, it was an enabler, a way to buy time for other instruments of American power to prove decisive, if the US government still had the will to employ them. At its hot core, that new American-style of warfare was predicated on hunting individual terrorists and other extremists who hid in the dark corners of the world, and in plain sight as well.

The intense battle rhythm behind that new style of warfare was unlike anything that had come before it. In the early years in Afghanistan and Iraq, McChrystal's Task Force 714 had launched an average of four or five targeted raids a month, looking for "high-value targets." At the height of the fighting five years later, they were launching dozens of raids each night, and hundreds every month. The intelligence-driven network that enabled, organized, and controlled all of that lethal action continued to grow more layered, its reach and data banks constantly expanding, and the hundreds of thousands of people that kept it pulsing became more tightly wired and connected with each passing year. By 2014 JSOC's style of operations had become, as Stan McChrystal once told me, the "Amazon.com of counterterrorism."

JSOC's multiagency joint task forces and intelligence fusion centers that combined the skills of many disparate players into a unified, mission-focused whole had become the new normal. That streamlined model greatly condensed the traditional military-targeting cycle of "find, fix, and finish" by constantly incorporating intelligence "exploitation and analysis," creating what the counterterrorism community called an F3EA style of operations, where the lines between intelligence gathering and operational targeting disappeared. The relentless demands of that new style of operations explained major reorganizations of DIA and the CIA, and the NSA's storage of vast amounts of electronic metadata in search of "patterns of life" among terrorists and their networks.

As the last US combat troops prepared to exit Iraq and Afghanistan and the government wound down the unpopular post-9/11 wars, the emerging US counterterrorism model centered on grafting that unique skill set—rapid network-centric operations by joint task forces and Special Operations Forces, advanced ISR (intelligence, surveillance, and reconnaissance), and precision strike power from the air—to enable local allies and proxies, much as the United States was already doing in such places as Somalia and Yemen.

I had witnessed that new style of warfare in Iraq and Afghanistan, in secret Special Operations Forces training and strike bases in Africa, and in intelligence fusion and drone operations centers inside the United States and overseas. I heard the mantra of the counterterrorism manhunt echo through a globe-spanning intelligence network, elegant in its simplicity and terrifying in its lethality: Find. Fix. Finish. Exploit. Analyze. And Reload.

What I didn't know was the answer to the big question: was the F3EA model of operations against discrete terrorist targets enough to keep the nation safe? The search for answers to that and related questions animates this book. Was the Islamist extremism that invaded these shores on September 11, 2001, sufficiently weakened or demoralized by a decade of war and global counterterrorism operations that the United States could now fight only from the air and in the shadows, without boots and reliable local partners on the ground, and without heavy-lifting nation-building to drain the swamps that breed extremism? What measure of security had the nation purchased with more than ten years of fighting in Afghanistan and Iraq?

What would become of this new war-fighting model once the originators passed from the scene, and the bonds of trust they had woven began to fray under peacetime pressures? The answer to those questions are revealed in the stories behind the unique brotherhood that gathered at DIA headquarters on August 7, 2014.

I WAS INTERESTED in the fraternity of soldiers, spies, and special agents that gathered for Mike Flynn's retirement primarily because the close relationships and bonds they forged in combat helped birth a new operational style of war. But I was also intrigued by what they represented. What united them to a person was a keen sense of duty to their country, and in that they were an apt metaphor for the less than 1 percent of citizens who had fought their nation's post-9/11 wars.

Self-selected over the decades since the abolishment of the draft in 1973, the all-volunteer, professional US military likewise hailed disproportionately from the working class and the heartland. Typically they are the sons and daughters not of Wall Street hedge-fund managers or the Northeast elite, or of the high-tech entrepreneurs on the West Coast, but of working-class cops, teachers, firefighters, and especially other soldiers. One 2007 US Army survey found that the 304 general officers in the army had 180 children serving in uniform, making military service something of a family business. By contrast, of the 535 members of Congress, the country's political elite, fewer than a dozen had children in uniform. By 2014 this wartime brotherhood was at the helm of a modern all-volunteer force that had largely become what its creators originally envisioned decades earlier—a truly professional army, with high degrees of competence and expertise in the increasingly sophisticated weaponry and tactics of modern war. By most quantifiable measures of discipline, reliability, education, and capability, it was arguably the best the United States had ever fielded.

The original architects of the all-volunteer force in 1973 could never have imagined, though, that the US government would treat it like an American Foreign Legion, sending the force to fight on its own for a decade without mobilizing the country with a draft or a full and sustained call-up of the reserves, or imposing so much as a war tax. That new compact between citizens and soldiers, where there is no shared duty to defend the country, created a sense of separateness and a dangerous perception gap, whether it was Congress's shrugging off dire warnings from Dempsey and the other joint chiefs about the harm in precipitous budget cuts, and ignoring Clapper and the intelligence community's advice against stringent post-Snowden surveillance restrictions, or the White House's dismissing Mike Flynn and the counterterrorism community's warnings about the growth in Islamist extremist groups. That gap between the nation and its defenders raises important questions that I also hope the life stories of these men will help answer.

Finally, there was the intriguing matter of genealogy to consider in trying to understand this unique brotherhood of warriors. Certainly the backstories of many of those present at the retirement ceremony or leading US security services were immigrant tales, full of deprivation and the kind of grit and determination that drives families forward as those traits are passed through the generations. Which is to say, quintessentially American stories. Of course, their backgrounds traced in many different directions, to include prominently David Petraeus, son of Sixtus Petraeus, a Dutch sea captain who commanded a Liberty ship for the United States during World War II. And then there were Flynn, McChrystal, Dempsey, McCauley, Campbell, McNeill, Mulholland, McRaven, Kelly. That the ranks of senior US national security officials read like an Ellis Island logbook during the 1840s potato famine was not lost on its membership, nor altogether coincidence. Some of them even joked about it, calling themselves part of a modern "Irish Brigade."

As Terry Golway notes in *The Irish in America*, the Irish have a long military tradition in the United States, tracing back to George Washington's Continental Army. During the Civil War newly minted Irish immigrants joined the armies on both sides of the conflict in such large numbers that the Union and Confederate armies formed Irish brigades. The wave of Protestant Scots-Irish immigration that began in the early 1700s also produced more than its share of soldiers, who composed roughly 40 percent of the Revolutionary War army, as noted in *Born Fighting* author, senator, and Vietnam veteran Jim Webb's paean to his own Scots-Irish ancestors.

Notable American military figures of Irish and Scots-Irish descent include the pioneers and Indian fighters Daniel Boone, Davy Crockett, and General Philip Sheridan; Civil War commanders Stonewall Jackson and Ulysses S. Grant; World War I hero Sergeant Alvin York; and General George Patton and Medal of Honor recipient Audie Murphy, the most decorated soldier of World War II. You could add to that long list General William "Scott" Wallace, who I embedded with as he led the 2003 invasion of Iraq, and who was the descendant of William Wallace of *Braveheart* fame.

At the reception following Mike Flynn's retirement, I came upon the FBI's Brian McCauley, who was joking about the modern "Irish Brigade" with retired general Dan McNeill, the former top US commander in Afghanistan. McNeill quipped that his ancestors were Scots-Irish, and would probably have been Irish if the Irish and Scottish hadn't managed to lose the Wars of the Three Kingdoms in the 1600s. "Look around at the bunch of us Micks," McCauley joked, ticking off the names of some of the senior officers and officials at the reception. "We sound like a lineup of the Westies gang."

I LEFT MIKE Flynn's retirement ceremony with McCauley, waiting as he stopped to shake hands with just about everyone we passed. Flynn and McCauley were especially close friends, and on weekends they often met for breakfast at Bob & Edith's Diner near the Pentagon. Their discussions of growing up as Irish American kids in nearby neighborhoods in Rhode Island, where families tended to be working class and their children were sent to Catholic schools, were often hilarious. Even though Flynn had grown up in a small house full of brothers and sisters, McCauley liked to kid him that the Flynn clan came from the better side of the tracks in Middletown where they ate watercress sandwiches instead of the mayonnaise variety favored by the McCauley kids. In their stories of Rhode Island virtually everyone was a cop, a soldier, a crook, or a corrupt politician.

Weeks before the retirement ceremony, I had joined McCauley and Flynn for breakfast at Bob & Edith's. The mood had been far more somber than usual. The offensive juggernaut launched by Islamic State extremists had rolled through much of Iraq and was threatening Baghdad. McCauley had requested that the FBI team be evacuated from the US embassy, but the ambassador was afraid that it would look like a routed retreat—which it would soon become absent quick action. Flynn said the military attaché in Baghdad had been warning about the rapidly deteriorating situation for more than seven months, but no one in Washington much heeded reports about what was happening in Iraq anymore.

Later, as McCauley and I were leaving Flynn's retirement ceremony, it occurred to me that JCS chairman General Martin Dempsey had been scheduled to present at the event, but he had canceled at the last minute. The cancellation was a shame, as everyone hoped he'd sing "Danny Boy" and bring the auditorium to tears. Later that same day, August 7, 2014, the reason for Dempsey's absence became clear when President Obama announced that US war planes had begun bombing Islamic State targets and flying humanitarian relief missions inside Iraq. So, the US military was officially going back to Iraq as part of the global war against radical Islamic terrorists. It was starting all over again.

# PART I

# ONE

# Where There's Smoke

## 1998–2001

M EMBERS OF THE FBI FIELD TEAM WERE SHUFFLING IN THE DAMP chill, rubbing their arms and clutching Styrofoam cups of hot coffee in an effort to keep warm. Dawn announced itself weakly on a wet, overcast day. The rural land outside Frederick, Maryland, is hill country, where the Catoctin Mountains spill onto the coastal plains, thick with forests and open fields and ravines with noisy streams. It is tough land, and the weather was miserable for an evidence search, the kind of unglamorous grunt work that is rarely depicted in movies and television shows about life in the FBI. The field team was waiting around for some gear to arrive so it could begin its search.

Lights approached in the gloom on the mostly deserted country road, and as the vehicle drew near the team leader noted to his surprise that it was a US Army Humvee. It pulled up to the group of civilians and a soldier in combat fatigues got out. "So, which one of you is General McCauley?" he asked. The FBI team leader looked at Special Agent Brian McCauley and got the shrug and smile that they were all coming to know so well.

"I told you, boss, I got a guy I know," said McCauley. Turns out the "guy" was a senior officer in the Maryland National Guard, who was more than happy to lend a hand in a real-world FBI evidence search as a way to log some monthly drill time. What never failed to astound his FBI teammates was that McCauley always seemed to "have a guy" to fit every occasion. He was a one-man networking machine with a seemingly inexhaustible Rolodex. McCauley hopped in the open rear bay of the Humvee, pulled out a cigar, and with a typical grin announced that the search could commence.

When McCauley had reported for duty at the bureau for the first time on Saint Patrick's Day 1997, the FBI was still an old-school criminal investigative organization focused primarily on bringing perpetrators to justice after the fact of a crime. J. Edgar Hoover would have recognized its straitlaced, G-man culture that still valued face-to-face interviews and interrogations over written reports, and shoe-leather detective work over technical finesse. If the bureau tended not to play particularly well with others, it was big enough that it didn't have to.

Only the end of the Cold War had unleashed forces and rapidly evolving threats that were outpacing such mammoth and slow-moving US government bureaucracies as the FBI. The phenomenon of globalization and rapid advances in information-age technology were eviscerating national borders and shrinking distances, blurring traditional lines between what constituted an international versus a domestic threat. Transnational drug cartels, hackers, spies, and especially international terrorists were crossing those boundaries and exploiting with impunity the gaps between US law enforcement, intelligence, and military jurisdictions. And the FBI that McCauley joined in 1997 had been slow to react.

At that time McCauley was already thirty-six years old and on his third career. He was a natural team player, an Irish American kid from a working-class neighborhood of immigrants in Providence, Rhode Island, where he had played basketball for St. Patrick's High School. He was one of five siblings, including a brother who was an "Irish twin," born less than a year apart. His mother had sent young Brian to Our Lady of Providence Preparatory Seminary in hopes of steering him toward the priesthood. Her plans were dashed the instant her son first laid eyes on young Rose Kelly. Ultimately, McCauley's ticket out of Providence was the same punched by his dad, and his grandfather, and his maternal great-grandfather before that, all of whom had joined the US Marine Corps. On his wall McCauley kept his honorable discharge right alongside that of his father, the dates thirty-four years apart almost to the day. Legendary Secret Service agent Tim McCarthy, who had taken the bullet for Ronald Reagan, had helped McCauley get on with the uniformed Secret Service. Then McCauley had returned to Boston to be near his ailing father, taking a job with the US Marshall's Service and attending night school at a satellite campus of Notre Dame, where students jokingly called themselves the "Fighting Nuns."

From the outset of his FBI career, McCauley had experienced the joy of someone who discovers late the work he was meant to do, the meshing of FBI organizational culture and his personality practically seamless. He wasn't one to write long reports or detailed analyses, but the FBI at the end of the 1990s was still more of a spoken-word kind of operation focused on shoe-leather investigations, takedown arrests, and successful prosecutions. He could charm the keys off a jailer, and he had an instinct and bias for action that perfectly suited the demands of FBI work. As one of his colleagues put it, you sometimes had to step on Brian McCauley's foot to stop him from making the most inappropriate comments imaginable, but he had also seen McCauley literally drive over the foot of a fleeing suspect rather than let the man escape.

There was a confluence between McCauley's career at the FBI and the rise of increasingly deadly terrorist attacks that had some analysts writing about the "Age of Superterrorism," and it would ultimately transform both his life and the bureau he loved. In his earliest days on the job, he had been assigned to a multiagency Joint Terrorism Task Force in Washington, DC, investigating a fund-raising operation run out of the Northeast in support of the Irish Republican Army (IRA). That investigation led him to what was known as the *Valhalla* case, a twisted scheme of gun-running and treachery that revealed the dark side of the tightly knit Irish American community in the Northeast, as well as the dangers that lurked at the shadowy intersection of transnational criminal cartels and terrorism.

The *Valhalla* was a 77-foot fishing trawler operating out of the hard-scrabble port of Gloucester, Massachusetts, where Irish mobster James "Whitey" Bulger used it to smuggle narcotics and run guns to the IRA.

Back in 1984 the *Valhalla* had transferred 7 tons of weapons and ammunition worth $1 million to an IRA boat named the *Marita Ann*. Thanks to an informant, the *Marita Ann* was intercepted by the Irish Navy before it could distribute to IRA gunmen a cargo of rockets, submachine guns, rifles, handguns, bulletproof vests, and seventy thousand rounds of ammunition. One of the crewmen on the *Valhalla*, John McIntyre, was later picked up by police and interrogated by drug enforcement officials, and he agreed to turn informant and reveal the links between the Irish mob in Boston, drug trafficking cartels, and the IRA.

Unfortunately for McIntyre, that information was eventually shared with FBI agent John Connolly, another first-generation Irish American, who had befriended Bulger as a kid on the tough streets of South Boston and was secretly funneling him intelligence, protecting the Irish mob boss from investigations into as many as nineteen murders. Weeks after talking with the Drug Enforcement Administration (DEA), McIntyre disappeared. He wasn't heard of again until 1999, when Whitey Bulger's lieutenant, Kevin Weeks, led investigators to his remains in a makeshift grave in Dorchester so as to lessen his own racketeering charges.

As a kid McCauley had always heard the Irish Republican Army romanticized as "freedom fighters," and it was an open secret that many wealthy Irish Americans gave them money for the cause of freeing Northern Ireland from British rule. But the *Valhalla* case and his subsequent investigations opened McCauley's eyes. IRA operatives were training in Libya right alongside other members of the global terrorist pantheon, including the Palestinian Hamas and the Lebanese Hezbollah. The IRA operatives were also early pioneers of the car bomb, a devastating weapon used repeatedly by the group to indiscriminately murder scores of Irish men, women, and children. The fact that the IRA was also in league with a murderer and mobster like Whitey Bulger, who had infiltrated and compromised McCauley's beloved FBI, only underscored his growing conviction that they were just another band of vicious killers hiding behind a supposedly noble cause and purifying ideology.

As he worked the IRA investigation with the multiagency Joint Terrorism Task Force, McCauley was struck by the fact that none of the many US intelligence agencies sat at the table crowded with local, state, and federal police agencies. In particular, he had virtually no contact with CIA operatives and analysts who ostensibly were responsible for tracking foreign terrorist groups, such as the IRA. That disconnect was largely the result of US laws that purposely erected a wall between domestic and foreign intelligence gathering, and between law enforcement and military operations. Those laws were part of groundbreaking reforms of the mid-1970s resulting from investigations into intelligence abuses by the Church and Pike Committees in Congress. Evidence collected by the committees and investigative journalists back then revealed myriad abuses, including CIA assassination and coup plots against such foreign leaders as Fidel Castro of Cuba, Patrice Lumumba of Congo, and Salvador Allende of Chile; CIA dossiers on more than ten thousand US citizens; FBI spying on antiwar dissenters and civil rights advocates; and National Security Agency domestic spying. As a result of the Church and Pike investigations, Congress established the Senate and House Select Committees on Intelligence to conduct oversight of the intelligence agencies, and passed the 1978 Foreign Intelligence Surveillance Act (FISA), requiring court approved warrants for national security wiretaps.

For all the good intention, these walls of separation enabled the IRA and other terrorist organizations to thrive in the gaps between US law enforcement, intelligence, and military jurisdictions. Some, including the IRA as well as al-Qaeda, also had tentacles that reached deep into the US homeland. It was while working on the *Valhalla* case that Brian McCauley first began to wonder what it would take to finally overcome the cultural and bureaucratic barriers that prevented US law enforcement and intelligence agencies from jointly confronting a common enemy.

BY THE LATE 1990s, increasingly lethal attacks by shadowy Islamic terrorist groups—to include the 1993 bombing of the World Trade Center that killed six civilians and injured more than a thousand, the 1996 bombing of the Khobar Towers housing complex in Saudi Arabia that killed nineteen American servicemen, and the devastating 1998 bombings of the US embassies in Kenya and Tanzania that killed more than two hundred people and wounded thousands—had exposed the gaps and disconnects between stove-piped US intelligence and law enforcement agencies. Nowhere were concerns about those disconnects more acute than at the CIA's campus in Langley, Virginia, and the FBI's J. Edgar Hoover Building in Washington, DC.

Over decades the CIA and the FBI had built cities on separate hills, and by their own admission they stared across a largely impassable gulf of cultural ignorance, mistrust, and downright disdain. Whenever the two agencies were forced to work together—an increasingly common occurrence in the post–Cold War thaw during the 1990s, with criminal cartels and transnational terrorist groups trampling the borders between their jurisdictions—CIA and FBI agents clashed openly and often, with the former playing to type as tweedy Georgetown intellectuals, and the FBI agents coming across as blue-collar beat cops.

Even in the field and on overseas postings, the two stubborn tribes often seemed to spend as much time competing with and even undermining each other as they did chasing bad guys. From the point of view of CIA station chiefs at US embassies overseas, who often served as an ambassador's point person on major strategic issues, the FBI legal attachés at the embassy seemed to rank somewhere just above chauffeur in the embassy hierarchy. "They had very little international experience or foreign language capability, and their main concern seemed to be catching fugitive bank robbers," a senior CIA official told me at the time, talking about his FBI counterparts. "It was almost embarrassing."

Given a CIA culture that prized the care and cultivation of sources and golden nuggets of secret information, CIA station chiefs were also disdainful of the FBI's focus on gathering evidence and building criminal indictments so as to prosecute perpetrators in open trials. Never mind that the counterterrorism strategy the United States followed throughout the 1980s and 1990s was to bring terrorists to justice before US courts, with the possibility of tough sentences in US prisons or even the death penalty.

For their part, FBI special agents who worked for the Justice Department and were the primary enforcers of the nation's laws tended to view their CIA counterparts as rogues and scofflaws, chronically stretching the rules until they broke, and operating overseas outside any recognizable legal regime. Never mind that covert activities ordered by the president and overseen by congressional intelligence committees, even if they broke foreign laws, were a legal and a critical tool of the US government. More to the point, the FBI agents sensed acutely the disdain and Ivy League arrogance of their CIA counterparts, and they returned it in kind.

The keystone cops routine between the nation's premier intelligence and law enforcement agencies might almost have been amusing if foreign intelligence agencies and transnational criminals and terrorists weren't increasingly exploiting the legal and cultural barriers between them.

Largely as a result of miscues that enabled the spying of CIA agent and Soviet mole Aldrich Ames, the Clinton administration had instituted in 1994 sweeping reforms designed to close the dangerous gap in operations and culture between the CIA and FBI. In a move that would have been heresy prior to Ames, Presidential Decision Directive 24 placed a senior FBI official in charge of counterespionage—the spy-versus-spy operations at the heart of the Ames scandal—and located him inside CIA headquarters in Langley, Virginia. The reform also established the National Counterintelligence Center at the CIA—run by an FBI official—to take on the broader mission of protecting American secrets and assets. The idea to trade counterterrorism and counterespionage deputies between the agency and the bureau was referred to unlovingly as the "hostage exchange program."

By decade's end it was also abundantly clear that the transnational threat on which the fortunes of the CIA and FBI would be tied most closely was international terrorism. Although the US counterterrorism strategy in the 1990s centered on law enforcement, that goal required cooperation between the CIA operatives responsible for surveillance and infiltration of foreign terrorist groups overseas, and FBI agents tasked with making arrests and gathering evidence that could be used in court.

As a result, FBI and CIA agents increasingly found themselves thrust into ad hoc joint task forces to go after specific targets, usually after an attack or incident. Some of the early successes of these joint task forces offered a glimpse of the synergy possible in field teams that, in their enthusiasm and desire to accomplish a common mission, put aside their differences and overcame institutional barriers, at least temporarily. Such joint task forces were responsible for apprehending and successfully prosecuting the terrorist cell responsible for the 1993 World Trade Center bombing, an attack designed to topple the North Tower of the trade center into the South Tower and kill untold thousands. The ringleader in that attack was Ramzi Yousef, a Kuwaiti who had spent time in an Afghanistan training camp run by the shadowy Islamist terrorist group al-Qaeda. Yousef's uncle was Khalid Sheikh Mohammed, who at the time was considered a dangerous freelance terrorist.

In 1997 FBI and CIA agents also successfully tracked down Mir Aimal Kansi, the gunman who killed two CIA employees in a 1993 attack outside the main gate of their headquarters in Langley. Other joint apprehensions in the 1990s included Omar Ali Rezaq, for the hijacking of an Egyptian Air flight in which fifty-eight people died; Mohammed Rashid, for the 1982 bombing of a Pan Am flight; and Tsutomu Shirosaki, for a rocket attack against the US Embassy in Jakarta.

One of the most successful preemptions of a terrorist plot came with the Y2K terrorist operation, a massive plot hatched by al-Qaeda involving planned attacks in multiple countries designed to kill thousands of people. Alerted to attacks that were planned to coincide with the turning of the clocks on the new millennium, CIA and FBI officials worked with foreign intelligence and police services to disrupt al-Qaeda cells in eight countries, with arrests made in the United States, Jordan, Pakistan, and Canada. The plot fizzled, and both the FBI and CIA communities breathed a collective sigh of relief.

If al-Qaeda and Osama bin Laden were deterred by the disruption of a major plot and the apprehension of many top operatives from earlier attacks, however, it didn't show. On October 12, 2000, two al-Qaeda operatives piloted a small boat toward the US Navy warship USS *Cole*, anchored in the Yemini port of Aden. Hassan al-Khamri and Ibrahim al-Thawar pulled their explosives-laden boat alongside the *Cole*, waving at the sailors and making friendly gestures right up until the moment they ignited the explosives, obliterating themselves in a blast that also killed 17 US sailors, wounded 40, and very nearly sank a US Navy ship of the line. When the United States mounted no counterattack, al-Qaeda leader Osama bin Laden was reportedly frustrated, and vowed to launch an even bigger attack to goad the superpower into lashing out in a way that would spark his longed-for war between Islam and the West.

Meanwhile, the steady drumbeat of sophisticated terrorist attacks sounded warning alarms in Washington, DC. A congressionally mandated report by the National Commission on Terrorism released in 2000 faulted both the CIA and FBI for being "overly risk averse" and insufficiently aggressive in investigating terrorist organizations. The House Select Committee on Intelligence released its own scathing assessment of the US intelligence community the same year, faulting it for poor organization and calling for a more corporate approach to intelligence gathering that included the entire intelligence and national security complex. The Senate Appropriations Committee, citing the FBI's lack of adequate focus on new threats, approved funds to establish a new domestic counterterrorism "czar" at the highest levels of the Justice Department. The idea never got off the ground.

By the late spring and early summer of 2001 the various threat warning systems of the FBI and CIA as well as the National Security Council's Counterterrorism Security Group started blaring in unison, reaching a deafening crescendo by midsummer. National Security Council counterterrorism coordinator Richard Clarke warned the White House that he was tracking six separate intelligence reports on al-Qaeda personnel talking about a pending attack that, in one typical description, would be "very, very, very, very" big. Clarke stressed that there were al-Qaeda terrorist cells already within the United States, and he was especially worried about reports indicating that Abu Zubaydah, suspected as a major planner of al-Qaeda's millennium plots, was cooking up another spectacular for the near future. The headline of a June briefing to top officials stated, "Bin Laden Planning High-Profile Attacks." The FBI Counterterrorism Division sent a message to federal agencies and state and local law enforcement, noting an increased potential for al-Qaeda attacks abroad, though it stressed the bureau had "no information indicating a credible threat of terror attack in the United States." The CIA briefed Attorney General John Ashcroft that al-Qaeda's preparation for multiple attacks, presumably overseas, were "in the late stages or already complete."

As the threat reporting built to a climax in late July, with CIA director
George Tenet noting that the entire system was "blinking red," the intelligence chatter about an imminent al-Qaeda attack abruptly stopped. The
circuits of the intelligence network went largely silent, though there was at
least one report that an attack had only been postponed by a few months,
not abandoned altogether. A vast counterterrorism system seemed to stand
momentarily down.

At the FBI Counterterrorism Division, Chief Dale Watson felt in his
bones that the danger had not passed, even though the threat reporting was
so nebulous, describing an apparition whose shape kept shifting and could
only be guessed. FBI field offices were tracking down seventy al-Qaeda–
related leads, but in reality Watson only had a handful of analysts at headquarters devoted full-time to the al-Qaeda account. For its part, on August
6, the CIA delivered a Presidential Daily Brief to the White House entitled
"'Bin Laden Determined to Strike the U.S.," though the evidence it offered
was mostly historical.

As the threat reports surged in the late spring and early summer of
2001, "John," a CIA official attached to the FBI's International Terrorism Section, began reexamining old surveillance photos and communications intercepts from a key January 2000 meeting of senior al-Qaeda
operatives in Kuala Lumpur. The cables indicated that an al-Qaeda operative, Nawaf al-Hazmi, had been in Los Angeles in January 2000, and
another, Khalid al-Mihdhar, had a US visa that stated his intention to
travel to New York.

Remarkably, "John" did not feel he could share that intelligence with
the FBI counterparts he worked with daily. He did give three surveillance
photos from the Kuala Lumpur meeting to a joint FBI-CIA task force working the USS *Cole* bombing. He also asked an FBI analyst detailed to the
CIA's bin Laden unit to review the Kuala Lumpur materials one more time.
That FBI analyst soon realized that there was no record that al-Hazmi had
ever left the United States, and Immigration and Naturalization Service records showed that al-Mihdhar had entered the country on July 4. Al-Qaeda
had come to America.

The FBI analyst "Jane" saw to it that al-Mihdhar and al-Hazmi were added to the TIPOFF watch list, a compilation of some sixty-one thousand suspected terrorists that is supposed to alert authorities whenever any of them enter or leave the United States. She also issued a lead alerting FBI field offices to be on the lookout for the men. An FBI field office agent also involved in the *Cole* case read the lead and contacted "Jane" looking for more information, but because he was designated as an FBI agent working criminal rather than intelligence cases, he was blocked by an internal intelligence-sharing "wall" from seeing the information. Furious, the FBI field agent fired off a prescient reply: "Whatever has happened to this—someday somebody will die—and wall or not—the public will not understand why we were not more effective and throwing every resource we had at certain 'problems.'"

It was during this period that FBI field agents began noticing that individuals with alleged ties to al-Qaeda were enrolling in flight schools in the United States. Noting the "inordinate number of individuals of investigative interest" doing so in Arizona, an FBI agent in the Phoenix field office sent a memo to headquarters warning of the "possibility of a coordinated effort by Usama Bin Laden [*sic*]" to send students to the United States to attend civil aviation schools. The memo was buried in the clutter of reporting between FBI field offices and the agency's headquarters in Washington. No managers would see it until after September 11.

At the same time, the FBI field office in Minneapolis was investigating a man with "jihadist beliefs" who was taking flight training in Minnesota. After an interview in which Zacarias Moussaoui became extremely agitated when questioned about his religious beliefs, the FBI agent concluded that he was "an Islamic extremist preparing for some future act in furtherance of radical fundamentalist goals." Moussaoui was arrested on immigration violations on August 17, 2001, and agents at the FBI field office sought a special warrant to search his computer under the Foreign Intelligence Surveillance Act. That required showing probable cause that Moussaoui was an "agent of a foreign power," however, and FBI headquarters doubted he rose to that level of threat. The Minneapolis field office supervisor was criticized by an FBI supervisor for trying to get people "spun up" about Moussaoui. "That's precisely my intent," the Minneapolis supervisor replied.

"I'm trying to keep someone from taking a plane and crashing into the World Trade Center."

On August 23, CIA director George Tenet was filled in on the Moussaoui case in a briefing titled "Islamic Extremist Learns to Fly." Because there was not yet a clear connection between Moussaoui and al-Qaeda, Tenet decided to let the FBI handle the case. As a result the CIA failed to track down intelligence overseas that would soon be unearthed by Britain's MI-6 foreign intelligence service, indicating that Moussaoui had attended an al-Qaeda training camp in Afghanistan, and to share that information with FBI agents who could have interrogated him again armed with new information. Nor did Tenet feel it necessary to discuss the case with anyone at FBI headquarters or in the White House.


"JUST FOLLOW THE smoke." The car carrying Brian McCauley and another FBI special agent raced from the FBI headquarters building near the Capitol Building and along the grassy expanse of the National Mall. A billowing plume of black smoke loomed ominously over white marble monuments still gleaming in an otherwise clear morning, the leading edge of an encroaching shadow. There was a report that the State Department had been hit, but as they closed on Foggy Bottom, the FBI agents saw that the smoke was drifting from across the Potomac River, and they turned toward the nearest bridge.

The fires were burning uncontrollably when McCauley reached the partially collapsed western diagonal of the Pentagon, and wreckage and human detritus from American Airlines Flight 77 were strewn across parking lots and nearby lawns. All 64 people aboard the airliner had been instantly killed on impact, and 125 military personnel and Defense Department civilians would die inside the building. Fire trucks, police and sheriff cars, and emergency response vehicles were converging from numerous jurisdictions, everyone rushing to try to help the scores of seriously injured people who lay on the ground or were staggering from the burning building, some of them on fire.

The FBI agents rushed to help the wounded, triage taking precedent over evidence collection. The Arlington County Fire Department was acting as the incident commander on scene, but McCauley had watched on television as two other airliners hit the World Trade Center towers in New York. Everyone understood this was a terrorist attack, which meant that the FBI was the lead federal agency officially in charge as the Justice Department's on-scene representative. This was now a crime scene investigation, one that McCauley could not have conjured in his own worst nightmares.

Some of the FBI special agents who would work twelve-hour shifts at the Pentagon crash site for weeks were familiar with the drill, having investigated the terrorist bombings of a US Air Force barracks at Khobar Towers, Saudi Arabia, in 1996; the US embassies in Kenya and Tanzania in 1998; and the attack on the warship USS *Cole* in Yemen in 2000. But picking through the smoldering wreckage in the heart of the nation's capital, recoiling from the unspeakable sights and smells on home soil, was an altogether more disorienting experience. No first responder on September 11, 2001, had any doubt that war had come home to America.

FOR BRIAN MCCAULEY and many other first responders, the 9/11 attacks struck close to home. They were connected by family or friendship to the more than 340 New York City firefighters and medics and the roughly 60 police officers killed at the Twin Towers site. They knew personally many of the 184 people killed at the Pentagon. The FBI lost one of its own when John Patrick O'Neill, until very recently the special agent in charge of the FBI's National Security Division in New York, and arguably the nation's most dogged investigator of al-Qaeda's string of terrorist attacks, died in one of the Twin Towers. O'Neill had only started his new job as chief of security at the World Trade Center the previous month. His insights into the nature of the al-Qaeda threat were spot on, and later would be captured in a book about his exploits: *The Man Who Warned America*.

In the frantic days and weeks after 9/11, McCauley was assigned to a special joint terrorism task force targeting the perpetrators of the attack, and tasked with foiling any follow-on plots. The deaths of more than three thousand civilians in the worst attack on the homeland since Pearl Harbor had inalterably skewed the known universe. Everyone understood it was a game changer. For CIA and FBI officials who had failed to share critical intelligence that might have foiled the attack, it was a defining moment, a chance to recalibrate a still dysfunctional relationship and work together to exact retribution. Everyone threw themselves into the manhunt with grim resolve.

Every special agent and intelligence operative was querying their network of sources for possible clues. McCauley learned of an Arab man who received a money transfer from the Middle East and left the money exchange in a red Volvo with a dented fender. An FBI colleague queried car rental agencies that rented Volvos and had cars overdue for return, which led them to the dented red Volvo that Hani Hanjour, Khalid al-Mihdhar, and Salem al-Hazmi (brother of Nawaf) had driven from the Marriot Residence Inn in Herndon, Virginia, to Washington Dulles International Airport on the morning of September 11, before hijacking American Airlines Flight 77 and flying it into the Pentagon.

The investigation into the hijackers' movements in northern Virginia led to the Dar al-Hijrah mosque in Falls Church. Both al-Hanjour and al-Hazmi had met the new imam, Anwar al-Awlaki, at Dar al-Hijrah before, when he was preaching at a mosque in San Diego. The US-born imam was a charismatic speaker and professed moderate who offered himself as a useful "bridge" between US authorities and the American Muslim population in the immediate aftermath of the attacks. McCauley and other FBI investigators privately suspected he had a role in the 9/11 plot, but they were unable to prove it during multiple interviews. Al-Awlaki was eventually dropped as a person of immediate interest.

During the investigation McCauley became friendly with Steve Gaudin, a wiry FBI agent with sandy hair and a quick, lopsided grin. Gaudin was assigned to the Joint Terrorism Task Force in New York, but had been dispatched to the special bin Laden project run out of Washington headquarters immediately after 9/11. As McCauley was soon to learn, the profane former Special Forces paratrooper from Boston arguably knew more about al-Qaeda than did any other agent in the FBI. Just that summer, Gaudin had also become the first FBI agent to complete the Arabic language course at Middlebury College, Vermont, a timely credential that was soon to pay high dividends.

He had been one of the FBI agents who deployed to Kenya in August 1998 in the aftermath of the bombing of the US embassy in Nairobi, one of the most devastating terrorist attacks in history up to that point. So little was known about al-Qaeda at the time that the US investigators weren't sure who exactly was behind the attacks, nor what their connection was to Osama bin Laden. As luck would have it, as part of the investigation Gaudin had interrogated a suspect in the bombing.

After reading the suspect his Miranda rights, Gaudin employed what FBI agents refer to as their "Mountain Dew" interrogation techniques, slowly winning a suspect's cooperation by subtle stroking of his ego, piecing together his story looking for holes and inconsistencies, and then gently prying at these until the story cracked. In the case of the self-professed Yemeni arrested in Kenya, he stuck to his story for nearly a week, and then on August 20, 1998, the truth came tumbling out in a torrent.

His real name was Mohamed Rashed Daoud al-Owhali. He was a Saudi from a wealthy family who had been trained in explosives at al-Qaeda's Khalden training camp in Afghanistan. Osama bin Laden had handpicked him to be part of the "martyrdom" operation in Nairobi.

The capture of a senior al-Qaeda operative and would-be suicide bomber was the biggest break to date in the US efforts to decipher the web of relationships that undergirded al-Qaeda's globe-spanning network. Steve Gaudin had built a rapport with the terrorist in countless interviews. In the three years it took to build a federal case against the conspirators in the embassy bombings, Gaudin went from knowing almost nothing about the inner workings and relationships at the core of al-Qaeda to arguably knowing as much or more than anyone in the US government.

When he was dispatched to FBI headquarters and the special bin Laden project after 9/11, his understanding of al-Qaeda proved invaluable. Al-Owhali had reportedly tipped off US investigators to the 2000 Kuala Lumpur al-Qaeda summit, where plans for both the USS *Cole* attack and the 9/11 plot were thought to have been finalized. That summit was the target of a hard stare, a focused and sustained surveillance operation involving a panoply of surveillance platforms operated by US intelligence agencies. Early in Gaudin's interrogation of al-Owhali, the terrorist had surrendered the telephone number he called before executing the embassy bombing mission, which was eventually traced to Yemen, to the father-in-law of Khalid al-Mihdhar, one of the 9/11 hijackers.

The 9/11 attacks were a watershed for the FBI and CIA, offering an opportunity to finally leave their bureaucratic jealousies and squabbles behind. For a time their cooperation was never better. Yet when word came in March 2002 that Pakistani authorities, working with the CIA, had captured suspected senior al-Qaeda operative Abu Zubaydah, the CIA's bin Laden unit "Alec Station" worried that transferring him to the new military detention center at Guantánamo Bay, Cuba, would risk losing control of the prisoner to the US military system or the FBI, where interrogators would likely be under much stricter legal constraints and required to alert the International Committee of the Red Cross. As a result, Zubaydah was transferred to the first CIA secret prison that was hastily created in Thailand in March 2002 to receive the suspected terrorist.

The FBI immediately dispatched Steve Gaudin, along with Special Agent Ali Soufan, a Lebanese American and top counterterrorism expert who spoke fluent Arabic. Before boarding the airplane they were told to leave behind any Miranda forms, and to forget about writing up notes from the interrogation. Their purpose was not to build a case for prosecution; rather, to obtain any information that might stave off the next 9/11-like terrorist strike. In fact, in the infamous August 6, 2001, Presidential Daily Brief titled "Bin Laden Determined to Strike in U.S.," Zubaydah was specifically mentioned as having been closely involved in the Y2K terrorist plot and as someone planning further attacks on the United States.

In February 2002, President George W. Bush had signed an executive order to the effect that the Geneva Conventions, which prohibit "mutilation, cruel treatment and torture," did not apply to captured members of al-Qaeda or the Taliban, the regime of Islamic extremists who had ruled Afghanistan and provided sanctuary to bin Laden prior to 2001. Gaudin and Soufan were told they were to augment a CIA-led interrogation of an enemy combatant. When they arrived in Thailand, neither FBI special agent yet had any inkling that they were about to become the focal point of a controversy that would shatter the post-9/11 détente between the FBI and CIA and drive a wedge between the two agencies.

For McCauley, who would soon be swept up in the debate over who best to interview suspected terrorists, the controversy over interrogations pointed to a more profound problem. It wasn't just the different cultures and traditions of the various US agencies suddenly thrown into the fight. They lacked a common understanding of the strengths and weaknesses that each of them brought to the effort. The threat demanded a new style of counterterrorism operations based on synergy, the whole of their collective efforts being greater than the sum of its parts. The initial decision to put inexperienced spies and low-ranking and poorly trained soldiers in charge of interrogations was the opposite of synergy. Before it could be overcome, that ignorance would send the "global war on terrorism" down a dead-end alley that rekindled tensions between the CIA and FBI, and darkened the reputation of the United States for many years to come.

# TWO

# Another Kind of War

## October 2001–May 2002

Big John Mulholland stood on the wind-swept tarmac of a bleak former Soviet airbase in Uzbekistan in mid-October of 2001, the weight of America's response to the 9/11 attacks having fallen disproportionately on the broad shoulders of the Green Beret. Karshi-Khanabad Air Base, or K-2, had recently become the headquarters for Task Force Dagger. Helicopters and prop aircraft bristling with armament and antennas cycled through a nearly constant rotation of takeoffs and landings, creating a backwash of wind, thunderous noise, and the acrid stench of jet fuel. The armada before Mulholland operated mostly at night, and was rarely seen in public: chubby MH-53 Pave Low search-and-rescue helicopters; converted MC-130 Combat Talon transports bristling with 40 mm cannons and a Gatling gun; sleek MH-60 Black Hawks and the big, twin-rotor MH-47 Chinooks. Combined, they were the razor edge of the sword of Damocles that the United States was lifting over the heads of Osama bin Laden and Mullah Omar, the one-eyed mujahedeen and commander of the Taliban. And Colonel John Mulholland had been chosen to wield it.

A few weeks earlier, Mulholland was simply the commander of the Fifth Special Forces Group out of Fort Campbell, Kentucky, in charge of roughly 315 Green Berets broken down into twelve-man A-Team detachments, one of seven such Special Forces Groups in the wider US Army. By mid-October he was in command of Task Force Dagger, responsible for operations throughout all of Afghanistan and tasked with toppling the Taliban regime, routing al-Qaeda, and capturing Osama bin Laden. Seemingly in an instant Mulholland had been elevated to a level of command for which he had never trained, operating in a land about which he knew virtually nothing, fighting among allies and enemies that he could hardly tell apart. The eyes of a wounded nation were on him, and personally he found it all massively intimidating.

Mulholland was the Irish American son of a fighter-bomber pilot and veteran of the Korean War, and two of his uncles had also served as combat aviators. As is so often the case, the instinct for military service had been passed down in the family's DNA. Since boyhood he had known he wanted to be a soldier. From high school he went to college in South Carolina to play football. On one of his first days on campus a big redneck asked, "Which side are you on?" Mulholland was confused until he realized the guy was talking about Yankees and Rebels. When he gave the wrong answer, the redneck and a bunch of his friends pummeled him mercilessly, dishing out the worst beating of his life. He was saved when another big Irish guy and a stocky German came to the rescue. The next day the redneck asked the same question, and got the same answer in reply. Mulholland took his beating, but he never changed his answer.

The fact that a relatively low-ranking full colonel from the Special Forces had been chosen to command the United States' initial response to the 9/11 terrorist attacks and for a time take responsibility for an entire operational theater of war was virtually unprecedented. That watershed decision reflected both the unusual nature of President George W. Bush's declared "global war on terrorism" and Defense Secretary Donald Rumsfeld's predilection toward Special Forces.

Rumsfeld's team in the Office of the Secretary of Defense were forceful advocates behind the idea of a "revolution in military affairs," or RMA in military-speak. The concept held that advances in information-age technologies and precision airpower were changing the fundamental nature of warfare, making it possible to couple advanced US air and space power with lightly armed forces on the ground to achieve an unprecedented level of lethality and military effectiveness. Landlocked Afghanistan seemed an apt test case for that revolution, given the country's inaccessible terrain and notoriously fractious tribes. The Afghan tribes' reputation for fighting among themselves was only exceeded by the ferocity they had historically shown in repelling invaders. Rumsfeld and US Central Command commander General Tommy Franks figured that was a good argument for keeping the footprint of US forces on the ground small.

As a colonel in the Special Forces, Mulholland had no experience commanding a joint task force headquarters that included representatives of the Army, Air Force, Navy, and Marines. Special Forces were traditionally accustomed to operating behind the scenes in support of those conventional forces. He was even more concerned about going into Afghanistan blind. The hallmark of the Green Berets was an ethos that included immersion in the cultures and tribal dynamics of the areas within which they operate. Older and more experienced than conventional troops, they spent years learning the languages and getting to know the key players and operators in various geographical theaters. Unfortunately, the US command authorities had washed their hands of Afghanistan after the Soviet army withdrew in the late 1980s, having entered the country in 1979 to backstop a communist puppet regime. US Central Command, to which Fifth Special Forces Group was attached, was focused on the Middle East area of operations.

In terms of scope and command authority, the Afghan mission given to Mulholland and the Fifth Special Forces Group was unprecedented. The marching orders seemed custom designed to agitate resentments among conventional force commanders who ruled all the armed services, whose general view of Special Forces was memorably summarized by former army chief of staff Harold Johnson, who called the Green Berets in Vietnam "fugitives from responsibility." Yet the situation and the enemy they would confront in Afghanistan were remarkably true to the vision of the man considered by many as the father of modern-day Special Forces.

WHEN PRESIDENT JOHN F. Kennedy took office in 1961, the Cold War struggle between liberal democracies and communism was threatening to turn hot on multiple fronts. The Soviet Union's 1957 launch of Sputnik, the first satellite successfully sent into low-earth orbit, badly shook the confidence of the US national security establishment. In 1960, the Soviets had shot down a U-2 spy plane over their territory, capturing CIA pilot Francis Gary Powers. Tensions were flaring again in Berlin, where tens of thousands of East Germans were defecting to the West each month, and where US and Soviet tanks were facing off on opposite sides of a barbed-wire fence that within months would be fortified into the Berlin Wall. In Asia, communist China and North Vietnam supported a communist insurgency that was threatening South Vietnam, giving rise to the US doctrine of pushback based on the domino theory, the idea that if one Southeast Asian country was allowed to fall to the communists, others would rapidly topple in turn. Later in 1961, Kennedy would sign a military and economic aid treaty with South Vietnam.

The communist threat was even encroaching into the United States' backyard. Cuba's revolutionary leader Fidel Castro was nationalizing US companies, spouting anti-American rhetoric and moving into a closer alliance with the Soviet Union, foreshadowing the Cuban missile crisis of 1962. Under Eisenhower's direction the CIA had already trained and armed the group of Cuban exiles that early in Kennedy's first year in office would launch the ill-fated attack on the island that became the Bay of Pigs fiasco.

Given a nuclear weapons arms race that was gaining momentum, the United States could ill afford direct confrontations that routinely threatened to turn the Cold War into a nuclear Armageddon. As the two superpower blocks jockeyed for advantage in critical regions around the world, Kennedy foresaw instead a series of proxy and small wars, which inevitably drew his attention to the few thousands of volunteers in the US Army Special Forces.

The Special Forces were established in the early 1950s during the Korean War, but their lineage traced back to the World War II Office of Strategic Services (OSS), a precursor to the CIA that was charged with coordinating spying activities behind enemy lines. The OSS deployed three-man Jedburgh teams deep into Nazi-occupied territory to help organize and support partisan militias, such as the French Resistance. US Army Special Forces also had an antecedent in Ranger units in World War II; these unconventional light infantry units sometimes worked behind enemy lines in both the European and Pacific theaters, going under the monikers of their commanders, with such names as "Darby's Rangers" for Major William Orlando Darby, and "Merrill's Marauders" for Brigadier General Frank Merrill. Their mission of working behind enemy lines, conducting sabotage, and organizing local militias and resistance groups was institutionalized in 1952 with the formation of the US Army's Tenth Special Forces Group. Although there was only one unit numbering a few thousand soldiers, it was called the Tenth Group in hopes that the Soviets would conclude there were many more where these tough men came from. The soldiers specialized in airborne tactics, psychological warfare, and cultural expertise in the regions where they operated. The motto of the group was "De Oppresso Liber" (To free the oppressed).

As commander in chief, President Kennedy viewed US Army Special Forces as the epitome of the kind of troops needed to fight the unconventional wars to come. In that sense modern-day US Special Operations Forces (SOF) were birthed shortly after ten a.m. on June 6, 1962, in the field house of the US Military Academy, where Kennedy shared his vision of a new kind of warfare with the West Point graduating class. The president rejected the idea then in vogue that nuclear weapons had made land wars obsolete, and he presciently foresaw a long, twilight struggle ahead against an enemy that would try and impose death by a thousand cuts, "seeking victory by eroding or exhausting" the United States rather than engaging it. Such a patient and pernicious enemy, Kennedy recognized, required a new strategy and a very different kind of military force.

Rarely has a US leader's vision been more rapidly realized than Kennedy's call for a "wholly different kind of force" to fight another kind of war. The president backed his idea in both deed and symbol, promising $100 million to strengthen US Special Operations Forces and unconventional warfare capabilities. The increased attention and resources for unconventional warfare coincided with the United States' deepening involvement in the counterinsurgency war in South Vietnam—US Special Operations Forces were the first troops that Kennedy would deploy to the conflict. He also for the first time authorized the wearing of the previously banned green beret that SOF troops had traditionally received on graduating from a grueling commando training course administered by Britain's famed Special Air Service (SAS). Kennedy called the green beret "a mark of distinction," sealing in that moment the bond between the brash young president and the Special Operations Forces.

THERE'S NO DOUBT that the Rumsfeld Pentagon saw the "global war on terrorism" as just such a conflict as Kennedy envisioned—new in its intensity, ancient in its origin, war by insurgents and terrorist assassins bent on exhausting the United States rather than engaging it, preying on ethnic conflict—and thus believed that Special Operations Forces would have an outsize role in prosecuting it. And so, just days after 9/11, Colonel John Mulholland was running four of his A-Teams, or Operational Detachments Alpha, through a crash course on Afghanistan, conducting a compressed mission planning and rehearsal cycle in anticipation of a deployment. Since the CIA had the most institutional memory of the players inside Afghanistan from its long ties to the Afghan mujahedeen, they sent a top analyst to help bring the Fifth Special Forces Group up to speed with the latest developments there.

After getting the green light, Mulholland deployed Fifth Special Forces Group in mid-October 2001. He quickly began pairing his A-Teams with various warlords and tribal factions that were willing to fight the Taliban, which came from the Pashtun tribe dominant in the south and east. The legendary leader of the anti-Taliban Northern Alliance, Ahmed Shah Massoud, had been killed weeks earlier by al-Qaeda assassins, clearly in anticipation of a US response to 9/11. Massoud's successor, Fahim Khan, was eager to join the fight. Another Northern Alliance fighter, General Abdul Rashid Dostum, was a warlord and leader of Afghanistan's Uzbek community, and he had also fought the Taliban in the 1990s. Yet several of the proposed warlords concerned Mulholland because they were known to have radical Islamist leanings and were dependably anti-Western. Although he pushed back against forming alliances with the most questionable warlords, the final decision was made far above his paygrade. The operational imperative was apparently "the enemy of my enemy is my friend."

After the weather repeatedly delayed their operations, Task Force Dagger was able to insert most of its A-Team detachments by the end of October, and they made an immediate impact on the fighting and anti-Taliban air campaign. Once A-Teams were embedded, the disorganized Northern Alliance forces showed greater tactical discipline and direction. Each A-Team included one or two CIA operatives and an Air Force Special Operations Command combat air controller, the team's critical link to US airpower. US Air Force combat controllers were outfitted with portable global positioning satellite (GPS) receivers, laser target designators and a handheld device featuring a digital map display, and a digital radio to communicate directly with the Combined Air Operations Center (CAOC) at Prince Sultan Air Base in Saudi Arabia via a satellite data link. The combat controllers enabled the Green Beret A-Teams to call in air strikes against Taliban troop formations that were positioned dangerously close to friendly forces. They would "rack and stack" a dozen or more aircraft circling overhead and then talk their pilots' eyes onto Taliban positions in a process they called terminal attack. These US Air Force joint terminal attack controllers (JTACs), represented an unprecedented level of air-ground integration on the battlefield. The Special Forces A-Teams became so dependent on the air controllers that they began referring to them as their personal American Express cards: "don't leave home without him."

With the images of the 9/11 attacks vividly in mind, the A-Teams and CIA paramilitary forces shared a sense of common purpose not always evident in their quarrelsome relations. The failed attempt to rescue American hostages in Iran back in 1980 had created suspicions among Special Forces that the CIA had withheld critical intelligence from them. There was also a natural competitiveness between the elite groups owing to the fact that a majority of the CIA paramilitary troops were former Special Forces operators themselves.

The success of the US commando units in organizing fractious warlords and spearheading offensives on Taliban strongholds quickly paid dividends. The joint commando teams of Fifth Special Forces Group were effective as the conduit to US airpower, and at times even rode horseback and took part in cavalry charges on Taliban positions.

Despite concerns about the vulnerability of A-Teams' being thrown into an extremely chaotic and uncertain fight, Mulholland was soon able to report marked progress in his daily video teleconference with US Central Command (CENTCOM) headquarters at MacDill Air Force Base, Tampa, Florida. Perhaps the greatest attribute of US Special Forces is their ability to thrive outside their comfort zone and adapt to a fluid situation, not only with courage, but also creativity. Mulholland's A-Teams had been inserted into alien and dangerous country in the middle of the night, and the next day were fighting alongside people they had just met. Looking across a vast cultural chasm, the Green Berets and the tough Afghan warlords experienced the recognition of fellow warriors with a common enemy. For a time at least, that recognition was enough to bind them in combat.

With Mulholland's A-Teams calling in heavy air strikes on the Taliban's defenses on the outskirts of Mazar-i-Sharif, destroying hundreds of enemy vehicles and bunkers, and killing or causing thousands of Taliban fighters to flee, the city fell on November 9, 2001, marking the first victory of Operation Enduring Freedom in Afghanistan, the initial front in the Bush administration's "global war on terrorism." Four days later the capital of Kabul fell, and by early December the Taliban was losing its grip on its stronghold of Kandahar in the south. With al-Qaeda's terrorist infrastructure largely destroyed and its leadership's fleeing to the mountains, US airpower, several hundred Special Forces ground troops, and a handful of CIA paramilitary and their ad hoc allies were on the cusp of toppling the Taliban regime and routing al-Qaeda. The only unmet objective was capturing Osama bin Laden. For a brief, shining moment the revolution in military affairs seemed real, and America's enemies were fleeing before its seemingly invincible power.

THE AIR FORCE officer conducting the air war over the heads of Mulholland's Fifth Special Forces Group was a man with a vision. Like a maestro with baton in hand, Air Force Major General David Deptula orchestrated the air war of Operation Enduring Freedom. Each day Deptula stood before the giant video screens in the cavernous Combined Air Operations Center at Prince Sultan Air Base. Stretched out on the floor of the 70,000-square-foot facility were scores of computer stations in stacked rows, each manned by a mission specialist and connected to a global command-and-control system and an aerial armada unlike any ever assembled. Long-range bombers, tactical fighters, airborne command-and-control and electronic warfare and surveillance aircraft, midair refuelers—all circled above landlocked Afghanistan just weeks after the September 11 terrorist attacks.

Deptula was considered one of the preeminent airpower theorists of his generation of officers, a strategic thinker in the mold of General William "Billy" Mitchell, the airpower advocate regarded as the father of the US Air Force. He had spent much of his career contemplating next-generation uses of airpower. A decade earlier, in 1991, Deptula had been the de facto air planner for Operation Desert Storm. His performance in that conflict—one of the most lopsided victories in US military history—explained why he had been chosen to coordinate the air war over Afghanistan.

Deptula had something of the air of the passionate professor. He had earned a master of science degree in national security strategy at the National War College, along with other advanced degrees in warfighting, systems engineering, and science from the Armed Forces Staff College, the Air Command and Staff College, and the University of Virginia. In the student lounge, the soft-spoken and studious Deptula might have been mistaken for an adjunct professor, his theories about advances in the technologies of airpower representing a "revolution in military affairs" intriguing if slightly futuristic and far-fetched.

Like most of the US Air Force leaders who had been groomed since the 1980s, Deptula was a fighter pilot and a member in good standing with the fighter mafia that still ruled the service. He clocked nearly 3,000 hours in F-15 fighters, more than 400 of which were flown in combat. He had also graduated from the elite Fighter Weapons School, the Air Force's version of *Top Gun*. If Deptula came off like a well-mannered professor, there was one critical distinction: he routinely turned theory into practice, and if you were an enemy of the state, he would slit your throat in a heartbeat.

At Prince Sultan Air Base in 2001, Dave Deptula marveled at how precision-guided munitions and stealth technology had improved exponentially in the decade since Desert Storm. A second-generation B-2 stealth bomber was able to accurately destroy twenty targets on a single bombing sortie, representing a dramatic improvement over bombers' dropping unguided bombs. The relatively new Joint Direct Attack Munition (JDAM), provided an all-weather precision guidance system utilizing GPS technology.

Advances in the realm of reconnaissance and intelligence were even more dramatic, and Deptula was frustrated that the Air Force had yet to realign itself to leverage those advances. Instead, it continued to function as a group of interlocking "fiefdoms," distinct communities representing strategic nuclear missiles and bombers, tactical fighters, air transport and midair refueling aircraft, space systems and satellites, and reconnaissance and surveillance aircraft and systems. The vital mission of intelligence gathering did not even rate having its own major command. Perhaps the most dysfunctional wall was the one that separated operators from intelligence gatherers. He remembered vividly how during Desert Storm intelligence shops had clung to a methodical, Cold War mind-set that required three days just to conduct bomb damage assessments. Surveillance planes at that time took photographs on film that had to be developed at a common processing facility and then flown to the intelligence center, where they were then carefully analyzed and, only when absolutely necessary, hand-carried to and shared with units and command nodes that had a declared "need to know."

Worst of all the Cold War hangovers in Deptula's mind was the attrition-based mentality that held that little had been accomplished until everything had been destroyed. Deptula had read Sun Tzu's *The Art of War*, embracing the wisdom in the adage that "the supreme art of war is to subdue the enemy without fighting," and certainly not to slug it out with the enemy in a knife fight on ground of his choosing. Sun Tzu held that the goal of warfare is not to destroy, but to compel. That was the essence of Deptula's concepts of effects-based targeting. What really assaulted his keen sense of airpower theory was the belief that the old Cold War "bomb them until the rubble bounces" mentality was still blinding the Air Force to potentially transformative operational concepts. Billy Mitchell and Giulio Douhet, the early pioneers of aerial warfare and strategic bombing from the 1920s, had the airpower theories largely right, he believed, but they were ahead of their time. New technologies were finally catching up with the theory.

ON HIS RETURN to Prince Sultan Air Base in October 2001, Deptula was most thankful for the vastly greater flow of data and information. The CAOC had advanced from a single fiber-optic T-1 line used in Desert Storm to nearly one hundred high-speed T-1 lines, enabling a level of real-time communications and centralized command of far-flung operations that would have been unthinkable just a decade earlier. The amount of digital bandwidth at Deptula's fingertips on the first night of Operation Enduring Freedom had increased one hundredfold.

The real game changer was evident in grainy black-and-white video projected onto the large screen at the CAOC, fed from an MQ-1 Predator unmanned aerial vehicle (UAV). The Pentagon and the CIA had been experimenting with unmanned aerial reconnaissance drones since the 1980s, based largely on Israeli designs, and in the mid-1990s an early developmental model of the Predator reconnaissance drone had been deployed to the Balkans, where the United States and its NATO allies had interceded to halt a civil war and widespread ethnic cleansing. At the time, it had to be flown "line of sight," with a pilot and several payload specialists sitting in a van near the runway operating with direct radio signals. The key breakthrough had occurred in the 1999 Kosovo air campaign called Operation Allied Force, a new front in the Balkan wars, when operators figured out a method to bounce the Predator signal off a satellite to the nearest ground station in Europe, which could route it all the way back to the United States via fiber optic cables lying on the bottom of the Atlantic Ocean. That technique of remote split operations would revolutionize air reconnaissance by delinking the actual drone from the pilot and air support crew keeping it aloft, and from the analysts pouring over the drone's broadcast images.

In 2001 the exploitation of unmanned drones was still in its infancy, with only a few deployed to Afghanistan on the first night of Enduring Freedom. The drone that most interested Deptula was the one circling over a remote compound of mud-brick buildings occupied by Taliban chieftain Mullah Omar. Although he had Navy F-18 and F-14 fighter air-craft standing by, Deptula was especially intrigued that the Predator was armed with two laser-guided Hellfire antitank missiles. At that moment the United States had an opportunity to exact retribution for the crumpled ruin in lower Manhattan and at the Pentagon, and to send a powerful message to other terrorist leaders about the danger of awakening the sleeping giant.

Loitering over its target for more than twenty hours, the Predator drone followed Mullah Omar and his entourage to a remote compound roughly 15 miles southwest of Kandahar. Deptula watched the video feed as they entered one of the buildings. He had the top Taliban leader dead in his sights on the first night of the war, and Deptula itched to take the shot.

Because of a convoluted "Mother, may I" process, CENTCOM in Tampa had to first vet and approve all targets, so Deptula could not directly order the Predator pilot to launch the Hellfire missile. The fact that the Predator was operationally controlled by the CIA, and flown by an Air Force–trained CIA pilot out of Langley, Virginia, further muddled the command-and-control chain.

As CENTCOM commander, US Army General Tommy Franks was concerned about collateral damage from airstrikes that could reinforce al-Qaeda's narrative of a US war on Islam. Memories were still fresh of the errant US airstrike during the Kosovo war that had mistakenly destroyed the Chinese embassy, a strategic error caused by the CIA wrongly identifying the coordinates of a Serbian military facility on the same street. Yet Mullah Omar's compound of adobe-like buildings was surrounded by isolated farmland. And no one could guess when there might be another chance to eliminate such a high-value target.

The order that came from General Franks's staff that night was to first destroy one of the vehicles parked in the courtyard of the compound, in hopes of flushing Mullah Omar out into the open. Deptula and his team watched the Predator video feed as one of the parked SUVs disappeared into a blast cloud, followed by a mad dash by the occupants of the building, their vehicles speeding off in different directions.

Six hours later, CENTCOM headquarters called to give Deptula permission to destroy the building.

"Well, that's fine, but there's no one in it anymore! They're all gone!" Deptula had snapped, not even trying to hide his frustration. Mullah Omar had escaped because of an inefficient, needlessly complex chain of command. The first ever attack by an armed unmanned drone had missed one of the highest-value targets in the "global war on terrorism," and instead had scored a direct hit on an unoccupied SUV. Not for the last time, Deptula worried that the US military's operational concepts lagged far behind the game-changing technologies now at their fingertips. Rather than optimize the potential of an armed drone to reduce the all-important "kill chain" from days and hours to just minutes by combining sensor and shooter into a single platform, General Franks and CENTCOM had used advances in real-time communication to micromanage the operation from Tampa. That was a lesson Dave Deptula knew he'd never forget.

BY LATE OCTOBER 2001, the frustration Deptula felt that first night of the war had spread throughout the US military's chain of command. Most of the limited number of fixed targets had already been struck, and the CAOC was averaging only sixty strike sorties each day. Deptula and his staff lacked situational awareness on the ground of elusive Taliban formations that still retained control of the major Afghan cities. The Taliban were also often too close to Northern Alliance forces to chance striking them from the air and risk hitting "friendlies." With Operation Enduring Freedom having seemingly stalled, critics back home in the United States were already predicting that US forces would fail to dislodge the Taliban and become stuck in a quagmire.

Disputes between the CAOC in Saudi Arabia and US CENTCOM in Tampa over the target-approval bottleneck were also becoming bitter. Deptula and his air staff were convinced that CENTCOM commander General Franks and his team were stuck in an outdated, conventional ground force mind-set that was causing them to let senior al-Qaeda and Taliban leaders slip through their grasp.

When Northern Alliance forces massed outside of the key city of Mazar-i-Sharif in early November 2001, Deptula received a phone call from General Abdul Rashid Dostum, a Northern Alliance commander and

Uzbek warlord. Dostum had just gotten off the phone with the Taliban commander in Mazar-i-Sharif, who taunted him by revealing that he had just commandeered Dostum's house as his headquarters.

"You should bomb my house immediately," Dostum told Deptula by phone. "It's the only house within miles with a swimming pool and tennis court."

Deptula turned to the Navy captain who served as his intelligence officer.

"I want you to get imagery of that house right away." He then consulted the air operations flow chart and confirmed that a B-1 bomber carrying twenty GPS-guided JDAM bombs was within an hour's flight of the coordinates. Within minutes the intelligence shop produced a photograph of Dostum's house.

"That's the place," Deptula said. "Get word to the B-1 pilot to drop two JDAMs on those coordinates within the hour."

Deptula called the CENTCOM staff, explained the situation, and per regulations performed his "Mother, may I" request to please take out the Taliban leader who was commanding the defense of Mazar-i-Sharif. The answer was no, to stand down until Central Command could confirm that he had the right target. The CENTCOM staff then faxed the satellite photo of the town and Dostum's house to Colonel John Mulholland's Task Force Dagger headquarters at K-2 in Uzbekistan, 100 hundred miles north of the Afghan border. A Special Operations messenger carrying the photo was then flown by helicopter to just outside of Mazar-i-Sharif, where another Special Operations soldier took possession and delivered it by horseback into the hands of General Dostum, asking him if he was sure this was the right target.

After three days, Dostum sent Dave Deptula a new message: "If you want to bomb my house, go ahead. But there is no one there anymore."

The situation began to improve markedly as Task Force Dagger's A-Teams became more accustomed to working with various warlords and Afghan militia factions. When Deptula next communicated with General Dostum, the wily warlord requested that he target a Taliban formation of tanks and troops massing on a nearby ridgeline. An Air Force air controller attached to Dostum's A-Team relayed the target coordinates directly to the CAOC, and because it was in a designated free-fire zone, the CAOC was able to task an orbiting B-52 bomber. Just nineteen minutes after the initial request, the B-52 dropped sixteen GPS-guided bombs on the Taliban formation. With the memory still fresh of the days-long lag time for approval to bomb his house in Mazar-i-Sharif, Dostum was impressed. They were all learning.

AFTER MAZAR-I-SHARIF, KABUL, and Kandahar fell in rapid succession in November and early December, Operation Enduring Freedom shifted from an unconventional offensive to a manhunt for Osama Bin Laden, Mullah Omar, and their top lieutenants, who were likely hiding in caves and bunkers. This search drove the other great innovation of the initial stage of Operation Enduring Freedom—an expansive umbrella of air- and space-borne intelligence, surveillance, and reconnaissance (ISR) platforms that enabled the most persistent and detailed hard stare of a battle space in the history of modern warfare. Skies over Afghanistan were crisscrossed by the most advanced ISR aircraft in the US arsenal, including the still-experimental Global Hawk unmanned drone, and the RQ-1 Predator reconnaissance drone; the E-3 AWACs command-and-control aircraft; the E-8 Joint STARS surveillance and target attack aircraft; the RC-135 Rivet Joint signals-intercept aircraft; carrier-based EA-6B and EP-3 surveillance aircraft; and a host of fighters and strike aircraft outfitted with infrared targeting systems.

Because of its unique ability to remain airborne and loiter above a potential target for many hours, the RQ-1 Predator drone became a star of the manhunt operation. "Rivet Joint" aircraft would detect a spike in communications coming from suspected Taliban locations. Next, the Predator was dispatched to take a closer look, sending visuals in real time simultaneously to the CAOC in Saudi Arabia and to CENTCOM headquarters in Florida. After the target was approved, the Predator illuminated the target with a laser, and laser-guided bombs or precise cannon fire from AC-130 gunships circling overhead would strike. The Predator would stay on station and conduct immediate bomb damage assessment.

Deptula and his staff worked round-the-clock removing links and tightening the sensor-to-shooter "kill chain." The targeting flow became so fluid and dynamic that the vast majority of aircraft were launching without yet knowing what targets they might be asked to hit. In one instance, intelligence had alerted them to a possible meeting of Taliban leaders on the outskirts of Kabul, and one of the RQ-1 Predators was dispatched to confirm. The Predator video feed was relayed to the CAOC. Deptula contacted a US aircraft carrier in the Indian Ocean via a satellite link, which relayed his call through a Navy ES-3 surveillance aircraft operating off the coast to an Air Force AWAC command-and-control aircraft flying over Afghanistan. The call was then relayed into the cockpit of an F-14 "Bombcat." Deptula literally talked the pilot onto the Taliban target by telling him to go three blocks north of a Kabul traffic circle and then hang a left, third house on the right.

Each link in that convoluted sensor to shooter chain had cost roughly five minutes. Wouldn't it be nice, Deptula asked his staff, if the Predator video feed could be sent directly into the cockpit of a targeting aircraft via a satellite link and receiver? What if it could also be shared with Task Force Dagger's A-Teams on the ground, who were trying to capture senior al-Qaeda and Taliban leaders?

With the help of the Air Force's special-project operation Big Safari, the CAOC had a radio installed on the Predator that allowed its remote pilot and sensor operator to talk directly to targeters in Saudi Arabia and to pilots circling the skies above Afghanistan. The CAOC also devised methods for the Predator video to be streamed directly into the cockpits of AC-130 gunships. Soon after, the Air Force would field the first man portable ROVER (remotely operated video-enhanced receiver) system, allowing Predators to stream video directly to Special Forces ground troops, allowing them not only to accurately locate the enemy, but also to see over the next rise or around the corners of buildings.

Because they combined sensors and weapons on a platform that could linger over the battlespace for nearly a day at a time, the armed Predators became the ultimate short-linkage kill chain. In November, al-Qaeda's military chief Mohammed Atef became the first of the terrorist group's high-value targets to be killed by the Predator drone. Deptula knew Atef would not be the last terrorist to share that fate.

He also sensed that the new style of warfare he had glimpsed during the initial phase of Enduring Freedom was the start of a paradigm shift. The armed drone was at the center of that transformation, its power lying in the unparalleled persistence it brought to the mission of manhunting. Remotely piloted aircraft were now unconstrained by the physiological limitations of a single pilot. This fundamentally altered the intelligence, surveillance, and reconnaissance equation. With armed drones, the United States could also project power without projecting vulnerability. That was an asymmetric advantage for the ages.

The unmanned drone and other advanced ISR platforms were part of a much larger revolution that Deptula believed had only just begun. Precision strike was another key enabler. Enduring Freedom represented the first combat use of the JDAM. In the 1991 Persian Gulf War, precision weapons had accounted for only 9 percent of the bombs dropped. In Operation Enduring Freedom, 70 percent of the munitions launched were precision guided. Deptula knew that percentage would only grow in future operations. The use of ground-based Special Operations Forces to enable an air campaign, as opposed to having aircraft primarily provide close air support to maneuver units on the ground, was also a novel approach that greatly increased the effectiveness of airpower.

Arguably the centerpiece of the transformation taking place was the global communications network that connected and controlled all those moving pieces. Deptula now commanded far-flung operations and units dispersed around the world, all acting in relative unison. A drone pilot sitting at a consul in Langley, Virginia, could launch precision weapons at enemies halfway around the world, even as the video feed from his aircraft was being analyzed by an intelligence specialist in Sacramento, California, and shared with a joint terminal attack controller on the ground in Kandahar. The Air Force didn't even yet have a name for those kinds of globe-spanning, network-centric operations, though one would soon be invented: extended range reconnaissance strike.

Precision strike. Stealth. Persistent surveillance. Cyber. Real-time intelligence. All of those capabilities were the result of decades of technological advancement, a process of constant self-improvement on the part of the US military whereby new technologies and concepts migrate from research-and-development laboratories to testing centers and training bases, and eventually to operational forces in the field. The dire necessities of conflict greatly accelerate and compress that cycle, pushing new technologies directly into the field where they immediately undergo real-world test and evaluation in the crucible of war.

Even in the early months of Operation Enduring Freedom, Deptula sensed that the technologies at the fingertips of operational commanders far outpaced the organizational processes and social relationships that dominated the US national security apparatus. Culturally and conceptually they were still operating within a twentieth-century paradigm, but there were now twenty-first-century arrows in the US military's quiver that were exquisite in their potential. Once new operational concepts caught up with technology—just as Blitzkrieg land warfare doctrine had exploited the capabilities of the tank, and aircraft carriers leveraged the range and lethality of manned aircraft to redefine sea power—Deptula thought US commanders might actually achieve the goal of effects-based targeting: they could make real Sun Tzu's vision of vanquishing a foe or bringing a fortress to heel with a single shot.

Afghanistan truly was the first front of another kind of war, and Deptula believed he had glimpsed the wholly different kind of military force needed to fight it, just as John F. Kennedy had so long ago. What looked revolutionary from the bird's-eye view of the Combined Air Operations Center at Prince Sultan Air Base in Saudi Arabia, however, looked very different to Colonel John Mulholland and the Special Forces troops on the ground at the tip of the spear. For them, the new style of warfare looked much like the old: a fight to the death in a fog-shrouded landscape, random violence, and unknown catastrophe always lurking around the next bend. There were times when all the cutting-edge technology just seemed designed to get you killed twice as fast.

FOR MULHOLLAND AND the Fifth Special Forces Group, disaster struck on December 5, 2001. The Bonn Conference to decide Afghanistan's political future had recently concluded, and dignitaries had identified a potential leader for the country who did not carry the baggage of corruption and cruelty common among the Afghan warlords. Hamid Karzai was an educated man, known as a person of character, and as a Pashtun he had already shown he could rally the Pashtun tribes. That was enough to make him a prime threat to the Pashtun Taliban. Their pledge to destroy him had prompted Mulholland to assign one of Task Force Dagger's A-Teams to serve as the personal protection of the future president of Afghanistan.

Instead, the Green Berets very nearly caused his death. Karzai's band of fighters and the A-Team were fighting to push the Taliban out of the town of Showali Kowt, roughly 10 miles from the Taliban stronghold of Kandahar. During the fighting, an Air Force tactical controller attached to the team called in an air strike on Taliban positions. He apparently punched the correct enemy coordinates into his global positioning unit, but had to change batteries before they were transmitted. During the reboot, the system defaulted to its own location and sent those coordinates to a B-52 bomber. The 2,000-pound bomb dropped into the A-Team's midst killed three Green Berets and an estimated twenty-five of their Afghan allies. The entire A-Team was taken off the battlefield, its members either dead or wounded. Hamid Karzai survived, but the Afghan next to him was decapitated by the blast. That was the worst day of the war for John Mulholland, but there were plenty of bad days to come.

Just days earlier Task Force Dagger had helped launch an operation to clear al-Qaeda fighters out of Tora Bora, a cave complex near the Khyber Pass connecting Afghanistan and Pakistan. Mulholland dispatched an A-Team to the operation, which also included a few score "black ops" — Special Forces commandos from Delta Force, the US Army's elite, direct-action counterterrorism force. Their role was to support more than two thousand Afghan irregulars. There was strong suspicion that Osama bin Laden was hiding in the caves with his most loyal fighters. Although Mulholland lacked conclusive evidence, the location of the complex high in the Hindu Kush and near the border with Pakistan made it a logical fallback for bin Laden and his top lieutenants.

The insistence of Rumsfeld's Office of the Secretary of Defense and CENTCOM commander General Tommy Franks that the United States maintain a light footprint inside Afghanistan severely hamstrung the operation to clear the Tora Bora complex. That forced Mulholland and other commanders to rely heavily on Afghan warlords of dubious reliability. There were already strong suspicions inside Fifth Special Forces Group that one of the first Green Berets to die in Afghanistan was killed in an ambush ordered by one of the Afghan warlords they were supporting. Privately, some of the Green Berets aimed to kill the warlord if the opportunity arose.

Lacking regular army forces to conduct a conventional isolate, cordon, and search operation around Tora Bora, US commanders relied on the Afghans to pull the noose tight, with disastrous results. In the midst of what became known as the Battle of Tora Bora, US Special Forces reported hearing bin Laden's voice in radio transmissions. But with a thunderous bombardment raining down on the cave complex, one of the Afghan commanders inexplicably declared a ceasefire. When Delta Force tried to push the militia to attack, the Afghans troops pointed their weapons on the US commandos. By the time the standoff was over, bin Laden and his bodyguards had apparently escaped into Pakistan.

BY THE SPRING of 2002, it was abundantly clear that in this new style of twenty-first-century warfare, air controllers who served as the link between advanced US airpower and Special Operations Forces on the ground would play a critical role. That became evident in March when Central Command launched Operation Anaconda in the Shah-e-Kot Valley to clear out a few hundred al-Qaeda and Taliban fighters. US commanders were concerned that the enemy was gathering to launch a spring offensive once the snows melted and the fighting season began again. After the fiasco at Tora Bora, some 1,700 US air mobile troops from the 101st Airborne and Tenth Mountain Divisions were the primary assault force for Anaconda. John Mulholland's Task Force Dagger was in support.

The night of March 4 was frigid as one of the task force's Chinook helicopters approached Objective Ginger, a knifelike ridge that ran along the spine of an 11,000-foot mountain called Takur Gar. The joint special operations reconnaissance team inside the helicopter knew Objective Ginger represented valuable high ground with a commanding view of the entire

Anaconda battlespace. The al-Qaeda fighters secretly dug in atop Takur Gar knew it, too.

As the Chinook helicopter Razor 3 approached the snow-covered landing zone, Tech Sergeant John Chapman, an Air Force combat controller, and the Navy SEAL team onboard all felt a mixture of cold air and engine backwash pouring through the open rear door. Just before the aircraft touched down, machine gun fire erupted and raked the fuselage. There was a blast and then a sickening lurch as a rocket-propelled grenade scored a direct hit, severing hydraulic lines and puncturing the fuselage. The pilots veered sharply away from the hot landing zone and struggled to get the aircraft back under control, scanning the terrain through night vision goggles as they searched for some place to bring the crippled helicopter down. Before they could land at an alternate site, the SEAL team realized that during the chaos and confusion one of their own, Petty Officer First Class Neil C. Roberts, had been knocked from the helicopter and into a hot landing zone under control of the enemy. After the helicopter landed on a flat patch of hillside roughly 4 miles away from the hot landing zone, Chapman and the SEAL team made a fateful decision. They would keep the promise that no man is left behind. They were going back up to the top of Takur Gar.

Like other combat controllers, Chapman had completed the highly technical combat control operator course in air traffic control, air navigation, and communication procedures. To earn the signature red beret of an Air Force combat controller and the combat control badge with the motto "First There," Chapman had also completed one of the most rigorous training regimes in the entire US military. Each combat controller was an airpower-savvy commando who could run, jump, or swim with members of any other special operations unit, and act as their conduit for close air support, airborne reconnaissance and surveillance, and air insertion and extraction. As Chapman's instructor in special tactics had said when asked if he were trying to turn the Air Force combat controllers into Navy SEALs, "No, I'm training them so that they don't slow the SEALs down."

Less than an hour after Razor 3 made its forced landing, Chapman and the five SEAL commandos were aboard another MH-47E helicopter and speeding back to the top of Takur Gar. The pilots received updates on the suspected whereabouts of the al-Qaeda fighters who had taken Roberts prisoner. As the helicopter approached the selected landing zone, the team once again began taking enemy fire. The pilots were able to set the helicopter down long enough to offload the commandos, and then veered off the mountainside.

Chapman and the SEAL team were alone in the dark and bitter cold, on a mountain swarming with al-Qaeda fighters. They quickly found themselves pinned down by blistering automatic weapons fire pouring in from multiple directions and positions. Chapman shouted into his radio over the din of the firefight, trying to call in close air support to keep the enemy at bay while the SEAL team assaulted an enemy position. Seeing that his team was effectively in a kill zone—taking enemy fire from three directions—Chapman advanced on a dug-in enemy position, firing his weapon. He and a SEAL commando killed two of the al-Qaeda fighters. Crawling into the enemy position, Chapman turned his fire on a second machine gun nest, and exchanged fire with the al-Qaeda fighters at close range.

With the enemy momentarily distracted by Chapman's assault, the leader of the SEAL team gathered two wounded members and pulled back down the mountainside, repositioning his team down the slope just as the sun was rising over Takur Gar. At that moment, a rapid-reaction rescue force of Army Rangers arrived in another Chinook helicopter. Because of a miscommunication, Razor 1 did not realize it was entering a hot landing zone. The Chinook was forced into a crash landing after being hit repeatedly by enemy fire. As the Rangers scrambled out of the downed helicopter into a withering barrage of machine gun fire, four were killed and others were wounded. Another Air Force combat controller assigned to the Rangers used his radio to call in close air support. Since the al-Qaeda fighters were in such close proximity to the downed helicopter, he waved off an aircraft from a bombing run with 500-pound bombs, instructing it to strafe the enemy positions with machine guns instead.

In the intense, fifteen-hour firefight on Takur Gar, seven US service members were killed in action, including Navy SEAL Neil Roberts, who after being captured by al-Qaeda fighters had been summarily executed. By the time night fell, close air support and the determined fighting of the joint special operations team of Army Rangers, Navy SEALs, and Air Force combat controllers and pararescuemen had driven the al-Qaeda fighters off what became known as "Roberts Ridge." US commanders estimated between forty and fifty enemy fighters had been killed in the firefight.

John Chapman was found where he had succumbed to numerous wounds after exchanging fire at close range with the al-Qaeda machine gun emplacement. Two dead enemy fighters lay nearby. One SEAL team leader credited Chapman with saving the lives of his entire team. For his actions at Roberts Ridge, Chapman was posthumously awarded the Air Force Cross, his service's highest award for valor. His death was an early harbinger of the critical role that Air Force forward controllers would play in linking advanced US airpower and Special Operations Forces in a new style of warfare.

ALREADY BY THE spring of 2002, the initial objectives of Operation Enduring Freedom had largely been met. Al-Qaeda was routed and its training bases destroyed, the Taliban regime was toppled and dispersed, and a friendly government had been installed in Kabul. In that newly permissive environment, US military forces shifted to a more traditional peacekeeping mission.

By the time Colonel John Mulholland prepared to leave Afghanistan in April 2002, more regular Army forces and higher headquarters staff were deploying into the country. That a Special Forces colonel had for a time commanded a combat theater that spanned an entire country was an anomaly, and Mulholland was proud of what Task Force Dagger had accomplished. A few hundred highly trained Special Operations troops had quickly deployed into a remote and utterly alien land, and after forging relationships with other agencies and local fighters, they had defeated a hated Taliban regime and sent al-Qaeda scurrying over the mountains in retreat. The operation wasn't perfect by any means—Mulholland would have liked to have walked out of the mountains of Tora Bora with Osama bin Laden in tow, either dead or alive. In his mind a lot of people underestimated just how hard it was to find a single individual who was hiding in his own backyard, let alone one of the most inhospitable and rugged backyards on the face of the Earth.

The overriding lesson Mulholland took from the experience was the synergy created when all elements of the vast US national security apparatus were united with a terrible purpose. "Whether it was working alongside our CIA brothers, or US Air Force combat controllers embedded with our ODAs [Operation Detachment Alpha], bringing twenty-first century joint firepower to bear, or a Navy F-18 screaming down on the deck to save an ODA from being overrun; when we quit worrying about who gets the credit and just focus, it is simply awesome to see how powerful our integrated capabilities really are," he recalled years later in an interview with the Defense Media Network.

Yet he also knew that the early stages of Operation Enduring Freedom had proven controversial, and had stirred up a lot of old jealousies and recriminations between the conventional US military and Special Forces. As later events would prove, the failure to bring enough forces to bear to capture bin Laden when he was within reach at Tora Bora, which a US Senate report would later place squarely in the laps of Secretary of Defense Rumsfeld and CENTCOM commander General Tommy Franks, was a blunder of truly strategic proportions. The very survival of the archterrorist in the face of overwhelming US force would become a rallying cry for Islamic extremists worldwide.

That failure and the miscues evident in the Battle of Anaconda, which was the deadliest military engagement in the "global war on terrorism" up to that point, led to an extended round of interagency finger-pointing, and resurrected the old quarrel between the Special Forces community and the conventional Army. Before he left Afghanistan, a senior Army general from the conventional forces drew Mulholland aside to drive home his view that a Special Forces colonel should never have been given so much authority in the first place. "We're never going to do *that* again!" the general said, the reproach in his voice like a slap in the face.

# THREE

# Descent into Darkness
## March–October 2002

E VEN AS THE INITIAL POST-9/11 BATTLES IN AFGHANISTAN WERE RE-
kindling long-dormant tensions and jealousies between US conventional military and Special Operations forces, the jockeying over terrorist
interrogations between the FBI and the CIA was threatening to undermine
the uneasy détente between those two agencies. In April 2002, FBI special
agents Steve Gaudin and Ali Soufan arrived in Thailand at Cat's Eye,
the CIA's first secret prison, or "black site," for interrogating captured al-
Qaeda operatives. The CIA interrogation team was nowhere to be found,
and suspected al-Qaeda operative Abu Zubaydah was barely alive. He had
been shot multiple times during his capture by Pakistani security forces in
late March 2002, and was bedridden and hooked to a phalanx of medical
monitoring equipment. Since the CIA's own interrogation team had not
yet arrived, it was up to the FBI agents to figure out how to extract the information that would prevent the next terrorist attack, which many counterterrorism officials feared was imminent, and keep Zubaydah alive.

Gaudin and Soufan were trained to first establish a rapport with Zubaydah, and then meticulously compare his statements to known facts so

as to find the cracks that would break down his story. There was no magic bullet or shortcut to a successful interrogation. Fortunately the two agents already knew quite a lot about the inner workings of al-Qaeda—Gaudin from his long interrogation and subsequent testimony at the trial of Mohamed al-Owhali following the 1998 US embassy bombings in Africa, and Soufan from leading the investigation into al-Qaeda's attack on the USS *Cole*. The first step was to ask Zubaydah a series of questions whose answers they already knew, to establish a level of baseline truth, the better to judge his level of cooperation.

Right away Zubaydah lied to the agents, insisting his name was "Makmoud Maliji," the equivalent of a World War II prisoner's saying his name was Charlie Chaplin or Kilroy. The agents laughed at the obvious ruse, taking it as a good sign. "As we were laughing, I was thinking to myself, 'This is good, he's got a sense of humor,'" Gaudin recalled thinking. "At that moment I felt very confident we could talk to this guy, and lead him down a certain line of questioning."

"Instead of 'Makmoud Maliji,' how about we call you Zayn al-Abidin Muhammed Hussein Abu Zubaydah," Gaudin replied, and then recited the names of the man's father and brothers. "You were raised in Saudi Arabia, and your father is an engineer."

Zubaydah was pensive. "So, I guess there's no point in my denying it," he finally replied in Arabic.

"Exactly, that's where we're going in this discussion," said Gaudin. "You decide you don't want to talk to us, the best thing for everyone is for you to just say so. But don't jerk our chains and lie to us. Because we're going to know if you do, and then this discussion is going to go in a way that's not productive for anyone."

Both Gaudin and Soufan felt they were making good progress in their first few interrogation sessions with Zubaydah. They reported back to Washington having established his true identity, and that he had provided answers to questions about al-Qaeda that only an insider could know. The pressure from Washington for more information was intense, and though the CIA interrogation team had still not arrived after a number of days, the CIA managers of the black site were growing impatient with the FBI agents' methodical approach.

At one point the CIA agent in charge tore into Gaudin. "Look, we don't care about his family history or what Zubaydah did back in the day," he argued. "We just want to know where the next bomb is going to go off."

"Well, that's what we want to know, too!" Gaudin shot back. "But if I go in there and ask him that question right off the bat, we're not going to get anywhere." He explained that the FBI had a successful template for conducting interviews that had produced results over many, many years. "So, don't have me go in there and try and play a different role, because I won't be able to sell it. Let me do my job, and I'll get you answers."

The pace of the interrogations was also hindered by Zubaydah's poor health. There were interruptions to change his bandages, and to let him use the toilet. At one point he had to be moved into a hospital, but still the questioning continued. In the hospital Zubaydah went septic, losing all control of his bowels and fouling his bed. Gaudin immediately grabbed a roll of paper towels and helped wipe him off, trying to comfort an obviously mortified Zubaydah, understanding his sense of vulnerability and shame.

"Listen, don't worry about it; we're going to take care of you," Gaudin said. "The doctors are going to save you."

Afraid they were losing him, Soufan held ice to Zubaydah's lips and began reading him verses from the Koran. The FBI agents were rediscovering what Israel's Shin Bet intelligence officials had learned in their own twilight struggle with terrorism: this was an intensely personal conflict, and to succeed required knowing your enemy and every detail of his backstory, the better to understand his motivations and circle of contacts. All of which inevitably meant confronting his essential humanity.

Later, when he was being prepped for an MRI exam, Zubaydah was obviously terrified of the claustrophobic machine. "Please don't leave me here alone," he muttered. Without thinking about the bizarre direction the interrogation had taken, or the alleged crimes of this man suspected of involvement in the 9/11 attacks, Steve Gaudin reached out and held Zubaydah's hand.

WHEN THE BUSH administration declared a "global war on terrorism" against al-Qaeda, it launched a hybrid war unlike any the United States had confronted in modern times. There were inevitable bureaucratic clashes and tensions as the various US intelligence, law enforcement, and military departments and agencies jockeyed for position and sorted out their critical roles and missions in that campaign. None of the bureaucratic jostling would prove more controversial or consequential than the clashes over the detainment and interrogation of terrorist suspects.

The chief advocate for a new gloves-off approach to interrogations was Vice President Dick Cheney, who had been delegated oversight of the campaign against al-Qaeda. Cheney wanted terrorist suspects placed beyond the reach of national or international legal protections. That was the purpose of the Guantánamo Bay detention camp in Cuba, which began accepting suspects early in 2002, as well as such CIA secret prisons as Cat's Eye. In February 2002, the administration also circumvented prohibitions against torture by declaring in a secret directive that the Geneva Conventions against the use of torture did not apply to enemy combatants captured in the "global war on terrorism."

The State Department and some other top officials in the US government opposed the directive and its implications. Acting through the United Nations, the State Department had successfully rallied much of the world against al-Qaeda after the outrage of the 9/11 attacks, and that support would clearly weaken if those in US custody routinely disappeared down the black hole of secret CIA prisons, where they were subject to abuse and even torture. There was also a strong ideological context to the conflict with al-Qaeda, and such practices threatened to turn the strength of widely recognized US values—such as respect for the rule of law—into a weakness. That played into the terrorist narrative of a war between Islam and a corrupt West.

The FBI opposed brutally coercive interrogation techniques mostly for a more prosaic reason: they produced unreliable information. Waging a war against an enemy that hid in the shadows was by nature heavily reliant on intelligence, and there was no more important intelligence-gathering technique than interrogation of suspected terrorists. Much of what the US government knew about al-Qaeda's networks and webs of relationships on 9/11 had been gleaned from FBI interrogations. The long experience of building criminal conspiracy cases that held up in a court of law had taught the bureau that its methodical approach to interrogations worked.

Its methods required patience, however, which was in short supply in the months after the 9/11 attacks.

Finally, there was the matter of core competencies to consider. The new, post-9/11 counterterrorism model being birthed required a clear understanding of the strengths and weaknesses that each agency brought to the fight. The CIA had many strengths, including operating in secrecy, developing sources, and analyzing intelligence. But conducting interrogations was not among them.

The capture of the first suspected senior al-Qaeda operative and his transfer to Cat's Eye brought those divergent views and approaches into direct conflict for the first time. The US government had come to a fateful fork in the road, and the direction it chose would have consequences that helped shape the post-9/11 war on al-Qaeda for years to come.

AFTER A WEEK of questioning Zubaydah, Steve Gaudin felt his man was almost ready to make a breakthrough. He had read the same signs just before al-Owhali came clean about the US embassy bombings after more than a week of denying his involvement.

"Look, you are off the battlefield now, and you are never going back to the fight. My advice to you is that it's in everyone's best interest now, including your own, for you to cooperate," Gaudin told Zubaydah. "You should try and explain to the world why you did what you did, because right now most people think you guys are just a bunch of bloodthirsty savages. You can't fight with a gun anymore, so why not pick up a pen and tell the world why you did it?"

He and Soufan had reached the point where Zubaydah was truthful, but not entirely forthcoming about all that he knew. They knew that once the CIA interrogation team arrived at Cat's Eye, they would likely lose control of the interrogation. To draw Zubaydah out, the FBI agents showed him photos of the FBI's twenty-two most wanted terrorists, and asked him to pick out Saif al-Adel, a former Egyptian explosives expert and top al-Qaeda operative under indictment for his role in the embassy bombings. If Zubaydah fingered al-Adel, Gaudin believed it would represent a breakthrough in the interrogation, and signal a deeper willingness to cooperate.

As Gaudin scrolled through the photographs, Zubaydah suddenly grabbed his arm. The photo on the Palm Pilot wasn't of Saif al-Adel, and Gaudin's anger took hold.

"Are you trying to tell me that's Saif al-Adel? After everything we've been through the last few days, with me holding your goddamn hand in the MRI room! I told you, don't try and bullshit me!" Gaudin knew the man in the photograph well: Khalid Sheikh Mohammed, the uncle of 1993 World Trade Center bomber Ramzi Yousef. They were both involved in the failed, mid-1990s Bojinka plot to bomb eleven commercial airliners flying between Asia and the United States. In an interview with the author, Gaudin recalled the exchange that followed.

"You need to stop bullshitting me!"

"I never said that was Saif al-Adel," Zubaydah replied defensively.

"Good, just don't bullshit me. Wait until you see Saif al-Adel's photo."

When Zubaydah stopped him at al-Adel's photograph, Gaudin was inwardly ecstatic, though he didn't let it show. Finally they had fresh intelligence to show for days of interrogation. As he was putting away his Palm Pilot, he asked Zubaydah to get off his chest whatever it was he wanted to say about Khalid Sheikh Mohammed.

"How did you know that Muktar was the mastermind of 9/11?" Zubaydah asked.

Gaudin was afraid he'd have a stroke trying to keep the shock and surprise off his face. No one in the US government suspected any such thing. They knew from communications intercepts that there was a "Muktar" at the center of the plot, but no one knew who he was. Suddenly Zubaydah was tying together all the loose threads, and telling them that Khalid Sheikh Mohammed was the 9/11 mastermind. Gaudin used every ounce of self-control he possessed to maintain a poker face. At the foot of the bed he saw Ali Soufan looking at him incredulously, wondering what the hell had just happened.

Gaudin turned back to Zubaydah and answered matter-of-factly. "Why else would we have showed you Khalid Sheikh Mohammed's photo if we didn't know?"

Steve Gaudin excused himself, afraid his poker face would crack. Once outside Zubaydah's hospital room, he grabbed the CIA manager of the black site. "Listen, you need to get this information back to CIA headquarters immediately, and we need you to loop in the following people at the FBI," he said in a rush, writing the message. "Abu Zubaydah just identified Khalid Sheikh Mohammed as the mastermind behind 9/11!"

THE CIA INTERROGATION team arrived at Cat's Eye a short time later. A senior FBI liaison at CIA headquarters told the agents that CIA director George Tenet had been on the phone with the president, who wanted to personally congratulate the CIA interrogators for learning about KSM's central role in the 9/11 plot. But when Tenet learned it wasn't CIA operatives who had interrogated Zubaydah—rather, two FBI agents—he apparently went ballistic, ordering his interrogation team to Thailand on the next available plane.

Immediately on arrival in Thailand, the CIA team informed Gaudin and Soufan that they were going in a different direction with the interrogation. Gaudin knew the CIA team leader from the embassy bombing investigation, and respected him as a competent and well-intentioned operator. He also knew the man had absolutely no experience conducting interrogations. The CIA also brought along a former Air Force psychologist named James Mitchell, who along with a colleague, John "Bruce" Jessen, had once run a training program designed to give US service members a taste of the harsh treatment they could expect as prisoners of war, including a form of simulated drowning used by the Chinese on American airmen during the Korean War. Under contract to the CIA, Drs. Mitchell and Jessen had developed a theory that waterboarding, as the technique was called, along with other harsh interrogation techniques, could produce a sense of "learned helplessness" that would render detainees incapable of withholding information. Abu Zubaydah was going to become the first human guinea pig in their experiment in learned helplessness.

As a former Special Forces infantryman, Gaudin had undergone the training, called SERE for "survival, evasion, resistance, and escape." He knew from personal experience that if waterboarding was used, prisoners were likely to say whatever they thought the interrogators wanted to hear, resulting in corrupted intelligence. What he couldn't figure out was why the CIA was going to embrace interrogation techniques based on the theories of two Air Force psychologists who had never actually conducted a real-world interrogation, and whose only experience was in interrogation techniques designed by totalitarian states to elicit false confessions and propaganda, not reliable intelligence.

"Hey, you guys are just getting here. We've been with this guy for nearly a week now, and we're just starting to get somewhere," Gaudin pleaded his case. He would have used the same argument even if the agency had suggested a softer approach to the interrogation, but he understood that was not what the CIA team had in mind. Their hard approach would include keeping Zubaydah in a bright, all-white room lit 24 hours a day, with frequent sleep disruptions and loud music constantly piped into his cell. The two FBI agents were told that they would no longer directly participate in the interrogation sessions.

"He's just giving you throwaway information," said the CIA team leader. Gaudin and Soufan looked at each other and just shook their heads. They knew what throwaway information was, and giving up the mastermind of the 9/11 plot didn't qualify by a long shot. The FBI special agents fired off an angry note to FBI headquarters: "[We] have spent an un-calculable amount of hours at [Abu Zubaydah's] bedside assisting with medical help, holding his hand and comforting him through various medical procedures, even assisting him in going [to] the bathroom. . . . We have built tremendous rapport with AZ and now that we are on the eve of 'regular' interviews to get threat information, we have been 'written out' of future interviews."

The FBI agents' objections were ignored, and for the next few days they observed the interrogation through a closed-circuit video feed, along with Dr. Mitchell. The CIA security officers wore all black uniforms, boots, gloves, balaclava face masks, and goggles. Zubaydah was restrained with handcuffs and leg shackles and typically kept naked and sleep deprived. Between interrogations, loud rock music or noise generators were used to enhance the prisoner's "sense of helplessness," all of which would be detailed in the Senate Select Intelligence Committee's report on the CIA interrogation program.

The CIA interrogators were following a script written by psychologists Mitchell and Jessen, and it went like this: you have a most important secret that we need to know, and we're willing to go at this until you're willing to tell us what it is. Zubaydah's face betrayed confusion. What is the question you want answered? More than once he asked where "Steve and Ali" were. His new interrogators were adamant: you know what we need to know, and we're not going to talk about anything else until you're willing to discuss the one key piece of intelligence we know you are keeping from us. Even observing from outside the room, Gaudin and Soufan had a hard time following the logic of the questioning devised by the psychological team. For four days the interrogation summary was the same: "Detainee hasn't said anything today." Zubaydah clammed up under the new approach.

Under Washington's relentless pressure for results, the CIA team leader was soon instructed to work the FBI agents back into the interrogation rotation. But the CIA scripted their questions. At one point Gaudin was given a photo and told to ask Zubaydah to identify the man, but the CIA team leader told him not to worry about his true identity, to just ask the question. When Gaudin showed Zubaydah the photo, he insisted he didn't recognize the man. They moved on.

Three days later, the CIA team leader revealed to Gaudin that the man in the photo was an old friend of Zubaydah's from his school days. When an obviously angry Gaudin confronted Zubaydah about the deception, he admitted to lying.

Walking out of the interrogation room, Gaudin was furious at the CIA's inept tactics. "Do you realize what you just fucking did?" he all but shouted at the CIA team leader. "You just taught him that he can bullshit me and I won't have any idea he's lying for three days!" Soufan was even more outraged at the illogical and, he believed, clearly illegal interrogation methods the CIA was using. At one point he called FBI headquarters and threatened to arrest the CIA agents on the spot if the abuse continued.

Washington's insistence on new information was relentless, and Gaudin and Soufan were eventually allowed once again to work together interrogating the prisoner. As the men who had all but saved Zubaydah's life when he went septic, they pleaded for useful information to justify their patience. Soufan left the room during one session, and Gaudin and Zubaydah were alone for hours. Gaudin was driving home the point once again that Zubaydah needed to tell the world why he felt compelled to act, and to justify his violence. The two men—the interrogator and the suspected terrorist—were literally sitting on the floor together in tears, until finally Gaudin couldn't take it anymore. He signaled for the handlers to open the door to the interrogation room.

Outside the room Gaudin was approached by one of the CIA team leaders. "I got nothing left; send someone in fresh," he told the man.

"No, you've got him! He's going to give it up! You can't see it because you're so wrapped up in the questioning, but we can see it from the outside," the CIA team leader said. "You've got to go back in there."

Zubaydah was somewhat sheepish on Gaudin's return, perhaps sensing exasperation in this man who had literally wiped his ass at one of the most vulnerable moments of his life. And as Gaudin began his questions again, Zubaydah interrupted him.

"There's this American, I think he's Mexican or Hispanic," began Zubaydah. And then he began telling the FBI agent a story.


As IT TURNED out, Zubaydah was not the senior al-Qaeda operations chief that the CIA suspected he was. He had helped run an al-Qaeda training camp, and when US forces invaded Afghanistan, he had played a major role in smuggling al-Qaeda operatives out of Afghanistan to safe houses across the border in Pakistan. Two of those operatives happened to have Western passports, though Zubaydah did not remember their names and could only describe the men. Yet he had clearly understood their potential value to al-Qaeda. After he stashed the two Westerners in a safe house in Lahore, Zubaydah brought them to the attention of "Muktar." Khalid Sheikh Mohammed would later encourage their plot to build a dirty bomb to disperse radiological material in a terrorist attack, understanding that their great value lay not in bomb-making expertise but, rather, in their Western passports and clean records.

Zubaydah's story offered exactly the kind of information on "where the next bomb was going to go off" that Washington had been demanding. The CIA wasted no time in feeding the intelligence into its vast counterterrorism database at Langley, searching for two people whose travel patterns fit the information supplied by Zubaydah. Within days CIA head-quarters forwarded a photograph to Cat's Eye, and Steve Gaudin showed it to Zubaydah.

"That's him! That's the guy I'm talking about," the prisoner confirmed. Not long after, on May 8, 2002, on returning from a trip overseas that included stops in Egypt, Saudi Arabia, Afghanistan, Pakistan, and Iraq, Jose Padilla, a.k.a. Abdullah al-Muhajir, was arrested by US Customs agents at Chicago's O'Hare Airport. A Muslim convert and former member of the Latin Kings street gang who had convictions for aggravated assault and manslaughter as a juvenile, Padilla was held as a material witness on a warrant stemming from the September 11, 2001, terrorist attacks.

Just as he had after Langley compiled a comprehensive case history on Khalid Sheikh Mohammed almost overnight on learning that he was the 9/11 mastermind, Gaudin marveled at the agency's analytic acumen and ability to quickly query vast counterterrorism databases. Despite the agencies' intense disagreements about interrogation techniques, the CIA's analysis coupled with the FBI's expertise in interrogations and investigations had achieved a synergy that quite possibly had averted another terrorist attack. In May 2002, the CIA disseminated no less than fifty-six intelligence reports based on the Zubaydah interrogations.

When Gaudin and Soufan returned to Washington, DC, a few weeks later to take part in discussions about the direction of the detainee interrogations, they discovered that a furious debate was under way about the program. In meetings at FBI headquarters they were both asked what lessons they had taken away from the interrogation of Abu Zubaydah, the first high-value target to undergo questioning. Between 9/11 and the anthrax attacks that followed just a week later, everyone in the US national security network was focused first and foremost on preventing the next attack. But the CIA interrogation team was already touting its harder approach as the reason that Zubaydah gave up Khalid Sheikh Mohammed and Jose Padilla. Both Gaudin and Soufan knew that was the opposite of the truth. Zubaydah was classified by the Bush administration as an "enemy combatant," which meant that he did not have to be read his Miranda rights and could be questioned indefinitely in secret. But the only important information he had surrendered had come about as the result of standard FBI interrogation techniques that comported with national and international norms.

"The truth is, only Zubaydah knows why he decided to talk. But I believe the US government will get more out of Zubaydah and these other terrorist suspects by having experienced subject-matter experts conduct the interviews like we've always done," Gaudin recalled telling his bosses. "All the intelligence we have backs that up."

At CIA headquarters at Langley, meetings were also being held in June 2002 to discuss the best way forward on interrogations. Air Force psychologist James Mitchell proposed using more "enhanced interrogation techniques," reverse engineered from the SERE training—to include face slapping, slamming against a wall, stress positions, use of diapers and insects, mock burial, and waterboarding—to break down Zubaydah's final defenses. Mitchell also proposed that the CIA enter into a contract with him and his partner Bruce Jessen, who had likewise never actually conducted an interrogation before, to design and execute the CIA's new interrogation protocols.

After the meetings, the CIA's legal department drafted a letter to Attorney General John Ashcroft, asking the Department of Justice for "a formal declination of prosecution, in advance, for any employees of the United States, who may employ methods in the interrogation of Abu Zubaydah that otherwise might subject those individuals to prosecution." Vice President Cheney's chief counsel, David Addington, worked with like-minded lawyers in the Justice Department's Office of Legal Council (OLC) and the Pentagon to construct a legal basis for "enhanced interrogation techniques" that would protect interrogators from criminal liability. In what became known as the "torture memos," OLC lawyers led by Deputy Attorney General John Yoo adopted a narrow definition of torture that included only "the pain accompanying serious physical injury, such as organ failure, impairment of bodily function, or even death."

AT 11:50 A.M. on August 4, 2002, after Abu Zubaydah had been kept in complete isolation for forty-seven days, the psychological experiment in "learned helplessness" began. Security personnel at Cat's Eye entered his cell, hooded him, stripped him naked, and then slammed him against the wall. Only Air Force psychologists Mitchell and Jensen were to have direct communication with the prisoner. Most other CIA personnel, including the agency medical team, monitored the interrogation on closed-circuit video.

Zubaydah's hood was removed and interrogators grabbed his face in an "attention grab," forcing him to watch as a large confinement box that looked like a coffin was placed on the floor. The interrogators demanded detailed information on terrorist plots against the United States, including names, phone numbers, e-mail addresses, weapons caches, and safe houses. Every time Zubaydah denied having such information, the interrogators slapped him or forcefully grabbed and squeezed his face. After more than six hours of such questioning, Zubaydah was waterboarded for the first time. For over two and a half hours he coughed, vomited, and had involuntary spasms as a result of the water filling his lungs and inducing a sense of drowning, but still he offered no useful information. An e-mail sent to CIA describing the first day of the "enhanced interrogation" was entitled, "So it begins. . . . "

Thus commenced a 24-hour, round-the-clock cycle of torment in which Zubaydah was routinely slammed against a wall, slapped in the face, forced into stress positions, and subjected to loud white noise and sleep deprivation. Whenever he was left alone, he was placed in stress positions or left on the waterboard with a cloth still over his face. He was waterboarded as many as four times a day for varying lengths of time, at one point losing consciousness and, according to the Senate Intelligence Committee report, "becoming completely unresponsive, with bubbles rising through his open full mouth," until medical personnel revived him. For all intents and purposes, Zubaydah had just drowned.

Besides the waterboarding, one of the worst torments was being stuffed into tight boxes for hours on end. Besides the coffinlike confinement box, there was an even smaller one, only 21 inches wide, designed to induce claustrophobia. Zubaydah spent twenty-nine hours in the smaller box, and a total of more than eleven days in the coffin. The interrogators assured him that the only way he was leaving Cat's Eye was in the coffin.

Within just a few days, Zubaydah had been reduced to frequent crying, begging, pleading, and whimpering, yet he continued to deny having any additional information on terrorist plots. By August 9, the sixth day of the interrogation, the CIA team at Cat's Eye provided headquarters with a "collective preliminary assessment" that it was unlikely Zubaydah had "actionable new information about current threats to the United States," and that the interrogation was stretching the bounds of legality. The team was reprimanded by CIA headquarters for raising the question of legality, and ordered to continue. For many of the CIA personnel onsite, the ugliness and futility of the torture was beginning to severely impact morale. On August 8, just four days into the cycle of intense abuse, CIA records showed that "Today's first session . . . had a profound effect on all staff members present . . . it seems the collective opinion that we should not go much further. . . . Several of the team profoundly affected . . . some to the point of tears and choking up."

Three days later, on August 11, a number of the CIA personnel at Cat's Eye were openly discussing demanding a transfer from the black site. They had joined the agency to protect America, not trample its most fundamental values. The team leader wrote headquarters that viewing the torment of Zubaydah on the closed-circuit video "has produced strong feelings of futility (and legality) of escalating or even maintaining the pressure."

At some point the prisoner became a broken man. Frequently he was hysterical and so distressed that he was unable to even communicate. All that Mitchell or Justin had to do was raise his eyebrow without comment, and Zubaydah would obediently walk on his own to the waterboard. If an interrogator snapped his fingers twice, Zubaydah would compliantly lie flat on it to be drowned all over again. The psychologists had achieved the desired effect: the suspect was clearly reduced to a state of "learned helplessness." And still the experiment in psychological deconstruction continued.

On August 23, 2002, seventeen days after it had begun, and fourteen days after CIA officials at Cat's Eye had collectively assessed that Zubaydah had no actionable intelligence to surrender, the experiment was halted. Despite the fact that they extracted virtually no additional intelligence from the man, CIA contractors and psychologists Mitchell and Jensen proclaimed the experiment such a resounding success that it should become the model for future interrogations of suspected terrorists. In a self-serving recommendation that would eventually lead to an $80-plus million contract with the CIA for their company, Mitchell Jessen and Associates, Mitchell and Jensen suggested that in future only psychologists "familiar with interrogation, exploitation and resistance to interrogation should shape compliance of high value captives prior to debriefing by substantive experts."

In a Presidential Daily Brief prepared in October 2002, senior CIA officials characterized Abu Zubaydah as having resisted providing useful information "until becoming more cooperative in early August, *probably in the hope of improving his living conditions*" [emphasis added]. No mention was made of the "enhanced interrogation techniques" used to break him. The CIA documents identified the "key intelligence" gleaned from Zubaydah as information identifying Khalid Sheikh Mohammed as the mastermind of 9/11, and relating to suspected terrorist Jose Padilla. The documents failed to point out that all of that information was acquired by FBI agents Steve Gaudin and Ali Soufan before CIA interrogators ever arrived in Thailand.

In a later interview with the *Guardian* newspaper James Mitchell was unrepentant, giving a spirited defense of the CIA interrogation program as a huge success. The CIA's own Inspector General Report that said Mitchell and Jessen "probably misrepresented" their "expertise" as experienced interrogators was riddled with errors "like my Wikipedia page," Mitchell told the newspaper; the Senate Select Committee on Intelligence's five-year, $40 million investigation, and subsequent report, were the work of "partisan Democrats" intent on "throwing me under the bus" and "rewriting history"; the claims by FBI agents Ali Soufan and Steve Gaudin that their more traditional, rapport-building techniques elicited the most important intelligence, including the identity of Khalid Sheikh Mohammed, are simply unbelievable in Mitchell's recounting.

Mitchell argues more persuasively that in 2002 the "threat matrix was just on fire" and everyone was frantic to head off the next 9/11-style attack. "I'm just a guy who got asked to do something for his country by people at the highest level of government, and I did the best I could," he told the *Guardian*.

Regardless, the die was cast. Briefed on the details of the CIA's enhanced interrogations, FBI officials opted out of the interrogation program

altogether. Rather than recognize the synergy created when FBI interrogators were working hand-in-glove with professional CIA analysts to exploit
the initial intelligence provided by Zubaydah, the Bush administration and
the CIA leadership decided to follow two psychologists and neophyte interrogators down a detour into darkness, a miscalculation that would cast a
shadow on the US war on terrorists for years to come.

# FOUR

# The Crucible
## October 2003–May 2004

D AWN PAINTED BAGHDAD IN A PALETTE OF REDS AND EVERY SHADE of brown, and the city began to come to life. Venders opened their small shops and market stalls and swept dirty sidewalks in the Karadah shopping district in anticipation of the midday crowds looking to buy everything from chickens and newspapers to satellite dishes. A few beat-up cars were already on the road trying to get a jump on the inevitable traffic jams that had grown since the US invasion, or an early place in the long lines that formed each day at gas stations low on petrol. Roadside peddlers were just taking their place on the sidewalks, ladling black-market gasoline from open barrels into small plastic containers for resale, their arms shiny and black up to their elbows.

A car pulling a portable generator crossed the newly reopened 14th of July Bridge, a suspension bridge and major artery over the Tigris River named to celebrate the beginning of Baathist rule. The vehicle turned down a largely deserted road outside the barricaded complex of the Coalition Provisional Authority, parking just outside a high security wall. Against the crimson and brown backdrop of Baghdad at dawn, the car and its generator, painted an incongruous bright blue, caught the eye of a US security officer stationed on a nearby rooftop. As a precaution an Iraqi police patrol was dispatched. Just the day before, October 25, 2003, Major General Martin Dempsey, the US commander responsible for Baghdad as head of a reinforced First Armored Division called Task Force Iron, had reopened the bridge and relaxed curfews as gestures of goodwill on the eve of the Muslim holy month of Ramadan, a concession that created a traffic thoroughfare in the middle of the protected Green Zone.

On the upper floors of the nearby Al Rashid Hotel, Deputy Secretary of Defense Paul Wolfowitz and his entourage were answering six a.m. wake-up calls and just getting out of bed. There had been a dinner reception for the group the night before, followed by drinks at the hotel bar that was packed with soldiers, contractors, journalists, and mercenaries of every conceivable stripe. Not everyone was happy to awaken to early alarms.

A noise outside like the sizzling of bacon on a giant skittle drew many of the hotel guests, including Wolfowitz, to the windows. At that moment between the lightning and the thunderclap, the contrails of the approaching rockets reached out like the fingers of a malevolent hand. Everyone who saw them knew they shouldn't be looking.

The fusillade of 85mm and 68mm rockets took the Al Rashid broadside, shearing off massive chunks of concrete wall, bursting into hotel rooms through shattered windows, blowing locked doors into the hallways like plywood. For a few moments after the attack the hotel was eerily quiet except for a distant alarm and the sound of rushing water from severed water pipes, as if the building itself was in shock. And then the Al Rashid awoke to pandemonium.

Wolfowitz's security detail hurried him toward the stairway from the top floor, the hallway filled with acrid smoke and already ankle-deep in water. Bare-chested men carrying guns spilled into the hallway, and shouts of "Fire!" and "Evacuate!" echoed through the smoke. In the emergency exit stairway glass from shattered partitions crunched underfoot, and the wounded were being carried down in sheets used as makeshift stretchers. Even through the thick smoke the way down was clearly marked by the footprints of boots' stepping through thickly pooled blood.

By midmorning on October 26, Dempsey was trying to explain to Wolfowitz how he had very nearly been killed on the major general's watch. The attack had killed Lieutenant Colonel Charles Buehring, who was in a room one floor below Wolfowitz's, making Buehring the most senior US officer to die in Iraq to that point. Many more guests had been critically injured.

"They do this every time. Every time we do something positive, the bad guys try to reverse the psychology with their own negative act," Dempsey told his civilian boss, revealing not a little frustration with the dynamic of nation building in a time of guerrilla war and terrorism that was increasingly coming to characterize Iraq. The positive concession had been the decision to reopen the 14th of July Bridge, which Dempsey would have to order closed again.

His troops had already captured and were examining the blue "generator" that had turned out to be a homemade multiple rocket launcher. It was an improvised piece of equipment that Dempsey described as a Rube Goldberg–like contraption, indicating the enemy's lack of sophistication. Cleverly improvised explosive devices had yet to become the enemy's weapon of choice in both Iraq and Afghanistan. He and his top commanders were clearly relieved that Iraqi terrorists had not successfully assassinated the Pentagon's number two official.

Before leaving Iraq later that day, Wolfowitz visited those seriously wounded in the attack at a hospital in the Green Zone. Once again he described the attack as a desperate final act of a few of Saddam Hussein's irredeemables. "The victims of this attack, including our colonel who tragically died, are real heroes," Wolfowitz said. "The criminals who are responsible for their deaths and injuries are the same people who have abused and tortured Iraqis for thirty-five years. There's a small number of bitter-enders who think they can take this country back by destabilizing it and scaring us away. They are not going to scare us away. We're going to finish the job despite the last, desperate acts of a dying regime of criminals."

MARTIN DEMPSEY AND his commanders knew the enemy was not a handful of dead-enders of Saddam Hussein's regime. Every morning he

confronted the signs as his staff went through the operational situation report for Task Force Iron's area of operations, which included Baghdad and
its sprawling suburban belts. Indeed, if you were looking for the high-water
mark of the Bush administration's "global war on terrorism," the farthest
reach of the post-9/11 offensive whose momentum carried the US military
through the capitals of two Muslim-majority countries before finally stall-
ing, it was roughly discernible in the static line of Task Force Iron's forces
dispersed throughout Baghdad. Dempsey and the other top commanders
in Iraq didn't yet know it, but the years ahead would be spent trying to consolidate ground already gained, and defend increasingly exposed positions,
an effort that would come to define the post-9/11 wars and ultimately shape
a new model for American warfighting.

By training and doctrine they were the masters of maneuver warfare,
leaders of the air-ground juggernaut that in 1991 routed the Iraqi army in a
matter of days in Operation Desert Storm, and finished the job by toppling
the Iraqi regime in just three weeks of "shock and awe" in the spring of 2003
in Operation Iraqi Freedom. In those campaigns, an Army armored division on the move was highly centralized and hierarchal. Intelligence on the
enemy's whereabouts flowed from the top down, and subordinate brigade
and battalion commanders distinguished themselves by adhering to time-
worn doctrine that prescribed a set of solutions for battlefield challenges.

By contrast, when Dempsey studied the video map in his operations
center in the fall of 2003, Task Force Iron was spread out all over hell's half-
acre, on both sides of the Euphrates and Tigris Rivers that dissected Baghdad. The screen also displayed the Blue Force Tracker, a satellite-linked
intelligence system that showed "friendly" forces with blue arrows, and
known enemy forces with red ones. The Blue Force Tracker display said it
all: Dempsey's units were isolated and spread throughout the city. There
were few red arrows on the entire map. The cold truth was, he and his
commanders didn't even know the enemy's identity, let alone where it was
located.

Dempsey was also learning that their best intelligence flowed from the
bottom up, gathered by companies, platoons, and individual patrols that
were closest to the Arabs on the streets, which turned the Cold War model
of military intelligence on its head. Saddam Hussein's elite Republican

Guard divisions and fanatical fedayeen irregulars that were decimated by US combat power during the initial invasion had melted away in the months since Baghdad fell in mid-April 2003. As a matter of survival they were reforming into a network of attack cells throughout Baghdad, operating mostly independently, albeit seemingly with some central coordination. Dempsey and his commanders had no doctrine for breaking down and disaggregating a US armored division in order to fight a shadowy enemy composed of loosely linked cells and networks.

That shadowy enemy was landing increasingly heavy blows that limited Task Force Iron's freedom of action and room to maneuver. The first major blow had landed on August 7 with a car bomb attack on the Jordanian Embassy that killed 11 people and wounded at least 65 others—retribution for Jordan's having sided with the United States in the Iraq invasion by allowing some six thousand US troops to stage from its soil. On August 20 a suicide bomber driving a cement truck full of explosives had demolished the United Nations headquarters in Iraq, killing 17 people, including the UN secretary general's special representative in Iraq, Sergio Vieira de Mello, and wounding more than 100 others. The attack came less than a month after the UN Security Council voted to endorse the US-backed Iraqi interim government. The enemy Bush administration officials dismissed as "regime dead-enders" was attacking close partners and backers of the US-led coalition, leaving the burden of Iraq's stabilization and reconstruction overwhelmingly on US shoulders.

There was no reliable intelligence on who was behind the attacks. Speculation ranged from former Baathists still loyal to Saddam Hussein, agents of Iraq's neighbors Iran and Syria, and the shadowy Islamic extremist group Ansar al-Islam that had ties to al-Qaeda. Whoever was behind the car bomb attacks forced Dempsey to consolidate Task Force Iron's footprint, closing a number of small combat outposts scattered around the city because they were simply too vulnerable. Pushing US units into larger bases and behind massive blast walls greatly decreased their exposure, but it also had the adverse effect of limiting the interaction of US troops with the Iraqi populace, drying up a critical source of street-level intelligence and information.

The strategic nature of the Ramadan Offensive revealed itself the morning after the attack on the Al Rashid Hotel, and the growing sophistication and coordinated planning of whatever enemies were aligning against US forces in Iraq became clear. Before noon on October 27, a coordinated wave of four suicide bombings in Baghdad killed 40 people and wounded more than 220. Like the earlier attacks on the UN compound and the Jordanian Embassy, the chosen targets in the Ramadan Offensive—four Iraqi police stations and the offices of the International Red Cross—were chosen to counter the US strategy of accelerating the handoff of security responsibilities to Iraqi authorities. If anyone failed to receive the message that siding with the United States was hazardous to your health, the shadowy enemy made an example of Faris Abdul Razzaq al-Assam, one of Baghdad's three deputy mayors, who was shot at pointblank range at an outdoor café by two executioners on the same day as the Al Rashid attack. His assassination was just the latest in a string of murders of Iraqi officials who dared to cooperate with US authorities.

The rapid fall of Saddam Hussein's regime and the triumphalism of the Bush administration's "Mission Accomplished" symbolism had led the American public to believe that the Iraq campaign, like the toppling of the Taliban in Afghanistan, would be a short, rapid, and decisive operation. Wolfowitz's visit and his message to accelerate the handoff of security to the Iraqis themselves was meant to reinforce that narrative, and it was a sure sign that the Bush administration and the American public were getting restless.

Yet like all military men, Marty Dempsey understood that the enemy gets a vote. The Ramadan Offensive left little doubt that an enemy they all hoped had been decisively beaten had instead gone to ground and, after regrouping over the long, hot summer of 2003, was voting to fight on. The problem was that it was not an enemy the US military was prepared to fight. Not only had counterinsurgency lessons and doctrine been expunged from military school curriculums after Vietnam, but the military's high-tech training centers where Dempsey and the other masters of maneuver warfare had honed their craft had created a generation of officers conditioned to go by the book. Observer controllers often graded the performance of a commander who acted in accordance to doctrine and failed as better than that of one who adopted outside-the-box tactics and succeeded. And pity the poor officer who crafted unconventional tactics or solutions at the national training centers and failed.

But if the US Army in 2003 was doctrinaire, it also had its iconoclasts. Dempsey had grown up as an officer in an armored cavalry regiment, a unit that scouted out ahead of the main force and probed so as to force the enemy to reveal himself. Its mission rewarded boldness and a certain independence of mind-set and spirit.

Martin Dempsey's decision to attend West Point had been more a lark than a career choice. He grew up in an Irish American enclave in the ethnic patchwork of immigrant neighborhoods in Bayonne, New Jersey, his father delivering mail and his mother stocking shelves at a local grocery. All four of his grandparents were Irish immigrants.

He had gone to Catholic school through his senior year, meeting his future wife, Deanie, at John S. Burke Catholic High School in Goshen, New York. Because of the influence of a favorite uncle, his first choice had been the US Naval Academy. When he was rejected because of poor eyesight, a track coach pushed him to apply to West Point. But in the summer of 1969, with the country turning decisively against the Vietnam War, a commitment to the US Army was practically the last thing on young Dempsey's mind. He had received a New York State Regents scholarship to attend Manhattan College, and had already chosen a roommate and picked his classes. And then his mother called and told him that a telegram had just arrived: He had been accepted to West Point, and they needed him to report in less than a week.

At home Dempsey tried to explain that he had already made up his mind to attend Manhattan College. He was having a rational conversation, but his mother was having an emotional one. She saw something clearly that was hidden from him. The moment she burst into tears, Marty Dempsey knew: Oh my God, I'm going to West Point.

At West Point he heard the message drummed into all plebes in ways profound and petty: "You are not good enough to be here!" That spark lit a fire deep in Dempsey's soul, and the more his drill instructors pushed him toward the door, the more stubbornly he pushed back. He built his career by proving that message wrong. Dempsey liked to joke that he never worried about what to wear a day in his life, having traded the uniform of a Catholic school for the uniforms of a West Point cadet and finally a US Army officer.

There are plenty of officers who lead by bombast and steamrolling personalities, and others who build loyalty with a common touch. Dempsey fell in the latter category, and his leadership style was more cerebral and intuitive. Even at the senior level of command where nearly everyone is a type A personality, there is a dividing line separating the officers who know they are the most intelligent people in the room, and those with the requisite humility to lean on others in search for collective wisdom. The first can climb as high as individual smarts and well-rehearsed doctrine can take them; but the latter are instinctively better able to cope with unfamiliar challenges that arise beyond the realm of doctrine, and that defy the expertise of any one person or the capabilities of any single organization. With a nascent insurgency growing and the fires of terrorist attacks burning all around, Iraq in the sweltering early fall of 2003 was a forge almost uniquely suited to delineating that dividing line.

As fate would have it, at least two other Army iconoclasts and intellectuals were in Iraq during the Ramadan offensive of 2003 who fell on the collaborative side of that dividing line, both of them fellow West Point graduates. Whereas Dempsey represented the conventional Army and the masters of maneuver warfare who were suddenly struggling to adapt to unconventional warfare, his friend and former West Point classmate Major General David Petraeus stood in for the light infantry and air mobile side of the service. Petraeus had completed his doctrinal thesis on counterinsurgency warfare, and by all accounts he was successfully applying those lessons as the commander of the 101st Airborne Division in Mosul, in northern Iraq. Graduating a few years behind them at West Point was Brigadier General Stanley McChrystal, who was in Iraq as the newly minted commander of Joint Special Operations Command (JSOC), the US military's elite counterterrorism force and the operational arm of US Special Operations Forces.

The hard lessons those three leaders took from the crucible of Iraq in 2003–2004 would have a profound impact on the United States' post-9/11 conflicts. The strategies, doctrines, and operational concepts they helped pioneer to free Iraq and later Afghanistan from the grip of stubborn insurgencies and nihilistic terrorists would lead to unprecedented levels of cooperation between traditionally distrustful US conventional and Special

Operations forces, and between the US military and intelligence and law enforcement agencies. Their experiences in the coming decade would in many ways define the longest period of war in American history.

IN THE OPERATIONS center of the 101st Airborne Division in Mosul, Major General David Petraeus kept a sign posted on the wall: "Will this operation take more bad guys off the street than it creates by the way it is conducted?" The message was meant as a lodestar for his commanders, but by Petraeus's own reckoning US operations in Iraq generally were failing that simple test on a grand scale.

Among the handful of division commanders in Iraq, Petraeus was uniquely prepared to grasp the complexities of irregular warfare that they all now faced. In the top of his West Point class and the top graduate in his class at the US Army Command and Staff College, Petraeus had written his doctoral dissertation at Princeton on counterinsurgency warfare in Vietnam, lessons that the Army had largely expunged in the decades since the war. He had also commanded in both Haiti and Bosnia in the 1990s, conducting stability operations in traumatized societies and hunting for war criminals. His career was steeped in the lessons of counterinsurgency warfare, and in Iraq the United States was breaking them by the numbers.

Lesson number one was the need to have a nuanced and granular understanding of a country before you decide to invade it. The so-called Iraq experts that had been assigned to the 101st Airborne before the division fought its way up the country to Mosul didn't even know if the population in the cities and towns along the way were majority Shiite or Sunni Islam. Which is to say they knew virtually nothing. The focus of Operation Iraqi Freedom had been on Baghdad from the start, and Petraeus received almost no advance intelligence on the situation in Mosul, or guidance on what to do there. The edicts that did come down from the Coalition Provisional Authority (CPA) routinely broke his cardinal rule of not taking actions that created more enemies than they already faced.

Petraeus understood that insurgencies are essentially a contest for political power, meaning any effective counterinsurgency campaign requires a tightly coordinated civil-military partnership. And the relationship between

CPA head L. Paul Bremer and his military commanders was clearly dysfunctional. How else to explain Bremer's initial decision, against the advice of his top military commanders, to disband the Iraqi Army without so much as a stipend offered, putting hundreds of thousands of trained military men out of work? That decision had led to weeks of demonstrations in Mosul that nearly turned violent. Next came the CPA's overzealous "de-Baathification" campaign that rooted out fourth-tier technocrats and government functionaries, including 120 tenured professors in Mosul that Petraeus had hoped to employ so as to keep the local university open. De-Baathification broadcast the message to tens of thousands of additional Iraqis that they belonged on the ash heap of history.

Petraeus had finally objected personally when Bremer briefed US military commanders on a new campaign plan, written by one of his aides who had been in Iraq for a few weeks and had never stepped out of the Green Zone. With no input from his senior military commanders, Bremer proposed shutting down all the state-run industries, leaving hundreds of thousands of additional Iraqis without a job.

Petraeus raised his hand and cut in. "Sir, with great respect," he began, recognizing the phrase as the most insincere in the English language, "We have already fired the Iraqi Army without telling those men what their future holds. We've imposed de-Baathification without reconciliation. We've created hundreds of thousands of enemies of the 'new Iraq.' Now you want to tell everyone who still works for a state-run company in a statist economy that they no longer have jobs?" Luckily, Bremer's campaign plan was never fully implemented.

Petraeus's answer to those challenges was to spend an inordinate amount of energy and time establishing local governance in Mosul, an exhausting effort that required forming a fractious governing caucus that included Sunni and Shiite Arabs, Kurds, Turkmen, Christians, and Yazidis. Whenever someone questioned why they were spending so much effort in government formation rather than in aggressive stability sweeps or counterterrorism operations, Petraeus would direct them to the poster on the wall of the operations center: Because they needed Iraqi partners, not more people on the street nursing a grievance against the coalition.

Not that Petraeus shied away from aggressive manhunting and counter-terrorism operations. He considered them a vital element of his campaign plan to stabilize Mosul. In June the Special Forces task force attached to the 101st Airborne had successfully tracked down Saddam Hussein's sons, the noted rapists and torturers Uday and Qusay Hussein. Petraeus was proud that both were killed in Mosul during a fierce, three-hour firefight with his forces. That was good cooperation to build on, a point he made when fellow West Point alumnus Stanley McChrystal visited the 101st Airborne in October on his initial fact-finding trip to Iraq. Both generals had spent significant portions of their careers commanding in the Eighty-second Air-borne Division. The two liked each other and were on the fast track for top command, but neither Petraeus nor McChrystal could yet foresee how their careers would intersect fatefully in the years to come.

On the eve of Ramadan 2003, a Black Hawk helicopter carrying JSOC commander Brigadier General Stanley McChrystal and Delta Force deputy commander Lieutenant Colonel Austin "Scott" Miller sped back to Bagh-dad along the muddy ribbon of the Tigris River. Their initial fact-finding mission to Iraq nearly completed, both soldiers were lost in their thoughts.

Stan McChrystal had grown up an army brat always knowing he wanted to be a soldier like his father. Herbert McChrystal Jr. was a West Point graduate who had served in combat in both Korea and Vietnam, and had risen to the rank of major general. Over his career Stan had commanded as an officer in the Eighty-second Airborne Division, in elite Ranger light infantry regiments, in the Special Operations Forces (SOF), and in a heavy armored division. As the chief of staff of the Eighteenth Airborne Corps under General Dan McNeill, he had deployed to Afghanistan the previous year. His most recent assignment was as the director of operations, or J-3, on the Joint Staff in the Pentagon. That breadth of experience was unusual in the highly specialized and insular world of Special Forces that operated under the umbrella of Joint Special Operations Command, both "white" SOF units, such as the Green Berets, and secretive "black" SOF direct ac-tion counterterrorism units, such as SEAL Team Six and Delta Force. The

Special Forces "tribe of tribes" gathered under JSOC's banner were the best trained and most experienced in uniform, but McChrystal's broader perspective and diverse background gave him an appreciation for the talents and capabilities that each of the US Army's various fiefdoms brought to the fight, instilling an instinct for collaboration that was sometimes at odds with the more insular elitism of Special Operations Forces.

Once back at Task Force 714's headquarters element at the Baghdad International Airport, McChrystal began to diagram his findings on a whiteboard with Scott Miller. He drew an hourglass with the top half representing forward-deployed Special Forces units attached to the major US commands in such places as Mosul and Tikrit, and the bottom half depicting the rear-area headquarters in Baghdad. The skinny bottleneck in the middle represented the insufficient communications bandwidth and command relationships needed to effectively link the two.

Task Force 714, the umbrella command-and-control team for JSOC's forward-deployed counterterrorism units, was less a coherent organization than an assemblage of far-flung teams with a rear-area headquarters largely irrelevant to the fight. Scott Miller conceded that if the bottom half of the hourglass were eliminated entirely, it would hardly make any difference to his Delta Force detachments in the field. They lacked fundamental unity of command. Forward teams operated independently with only vague guidance from their distant headquarters. Intelligence gathering was haphazard and slow. Raw intelligence and evidence gathered on raids and snatch-and-grab operations was dumped on a single overwhelmed intelligence analyst. Captured computers, documents, maps, photographs, and all manner of information was thrown into large garbage bags, which together with important prisoners were flown back to headquarters, where they disappeared into a black hole.

As a JSOC staff officer back in 1990, McChrystal had lost twelve soldiers, killed in an air crash during a training exercise because of poor synchronization of unit movements, and ever since he had thought about how dispersed military forces could be more centrally commanded and tightly coordinated. Or maybe it was just that an officer who had been carefully groomed since West Point, and had excelled at every level of command, had risen into exactly the right job at precisely the time that the nation needed him most. The annals of US military history are strewn with such instances of serendipity, when a combination of careful military grooming and dire national need conspire to identify an exceptional leader.

At the end of his tour of discovery, McChrystal concluded that Task Force 714 suffered from exactly the same limitations that bedeviled the entire US military campaign in 2003: lack of a common strategy for winning, and of a network linking command-and-control elements and operational units that was capable of executing it. He began to visualize the changes that needed to be made for the task force to prevail in the fight that was clearly coming. He would need to tighten the linkages in a chain of command that stretched from Baghdad to the hinterlands, and across two war zones in Iraq and Afghanistan, to enable truly centralized command of decentralized operations. An unprecedented degree of intelligence exploitation was needed to identify and target an enemy that wore no uniform and hid in the shadows. He envisioned a pace of operations and a degree of cooperation between Special Operations Forces, conventional US military forces, and intelligence agencies that had never been achieved before. Above all it would require building a network of operators and analysts that could rapidly translate orders into action and prove agile enough to defeat the enemy's increasingly deadly networks of far-flung cells.

Early on McChrystal sensed the need to fundamentally transform Joint Special Operations Command and Special Operations Forces writ large, an effort he knew would meet with stubborn resistance. He had yet to realize the effort would also play a large role in transforming the vast US counterterrorism apparatus. Such profound seismic shifts require the buy-in and sacrifice of thousands, and they outlast the leadership of any one individual. And yet transformative change even on an epic scale can begin with a single catalyst, an innovator who inspires others and sparks a movement.

In Stanley McChrystal the US military had found one of its chief innovators for the post-911 "global war on terrorism," a lean officer of quiet intensity whose devotion to the cause and code of personal discipline reminded some of a warrior monk. He was driven by a mounting sense of urgency. McChrystal had been studying operations in Iraq from Washington as director of operations on the Joint Staff, so he knew that the situation had been deteriorating all summer. Although he was prepared to be disappointed by the situation in Iraq, what he found was nonetheless shocking.

The staff at the US embassy seemed as if it had been in-country for about sixty minutes, not six months. The most complex undertaking the nation had attempted in decades—invading a populous and strategically important country, destroying its government, and planting the flag of democracy—was being led by an ad hoc team of inexperienced civilians. Various intelligence agencies were working largely independently according to their own agendas, and militarily no one appeared to be in charge and able to organize a collective effort. The approaches adopted by division commanders, such as Dempsey, Petraeus, and Major General Ray Odierno of the Fourth Infantry in Tikrit, were all different, everyone learning on the fly. The campaign was fragmented, with very little clarity about the objectives and about the enemy that was trying to stop them. Senior US officials were still talking about finding stockpiles of weapons of mass destruction. No one was even willing to utter the words *terrorism, insurgency,* or *war.*

As the chief of staff of the Eighteenth Airborne Corps in Afghanistan the previous year, McChrystal had witnessed the same sense of drift and lack of coordinated effort. The secretary of defense had put an arbitrary cap of only 7,500 on US troop levels inside Afghanistan, severely hamstringing their operations. US forces were trying to stand up an Afghan army by dispensing hundreds of AK-47 rifles and offering slapdash training. Bagram Air Base was overrun by a host of weird international characters in beards, dressed as if they were going on safari at an animal park and wearing low-slung pistols on their hips, yet who never seemed to leave the base. At the same time, the US military was being seduced by warlords who had survived decades of conflict by perfecting the double and triple cross, running circles around American neophytes in a professional game of power politics. And now they were doing it again in Iraq, and it assaulted McChrystal's sense of the seriousness of the situation in both countries.

Before leaving Iraq in October 2003, McChrystal huddled one last time with Scott Miller to solicit his thoughts. As the head of JSOC and deputy commander of Delta Force, respectively, they commanded organizations that had not even existed twenty-five years earlier. Delta Force had been established in the late 1970s as a direct-action counterterrorism and hostage rescue force in response to the proliferation of terrorist groups at that time, many of them Palestinian. The unit's first mission in 1980 to rescue American hostages held by Iran failed spectacularly, with the death of eight service members at a rendezvous point inside Iran dubbed "Desert One." Delta Force commander Colonel Charlie Beckwith had recommended creation of a permanent counterterrorism joint task force with unified command-and-control of direct-action units, such as Delta Force and SEAL Team Six, which was created in 1980 as the Navy's answer to Delta Force. That idea came to life with the establishment of the Joint Special Operations Command in 1980. The Holloway Commission that investigated the tragedy at Desert One called for the establishment of a new Special Operations umbrella command with its own budget and centralized authority to oversee training, planning, equipping, and support of special operations units from all the various services. The idea eventually became the US Special Operations Command (SOCOM), established in 1987.

As Delta Force's deputy commander, Miller had been watching the violence in Iraq steadily increase throughout the summer and early fall. Iraqis were no longer throwing up their hands and surrendering; rather, they were standing and fighting to the death. The task force lost two commandos in a fierce firefight in Ramadi out in Anbar Province, and yet apparently the Powers That Be in Washington did not want to call what they were confronting an insurgency, and the US military commanders in Iraq dutifully fell into line.

Miller had served as the Delta Force assault commander during the ferocious Battle of Mogadishu in 1993, made infamous by the book and movie *Black Hawk Down*. The assumption back then was that UH-60 Black Hawk helicopters could operate relatively safely in a congested and contested urban environment, and after two Black Hawks were shot down, Miller and his Delta Team were part of a rescue force that fought through the night against thousands of Somali militiamen in the crooked side streets and back alleys of Mogadishu. The Battle of Mogadishu cost the lives of eighteen soldiers and wounded scores more, and it taught Miller to always be wary of false positives, those basic assumptions that rise to the level of conventional wisdom and are taken for granted as accepted facts.

The Office of the Secretary of Defense wanted to believe the US military was conducting stability operations in Iraq against a few "regime dead enders," which struck Miller as a false positive of the first order. If the leadership wasn't even willing to call the enemy by its proper name, they probably weren't adequately preparing for the fight that was surely coming.

"Sir, we're deluding ourselves if we don't think we're facing a full and growing insurgency," Miller told McChrystal.

AS DIVISION COMMANDERS and former classmates, Martin Dempsey and David Petraeus talked often in Iraq. During one of those conversations Petraeus had gone out of his way to recommend one of Dempsey's brigade commanders. The colonel commanding First Armored Division's Second "Striker" Brigade could certainly be a nuisance, and his unorthodox tactics and willingness to trample regulations had convinced a number of senior officers on Dempsey's division staff that he was practically a rogue commander. Staff frequently warned Dempsey that the man would break one regulation too many, and possibly end both their careers.

Dempsey also knew that Colonel Ralph "Rob" Baker had taught counterinsurgency warfare both at the Infantry School at Fort Benning, and at Britain's Royal Military Academy at Sandhurst, where he learned from the accepted experts the lessons from years of guerrilla warfare against the Irish Republican Army. As it happened, Second Brigade had responsibility for the Green Zone and much of central Baghdad that included 70 percent of the foreign embassies, so Baker was a natural choice to look into the attack on the Al Rashid and other targets of the Ramadan Offensive. At Dempsey's direction, Colonel Baker was given a mission that was unconstrained by brigade boundaries or a strict interpretation of by-the-book regulations: find the enemy cells behind the Al Rashid attack and other spectacular bombings that were making life increasingly untenable in Baghdad, and take them down. After the Ramadan Offensive, Dempsey had decided that maybe a rogue was what he needed.

Ever since the Al Rashid attack, Rob Baker had pressed his unique intelligence unit into overdrive to mine everything it could learn about the local insurgency, having grasped long before that human intelligence was the key to the kind of counterinsurgency war the US military was confronting in Iraq. As his soldiers had quickly learned while patrolling the unfamiliar streets of Baghdad, without the eyes and ears of local Iraqis they were fighting blind against an enemy hiding in plain sight.

As a result of that insight, Baker had created a brigade intelligence shop unlike any other in the conventional US Army. He enlisted the advice and help of a number of reservists on his staff who were detectives and police investigators in their civilian lives. Using stacks of captured US dollars that had been hoarded by Saddam's regime, and stretching Army regulations beyond recognition, he had established the "Striker Service Agency" and put on its payroll a host of Iraqi informants and surveillance teams throughout his area of operations in central Baghdad. His staff kept an account of every dollar spent, and Baker had discovered early on that while money may not buy you love, it could sure purchase a lot of cooperation in Iraq. Resistant at first, his battalion commanders had come to accept that they were graded on their ability to recruit and run informants in an ever-widening intelligence-gathering network. By the time of the Al Rashid attack, that network already included former Iraqi intelligence agents and military officers, police officers, university professors, local imams, politicians, taxi drivers—even prostitutes.

Rather than immediately send detainees to Abu Ghraib prison and captured documents and computer hard drives to division headquarters as stipulated in protocol, Baker had his intelligence shop build its own jail and conduct interrogations and document exploitation on its own. The jail itself was seasoned with Iraqi informants on Striker's payroll who often gleaned more from passing comments and conversations with fellow prisoners than was revealed in interrogations. Released prisoners were offered a taxi ride home, and those who unburdened themselves and admitted their complicity in the insurgency to a sympathetic Iraqi taxi driver were shocked to discover that they had been driven right back to jail, discovering too late that the drivers were paid informants of Striker Service Agency.

The production of "actionable intelligence" led to more arrests and more focused and probing interrogations and investigations, freeing the brigade from the need to conduct the broad security sweeps that earlier in the deployment had paralyzed entire sections of Baghdad and infuriated the locals. The result was a steadily increasing insight into the insurgency in and around Baghdad, and into the leadership hierarchies that guided it. Daily targeting briefs in Second Brigade's operations center came to resemble an Arab genealogy course, with the tribal and familial ties that connected various insurgents and their operating cells laid out in link charts favored by CIA counterterrorism analysts. In most cases each branch of the tree was capped with a picture, name, aliases, and preferred mosque of a suspected insurgent.

Just two weeks after the Al Rashid rocket attack, Colonel Baker and the Second Brigade launched Operation Striker Elton to take down the insurgent cell behind the operation, named in honor of pop singer Elton John's hit "Rocket Man." On the night of November 8, 2003, Baker's convoy of Humvees snaked through the largely deserted streets of Baghdad, the operation taking them well outside of the Second Brigade's normal boundaries. As they passed under each bridge, a gunner standing through the roof of the lead vehicle would swivel and aim a searchlight on the overpass above, while gunners in the trailing vehicles turned and swept their automatic weapons in the light's arc, looking for telltale movement. It was a tic of urban survival that Second Brigade soldiers had learned the hard way.

At a designated spot, the convoy turned into a darkened and deserted dirt lot, and the Humvees formed a circle and pulled tents off their back to set up a tactical operations post. A computer screen in Baker's command vehicle displayed a detailed city map and the positions, tracked by satellite and updated every few seconds, of the various units in his strike force. Striker Service Agency had Iraqi informants driving through the neighborhoods in civilian vehicles, dropping infrared chemical lights in front of the targeted houses where suspected members of the insurgent bombing cell lived. Unseen by the naked eye, the infrared lights shone like beacons through night-vision goggles.

Before long, another convoy of vehicles pulled into the dirt lot, and Major General Dempsey stepped out of a black, armored SUV with tinted windows. Baker knew that Dempsey was there to keep an eye on the unconventional operation, but he was glad to see his boss. Rather than being by-the-book, Dempsey was an intuitive leader who didn't carry the baggage of a big ego, which made him open to new ideas and unconventional methods. Baker also knew from backchannels at division headquarters that a number of his superiors on the division staff had wanted to shut the Striker Service Agency down. Dempsey was taking a risk by backing his operation. Before the operation could begin, however, Baker had to ask his boss to turn off the electronic jamming equipment that the general's vehicle used to disable radio-triggered improvised explosive devices, which was interfering with the brigade's communications.

After the signal was given, the strike teams descended on their targets. Team members broke the night's quiet, shouting in Arabic and hammering loudly on doors. Calls soon started flooding in over the tactical radio, repeating code names given each individual insurgent targeted and captured—"Zulu Zero Seven," "Zulu Zero Ten," "Zulu Zero Two." Before the night was over, Operation Striker Elton had netted three dozen suspected insurgents. After interrogations and evidence exploitation, twenty-nine of them would be imprisoned for their role in the Al Rashid rocket attack and other insurgent operations in Baghdad.

THE INTELLIGENCE BONANZA from Operation Striker Elton became the gift that kept on giving for Dempsey and Task Force Iron. Baker's Striker Service Agency discovered later that the operation had actually taken down one of Saddam Hussein's three insurgent cells in Baghdad. The loss dealt a serious blow to the Baathists' operations in the capital. Yet even as the Baathist insurgency began waning in late 2003, the face of the enemy was rapidly changing.

Operation Striker Elton had netted Shawki al-Kubesyi, thought to be the top financier of foreign terrorists entering Iraq from elsewhere in the Middle East to join Islamic extremist groups, most notably Ansar al-Islam, a shadowy Kurdish terrorist group that had operated in northern Iraq during Saddam's reign and had ties to al-Qaeda. Alleged connections between al-Qaeda and Saddam Hussein's regime trumpeted by Bush administration officials before the invasion were specious. But by the end of 2003 the shadow of Islamist terrorism, which intelligence analysts in Iraq sensed had been lengthening throughout the year, had finally grown substantial enough to take shape and be given a recurring name: Abu Musab al-Zarqawi, an itinerant Jordanian terrorist and top al-Qaeda operative who had ties to Ansar al-Islam, and was behind most of the attacks of the Ramadan Offensive.

Pulling the threads from Operation Striker Elton, the Striker Service Agency became an increasingly important player in the intelligence gathering community in Iraq. With their own homegrown product, Baker and his team became more adept at bartering and sharing intelligence data with other agencies operating in and around Baghdad, to include the CIA, Britain's MI6 intelligence service, and the FBI. By far the most fruitful and unusual collaboration was between the Second Brigade and the Delta Force detachment in Baghdad. As it happened, Rob Baker had only been one year ahead of Scott Miller at West Point, and the two men had become friends as young lieutenants in the Eighty-second Airborne Division. Together they would develop one of the most symbiotic relationships between a conventional US Army brigade and a "black ops" Special Forces unit in the entire military.

In November 2003 Scott Miller was back in Iraq conducting an interagency survey with an eye toward tightening some of the linkages between the major intelligence and military players in Baghdad. He stopped by Dempsey's Second Brigade headquarters to talk with Rob Baker and get acquainted with the Striker Service Agency. Miller believed his old friend from the Eighty-second had become one of the most innovative officers in adapting to the insurgency that they all felt brewing. The next time JSOC commander Stan McChrystal was in Baghdad, Miller brought him out to Second Brigade headquarters and had Baker walk his boss through everything they were accomplishing with Striker Service Agency. Baker's brigade was producing the one thing that was in shortest supply in Iraq in late 2003, and that was actionable intelligence.

Unencumbered by the suspicions so often at the heart of the relationship between conventional military units and Special Forces, Baker and Miller began planning joint operations between the Second Brigade and Delta Force that raised a lot of eyebrows around Baghdad. The partnership was a dramatic departure from standard operations. Typically, secretive Delta Force strike teams made unannounced raids in the night that inevitably spooked the locals and took conventional force leaders by surprise, leaving General Dempsey and his brigade commanders to handle the blowback from furious Iraqi officials. For his part, Miller was perplexed by frequent comments from other conventional force officers that Baker was some sort of renegade. He may be a rule breaker, Miller thought, but the rules had ceased making sense. At least he was an effective renegade.

After one of his visits to Second Brigade headquarters in the Green Zone, Scott Miller and his survey team were driving back to their headquarters at the Baghdad International Airport. At night there was rarely any traffic on the 7-mile stretch of road, and if there were ever any traffic lights on the highway they had long ago been shot to hell. The black SUV was speeding through the darkest stretch of road that Miller ever remembered seeing when it was hit by machine gun fire from multiple directions. The thump of impacts stitched down both sides of the truck like hammer blows, and multiple rounds exited the windshield just above Miller's head. The SUV swerved and lurched dangerously to one side. The driver, Jimmy Reese, was hit and slumped over, but he kept the pedal to the metal. Then Miller felt the impact of the bullet like a hard punch just below his body armor, and his breaths became shallow as the truck careened down the pitch-dark gauntlet. He would recover from his wound, but he added to his list of false positives the supposedly benign thoroughfare between Baghdad airport and the Green Zone called Route Irish.


AT THE ONE-YEAR mark the strategic incoherence at the core of Operation Iraqi Freedom had spread like rot through an increasingly shaky enterprise, manifesting itself in confusion and self-delusion. Senior Bush administration officials imposed a constant mismatch between goals, resources, and timelines in Iraq, and it bedeviled US military commanders, stunting progress and widening fissures in their own ranks on the best way forward. What felt haphazard and dangerously confused on the ground at the time, in a land that the Americans fundamentally did not understand, was in fact a pitiless strategic folly.

With the failure to find weapons of mass destruction, the White House had subtly changed the primary goal to establishing a functioning democracy in Iraq as a way to cure the autocratic sclerosis afflicting the Middle East, a precursor of Islamic extremism. Bush liked to use the analogy of his father's fighting the Japanese in World War II and living to see both Japan and Germany turned into vibrant democracies and key US allies. Never mentioned in that analogy was the inconvenient fact that more than half a century after those wars, the United States still stationed tens of thousands of its troops in those countries, as well as in South Korea. Having dismantled the institutions of the Iraqi state, creating fertile ground for an insurgency that attracted the fastest growing al-Qaeda franchise in the terrorist pantheon, the George W. Bush administration already had one foot out the exit door in Iraq by April 2004.

Adding to the troubles of Dempsey and the other division commanders in Iraq, the dead-end the Bush administration had initially steered down with its secret CIA prisons, "enhanced interrogation techniques," and legal opinions redefining *torture* had culminated in a controversy involving the sprawling prison on the rough outskirts of Baghdad called Abu Ghraib, where Saddam Hussein had enforced his iron-fisted rule with torture and executions. In January 2004, media reports and photos revealed that a US Military Police (MP) unit at the prison had routinely inflicted torture and sexual sadism on Iraqi prisoners there. The Bush administration tried to portray the abuse as the isolated acts of a rogue MP unit, even though many of the interrogation techniques approved by the chain of command at Abu Ghraib—to include temperature extremes, forced nudity, and extreme sleep deprivation—mirrored some of the "enhanced interrogation techniques" adopted by the CIA and signed off by the White House. The extrajudicial gloves-off approach to interrogations of high-value targets embraced by Vice President Dick Cheney had predictably filtered out into the wider national security structure involved in the "global war on terrorism," finding its logical expression in the abuses at Abu Ghraib.

The sickening photos from Abu Ghraib made the front pages of newspapers around the globe, and across the Middle East, and they couldn't have come at a worse time. In the spring of 2004 the US military was engaged in the largest replacement in force in half a century, with outgoing and incoming divisions swapping out responsibilities. US commanders were trying to ensure that the painstaking relationships of trust with Iraqi tribal and political leaders established over the previous year were maintained and passed along to incoming officers. That trust began to bleed out with the publication of each successive photograph of the torture and humiliation of Arab men by a female MP and her grinning colleagues. Worse, the Abu Ghraib photos became recruiting posters for Abu Musab al-Zarqawi and al-Qaeda in Iraq, spurring a wave of enraged jihadists from across the Middle East to flock to his black banner in Iraq to defend Islamic honor, giving the insurgency an even more pronounced religious dimension and further fulfilling Osama bin Laden's narrative of a war between Islam and the West.

Meanwhile, the internecine bureaucratic warfare between Donald Rumsfeld's Defense Department and Colin Powell's State Department, which had conducted nearly all of the preinvasion planning for stability operations in Iraq as part of its "Future of Iraq" project, had deprived US military commanders of needed civil support and guidance. The dysfunctional relationship between the Pentagon's chosen civil authority, L. Paul Bremer, and US generals was the opposite of synergistic.

Iraq was a tinderbox in March 2004, and two unforeseen incidents provided the match that ignited a general uprising against the US occupation by Iraqi Sunnis and Shiites alike. Predictably, Bremer poured fuel onto both fires. If the Bush administration's post-9/11 "global war on terrorism" really was another type of war, to paraphrase John F. Kennedy, war new in its intensity but ancient in its ethnic and religious origins, war by terrorists and insurgents who sought through ambush to erode and exhaust their enemy, then it was about to become clear that the United States was losing that war. For frontline US military leaders, such as Martin Dempsey, David Petraeus, and Stanley McChrystal, staring at the Iraqi bonfire and contemplating the once unthinkable prospect of a US military defeat offered a painful epiphany, and the lessons they took from the experience would reshape America's post-9/11 wars.

IN MARCH 2004, Bremer ordered Dempsey's First Armored Division forces to close the newspaper of the firebrand Shiite cleric Muqtada al-Sadr. A virulently anti-American cleric with close ties to Shiite Iran, al-Sadr had the backing of a large militia that called itself the Mahdi Army, or JAM (for "Jaish al-Mahdi"). The Mahdi Army held sway in many of the Shiite-dominated southern Iraqi cities, such as Najaf, Karbala, al-Kut, and al-Hillah, as well as in the teeming Shiite slums in Baghdad called "Sadr City." Muqtada al-Sadr had been a thorn in the side of US forces virtually since they entered Iraq, and at Friday prayers he frequently incited violence against the Coalition Provisional Authority and Iraqi "collaborators," incendiary comments that were reprinted in the newspaper *Al-Hawza* that served as his mouthpiece. Dempsey had developed a standing plan for capturing and arresting al-Sadr, but it had been repeatedly shelved for fear of sparking a general Shiite uprising against the coalition as US military forces were focused on a mostly Sunni insurgency led by al-Zarqawi and al-Qaeda in Iraq.

Especially with the replacement in force under way, those concerns were heightened, and Dempsey argued against closing al-Sadr's newspaper. In typical fashion, Bremer ignored the advice of his on-the-ground commander and insisted that the paper must be closed anyway. On March 26, First Armored forces backed by Iraqi police dutifully shut *Al-Hawza* down. Almost immediately, angry crowds of Shiites shouting insults and burning American flags began gathering at the newspaper's office in Baghdad each morning. Soon the crowds had swelled to more than ten thousand angry Shiite men, many of them carrying AK-47 rifles and rocket-propelled grenades, and there were reports of similar anticoalition demonstrations in a number of Shiite cities in the south.

Angered by Bremer's decision to close the al-Sadr newspaper, and inspired by a Sunni uprising centered in the town of Fallujah, the Mahdi Army went on a rampage, taking outright control of the southern strongholds of Najaf, Karbala, al-Hilla, and Kufa. Those rapid gains straddled the main US supply line that ran from Kuwait to Baghdad, threatening to cut the logistical lifeline for the main body of US forces in Iraq. In responding to the Shiite uprising in Baghdad's Sadr City, the newly arrived First Cavalry Division became embroiled in a desperate, twenty-four-hour firefight. Eight US soldiers were killed and sixty more wounded in the fighting.

Martin Dempsey was forced to extend the First Armored Division's combat tour an extra three months, sending his forces south to retake the southern cities from the Mahdi Army. He would never forget their shock at an uprising by Shiite militias that were not considered a major threat. He was also surprised by the utter collapse of a handful of Iraqi National Guard units that his forces had trained and mentored. After that "black swan" moment, Dempsey also began questioning some of the underlying assumptions behind the technological "revolution in military affairs" advocated by Rumsfeld.

"April 2004 in Iraq is when the lightbulb really went off for me," Dempsey would tell me later. "Here we were, an army that prided itself on being on the absolute leading edge of technology, of being able to see first, understand first, and if necessary shoot first; and suddenly we were facing these simultaneous uprisings! We all had this moment like, 'Wow, I just didn't see that coming!' That suggested to me that relying too heavily on technology in this era was dangerous. In April 2004 in Iraq, technology was less important than understanding anthropology and sociology and what was on the minds of Iraqis on the street."

Major General David Petraeus was dispatched back to Iraq during the twin uprisings of April–May 2004 to learn why US-trained Iraqi security forces crumbled in the face of the uprisings. To the list of missions the US military confronted in Iraq for which it had neither doctrine nor a core capability, he added standing up an indigenous army virtually from scratch in a populous country. Of the five Iraqi Civil Defense Corps battalions in Baghdad, almost a third of them failed to report to duty during the fighting. One battalion recruited mostly from the Shiite slums of Sadr City reported 80 percent absenteeism. The Civil Defense Corps unit in Fallujah disintegrated, and many of those that did not abandon their posts joined the Sunni insurgents outright. When the first battalion of the new Iraqi Army was ordered to deploy to Fallujah, roughly half of its members deserted.

"I found that Iraq had really blown up with the twin Sunni and Shiite uprisings, and Iraqi security forces that had been treated less like soldiers, and more like military daycare, predictably failed to show up for work when the fighting got tough and we really needed them," Petraeus recalled. After briefing the Pentagon and White House on the dire situation in Iraq, Petraeus would be deployed back to Iraq as the first commander of the Multinational Security Training program, the first serious effort to build Iraqi security forces from the ground up with a strong foundation. He would be followed in that job by Martin Dempsey.

Brigadier General Stanley McChrystal was in Fallujah on the one-year anniversary of the Iraq invasion. On March 31, four guards from the private contracting firm Blackwater, all of them former US Special Forces, had been ambushed in Fallujah, their bodies pulled from their SUV, set on fire, hacked with shovels, and dragged behind cars. At least two of them were strung up on the beams of a bridge like slaughterhouse carcasses.

After the outrage, Paul Bremer demanded that the US Marines in charge of the area clear Fallujah of insurgents. Newly arrived Marine Corps Major General James Mattis and his leadership team, which included Brigadier General John Kelly, objected. The Marine officers wanted to try a softer approach to Anbar Province. Bremer overruled them.

"I thought Bremer's ridiculous decision to disband the Iraqi army was perhaps the dumbest ever, because it poured gasoline on an insurgency that was just an ember at the time," Kelly later recalled. "Probably the only decision that was nearly as dumb was to order the Marines to take Fallujah in 2004. We were all begging Bremer to change his mind, because General Mattis had a plan for Fallujah that was less kinetic. Anyone can shoot and kill people, but what counts is imagining your way through these problems."

The ill-advised assault on Fallujah met heavy resistance, with the Marines suffering significant casualties. The fighting was depicted on Arab TV networks as indiscriminate shelling of the civilian population in the city. After the UN representative in Iraq and Sunni members of the Iraq Governing Council threatened to quit over the siege, Bremer reversed himself and insisted that the Marines cancel the Fallujah offensive.

On the one-year anniversary of the fall of Baghdad to US forces, Stan McChrystal was on hand when CENTCOM commander General John Abizaid flew out to the Marine Corps base at Camp Fallujah and told the Marines to do something that ran counter to every instinct ever drubbed into them from the moment they first stepped foot on Paris Island: to stand down and retreat in the face of a determined enemy. McChrystal knew that Abu Musab al-Zarqawi and his terrorist network's base of operations was centered in Fallujah, and that the Marines standing down would look to all Iraqis like a stunning victory for al-Qaeda in Iraq and the Sunni insurgency. The reports he was receiving from far-flung Special Operations teams were also dire and disorienting: the main supply route to Kuwait had been interdicted; rockets were being fired at the Baghdad airport and there were ambushes along Route Irish to the Green Zone; southern cities were falling like dominoes to the Mahdi Army; Abu Ghraib was being played up in the Arab press as the equivalent of a mini–My Lai, where US soldiers in Vietnam in 1968 massacred hundreds of unarmed civilians.

In the simultaneous Sunni and Shiite uprisings of April 2004, McChrystal and his JSOC team also had an early premonition of the civil war that al-Qaeda in Iraq was trying to ignite as a means to drive US forces from the country, and they could see how that strategy might well work.

"I remember how shocked we all were that everything blew up in Iraq all at once," he later recalled in an interview. "I became really convinced at that moment that we could lose this thing pretty quickly, and it was a message I stressed to my task force: 'This is how you lose wars!'"

The select group of US division and task force commanders in Iraq in 2003–2004 would form one of the most influential cliques of officers in modern US history, none more prominent than future four-star officers Dempsey, Petraeus, and McChrystal. While Dempsey and Petraeus would go on to institutionalize the lessons of counterinsurgency war in a time of terror as commander of the US Army's Combined Arms Center, and Training and Doctrine Command, respectively, McChrystal stayed in the fight. For much of the next five years he and Task Force 714 would hone to a lethal edge a new model of counterterrorism operations forged in the crucible of Iraq.

# FIVE

# Martyrs' Den
## 2006–2007

B RIAN MCCAULEY WAS AT THE US EMBASSY IN KABUL EARLY ON the morning of September 8, 2006, Afghanistan having exacerbated his lifelong inability to sleep through the night. McCauley often found himself wide awake when the rest of the world was sleeping, his mind racing over the events of the previous day or the one yet to come. He would just settle down with a cigar and take solace in the silence, his mind doing some of its best thinking unbidden. As the legal attaché at the US Embassy, he was the senior FBI official in country, and in the early morning office colleagues often found him already at work, looking fresh, as if he had been up for hours, which he had.

The Afghan capital was bustling, September 8 being a national holiday and day of commemoration for the legendary Afghan warrior Ahmad Shah Massoud, the Northern Alliance commander and ethnic Tajik who had helped drive the Soviet Army out of Afghanistan, and had then fought the Taliban until his forces were driven into the north. Massoud had been assassinated by two al-Qaeda operatives posing as television journalists on

September 9, 2001, setting in motion the events that led to the 9/11 attacks on the United States just two days later.

The busy traffic circle just outside the US embassy was named in Massoud's honor. The vast increase of automobiles and traffic jams in Kabul since the 2001 fall of the Taliban was a positive indicator of a return to normalcy. A convoy of three US military vehicles passed through Massoud Circle around 10:30 a.m., and a blue Toyota Corolla driven by a young, heavy-set man sped past another car in the inside lane before swerving toward one of the two US Humvees.

McCauley felt the explosion like a hammer blow inside his chest and head, the deafening blast wave vaporizing windows in the US Embassy and other nearby buildings. Outside, the trees in the traffic circle were on fire, pieces of bodies hung in their branches, and a thick plume of dirty brown smoke rose hundreds of feet in the air. Without stopping to think, he rushed out of his office toward the explosion.

The scene outside the fortified gate of the US Embassy compound was of devastation and pandemonium. The wide boulevard was strewn with charred pieces of a Humvee and the bodies of scores of the dead and wounded. Dozens of US and British soldiers were running through the smoke and attempting to help the wounded and cordon off the area. A giant crater smoldered where the Corolla had rammed the Humvee with US soldiers inside.

Along with other embassy officials, McCauley began searching for the wounded to help move them inside the embassy walls for emergency triage. He watched as someone carried the mangled body of a female US soldier toward the gate. The woman still wore her helmet but her face was gone, and she had lost a leg. McCauley knew from just looking that there was no saving her. He passed a wall where an Afghan woman and her daughter had been standing just before the explosion, the outlines of their bodies delineated by a bloody red mist.

International Security Assistance Force (ISAF) soldiers cordoned off the area, and Afghan police were soon swarming the scene, throwing body parts into plastic garbage bags and towing wrecked automobiles to unsnarl traffic. The Kabul police chief and criminal director, Ali Shah Paktiawal, was also soon sifting through the wreckage, though apparently doing little else to direct the response of the police. With no authority to intervene himself, McCauley just observed as police, soldiers, and detectives from countless different agencies and countries grabbed pieces of evidence in the most haphazard fashion. Before long the Afghans, assisted by ISAF troops, began washing down the gruesome scene with fire hoses.

McCauley had conducted onsite forensics before, including at the Pentagon on September 11, 2001. He had participated in numerous counterterrorism investigations, and had helped track down his share of ruthless killers, including IRA bombers and gun runners. The thrill and intrigue of the hunt was a large part of what drew him to the FBI. Witnessing the car bomb attack just outside his office, he realized just how dramatically the old dynamic had changed and the odds had shifted in this strange land. The hunters had become the hunted.

The mangled US soldier he had seen carried into the embassy compound was Sergeant First Class Merideth Howard. At fifty-two years old she was the oldest female soldier killed in the post-9/11 wars in Afghanistan and Iraq. Her colleague Staff Sergeant Robert Paul was also killed in the blast, along with fourteen Afghan civilians. More than thirty others were wounded, many of them seriously. The car bomb contained more than 600 pounds of explosive. The suicide bomber, whoever he was, had conducted the most successful and devastating attack in the capital since the Taliban regime was toppled in 2001, providing a horrific exclamation point to what was shaping up as the deadliest period of the Afghan war for US and allied forces.

In the late hours of the night McCauley didn't even bother trying to sleep, preferring to let his mind scroll through the bombing and its aftermath, searching for clues. So much about the bomb scene troubled him, beginning with the actions of the Afghan police and ISAF first responders. Within a few hours of the bomb blast they had moved the wreckage and hosed down the site, washing away critical evidence. The Afghan police had been all over the bomb site seemingly in minutes, but where were the checkpoints and roadblocks that might have averted the disaster? How had the bomber acquired 300 kilos of high explosive, and managed to smuggle it into one of the most closely guarded sections of the capital, without anyone having a clue? Who had recruited, trained, and indoctrinated the bomber so successfully that the man was not only willing, but also able to vaporize himself in a wanton act of violence on the doorstep of the US embassy? Who exactly was hunting them?

Most of all, McCauley was troubled by the memory of the mangled bodies of Merideth Howard and Robert Paul. Soon they would be identified on newscasts and in hometown newspapers as "military casualties" in a mostly forgotten war. Only they were no longer abstractions for McCauley. They were two Americans who had been murdered by terrorists before his very eyes. And the FBI was ultimately responsible for protecting US citizens from terrorists. That realization helped crystalize McCauley's thinking on what had to be done. The first steps would be to call the US ambassador in Afghanistan, and then FBI headquarters back in Washington, DC. What he would propose was unprecedented, and it would prove instrumental in changing the relationships at the core of US counterterrorism operations, leading to the closest-ever collaboration between the bureau and US Special Operations Forces. McCauley was about to launch one of the largest conspiracy investigations in FBI history, targeting the suicide bombing networks that preyed on US soldiers and civilians and their allies in Afghanistan.

By 2006 Afghanistan had become America's largely forgotten war. With Iraq sliding toward all-out civil war, the US government and military were in five-alarm-fire mode there, facing the very real possibility of a catastrophic defeat. The Iraq crisis had sucked all the energy and resources out of the Afghan campaign, revealing that the United States' relatively small, all-volunteer military simply was not big enough to fight on two major fronts. Afghanistan was a holding action until the dust settled in Iraq, one way or the other.

In the years since 2001 Operation Enduring Freedom had devolved into one of the most underresourced stability and reconstruction campaigns in modern history. In some particulars Afghanistan was even more difficult to stabilize than Iraq, starting with the fact that it was one of the poorest countries on earth, and its population of more than 25 million people was saddled with illiteracy rates of more than 90 percent outside major urban

areas. Building functioning Afghan security forces and government institutions in a country where most people could neither read nor write was a
Sisyphean task, one made all the more daunting by the rampant corruption
that was simply a way of life in an impoverished, tribal society. Constant
shakedowns by government and security officials were normal for the average Afghan, and entry into and advancement in those government bureaucracies was generally bought and paid for by the highest bidder.

With Iraq siphoning off military and intelligence manpower and resources, there were far too few troops on the ground in Afghanistan to
conduct a real counterinsurgency campaign of clearing out Taliban insurgents, keeping them separated from the population, and setting the
conditions for reconstruction and development that tie the population
to the central government. As it focused on Iraq the Bush administration
had already transferred chief responsibility for Afghanistan to the NATO
alliance, which thought it was taking charge of a peacekeeping mission.
The European allies had imposed a host of national caveats on their insufficient forces, restricting their ability to move around the battle-space
and actually engage in combat. The private joke among US military commanders in Afghanistan was that the NATO force called ISAF actually
stood for "I Saw Americans Fighting."

After finding uncontested sanctuary across the border in the wild tribal
areas of Pakistan, the Hydra-headed Taliban and allied Islamic extremist
groups had regrouped, and increasingly they were going on the offensive.
The Taliban controlled areas in southern Helmand Province, part of the
group's original stronghold, and frequently sent attack cells into Kabul
to take the fight directly to the central government and the US-led ISAF
mission.

US officials were also seeing a dramatic shift in Taliban tactics by 2006.
US and NATO airpower had conditioned the insurgents to avoid large-
scale field operations, and to focus increasingly on asymmetric attacks using roadside explosives and suicide bombers. Suicide attacks were alien to
the Afghan culture, and their increased use indicated to US intelligence
officials that al-Qaeda was importing to Afghanistan the terrorist tactics that
its Iraq franchise was perfecting, and teaching them to the Taliban. Already
the period of 2006–2007 was on course to becoming the deadliest to date

for US and allied forces fighting the Afghan insurgents. Largely as a result of the US decision to open a second front in the "global war on terrorism" in Iraq and drain off forces and resources from Afghanistan before the job there was completed, Osama bin Laden was tantalizingly close to realizing his original strategy of drawing US and other Western forces into a losing knife fight in Afghanistan.

BRIAN MCCAULEY WAS a one-man networking machine in Kabul. He had a gift—uncommon in the button-downed culture of the FBI—for putting people at ease with a sharp wit and self-deprecating humor. He would open meetings with diplomats and ambassadors by noting that they were real "pointy heads," whereas he was a former enlisted Marine who had earned his college degree in night school. And yet there was a method to his madcap wisecracking. He used it to personally get to know all the major players in the interlinking webs of intrigue that operated round-the-clock in wartime Kabul, from generals, diplomats, spies, and Special Forces commandos to phone bank operators, drivers, security guards, and journalists. He paid special attention to building relationships with his Afghan counterparts and security personnel. Everyone knew they could wake up McCauley in the dead of night to ask a difficult favor, and not have to ask twice. That was the real reason some of his colleagues affectionately called him the "mayor of Kabul."

One of the relationships he worked hardest to cultivate was with Victor (a pseudonym), the CIA station chief in Kabul. The previous FBI legal attaché and CIA station chief famously couldn't stand each other, so McCauley had showed up at his CIA counterpart's office door one day to introduce himself. "What are you up to in Kabul?" Victor asked. Chasing terrorists and investigating corruption, McCauley told the spy. "Oh, kind of like looking for sand on a beach, huh?" replied Victor. Before long the two men were fast friends, and in what was probably a historical first the CIA even gave the cash-strapped FBI legal attaché funds to pay confidential informants.

In putting together what later came to be known as the Kabul Counter-IED (Improvised Explosive Device) Initiative, McCauley first wrangled approval from headquarters to flood the zone. Up until that time the FBI's in-country team amounted to just the legal attaché and a handful of agents who were mostly there to keep their ears open to any intelligence linking captured al-Qaeda operatives in Afghanistan to plots involving the US homeland. That was about to change. The conspiracy investigation McCauley had in mind required the full bureau skill set, including bomb technicians, forensic specialists, interrogators, and even criminal profilers. As part of the initiative the FBI's in-country team would thus grow from a handful to well over one hundred agents. That kind of heft and capability for the first time made the bureau a key player on the US counterterrorism team in Afghanistan, whereas previously it was largely on the periphery of a show run mostly by the CIA and US Special Forces.

In personally recruiting agents to voluntarily deploy to a war zone, McCauley used a familiar pitch over and over. The same techniques you are using to build criminal conspiracy cases against mobsters and drug cartels? Let's use them to take down IED networks in Afghanistan that are targeting and killing young Americans every day. He even tried it on Special Agent Rich Frankel, who wasn't buying the recruiting pitch. "Brian, I'm a short, fat Jewish lawyer; how in the hell can I be a perfect fit for Afghanistan?"

The FBI could not simply serve a warrant on a would-be suicide bomber in a war zone. That meant the growing team would have to work hand-in-glove with the counterterrorist door crashers of the US Tenth Special Forces Group in Afghanistan. Once again McCauley's unmatched Rolodex and penchant for making friends and influencing people came into play. He had worked with a number of the key Special Operations Forces commanders on earlier stints in-country.

The commander of ISAF during the initiative's critical phases was Lieutenant General Dan McNeill, the tough Scots Irish paratrooper who had mentored so many of the officers who led US Special Forces, including JSOC commander Stan McChrystal, who was already pioneering a newly collaborative, multiagency counterterrorism model with his joint task forces in Iraq and Afghanistan. On first introducing McCauley to Major General John Mulholland and the other Green Berets of Tenth Special Forces Group, McNeill had cemented the close bond that would need to exist for either organization to be successful: "G-man," McNeill had said, "I want you to meet your SWAT team."

On an earlier stint in Afghanistan, McCauley had already broken protocol by sending his special agents into the field with Special Forces A-Team detachments. While McChrystal and other senior commanders had approved the experiment, the rank-and-file Green Berets had initially resisted it as a terrible idea. That resistance disappeared after the A-Teams discovered how FBI investigative and evidence exploitation techniques could quickly narrow their search for insurgents laying improvised explosive devices. The success of that experiment would pave the way for a program that assigned FBI Hostage Rescue Team members to "black ops" Special Forces units, such as Delta Force and SEAL Team Six, and they would jointly go on counterterrorism raids together.

WITH FBI AGENTS pouring into Afghanistan in unprecedented numbers as part of the Counter-IED Initiative, Brian McCauley embedded them in greater numbers at Task Force 714 headquartered at Bagram Air Base, understanding that the FBI would need a lot of help in identifying and exposing the IED networks operating in Kabul, and the effort would do little good if the Tenth Special Forces Group wasn't poised to capture or kill them at a moment's notice.

As commander of Joint Special Operations Command, Stan McChrystal was still in the early stages of transforming Task Force 714, the forward-deployed headquarters team that controlled JSOC's various subordinate task forces in Iraq, Afghanistan, and elsewhere. He envisioned a truly "joint" task force, combining under one roof all the military, intelligence, and law enforcement agencies that had a piece of the counterterrorism mission. And it still wasn't an easy fit. Intelligence agencies, such as the CIA, National Security Agency (NSA), and Defense Intelligence Agency (DIA), were still wary of sharing intelligence with one another, let alone with law enforcement entities, such as the FBI and Drug Enforcement Administration (DEA). All of them were still becoming accustomed to working under the auspices and leadership of a military organization, such as the Joint Special Operations Command, which had its own insular culture, one that such leaders as Stanley McChrystal, his deputy Bill McRaven, and his intelligence chief Mike Flynn were trying hard to transform. Their focus

was a more joint, network-centric model of operations that combined centralized command and widely dispersed operational and analytic units. It
didn't help that McChrystal, the predominant change agent, was absorbed
with the desperate fighting in Iraq.

Some of the traditional rivalry and animosities between the FBI and
CIA continued to grate just beneath the surface. When some of McCauley's special agents first arrived in Afghanistan a few years earlier, the CIA
station chief in Kabul had assigned them as bodyguards to his agents in the
capital, clearly viewing them as little more than unsophisticated muscle
and trigger pullers. Relations had improved somewhat since, but that was
the kind of slight that left a lingering aftertaste.

In truth the wartime experiment in joint, cooperative counterterrorism
operations combining the skills of all the US intelligence, law enforcement,
and military organizations was still very much a work in progress. Leaders
like McChrystal were preaching the gospel, but the institutions involved
had not yet converted, retaining distinctive and in many cases incompatible
operational cultures that were shaped far more by what was happening back
at headquarters in Washington, DC, than by events in Afghanistan and
Iraq. Until that changed, everything was personality driven and dependent
on a relative handful of true believers. Most of them could be found on the
front lines where Americans and their allies were fighting and dying every
day. That's where McChrystal had his most devoted disciples, and where
the FBI had found its own in Brian McCauley.

As he studied the IED attacks from the perspective of a conspiracy investigation, McCauley saw too many black holes in their understanding of
the threat. The FBI would need to illuminate those gaps. Almost all of the
attention was focused on trying to discover who a suicide bomber was after
the fact, when all that was left of him was literally a bloody and blackened
crater in the ground. And the number of craters and the human toll of
misery and grief left behind were surging, with a wave of suicide bombers
unleashed in Afghanistan in a full-scale offensive without precedent in that
part of the world.

The numbers of suicide bombings had ballooned from just 3 in 2004
and 22 in 2005, for instance, to suddenly 139 in 2006. In the weeks before
the suicide attack outside the US embassy that McCauley had witnessed

personally, there had been a suicide attack targeting a Canadian ISAF convoy in Kandahar that killed 6 soldiers and 19 civilians on August 3; a suicide bomber, or BBIED, for "body-borne improvised explosive device," blew himself up next to a former police chief in Helmand on August 28, killing him and 16 civilians while wounding 47 more; on September 18, another bomber tried to assassinate the deputy chief of police for Herat, killing 4 policemen and 7 civilians. On September 27, a suicide bomber targeting the governor of Helmand Province killed 9 Afghan soldiers and 9 civilians; on September 29, a suicide bomber tried to infiltrate the Interior Ministry in Kabul by joining a line of workers outside the gate, ultimately igniting his bomb prematurely and killing 12 civilians.

All of that nihilistic mayhem unleashed in just a matter of weeks by an apparent death cult was deeply unsettling not only to the Afghans and ISAF, and also to the international community writ large that had assumed Afghanistan was largely tamed. The wave of "human missiles" sent exactly the terrifying message that al-Qaeda and the Taliban wanted to deliver, that "we cherish death more than you cherish life."

But who had recruited, indoctrinated, and trained these killers? Who made the bombs, and how were they delivered into the hands of the bombers? How were the bombers fed and housed? From where did they travel? Who picked the targets? Given the rapidly growing number of attacks, McCauley could sense an unseen and malevolent intelligence orchestrating the networks behind all the mayhem and death, one that was sophisticated far beyond the fevered dreams of a suicide bomber intent on martyrdom. But who were these people?

To find answers McCauley knew he needed the help of the intelligence agencies, particularly the CIA, which by far had the best human intelligence (or "humint" in intelligence-speak) network of confidential sources. He reached out to Major General Steve Fogarty, director of the Joint Intelligence Operations Center in Afghanistan, and held a number of meetings with all of the intelligence agencies, with the aim of persuading everyone to show their cards on confidential sources.

"Look, we all have to agree not to try and poach each other's sources. Let's agree that no one can tell a source behind another agency's back,

'Hey, why don't you come to work for us?'" McCauley recalled a typical pitch. "Because at the end of the day, this is all about getting accurate intelligence. The last thing any of us want is to get the intelligence wrong, and be responsible for getting a Special Forces troop killed going on a raid based on our faulty intelligence."

As trust slowly built among the intelligence agencies at Task Force 714, McCauley and Fogarty got them to post photos and identify their confidential sources on a common wall, and they recognized a funny thing. Some of the sources were snooping for multiple US and allied intelligence agencies, and not just double-dipping in the till. Some of them were triple- and quadruple-dipping. Some of the sources were also telling different, and contradictory, stories to different agencies. So, the US intelligence agencies were being played by their own sources, something they would never have learned if they hadn't shown their cards and cooperated with one another.

With growing resources and manpower in Afghanistan, McCauley also directed his special agents to begin establishing their own network of informants, giving him more leverage and chips to deal in the interagency intelligence swap, and taking an important step toward infiltrating the suicide bombing networks, just as the FBI had infiltrated Mafia families. He thus became the first FBI legal attaché in history to operate his own extensive human source network overseas. Some other intelligence agencies initially viewed it as poaching on their turf, but there was no denying that the FBI was becoming a more prominent player in the counterterrorism war in Afghanistan.

McCauley also had the manpower to keep a 24/7 watch on US military radio traffic in Kabul reporting "significant events," which more often than not were IED attacks. An emergency response team was constantly on hand to rush to the site of a new bombing for careful forensic examination. McCauley was determined never to see Afghan police or ISAF troops hosing down a bomb site before his special agents could go over it with tweezers, looking for clues. Because Afghan police chief Ali Shah Paktiawal and his men were often the first officials on the scene after a bombing, McCauley had his men instruct and train the Afghan police in the importance of preserving a bomb scene until careful examination could reveal its secrets.

He also reached out and established a close working relationship with the Afghan National Directorate of Security (NDS), the country's chief intelligence agency, for the same reason.

In Kabul, McCauley also became friends with bomb technicians with experience in Britain's long war with IRA terrorists. They swapped IRA stories, with the FBI attaché recalling his work years earlier on the Valhalla case, and the British officers describing in horrific detail the scenes of carnage in Northern Ireland as a result of IRA car bombs. IRA operatives trained in Libya became masters of vehicle-borne improvised explosive devices, or VBIEDs, a fearsome weapon that Hezbollah terrorists had used to kill 241 US Marines in Beirut, Lebanon, in 1983, and domestic terrorists Timothy McVeigh and Terry Nichols had used to kill 168 people, and injure more than 600 others, in an attack on the Alfred P. Murrah Federal Building in Oklahoma City in 1995. VBIEDs were a weapon of mass destruction, and McCauley knew his team was in a race against time before such weapons increasingly came to define the Taliban campaign against ISAF.

Many of the FBI's own bomb technicians had trained in Britain, and it was fortuitous to link up with British bomb experts in Kabul. They all knew that each bomb maker had a unique "signature," some technique or tactic that to the trained eye was as identifiable as a fingerprint. In some cases it might be where the bomber places the bomb, or how he ties off wires. It might be the type and batch of explosives he uses. The best identifiers were radio power units used to trigger the blasting cap from a safe distance. If investigators could locate the power unit triggers, they were often treasure troves of information, including actual fingerprints and DNA. All such evidence was gathered by the FBI investigators in Kabul and immediately flown to the FBI forensics laboratory in Quantico, Virginia. Details on the unique signature of the bomber, and whether it had been seen at other blast sites, were soon back into the hands of McCauley's team, which shared them with Task Force 714.

At one particular blast site an FBI special agent found the power switch that detonated the IED. It was a unique device, with distinctive red and blue pressure switches. Roughly a month later, one of Task Force 714's Alpha Teams was searching an Afghan village with suspected Taliban links. In a house they found a bag full of power units with the same distinct red

and blue switches. Because they had learned about sensitive site exploitation from the FBI, the Alpha Team detained the man who lived in that
house and flew him to Bagram for interrogation, and he was later arrested
for complicity in an IED cell.

In a matter of months, McCauley sensed that some of the pieces of the
IED and suicide bomber puzzle were falling into place. The joint, counter-
IED task force's growing web of confidential informants, intelligence from
NSA communications intercepts, and evidence gathered at bomb sites and
in Special Forces Tenth Group raids all indicated distinct cells operating
independently in and around Kabul. But the trail grew murkier the farther from Kabul it led. To understand the forces that were directing and
motivating all that lethal activity, McCauley turned to some old friends at
Quantico who were better known for tracking serial killers. It had occurred
to him that this was exactly what they were hunting in Afghanistan.

"YOU KNOW WE'RE going to see this stateside sooner or later. It's already
happening in Europe. Look at London and Madrid. Suicide bombers and
improvised explosive devices are the next new wave of terrorism!" Brian
McCauley was speaking by phone with FBI special agent Scott Stanley,
and he was in full recruiting mode, which is to say Irish charming and persuasive in his logic. Stanley was an old friend of McCauley's and a top analyst in the FBI's elite Behavioral Science Unit, the psychological profilers
who track serial killers and terrorists. "We're always looking at these terrorist
cases in the 'incident management' phase, after the attack has already taken
place. But what if you had an opportunity to interview failed suicide bombers, the ones whose bombs don't work or who are subdued before they can
set them off? Would you be interested in that?"

Stanley didn't actually need much persuading. Every counterterrorism
expert knew that suicide bombers had become the asymmetric weapon of
choice for Islamic extremists, inflicting some of the worst acts of mass murder in history, to include the bombing of the US embassies in Africa in
1998 (more than 200 killed), the attack on the USS Cole in 1980 (17 sailors
killed), the 9/11 attacks (more than 3,000 killed), and the bombing of the
London transport system in 2005 (52 killed). In the pantheon of Islamic

extremist terrorism, suicide bombers were the ultimate weapon, and their frequent use had migrated from the Middle East to Afghanistan. The fact that they eviscerated themselves in the very act of their crime made suicide bombers not only psychologically unsettling—the gold standard in acts of terror—but also all but impossible to investigate using the FBI's standard methods. And here Stanley's old buddy Brian McCauley was offering him a rare chance to sit across an interview table and try to get inside the heads of would-be suicide bombers.

Much of the work done at the FBI's Behavioral Science and Analysis Unit at Quantico was based on groundbreaking research conducted in the 1970s by special agents who traveled around the country conducting exhaustive prison interviews with the most notorious serial killers in the land. That's how they got inside the heads of some of the most prolific predators in the annals of crime, such as Theodore Kaczynski, the brilliant loner who terrorized the country with letter bombs for more than a decade before his published "manifesto" was deconstructed by psycholinguistic analysis at Quantico, eventually leading FBI agents to his remote cabin in Montana.

The groundbreaking interviews with serial killers and such terrorists as Kaczynski and associated research formed the foundation of the Behavioral Science Unit, informing its analysts both on recurring methods of operations (MOs) adopted by serial killers, and on the unique "signatures" that pointed to individual motivations. The training and education that Stanley and the others at the Behavioral Science Unit received is considered the most rigorous and thorough of its kind. After foundational course work, the analysts are assigned to one of three sections, which specialized in serial killers, crimes against children, and terrorism. Collectively, these profilers are considered among the world's preeminent manhunters. Scott Stanley, a tall, rangy agent with a quiet demeanor and sharp mind, was assigned to the unit that tracked terrorists. He had been chosen for the elite unit in part based on his intuitive work on high-profile terrorist cases, including the investigation of the 2001 anthrax attack that killed five people and terrorized the country in the wake of the 9/11 attacks, and the investigation of the "Beltway snipers" who killed ten people and critically injured three others in a series of random shootings around the nation's capital in 2002. The snipers, who left Tarot "Death" cards with the words "Call me God" at some of the shooting sites, terrorized and largely paralyzed the nation's capital for nearly a month.

After talking to McCauley, Stanley received approval from his unit chief to deploy to Afghanistan. He would be traveling with another of the FBI's elite criminal investigative analysts (commonly known as profilers) named Tom Neer, a gifted agent who had been a chief interviewer of Saddam Hussein in Iraq, and who had visited the military prison at Guantánamo Bay, Cuba, numerous times to interview captured al-Qaeda operatives there.

At the US Embassy in Kabul, McCauley introduced Stanley and Neer to his regional team and then briefed them fully on his Counter-IED Initiative. The problem was well understood in its general dimensions. Every week US soldiers and Afghan civilians were suffering traumatic brain injuries, or losing their arms, legs, and often their lives to roadside bombs and suicide bombers. But the perpetrators didn't just appear at the site of the explosion and suddenly detonate bombs. Someone had recruited, indoctrinated, and trained them, and provided the logistics to get them to the target. Often a colleague observed the actual attack, either to ensure the bombers went through with the operation, or to video it for propaganda purposes, or for proof so that payments could be made to the bomber's family. It takes a village to raise a suicide bomber, McCauley said, and the FBI could use some of the same techniques that it employed in taking down Mafia families, drug cartels, and violent criminal gangs to identify those villagers. Then the Tenth Special Forces Group could bring them to justice.

To dismantle the bombing cells operating in Kabul, McCauley believed they would have to infiltrate them with confidential human sources. Doing so would require a far more granular understanding of how the cells operated and were directed. Which is where Stanley and Neer came in. Using close relationships he had established with senior officials at the Afghan National Security Directorate, McCauley had finagled permission for Stanley and Neer to interview would-be suicide bombers, ones whose vests or car bombs had failed to detonate, or who were subdued before pressing the igniter. Not for the last time, Stanley was impressed by the close working relationship that McCauley had established not only with the interagency intelligence community and the US military in Kabul, but also with the Afghan intelligence and security agencies. He was among the agents who gave McCauley his nickname the "mayor of Kabul."

As experienced agents, Stanley and Neer declined offers of a security detachment, believing it would slow them down and insulate them from the Afghan "street" and a culture they needed to understand. The two of them drove around the Kabul Red Zone together in an unmarked car, having meticulously established emergency communications protocols to the quick-reaction force back at the embassy, and multiple ingress and egress routes from the prisons and jails around the city which they visited to interview suicide bombers. Always have a "plan for pain," as Stanley put it.

They worked with a couple of translators, but quickly developed a preference for a clever Iranian woman. She had a disarming style with the young, religiously conservative prisoners, Muslim men unaccustomed to interactions with women outside their families, and an encyclopedic knowledge of the Koran that would prove essential. An Islamist suicide bomber was pretty much the definition of a "true believer." The rules the FBI profilers established were that the interpreter could never interrupt an interrogation with his or her own questions, and must repeat every word the interviewee said verbatim. The two FBI agents also insisted that no Afghan prison guards or police could be in the room during interviews, because their presence would distract the prisoners and alter the subtle dynamic at play in the interrogation.

The FBI agents made no attempt to hide who they were, and the reaction of the shackled prisoners was almost inevitably to start screaming and spitting at them, and often to try to attack them as well. This initially upset the Afghan guards monitoring the interview from outside the room, but the FBI profilers expected such behavior. The surprise would have been if the bombers weren't agitated by their presence and questions. In the second interview they would often talk to the prisoners for hours about nothing in particular, seemingly satisfied just to have a two-way conversation. The entire time the FBI profilers were eliciting answers that revealed the prisoner's level of education, worldliness, and sophistication, or lack thereof. Were they visual or auditory in their processing of questions and information? All of those subtle judgments informed how the profilers crafted an interview strategy. And then they would settle in and talk to these would-be mass murderers "until the paint comes off the wall," Stanley recalled.

The initial cadre of thirteen suicide bombers they interviewed included some of the smartest as well as some of the most ignorant people that Stanley ever questioned. The few that were truly ignorant lacked even basic knowledge on fundamental concepts, such as shapes and colors, which made them extremely hard to interrogate, but easy to understand from a motivational standpoint. One or two clearly had severe mental deficiencies. These illiterate young men were the easiest to manipulate, as the interviewers could point to nonexistent passages in an open Koran and insist that it ordered believers to be truthful and open about their deeds. If the prisoner asked to see the passage, they knew he was literate.

Typically the bomber had been first identified as a promising recruit or someone who was particularly compliant by an imam in a fundamentalist madrassa, or Islamic religious school. US intelligence agencies estimated that there were more than six hundred such madrassas in Pakistan, funded with money from Saudi Arabia and the other Persian Gulf monarchies, which taught the intolerant Wahhabi version of Islam that inspired al-Qaeda and other Sunni jihadist groups. The most promising recruits were separated from the rest of the class for more intense indoctrination and brainwashing. At some point, the young man's parents would be approached and asked to "donate" their son to the service of Allah, and on completion of his martyrdom the family would receive agreed upon compensation.

The FBI agents also discovered a major correlation between suicide bombers and birth order. In Afghan's rural and conservative culture, it was not unusual for families to consist of eight, ten, or even more children. And yet a disproportionate number of the suicide bombers were either the first- or last-born children. As they interviewed the prisoners it became apparent that in the predominant Pashtun culture of the Taliban, the first-born male child was treated as the "man of the house." He was expected to forage and toil to provide for the extended family, so few firstborns had the chance at a formal education. Their fathers also frequently burdened the firstborn son with the most distasteful menial jobs, creating a hostility and discontent that was easily manipulated by religious leaders and their emissaries, who whispered messages of empowerment and favor in the eyes of Allah: if only these put-upon sons would show their faith by doing this important job, they would reap the reward in a paradise of seventy-two virgins.

The youngest males in large Pashtun families were frequently doted on, and they accounted for nearly half of the cohort of thirteen suicide bombers. Unburdened by the need to provide for their families, they were the most likely male children to be sent off to get an education in conservative religious madrassas. There they, too, fell under the influence of charismatic imams who preached the fundamentalist, Wahhabi interpretation of Islam that glorified violent jihad and martyrdom as Islam's response to the encroachment of infidels and Western modernity. Conversely, some families also considered the youngest male the most expendable, and were thus willing to sacrifice him to the faith in exchange for payment from a well-connected religious figure.

After weeks and months of exhaustive interviews with suicide bombers, Stanley and Neer learned to craft their interrogation strategies very differently depending on whether the prisoner was a first- or last-born son. That one piece of information suggested different relationships with their brothers and sisters and other members of the extended family that could be used to tease out not only motivations, but also tactical intelligence that often revealed important details about operations. When chided by other members of the task force about spending so much time with often illiterate would-be suicide bombers, Stanley replied that there were no easy shortcuts to such interrogations. He compared them to "watering a flower," so that their understanding of the living organism behind a suicide-bombing cell grew a little bit more each day.

In terms of the all-important factor of motivation, the FBI profilers learned that you could no more interrogate would-be suicide bombers without deeply exploring their religious faith and beliefs, than you could interview serial killers without mentioning the psychosexual impulses that drove them. Virtually by definition, someone willing to commit mass murder and self-immolation in an act of faith was a true believer. The special agents thus had to become readily conversant in the basic tenets of the Islamic faith and the Koran, with its strong emphasis on such concepts as martyrdom, jihad, and infidels. Nor was it hard for the Americans to understand that the Afghans in their control group of would-be suicide bombers had a deep cultural aversion to the idea of foreign invaders. No doubt that belief had passed down in tribal lore and custom through centuries of conquest and war in a country that earned its nickname "graveyard of empires."

As the suicide bombing networks came into sharper relief through interviews and the Counter-IED Initiative's intelligence-gathering operations, Scott Stanley's unease about the threat they were facing grew. Some of the suicide bombers themselves might be illiterate country boys, and they were ruthlessly manipulated and sacrificed as little more than mules to deliver a bomb in person. Others were far more intelligent and capable, and these men were given much more complex operations to execute, usually against higher-value and more heavily guarded targets. And Stanley realized that these individuals had been carefully chosen as suicide bombers, shooters, facilitators, bomb makers, financiers, and cell leaders based on their level of intelligence and individual skill set.

Somewhere behind all of that complex activity Stanley sensed unseen hands, master manipulators using psychological profiling techniques and motivational tricks every bit as sophisticated as his own. In the deadly game of cat-and-mouse playing out in wartime Kabul, this was an unsettling thought, and Stanley couldn't shake it: If the FBI profilers had been asked to recruit personnel to man an operational unit using everything that the Behavioral Science Unit at Quantico and years of field experience had taught them, they would have recruited a team that looked a lot like the suicide bombing and IED cells that were hunting them throughout Afghanistan.

ARMED WITH THOSE insights into the origins and motivations of suicide bombers, and with evidence on bomb-maker signatures from the FBI forensics laboratory in Quantico, McCauley's investigators illuminated three distinct IED and suicide bomber cells working in Kabul. Working with the CIA and the Afghan National Directorate of Security, he began to infiltrate the organizations with confidential sources.

The trail typically began in such a place as the radical Muridke or Manba Ulom madrassas in Pakistan's tribal area, known centers of jihadi indoctrination where impressionable young Afghan men, often from dirt-poor villages, were enticed with promises of a better life in the hereafter and a chance to attain greatness in this earthly realm. There they were fed a strict diet of jihad, and nourished on hatred for infidels, or non-Muslims. Based on their acumen and level of intelligence, the young men were selected to serve as various cogs in the enemy network. Whether gunman, bomber, or facilitator, they were trained in one of the twenty-nine training camps that the Taliban and al-Qaeda were known to operate in North and South Waziristan.

Those "honored" to be chosen as suicide-bombers were isolated from the rest of the group, and subjected to a more intense round of indoctrination. Their families were promised martyrdom rewards of up to $15,000, and they made suicide videos for propaganda purposes so that later these young men might speak from the grave of their lofty ambitions and hunger for martyrdom. Before they left on their journey, suicide bombers often received an inspirational sendoff by one of the new lords of terror, men in the mold of Abu Musab al-Zarqawi, for whom indiscriminate killing was honored as a measure of commitment, and by such leaders as Siraj Haqqani, Baitullah Mehsud, and Mullah Dadullah. Haqqani had already proven much more extreme than his mujahedeen father, Jalaluddin, and he was fast developing the most sophisticated terror network of the various extremist groups united under the Taliban banner. As the leader of the Pakistan Taliban, Mehsud was behind the wave of suicide terror spreading into Pakistan, launching nearly fifty suicide bombings in 2007, including an attack on the convoy of former prime minister Benazir Bhutto that left her unhurt but killed approximately 150 civilians. None was more bloodthirsty than Dadullah, who was filmed in a cave in Pakistan before a cadre of suicide bombers, handing out "passes to paradise." Entry to that utopia was even extended to a six-year-old boy whom the Taliban fitted with a suicide vest and then instructed to walk up to a US patrol and press a button to "spray flowers."

The trail of the suicide bombers included facilitators who journeyed with them, bribing police at checkpoints and stopping along the way to visit friends and safe houses. The final destination was a safe house in the capital, where they waited until a separate manufacturing operation could produce the suicide vest, car bomb, or roadside explosive. Targets were typically vetted with senior leaders, such as Mehsud and Dadullah, and the leader of an eight-man bombing cell would rehearse the tactics for the attack.

In the parlance of counterterrorism, Brian McCauley's investigators had gotten "to the left of the boom." Instead of wading through blood and gore at the smoking scene of a surprise attack as he had outside the US embassy in 2006, the conspiracy investigation had revealed the intricate networks behind the suicide bombers. And with the networks so exposed, Major General John Mulholland's Tenth Special Forces Green Berets lived up to their promise to serve as the SWAT team.

By far the most prolific IED cell operating in Kabul was run by the Brothers Dabazorai, three hard-core Taliban siblings led by the eldest, Zaher. The Brothers Dabazorai were responsible for the car bomb that had killed Sergeant First Class Merideth Howard and Staff Sergeant Robert Paul outside the US embassy, the attack that proved the genesis of the Counter-IED Initiative. McCauley's team had successfully infiltrated the Dabazorai cell with a confidential source, code-named "Sunshine." Their double agent was clever but uneducated, and he was unable to operate a GPS device to reveal the coordinates of the Dabazorai compound. McCauley's Afghan right-hand man, a brave and resourceful former Northern Alliance fighter named "Mohammad," had dressed in traditional Afghan clothes and impersonated a taxi driver, taking "Sunshine" to a remote, walled compound and farm in Logar Province. After dropping the source off, Mohammad discretely recorded the GPS coordinates of the compound.

Retribution was served by a Tenth Special Forces Group A-Team, which swept in on the Dabazorai compound in a raid. None of the brothers chose to surrender, and Zaher and another brother were killed in the ensuing firefight. The Green Berets found the last brother hiding down a well. Ordered to surrender, the man opened fire with a pistol instead. A hand grenade tossed down the well brought to a close the cycle of pain and indiscriminate murder that gave the Brothers Dabazorai purpose in life, and set Brian McCauley on the quest that ended in their death. Before that journey was complete, the FBI had forged the tightest bonds in its history with US Special Operations Forces, and for the first time developed a detailed understanding of the ticking time bomb that is the mind of a suicide killer.

# SIX

# Five Assassins
## May–July 2006

B Y THE SPRING OF 2006 THE MOST MALEVOLENT FIGURE IN THE pantheon of global terrorism was hiding not in Taliban-controlled territory in southern Afghanistan, nor in the tribal areas of Pakistan where much of al-Qaeda's leadership had sought refuge, but in the hard-scrabble towns along the Euphrates River in Iraq's western Anbar Province. That was the base of operations for the ascendant franchise al-Qaeda in Iraq (AQI) and its Jordanian leader, Abu Musab al-Zarqawi, who had the blood of thousands on his hands. Because al-Zarqawi was close to succeeding with his strategy of igniting a sectarian civil war that would drive US forces from Iraq, Task Force 714's manhunt for this terrorist was in a desperate race against time. That desperation was a catalyst for many of the innovations that would come to define US counterterrorism operations.

Certainly al-Zarqawi's appetite for slaughter even of fellow Muslims represented something new and ominous in the evolution of jihadi terrorism. In the single month of May 2006, nearly 1,400 Iraqis died violently in the mayhem unleashed by al-Zarqawi, the highest death toll since the US invasion in 2003. With each new body tossed into his charnel house, his infamy grew in a terrorist milieu where bloodshed remained the coin of the realm, and money and foreign fighters flowed to his black banner from the wider terrorist networks as offerings to a rising al-Qaeda warlord. Osama bin Laden had lured the "far enemy" to Afghanistan in hopes of delivering the fatal blow in the familiar graveyard of empires, but with bin Laden and his top lieutenants hiding in Pakistan the baton of leadership in the organization was being not so much passed as wrested away by the brutish al-Zarqawi. Bin Laden had already named al-Zarqawi the "emir" of al-Qaeda in Iraq, and urged young Muslims to join him there and take advantage of a "golden opportunity . . . to make Americans bleed in Iraq."

The Jordanian was a constant presence inside the headquarters of JSOC's task force in Iraq at Balad Air Base. On a wall of the operations center hung a poster-size photograph of a masked and knife-wielding al-Zarqawi, flanked by four similarly masked murderers, their faces glaring into the camera insolently as they stood over an American who sat before them handcuffed and in an orange jumpsuit of the kind prisoners wore at Guantánamo Bay, Cuba. Just about everyone in the task force had seen the video, could hear Nick Berg's screams as the assassins went about their grisly work of beheading him while shouting "Allahu Akbar!" ("God is Great!"). The memory was indelible no matter how hard you tried to forget it.

When they were not out observing raids by their Special Forces units, Major General Stanley McChrystal and his intelligence chief, Colonel Mike Flynn, could usually be found huddled together before the video screens in the operations center. All that either of them had to do was look at the poster in the midst of another endless cycle of operations and intelligence analysis, and they could feel their resolve harden. No way that poor kid deserved what those men did to him. For that and a thousand other reasons, the task force was committed to avenging Berg's death and bringing down the AQI leaders who had been captured in the photo image. Both McChrystal and Flynn knew better than most that al-Zarqawi used the human sacrifice of Nick Berg as a metaphor, a message to Americans and anyone else who dared stand in the way of his plans to set Iraq on fire so that his vision of a Sunni Islamic caliphate could rise from the ashes.

The nature of that nascent regime was revealed in intelligence reports of "significant events" that McChrystal and Flynn pored over each day. An

AQI suicide car bomber had attacked a ribbon-cutting ceremony for a new reconstruction project in Baghdad, killing 35 Iraqi children in a massive blast that wounded more than 140 civilians and 10 Americans who were on hand. Simultaneous suicide bombings—an al-Qaeda signature embraced by the Iraq franchise—targeted three hotels in Amman, Jordan, in late 2005. Al-Zarqawi had tried to destroy those same buildings years earlier during millennium celebrations, revealing al-Qaeda's penchant for following through once a threat has been made and a target has been identified. Khalid Sheikh Mohammed had similarly succeeded in destroying the World Trade Center buildings on 9/11 after his nephew Ramzi Yousef had failed in his attempt to topple the towers with a truck bomb in 1993. In the case of the Jordanian hotels, three AQI suicide bombers killed more than 60 people and wounded 115 others, including many members of a wedding party at the Radisson Hotel. Outrage over the grisly slaughter at a wedding celebration prompted thousands of Jordanians to take to the streets in protest, but al-Zarqawi was unmoved by the grief of his countrymen. As the shadow of his menace grew with each attack, fear gripped the Iraqi countryside, and during a recent Shiite pilgrimage just the unfounded belief that his suicide bombers were on hand triggered a stampede in northern Baghdad by the terrified crowd that killed more than 950 Iraqis, including many women and children trampled underfoot.

In February 2006 al-Zarqawi's network had bombed the Golden Mosque in Samarra, one of the holiest sites in Shiite Islam. The dome of the Golden Mosque was reduced to rubble, igniting a spasm of sectarian killing that claimed the lives of roughly one thousand Iraqis in just the first days after the bombing. US commanders would soon recognize the bombing as a turning point in the Iraq campaign, the moment when an operation that had long ridden on the cliff edge of failure started to topple into the abyss. The destruction of the Golden Mosque unleashed Shiite death squads that nearly matched al-Zarqawi's legions in depravity. Their ethnic cleansing campaigns quickly displaced more than eighty thousand people in the capital and led to the daily discovery of scores of bodies on city streets each dawn, the majority of them bearing unmistakable signs of torture.

Al-Zarqawi's improbable rise from a street thug to the leader of al-Qaeda's most important franchise had followed an increasingly familiar arc. At the insistence of his mother, the hotheaded young Jordanian had begun attending a mosque in Amman known for its fundamentalist Salafist ideology. His personal journey of jihadism led, like so many others, to Afghanistan and the mujahedeen who were glorified for expelling the Soviet infidels from that Muslim country. Back in Jordan, al-Zarqawi had fallen in with an insurgent group led by the Islamist ideologue Abu Muhammad al-Maqdisi. Both men were imprisoned for running guns and explosives, and during his five years in prison al-Zarqawi was further radicalized, using his physical bulk and penchant for violence to become the enforcer of the fundamentalist block of prisoners. Back in Afghanistan in the late 1990s, he established his own training camp and developed a relationship with Osama bin Laden's al-Qaeda organization. After the US invasion in 2001, al-Zarqawi was nearly killed by a US bomb and fled to Iraq, reportedly seeking revenge.

On his own release from prison, al-Maqdisi had criticized his former protégé for his wanton killing of fellow Muslims, even if they were of the Shiite sect. Al-Qaeda's second-in-command, Ayman al-Zawahiri, weighed into the debate, praising al-Zarqawi's effectiveness but also chastising him for attacks on Shiite Muslims, reminding him that the first priority of al-Qaeda was to drive US forces out of Iraq. Al-Zarqawi's answer to both men was a message posted to al-Qaeda's website, declaring "total war" against Iraqi Shiites. In typical fashion he punctuated the declaration with a deadly exclamation point: on the same day that his message appeared online, twelve separate bombs exploded in Baghdad. Targeting Iraqi Shiites, the explosions killed 114 civilians and wounded 600 more.

Certainly Mike Flynn didn't need help interpreting the metaphor of Nick Berg's beheading, or recognizing in the mass slaughter of civilians the merciless tyranny at the heart of al-Zarqawi's twisted worldview. The evidence greeted him each day as Flynn took his seat at the giant horseshoe desk at the center of the task force's headquarters at Balad Air Base for the daily operations and intelligence (O&I) briefing by video teleconference. The only real surprise was just how close al-Zarqawi was in 2006 to achieving his dream of an all-out sectarian civil war. If they couldn't stop the arsonist, then Iraq would surely go up in flames.

COME RAIN, SHINE, or catastrophe, Stanley McChrystal gathered the leadership of his task forces in Iraq and Afghanistan together for a ninety-minute video teleconference briefing. It was a ritual conducted each day, six days a week, precisely at twelve noon Zulu time, which was four p.m. in the afternoon in Iraq, and more important, nine a.m. in Washington, DC. Having built a globe-spanning, manhunting network unique in the annals of counterterrorism, McChrystal used the O&I briefings to keep it focused and tightly strung together. At his spot at the top of the horseshoe of computer stations in the operations center, he was usually flanked by his intelligence chief, Mike Flynn, and his operations chief, Delta Force deputy commander Colonel Scott Miller, which was fitting: the task force was becoming as much an intelligence-gathering organization as a counterterrorism gun outfit, and breaking down the walls that traditionally separated intelligence analysts and operators was just the first bit of crockery McChrystal had smashed in building Joint Special Operations Command's counterterrorism network.

For officials at the alphabet soup of intelligence, military, and law enforcement agencies in the capital, the workday was just getting started at the time of the briefings, and there was no better place to check the beating pulse of the United States' "global war on terrorism" than Task Force 714's video teleconference. The simple fact that scores of agencies and commands scattered across the globe in more than two dozen countries would meet in a secure virtual space each day to share their insights face-to-screen represented a quantum leap not only in capability and cooperation, but even more important, in trust. If the intelligence shared in the daily O&I was leaked, it could get people killed, most readily the Special Operations Forces direct action teams whose raids formed the hot core of task force operations, but also intelligence sources whose lives depended on anonymity. McChrystal considered the O&I his most powerful tool for instilling an ethos of centralized command and decentralized execution into a far-flung network anchored in Iraq and Afghanistan, but increasingly spanning the globe.

Al-Qaeda's own network was growing inside of Iraq, with seasoned foreign fighters pouring into the country from Pakistan, Afghanistan,

Chechnya, Bosnia, Kosovo, and all points in the Middle East. That vanguard included many of the suicide bombers that were al-Qaeda in Iraq's most fearsome weapon, and they called their pilgrimage to Iraq the "Caravan of Martyrs." Task Force 714 had been forced to rapidly thicken its own network to try to trace their movements and stem the flow. The critical thread of intelligence that led to the archterrorist might come from a conversation overheard in a Pristina café, or from a courier recognized on the streets of Karachi. McChrystal and Flynn had thus seen to it that more than eighty of Task Force 714's most able intelligence analysts were deployed as liaisons inside embassies and friendly intelligence services around the world, making each a new node and sensor in their expanding network. The task force analysts jokingly referred to the liaison program as a "hostage exchange" program, but it was crucial in expanding their reach. Flynn had even developed a detailed video tutorial "How to be a Liaison Officer."

"It takes a network to defeat a network" was an oft-repeated mantra for McChrystal and the rest of the task force's leadership. Al-Qaeda had gotten a nearly decade jump on them in building its own networks. The daily O&I briefing was McChrystal's way of catching up, summoning his own growing network out of the electronic ether each day, giving it names, faces, and substance. McChrystal and Flynn constantly stressed that agencies don't cooperate with one another, people do, so they spent an inordinate amount of time establishing and nurturing multiagency and multinational relationships. By the summer of 2006, the audience for the worldwide teleconference thus stretched into the thousands, all united by a singular purpose.

Watching his boss conduct the O&I briefing like an orchestra, eliciting a coherent intelligence piece with subtly probing questions, thoughtful asides, and bits of encouragement, Flynn marveled at McChrystal's mastery of the art form. Initially there had been a lot of resistance to the virtual pow-wows. The US military in general, and Joint Special Operations Command (JSOC) in particular, were used to operating by video teleconference. Yet discussing sensitive intelligence in that kind of open forum was anathema for many intelligence agencies, whose cultural default was the jealous guarding of secrets.

McChrystal and Flynn understood that human instinct in any transaction was for face-to-face communications. You naturally wanted to smell the coffee on people's breath, sense their body language. Yet they also knew that the kind of globe-spanning network they envisioned would be damn near impossible to manage on a face-to-face basis. So, they spent an inordinate amount of time building greater bandwidth for secure communication across multiple agencies, and insisting on absolute integrity in the handling of intelligence. No poaching of sources, no leaking of sacrosanct sources and methods. McChrystal also constantly used the O&I both to drive home his "commander's intent" to far-flung forces and to reinforce the message to Washington bureaucrats, working nine-to-five days, that this really was war.

Like that of the terrorist leaders he was pursuing, McChrystal's own reputation within the tightknit counterterrorism and military communities had grown in the three years since he had taken command of JSOC. Word spread of a warrior monk who slept on a cot and got by on one meal and a few hours of sleep a day, and of his band of devotees who stayed in the fight for years with only brief breaks while others tended to rotate in and out on six- or twelve-month deployments. McChrystal and Flynn slept next to their operations center and frequently went out into the field with their raiding teams. And with each Task Force 714 night raid's gutting another node in the enemy's network, success bred success, and elicited more buy-in from intelligence agency and law enforcement officials who badly wanted to be part of a winning team. A stint serving on one of JSOC's joint interagency task forces at Bagram in Afghanistan or Balad in Iraq became a career enhancer and point of pride for those in the counterterrorism trade, civilian as well as military, and a point of common reference when they took those lessons in collaborative manhunting back to their respective agencies in Washington.

Again like their prey, McChrystal, Flynn, and the rest of Task Force 714 leadership were also learning that success was infectious. With each passing day their network became more layered and tightly wired, with more players in the counterterrorism community operating on a common wavelength. The problem was al-Qaeda and its chief affiliate had a head start, and the question hung heavily in the stifling air of Iraq in the summer of 2006—which network would prevail?

DURING THEIR MOMENTS of reflection, Stan McChrystal and Mike Flynn sometimes marveled at how far the task force had evolved in just a few years. The epiphany for McChrystal was hunting al-Qaeda in Afghanistan and seeing how fluidly the organization transformed orders at the top into action among a far-flung rank-and-file, and then watching Iraq nearly melt down in the spring of 2004. He sensed that the events were connected, but he didn't understand how. When he had originally described the kind of organization that he thought Task Force 714 would have to become to succeed in fighting al-Qaeda's networks, his deputy, Rear Admiral Bill McRaven, cut in: "You're describing a JIATF," using the acronym for a joint interagency task force that united multiple agencies under a single roof.

The concept of a JIATF wasn't altogether new. Most notably, the government had established JIATFs to combat drug smuggling by major Latin American drug cartels in the 1990s, another threat that crossed myriad agency boundaries. Joint Interagency Task Force South in Key West, Florida, commanded by a Coast Guard admiral who wore dual hats as both a military and law enforcement commander, was considered the gold standard of the multiagency task forces before 9/11. But it was primarily an intelligence fusion organization that tried to loosely coordinate interagency operations top-down at an operational level.

What McChrystal and Flynn demanded of Task Force 714 was on a different order of coordination altogether. Tracking the leadership of al-Qaeda and its affiliates and dismantling their networks required a mind meld that combined in one team the skill set of all the different agencies under their roof, operating as a coherent whole. It also demanded a level of centralized command and decentralized execution by multiple agencies that had never before been achieved.

In the early days, suspicions between the various intelligence, law enforcement, and military agencies gathered under Task Force 714's umbrella were still so strong that some agencies cordoned off their workspaces with yellow police tape, as if protecting a crime scene. "You are hereby charged with the felony of interagency cooperation." Overcoming those cultural barriers was the most difficult challenge McChrystal and Flynn initially faced. Hard-wired into those disparate cultures were different mind-sets for viewing a problem, with the State Department inclined to take the long view, the CIA focused on the middle distance, and the US military absorbed with the immediate. Then, you had the personality clashes. Nobody initially wanted to work for someone else.

Certainly guilty parties included the Special Operations Forces direct action units Delta Force and SEAL Team Six, which were called black ops units for a reason. Their culture was hypersecretive and insular, and from the outside, at least, arrogant. McChrystal had spent much of his career in Special Forces, and he always felt the "we're too cool for school" attitude—"we are *very* special and *very* elite"—was a hindrance to cooperative operations. It simply rubbed a lot of people the wrong way. Even Special Forces doctrine reinforced the idea that members were only interested in conducting certain missions of their own choosing: "We'll be gone from our objective by daylight, and we'll turn it over to competent authorities." What the hell did that even mean? McChrystal wondered. Turn over what, exactly, and to whom?

Breaking down those walls of cultural mistrust and suspicion had been the first order of business, and it was done one sledgehammer blow at a time, and not without a lot of broken furniture and bruised feelings. The trick in McChrystal's mind was to align objectives, metrics for success, and incentives in a way that naturally forced cooperation. Even in a war zone, incentives still matter to government agencies. His message, drummed in at each daily O&I briefing, was simple: "This is a war, and it will have a winner and a loser. And unless we can find a way to work together, it is not at all clear to me that we will be the winner."

The throbbing heart of McChrystal's vision remained the cycle of operations JSOC commanders dubbed F3EA, or "find, fix, finish, exploit, and analyze." Perhaps not surprisingly for an organization created by JSOC, the overwhelming focus early on was on Special Operational Forces (SOF) direct action units finishing terrorist and insurgent targets. For about a hundred years that had also been the focus of US military operations writ large, because it was relatively easy to find a Soviet or Warsaw Pact tank division.

Destroying it was the problem. Now advances in precision guided weapons and airpower meant you could destroy virtually anything you could locate on a grid coordinate. The problem in counterterrorism operations was finding out where the enemy was located, who it was, and, most important, why your enemy was your enemy in the first place.

The realization that the F3EA cycle would be weighted toward the "find" and "fix" imperative in counterterrorism operations led to the other transformative change in Task Force 714. Traditionally, intelligence was considered an enabler of US military operations, but the fighting in Afghanistan and Iraq had turned that maxim on its head. Increasingly, the task force was conducting raids and operations specifically to gather more intelligence, which prompted yet more raids, in what was becoming a virtuous cycle. The man most responsible for that particular epiphany was the task force's intelligence chief, whom McChrystal first met when the Ranger regiment he commanded cycled through the hyperrealistic training at the Joint Readiness Training Center (JRTC) at Fort Polk, Louisiana. McChrystal had reason to be thankful that the JRTC evaluator who helped rate the performance of his unit on that rotation was Mike Flynn, who was already making a name for himself as one of the US Army's most talented, up-and-coming intelligence officers.

WITH HIS FAMILIAR green notebook crammed with notes and diagrams nearly always in hand, Mike Flynn had set about early on deconstructing F3EA into its component parts, putting each phase of operations under the microscope. He pored through the plastic garbage bags filled with seized materials from night raids, stared at documents in Arabic he could not decipher, palmed thumb drives and laptops that no one had searched, and asked his intelligence analysts futilely where certain pieces of evidence had been collected, and from whom? He had accompanied the SOF direct action units on night raids to witness firsthand how they collected materials, what they looked for, and for how long. At the end of the review Flynn had concluded that to be successful, Task Force 714 had to become as much an intelligence gathering and exploitation organization as a direct action outfit. It didn't need more shooters, but a more finely calibrated scope and better trackers. Flynn had looked at the critical "find," "exploit," and "analyze" pieces of the puzzle, and determined that the task force's capabilities fell woefully short.

The need to check AQI and stop Iraq's slide toward all-out civil war drove the task force relentlessly, and that made it an almost perfect incubator for the new style of multiagency, intelligence-driven operations he and his boss were pioneering. They enjoyed an almost unheard-of level of autonomy and were able to launch night raids and lethal strikes virtually at will in Iraq and Afghanistan without having to ask, "Mother, may I?" from higher headquarters. More broadly, no one in Washington had specifically empowered JSOC to form a globe-spanning, multiagency counterterrorism network, but neither had anyone specifically forbidden it, either. Stanley McChrystal and company built their counterterrorism network out of necessity, and in *Field of Dreams* fashion, other counterterrorism players came to join the team.

Working closely with FBI and other law enforcement members of the task force, and building on early FBI and SOF cooperation in Afghanistan, Flynn implemented evidence collection protocols for the Special Forces night raids that closely mirrored techniques the FBI used in executing search warrants. Although it meant that the night raiders had to linger longer on target and take additional risks, each computer, thumb drive, cell phone, and document captured was catalogued and filed according to which room it was seized in, and whenever possible to which prisoner it was linked. No longer did operators simply dump plastic garbage bags of captured material tagged with sticky notes into the laps of bewildered analysts and consider their job done.

To pore through and analyze the mountains of captured materials, Flynn enlisted the help the Defense Intelligence Agency's National Media Exploitation Center. Large satellite dishes were placed on the roof of task force headquarters so that terabytes of data could transmit to the agency's Arabic linguists in Washington. Flynn would quickly receive their translations and analysis in an increasingly common process that became known as reach back. He also created multiagency intelligence fusion cells that mirrored operations at Balad and Bagram on a smaller scale, and deployed them throughout Iraq and Afghanistan. Analysts were organized into joint exploitation teams, or JETs, whose sole focus was massing intelligence against specific targets.

Task Force 714 was also frequently able to bypass a normally ponderous Pentagon acquisition and supply bureaucracy, receiving top priority for much of what they asked for. What it couldn't get from the acquisition bureaucracy, the force improvised. When the system was slow to supply requested Predator drones, the Task Force created what its members lovingly referred to as the Confederate Air Force, a motley collection of airframes that included six commercial single-engine turboprops and various helicopters. The Confederate Air Force employed equipment and expertise honed by the Army's supersecret signals intelligence unit called the Intelligence Support Activity (ISA), or simply "the Activity" in the Special Operations community. US Army Special Operations Command had invested heavily in creating its own signals intelligence expertise, with the "knob turners" of the ISA becoming the best tactical unit in the world at intercepting and tracking electronic communications, whether cell phones, satellite phones and radios, or fiber-optic communications.

Al-Zarqawi's AQI was the first terrorist group to arise in the age of cell phones and broadband Internet, and it relied heavily on electronic communications both to organize its far-flung operations and to recruit and spread terrorist propaganda via the web. A terrorist enterprise as ambitious and hyperactive as al-Zarqawi's required rapid communications, and that was a vulnerability that Task Force 714 was determined to exploit. In the hunt for al-Zarqawi, the Activity was using new intercept techniques, such as tracing cell phones even when they are turned off, and advanced software that revealed the patterns of relationships hidden in the numerology of captured phones.

The ability to follow those electronic leads was vastly improving with the emergence of drones, a superstar node in the network of intelligence, surveillance, and reconnaissance (ISR) assets. By 2006 the task force had three dedicated Predators that had flown more than five hundred hours, following known or suspected al-Zarqawi accomplices. The video feed from a remotely powered drone was a constant companion in the task force's operations center, visual white noise that at any moment might surrender the clue that led to the AQI leader.

As he watched the task force's increasingly sophisticated array of electronic divining rods probing for golden nuggets of intelligence, Mike Flynn sensed that they were closing in on al-Zarqawi. The entire task force felt it, and the resultant vibe was like a low hum in the operations center. Their improved intelligence analysis and exploitation had ratcheted up the operations tempo from just 18 targeted raids a month a few years earlier to nearly 300 a month by the summer of 2006. Their evidence collection techniques had become so solid that more than 80 percent of the insurgents the task force captured were being convicted in Iraqi courts of law, versus roughly 20 percent of suspected insurgents captured in traditional sweeps that netted "military-aged men" of indeterminate guilt.

In one instance, an FBI agent working on the task force was taking a pro forma statement from an insurgent before turning him over to Iraqi authorities, and the man revealed a new piece of intelligence that was missed in his initial interrogations. The intelligence was passed to Flynn's fusion cell in Mosul, which used it to identify the commander of AQI's northern network, a former member of the Iraqi Olympic soccer team named Abu Talwa. Because Talwa was deemed close to al-Zarqawi, the interrogation team was eager to talk with him, but when confronted with a SOF raiding team, he blew himself up with a suicide vest. Flynn discovered that he was one of the five assassins in the poster photo of al-Zarqawi and Nick Berg, and the whole team was encouraged by his photo on the wall now being crossed out with a prominent X. They were getting close.

CHANGES AT THE top were also transforming the task force's direct action units, never more so than when McChrystal surged Delta Force into the Western Euphrates to try to stem the flow of foreign fighters down the smuggling ratlines that ran through the river valley into Syria. The plan was controversial because it required committing two of only three Delta units into the fight, an unsustainable level of effort for the elite but small commando force. Delta was accustomed to executing discrete missions, not military campaign plans, but the entire Iraqi enterprise was on the cusp of potential failure. Despite grumbling from some quarters, Delta's deputy commander Scott Miller backed the plan. Counterterrorism was Delta's reason for being, and if it didn't disrupt al-Zarqawi's "Caravan of Martyrs," then the terrorist leader might well succeed with his outlandish strategy to massacre Iraqi Shiites until it provoked a sectarian civil war. It was a lesson none of them would forget: when al-Qaeda and its jihadist brethren promised to do something—say, defeat the Soviet Union or bring the United States to its knees—they meant to do it, or die trying.

The Western Anbar campaign tightened the handshake not only between the various elements of Special Operations Forces, but also between SOF and conventional forces in Iraq. Borrowing a page from his boss's notebook, Scott Miller held a weekly video teleconference with the conventional brigade commanders in Iraq to share intelligence and build a common picture of the contested battle space, a level of transparency and coordination that would have been unthinkable a few years earlier. The fighting was becoming so intense throughout Iraq in 2006 that it was necessary to "de-conflict" targets lest US units fall in on the same insurgent groups and end up shooting at each other.

Army Ranger battalions became a critical part of the SOF mix, routinely cordoning off city blocks and providing overwatch and egress routes for Delta's night raiders. In a division of labor dating to earlier in the war, SEAL Team Six had been given primary responsibility for Afghanistan, while Delta Force was charged with Iraq. As a result of the need to surge forces in the Western Euphrates and reinforce Delta, Task Force 714 had Navy SEAL Team Six commandos join the fight in Anbar alongside their Army counterparts. The natural rivalry between the United States' two elite counterterrorism outfits was set aside as they fought together against a determined enemy. The close relationships and bonds of shared sacrifice that developed between the junior officers and enlisted noncommissioned officers in all of those units would only grow tighter as they were promoted up the chain of leadership in the years to come.

The greatest adaptation in Task Force 714 raids was evident after targets were secured. The symbiotic relationship between the Special Operations forces and the FBI that legal attaché Brian McCauley and his colleagues in Afghanistan helped pioneer had become increasingly institutionalized and routine. After securing a target, Delta and SEAL Team Six commandos became forensic specialists, taking photographs of each room and carefully cataloguing evidence as if executing a search warrant, revealing their evolution into an intelligence-gathering force.

In many cases the raiders even included members from the FBI's own Hostage Rescue Team (HRT), revealing the bureau's parallel transformation into a counterterrorism organization. Stanley McChrystal and Mike Flynn had pushed the FBI to become an even more integral part of the Task Force 714 team and lend its expertise in evidence collection, forensics, and interrogations. The bureau had responded by assigning twelve agents from HRT to the task force. The HRT was an elite counterterrorism unit the bureau had established in 1983 on the eve of the Los Angeles Olympics, mindful of the inadequate response of German police to a Palestinian terrorists attack that killed eleven Israeli athletes at the Munich Olympics in 1972. HRT members were trained in close-quarter fighting and house breaching by Delta Force instructors at the US Army's Special Operations Command training ground in Fort Bragg, North Carolina.

The rewards and risks of the FBI partnership were exposed during the Western Anbar operations. On a night raid in Ramadi in March 2006, two Rangers were killed by gunfire after entering the ground floor of a target house, and a third team member was knocked unconscious and wounded by shrapnel when an insurgent triggered his suicide vest. The wounded raider was later revealed as FBI special agent Jay Tabb, a member of the HRT unit who was embedded with the Rangers, and who would later go on to lead the Hostage Rescue Team.

Often at night when Scott Miller was commanding Delta Force from the Operations Center and monitoring the progress of multiple raids, Stan McChrystal would come in and quietly observe from the periphery. As a point of leadership in emphasizing decentralized execution, McChrystal rarely inserted himself into or interrupted tactical operations. When the raids were completed and his subordinates had the operations in hand, Miller would often go and sit with McChrystal, and the two soldiers who had fought so long together would talk, sometimes well into the early morning hours— about sports, or missing their families and home, anything but the war. Other times, the war was the elephant in the room you couldn't ignore.

The tempo of their F3EA operations was industrial strength by 2006, with nearly every kink in the find, fix, finish, exploit, and analyze cycle eliminated by constant repetition and a disciplined after-action review process of continual self-improvement that they called a hot wash. The task force had become a manhunting machine in perpetual motion.

And yet each night at its nightly briefing, where Miller was responsible for summarizing the "significant activities," he knew violence was continuing to spike upward in Iraq. More than one thousand Iraqi civilians continued to die each month, and the number was climbing. More than one hundred thousand were fleeing the country each month in a desperate attempt to escape the ethnic cleansing and violence—mostly the educated upper and middle classes who could afford to leave, and whom Iraq could not afford to lose. US casualties were also spiking, with more than one hundred troopers killed in action in some months, and many hundreds more wounded.

The questions and doubts swirled through everyone's head. Was their near obsession with hunting down one man blinding them to the bigger picture? What if they finally killed al-Zarqawi the man, but the myth and ideology behind the man endured and simply awaited the next flesh-and-blood vessel to claim the mantle of al-Qaeda emir? What if, despite this massive manhunt and all of their sacrifices, the furies of sectarian hatred and vengeance continued to tear Iraq apart? What if al-Zarqawi's strategy worked?

Iraq was Scott Miller's second war after Somalia and there were times when it felt as if he was batting 0 for 2. There was calm and steadiness at the core of Stan McChrystal, however, and it gave Miller confidence. McChrystal had already concluded that decapitating al-Qaeda's leadership was not a war-winning strategy. That was one reason why he decided to aim relentless body blows not only on AQI's leadership, but also on the entire network and middle management. Their job was to keep the terrorist and insurgent leaders and their networks on the defensive until longer-term efforts to stand up Iraqi security forces and build governing capacity hopefully tipped the balance.

The talks with McChrystal always helped Miller see the longer view. The man could deliver a world-class ass-chewing, but he was a good listener and as smart as they come. As a career soldier Miller had always been on the lookout for that one leader that he would gladly follow anywhere.

In McChrystal he found that guy, even if the hardscrabble Anbari towns along the Euphrates where Miller had followed him—Fallujah, Ramadi, Haditha, Hit—would always recall desperate fighting and a long roll call of fallen friends.

THE TRAIL THAT eventually led to their biggest break in the al-Zarqawi manhunt was typical of their network-centric operations by the summer of 2006. Earlier in the year, one of the task force's liaison officers embedded with Iraqi security forces reported that they had captured a man believed to be Abu Zar, a native Iraqi and a key leader of AQI's car-bombing operations. Under extended interrogation, Zar had identified a safe house in Yusufiyah sometimes used by Abu Ayyub al-Masri, an Egyptian and AQI's second-in-command, whose ties to al-Zarqawi stretched back to 1990s Afghanistan. Dubbed "Named Area of Interest 152," the safe house became a frequent point of observation for Predator unmanned drones whenever the task force was flying them in the vicinity. For three months, the task force periodically monitored the safe house from the air, and when a convoy of vehicles was spotted there, a daylight strike raid was immediately launched, consisting of SEAL commandos and Army Rangers. In the ensuing firefight, five insurgents were killed, and a treasure trove of intelligence and bomb-making materials was captured. More important, just before the raiding team's helicopters landed at safe house "152," surveillance aircraft detected a car driving away from it to a second compound just up the road. A second raiding team was launched on that house—"Objective Mayers"—where they captured twelve men who were unlike any of the al-Qaeda thugs the task force had yet encountered.

Sitting across from one of those men at the interrogation table in the task force's well-lit detainee screening facility, Mike Flynn wondered why such an obviously educated and intelligent person was devoting his life to tearing his country apart, rather than rebuilding it. For Christ's sake, you have an electrical engineering degree, he thought to himself, and instead of building a bridge or helping establish a functioning government, you are applying your talents to identifying societal weaknesses and attacking vulnerable governing institutions in order to terrorize and intimidate.

The network al-Qaeda in Iraq had established for that purpose was sophisticated far beyond the early reckoning of US commanders, with interlinked logistics, transportation, information, money management, and strike operations worthy of a multinational conglomerate. After just a few interview sessions, it became clear that the older men captured at Objective Mayers were the senior managers and vice presidents of that terrorist enterprise. The first clue was the fact that they were not armed; another was that, between them, they carried only a single cell phone, an unusually disciplined level of trade craft.

The task force's interrogation teams had quickly focused on four of the detainees in particular as the most senior AQI leaders. Triangulating their responses during extended interrogation sessions and playing them off against one another, as well as expertly appealing to the obvious ego and sense of pride of the detainees, task force intelligence analysts began focusing special attention on Abu Mubassir, a former Iraqi soccer player and wrestler in his thirties who spoke good English and seemed to delight in matching wits with his interrogators. After weeks of exhaustive interplay and the establishment of that unique bond between detainees and analysts trained in the subtle arts of interrogation, Mubassir had given up a critical piece of intelligence: the name and general location of Abu Musab al-Zarqawi's spiritual adviser, Sheikh Abd al-Rahman.

By the summer of 2006 perhaps no task force operation had undergone a more fundamental transformation than detainee interrogations. After JSOC personnel were disciplined for prisoner abuse in 2004, including two who were expelled from the task force for using a Taser on a prisoner, and especially following the black eye of the Abu Ghraib detainee abuse scandal that became a worldwide recruiting poster for al-Qaeda, McChrystal had instructed Flynn to thoroughly professionalize their interrogation operations. Flynn reached out for additional interrogators at the US Army Intelligence Center at Fort Huachuca, Arizona, where he had commanded the intelligence school, and to the reserve component. He scoured the government for Arabic speakers and supplanted their ranks with local hires. By 2006 the task force boasted six times as many interrogators, interpreters, and analysts as detainees. They opened the interrogations to the FBI and other interested agencies as a move toward greater transparency, and to learn best practices. Paper maps on the walls of interrogation rooms were replaced with computers and flat-screen desktop monitors, and detainees were shown satellite imagery and asked to indicate with the click of a computer mouse where safe houses and rendezvous points were located. Each click of the mouse was automatically recorded into a database that tracked all known addresses associated with the insurgency.

"We had to teach ourselves how to conduct high-end interrogations, and then train that expertise to a complex, multiagency task force of people from very different backgrounds and organizational cultures, to include Special Operations Forces and intelligence and law enforcement agencies," recalled Flynn. "As a result we were able to mass so much information against individuals we captured that at some point they realized it was no use lying any more. We knew more about many of these guys than their closest friends or even families. We knew more about some of these guys than they knew about themselves. That just broke their fabricated stories down. I witnessed that happen hundreds of times."

Armed with the name and address of Sheikh al-Rahman, the task force directed a hard stare that monitored his comings and goings 24/7, tracking him with unmanned drones and establishing a "pattern of life" so that any anomaly in his activities would stand out. One of the task force analysts became so familiar with Sheikh al-Rahman's demeanor that he was able to pick him out of a crowd following Friday prayers just by the way he walked.

Given that Flynn's intelligence shop was following its most promising lead ever on a close al-Zarqawi associate, they wanted to devote the preponderance of the ISR assets of manned and unmanned surveillance aircraft to the hunt. With roughly 70 percent of the task force's critical ISR diverted to the hunt for al-Zarqawi, the relentless pace of Delta's F3EA operations, which had been averaging three hundred raids each month, began to slow and sputter. The breakneck cycle of operations the task force was pioneering was heavily dependent on unmanned drones' persistent stare in particular, and on advanced ISR in general, to grease the machinery. Without those enablers, the task force was forced to ease its relentless pressure on al-Zarqawi's network. If the intelligence the analysts were pursuing turned out to be yet another false lead, they would have ceded critical momentum to AQI that would be hard to recapture. Mike Flynn and the intelligence shop were asking Delta Force to be patient, but by nature Scott Miller and his commandos were not patient men. Left idle, they tended to get ill-tempered. Everyone was feeling the push-and-pull tension between a deliberate and analytical intelligence shop's tapping on the brakes, and gung-ho operators with their foot on the gas, and that tension was central to the new style of warfare that was emerging from the crucible of Iraq.

"THAT'S AMZ," McCHRYSTAL said, using the task force's shorthand for "Abu Musab al-Zarqawi."

McChrystal was sitting with Mike Flynn and his command team at the U-shaped table that fronted the Joint Operations Center on June 6, 2006. On the large screen, the video feed from a Predator drone showed a lone figure emerge from an isolated two-story house tucked away among palm trees outside the fly-speck town of Hibhib. The figure walked down a long driveway to a dirt frontage road bordered by an irrigation canal, and looked both ways to see if his spiritual adviser, Sheikh al-Rahman, had been followed. The man in the video was heavyset and dressed all in black, al-Zarqawi's signature. No one in the Joint Operations Center doubted that the most wanted terrorist in the world was in their sights at last.

Even if al-Zarqawi had looked up into the early evening sky, it's doubtful he would have detected the nine ISR platforms orbiting above like moons drawn to his dark gravitational pull. The aircraft had tracked the silver sedan that drove Sheikh al-Rahman out of Baghdad; the blue truck that had picked him up after a vehicle switch designed to throw off any pursuers; the restaurant where he had switched cars yet again in Baqubah, the capital city of Diyala Province north of Baghdad; and the white pickup truck that had driven him to al-Zarqawi's safe house on the outskirts of Hibhib. The task force's remotely piloted drones had logged more than six hundred hours following accomplices to this fateful rendezvous. Even as McChrystal and Flynn and the rest of the task force watched from the Joint Operations Center, an F-16 fighter from the Iowa National Guard was streaking toward the house's coordinates.

Stan McChrystal was irritated. He wanted to capture al-Zarqawi alive and give his team a chance to interrogate the al-Qaeda princeling. Task force operators determined that a raid on the compound in the waning light was too risky, and that their prey might well escape in the chaos. Then one of the Night Stalker's two helicopters that was ferrying Delta Force troops to the site to secure it after the bomb blast malfunctioned on the flight line, a rare snafu. The decision was made by the operational commander that they couldn't afford to wait and risk having al-Zarqawi escape.

"Blow the motherfucker up," he told the operations center in Baghdad.

Task Force leaders watched the video screen as the F-16 made a pass over al-Zarqawi's compound, and stared in disbelief when it failed to release its bombs because of a garbled command to engage. They half expected to see the man in black flee out the backdoor into the palm groves. On the next pass, the screens in the Operations Center flashed a blinding white as the 500-pound GBU-12 bomb hit the compound. On a second pass, another bomb found its target, the house disappearing into billowing clouds of smoke.

At sunset McChrystal and Flynn walked together to the screening facility where the Delta raiding team had left the bodies of Sheikh al-Rahman and al-Zarqawi. Their bodies lay atop separate tarps on the cement floor. Because they had been killed by overpressure from the bomb blast that ruptured internal organs but left their bodies intact, both men looked in death much as they had appeared in life: the surprisingly young imam and spiritual adviser, and his most accomplished disciple, a mass murderer for the ages.

That night, McChrystal and Flynn participated via video teleconference in a change of command ceremony for Admiral Bill McRaven, one of JSOC's assistant commanding general officers who was moving on to become the commander of all Special Operations Forces in Europe, and would later succeed McChrystal as JSOC commander during the seminal operation targeting Osama bin Laden. By any measure it was a moment to celebrate, though bittersweet. Both McChrystal and Flynn recognized the faces of friends and family in the audience at Fort Bragg that they had seen little of in the previous three years of fighting. McChrystal caught himself staring into the audience at his wife, Annie, who had endured three Christmases with her husband away on foreign battlefields. Flynn thought of his own wife, Lori, and his brother Charlie, who was a commander with the

Eighty-second Airborne Brigade at Fort Bragg. The two brothers had been neighbors for three years at Fort Bragg, with houses just down the street from each other, during which time Mike had seen Charlie a sum total of one time.

Before long, the poster on the wall of Task Force 16's headquarters had an X crossing out each of the five assassins of Nick Berg. One had been captured, and like al-Zarqawi the rest had been killed. There was satisfaction in avenging the death of an innocent American, though it was more than tempered by the fact that many more Americans and Iraqis would die in the Iraqi civil war. Just in the month of June 2006, 3,149 Iraqis would be killed in the sectarian violence gripping the country, followed by a record 3,400 in July. The vast majority of those killed, an estimated 90 percent, showed signs of summary execution. Al-Zarqawi might as well have been laughing from his grave.

# SEVEN

# Prodigal Soldiers

## January–December 2007

B Y THE END OF 2006, THE UNITED STATES' POST-9/11 WARS HAD reached a critical inflection point. After Republicans were trounced in midterm congressional elections in large part due to the unpopularity of the Iraq conflict, President George W. Bush replaced Defense Secretary Donald Rumsfeld. He subsequently announced that Lieutenant General David Petraeus would lead a 30,000-troop surge in Iraq, and with roughly 140,000 soldiers and Marines execute a holistic counterinsurgency campaign to try to stabilize a country coming apart along its sectarian seams, and salvage an acceptable outcome to one of the greatest strategic blunders in modern American history.

Only this was not the same uninformed and inexperienced US force that invaded the country in 2003. Most of the senior commanders who led during the 2007 surge—notably to include Petraeus, Martin Dempsey, and Stanley McChrystal—had been part of that initial rush into Iraq. They had gone to school on the mistakes. Their collective actions over the next twelve months would help form the definitive narrative of a new American style of war. That model relied on unprecedented civil-military coordination, and leveraged counterinsurgency operations to protect the population and win the battle for hearts and minds. It would deny terrorists and insurgents sanctuary by maneuvering forces on the ground, both US and Iraqi, to clear and hold territory, and maximize the lethality of targeted counterterrorism operations through the application of new intelligence-gathering and code-breaking techniques. Above all else, it recognized the truth in Carl von Clausewitz's maxim that war is a continuation of politics by other means, and thus embraced political reconciliation as the fastest way to drain the swamps of extremism.

The small clique of US leaders who returned to Iraq in 2007 quickly discovered that what had once been all but unthinkable had become undeniable: the United States was losing the war. As with Vietnam, the defeat would not be theirs alone to bear, but the stain of that legacy and their part in it would endure for the rest of their lives. In that sense they were prodigal soldiers being given one last chance at redemption, and it bound and united them in a hellish landscape redolent of Dante's Inferno.

THE SEVENTH CIRCLE of that inferno was a road the locals called Sharia al-Dagat. Al-Qaeda in Iraq's bombing of Samarra's Golden Dome mosque in February 2006 had initiated an unchecked, eye-for-an-eye cycle of sectarian violence by Sunni suicide bombers and Shiite death squads that set Baghdad afire, and no suburb was worse than the mixed neighborhoods of the northwest. The northern section was overwhelmingly Shiite and dominated by the Jaysh al-Mahdi militia, but the southern section was predominately Sunni and thoroughly infiltrated by al-Qaeda in Iraq (AQI). In the middle, once peaceful mixed neighborhoods had become raging battlegrounds, with more than ten thousand families displaced from their homes in deliberate campaigns of sectarian cleansing. Iraq now suffered over two hundred car and suicide bombings each month. In early 2007, Baghdad was averaging 370 murders each week, many of the victims bound, tortured, and killed execution style and dumped on the side of Sharia al-Dagat and other lonely roads just like it.

As part of Petraeus's last ditch counterinsurgency offensive, the First Infantry Division's "Dagger Brigade" had been placed in the middle of the warring factions on either side of Sharia al-Dagat. For the US soldiers, it wasn't just the bound and mutilated bodies lying beside the road that brought Baghdad's tortured soul into unforgettable relief: dumped bodies had become a disgustingly routine fixture of the city's morning landscape. Rather, it was the Iraqi children blithely playing soccer among the corpses— harbingers of a dark psychosis that promised to shadow that land for genera- tions, a sickness that would become evident years later in the willing recruits who flocked to the banner of the Islamic State.

The Dagger Brigade's response was to establish in the mixed Sunni- Shiite neighborhoods of northwest Baghdad a compound of forty-five houses called Combat Outpost Casino. Protected by blast walls, it sheltered a battalion of several hundred US soldiers.

The soldiers at Outpost Casino were soon joined by a battalion of the Sixth Iraqi Army, evidence of a reenergized train-and-equip program led first by Petraeus and in 2007 by Major General Martin Dempsey. The Iraqi troops joined with their US counterparts in conducting joint patrols and operations. Living among and working side by side with the Iraqis around the clock gave the US officers insight into which Iraqi commanders were trustworthy, and which were in league with the militias and insurgents, or were simply corrupt. The joint patrols and operations also pulled Iraqi army troops and police off their own major installations and helped give them increased visibility and legitimacy in the eyes of local Iraqis.

Combat Outpost Casino became of one of seventy-seven so-called joint security sites that General Petraeus established throughout Baghdad. In each case, death squad murders dropped dramatically. Locals began giving US commanders more accurate intelligence on insurgent and militia ac- tivity, helping the security forces and Stanley McChrystal's Task Force 16 identify and destroy many suicide bombing and death squad cells. By the summer of 2007, the joint security sites were showing unmistakable signs of curbing the runaway cycle of sectarian violence. Commerce began flour- ishing as the violence gradually tapered off, and children began returning to schools. Kids could be found playing soccer in fields no longer littered with dead bodies.

But putting US troops on the fault line of Shiite-versus-Sunni tensions was costly. In the first six months of 2007, 575 US troops died in Iraq, a 62

percent increase over the same period in 2006. The 332 service members
who died in a three-month stretch in the summer of 2007 made it the most
lethal quarter yet for the US military in Iraq. The sound of "missing man"
roll calls and bugles playing taps at memorials for the fallen was a frequent
refrain heard around Baghdad, underscoring the grave toll that the new
counterinsurgency campaign was exacting on US forces. Given the many
years of war in Iraq, it was anyone's guess how long the American public
would support such a costly campaign in what many had already written
off as a lost cause.

IN THE HEADQUARTERS of Multi-National Force–Iraq inside Baghdad's
Green Zone, David Petraeus constantly poured over the metrics tracking
his comprehensive, civil-military counterinsurgency campaign. Along with
a lot of smart people at the US Army Combined Arms Center at Fort Leav-
enworth, he had spent two years researching and writing the US Army's
counterinsurgency doctrine. On his third command tour in Iraq, Petraeus
was confident his strategy would work. Which truly made him an army of
one.

The problem was that Petraeus couldn't predict when the counterinsurgency operations would start paying dividends and Iraq would flip for the
better. There was a cycle to this type of conflict, but each was unpredictable
in its own way. Looking at the horrific US casualty figures for June and July,
he understood that the sands in the hourglass tracking Washington's perse-
verance with this last-ditch campaign were slipping away.

Petraeus constantly reminded his commanders that the surge that mattered most was not of troops but of ideas. He knew his doctrine sounded
Zen-like to some hard-charging traditionalists, but it drew lessons from
some of the dirtiest and most protracted wars in history: *The most important terrain is the human terrain.* The imperative was securing the population, not hunting terrorists or fighting insurgents. That meant US troops
would have to leave their massive forward operating bases and live among
the Iraqis so as to protect them, while exposing themselves to greater danger. The casualty figures on his desk confirmed Petraeus's early assessment
to President Bush that the situation in Iraq would get worse before it got

better. But the numbers also indicated that Iraqi civilian casualties had dipped in June to the lowest level in a year, suggesting his campaign was gaining traction.

Perhaps the greatest difference in the new US campaign in Iraq was the tight civil-military bond Petraeus formed with US ambassador to Iraq Ryan Crocker. That relationship stood in stark contrast to the utterly dysfunctional relationship in 2003–2004 between Coalition Provisional Authority (CPA) head L. Paul Bremer and his military commanders. Having personally witnessed the folly that flowed from that dysfunction like blood from a wound, and understanding that political progress and reconciliation were equally as important in counterinsurgency campaigns as military operations, Petraeus and Crocker had joined themselves at the hip. Their offices shared a common reception room, and both men agreed early on that theirs would be an equal partnership: if either man disagreed with a course of action or policy decision, it would not go forward.

Whenever Crocker and Petraeus visited the always difficult Iraqi prime minister Nouri al-Maliki, it was as a tandem. Al-Maliki was upset with the entire direction of Petraeus's counterinsurgency strategy. He wanted the United States to transfer security responsibilities to Iraqi security forces even faster so as to consolidate his own power base, a strategy that was already failing. He also believed any new US forces should be stationed on large bases away from the major cities, and wanted US commanders to release detained insurgents from captivity quicker. Petraeus essentially overrode the Iraqi leader on all counts, and relied on the always diplomatic Crocker to handle the inevitable al-Maliki blowback.

Their unique partnership was aided by Crocker's deep experience and background in the Middle East. He was the closest thing to Lawrence of Arabia that the US Foreign Service had produced. A military brat, Crocker had made his first trip to the Middle East at the age of three, attended high school in Turkey, and in college hiked to Calcutta. On a diplomatic posting to Beirut during the Lebanese civil war in the early 1980s, he personally investigated a right-wing Christian militia's massacre of more than one thousand Palestinian men, women, and children at the Shatila refugee camp, so he understood the dark tribal and sectarian currents that flowed just beneath the thin crust of civilization in the Middle East. Crocker was injured and very nearly killed by a suicide truck bomber when the US embassy in Beirut was hit in 1983.

More recently, Crocker had reopened the US Embassy in Kabul in 2002, and he cowrote the prescient 2002 State Department memo entitled "The Perfect Storm," which warned that the invasion of Iraq could unleash long-repressed sectarian and ethnic tensions; invite meddling from Iraq's neighbors Iran, Syria, and Saudi Arabia; and saddle the United States with onerous nation-building duty in a country with dilapidated infrastructure. Personally he felt it was the worst idea since Israel decided to invade Lebanon in 1982, to its lasting regret.

Crocker had never forgotten the utter contempt Defense Secretary Rumsfeld and his band of neocons had shown in dismissing the memo. They treated the Foreign Service not as experts to be consulted but, rather, like saboteurs not to be trusted. They seemed to believe that once Saddam's boot heel was off the necks of the Iraqi people, then the arc of humanity would bend toward democracy and justice. In Ryan Crocker's experience in the Middle East, the more likely reaction to such a chaotic situation would be a fierce competition for power among people who reverted to their primordial identity as sect, tribe, and family. Sadly, events had proven him right.

Having grown up in a military family, Crocker was comfortable with the culture, and he warmed immediately to Petraeus, who grasped the political dimensions of conflict better than most other generals did. "There was also the gravity of the situation in Iraq when we arrived in 2007," Crocker later recalled. "It went back to the dawn of our own American history. Both David Petraeus and I understood that we had to hang together, or we would surely hang separately."

Nowhere did their close collaboration pay greater dividends than on the issue of reconciliation in general, and in Anbar Province in particular. The Sunni province was the vortex of the insurgency and the base of operations for al-Qaeda in Iraq. Under an outreach program that became known as the Anbar Awakening, a number of Sunni sheikhs and tribes had banded together to form the Anbar Salvation Council, splitting from al-Qaeda in Iraq and finding common cause with US forces in their fight against the terrorist group. On one of his first days back in Iraq, Petraeus traveled to

Anbar to meet with Sheikh Abdul Sattar Abu Risha, a ringleader of the Awakening movement, who had issued a manifesto denouncing al-Qaeda in Iraq. Sheikh Abu Risha backed his words with 1,500 men from his tribe who were recruited to join the police force in the key city of Ramadi.

Petraeus was determined to expand the Awakening model, and he started a chain reaction up the Tigris River Valley by deploying new US battalions to the towns and cities along the river upon their arrival in-country as part of the troop surge. As soon as the new units established greater security, Petraeus asked local leaders in neighboring towns whether they wanted a similar US troop presence to protect them from al-Qaeda. Many said yes, and soon the Anbar Awakening was reaching critical mass. Tragically, for his efforts in launching the Awakening movement Sheikh Abu Risha would later be assassinated by an AQI car bomb.

The Shiite-dominated government of Prime Minister al-Maliki was very reluctant to arm Sunni militias at the heart of the Awakening, or to put them on the government payroll. Crocker worked that political end by constantly pressuring al-Maliki to make a gesture of goodwill to these militias, who were fighting a common enemy. Al-Maliki finally relented. On a sweltering summer day, Crocker traveled to Anbar with a Shiite vice president and a Kurdish deputy prime minister, and handed the provincial governor in Anbar a check for $250 million.

As it happened, the commander of Multi-National Force–West (MNF-West) in Anbar was Major General John Kelly, the rangy Bostonian who had joined the Marine Corps as an enlistee and had risen through the ranks to three-star general. Petraeus's more holistic counterinsurgency campaign of clearing insurgent pockets, holding territory, and building governance comported perfectly with the lessons Kelly and other Marine Corps leaders had drawn from multiple tours in Iraq. In the early days, US forces had been trained and indoctrinated to consider themselves a hammer, so naturally everything in Iraq looked like a nail.

On a regular basis Kelly would sit down with Sunni sheikhs in Anbar who on earlier tours had been his sworn enemy. "My brother, last time I was here I spent all my waking hours trying to capture or kill you," Kelly would say. "That's funny," the sheikhs would inevitably reply, "because I spent all my waking hours trying to kill you."

When Kelly asked the sheikhs why they had stopped fighting US forces, and instead found common cause with them against al-Qaeda in Iraq, they gave a version of the "if you can't beat them, join them" rationale. The Bush administration's announcement of a troop surge was taken as further evidence that the Americans weren't going away. The Sunni tribes had lost so many of their young men in battles with US soldiers and marines that there was no one left to marry their daughters. And no self-respecting father would marry his daughter to an al-Qaeda fighter, knowing that the fanatics were likely not long for this world.

BY 2007 IT was understood that Petraeus's "clear, hold, and build" counterinsurgency campaign required boots on the ground to hold territory cleared of insurgents, and that eventually the soldiers wearing those boots would have to be Iraqis. Building viable Iraqi security forces was thus the ticket home for US troops. The leader responsible for purchasing it was Lieutenant General Martin Dempsey, the commander of the Multi-National Security and Transition Command–Iraq, or "Min-Sticky" in military-speak.

Like the other commanders in Iraq, Dempsey saw the 2007 campaign as a last chance to get right what had gone so terribly wrong in that country. He had never forgotten the 2004 Sunni and Shiite uprisings, when he commanded Task Force Iron and the Iraqi National Guard units he trained had refused to fight. In 2005 and again in 2006, US attempts to speed up the handoff to Iraqi forces and begin pulling out of Iraq similarly collapsed when the Iraqis proved unable to cope with militia attacks and rising sectarian violence. The primary challenge they still faced was evident in the mounting violence in the country: the mostly raw Iraqi recruits and inexperienced leaders they were training were quickly being thrown into a maelstrom.

In fighting al-Qaeda–inspired terrorist insurgencies in Iraq and Afghanistan, the US military was learning that creating indigenous security forces almost from scratch was nation-building on a scale and complexity that the United States had not confronted since the aftermath of World War II. Only this time they were attempting it while the war still raged.

Dempsey was responsible for training, equipping, and supporting 348,000 Iraqi security personnel, including 151,800 Iraqi army troops, a 26,300-member national police force, and 135,000 local police officers. Eight of ten Iraqi army divisions were already battling insurgents in their assigned areas of operations, and all nine national police brigades were committed to the fight alongside US troops. Dempsey was learning that building a foreign army that was heavily engaged in fighting was more art than science, and required a skill set the US military had never developed on this scale.

Perhaps the greatest surprise was the amount of energy Dempsey had to expend in reforming Iraq's Defense and Interior Ministries, which were respectively responsible for army and police. One of the chief lessons of 2004 was that because the United States paid the salaries of security forces, they were more loyal to US overseers than to their own government. Moreover, when pressed, they weren't willing to put their lives and possibly their families at risk for a US–led coalition that might not be around very long. So, Dempsey had taken responsibility for reforming the ministries, giving him visibility and influence over the entire system from the individual soldier or policeman all the way up to the minister's office where strategy and policy were decided.

What he discovered was rampant corruption, cronyism, and signs of sectarian influence. His intelligence briefers had evidence of a senior Iraqi officer with ties to Iranian intelligence, who ran a kidnapping, extortion, and murder ring on the side. Another general who had been fired for corruption still met with his former subordinate officers for private dinners. Still another Iraqi commander was directly tied to insurgent cells that planted roadside bombs targeting US forces. Arrest warrants had been issued for some of those officers, but others were considered virtual "untouchables" because they enjoyed protection from well-placed Iraqi politicians, including Iraqi prime minister Nouri al-Maliki. At one point, a senior Iraqi general that the Americans trusted had been replaced by an officer close to al-Maliki who had a clearly sectarian agenda favoring his Shiite sect. Dempsey and his former West Point classmate David Petraeus had threatened to withhold all US training and support from the brigade in question, until finally al-Maliki relented and reinstated the original officer.

The incident drove home the point to Dempsey that the United States was going to have to stay closely engaged in mentoring Iraqi security forces and in keeping the Iraqi political leadership honest. Otherwise, the Iraqi army that was being built to serve as an instrument of national unity could become little more than a club in the hand of a sectarian tyrant. Years later that lesson would be ignored, and the results would come back to haunt Dempsey and the rest of the US high command.

THE MARCHING ORDERS that David Petraeus gave to Stan McChrystal and the Joint Special Operations Command (JSOC)'s hunter-killer teams was straightforward: we'll do the net fishing, you do the spear fishing. In the summer and fall of 2007, the spear fishing in Iraq was abundant. The synergy of targeted counterterrorism operations as part of a broader counterinsurgency campaign was evident for all to see. As Petraeus and Crocker expanded the Anbar Awakening outreach and used those relationships to begin a serious reconciliation process between Sunni tribes and the government in Baghdad, it became far easier to gather intelligence and target the irreconcilables of al-Qaeda in Iraq.

Petraeus also received extra Special Forces units as part of his troop surge, and soon McChrystal established a task force to exclusively go after Shiite militia leaders and death squads. The only raids that required permission from Petraeus's headquarters were those into the Shiite slums of Baghdad's Sadr City, a mazelike mini-metropolis of ramshackle buildings and back alleys. Delta Force or SEAL Team Six strike teams could and sometimes did launch on targets inside Sadr City, but they usually had to fight their way out, and in the tight confines that almost inevitably involved civilian casualties. The blowback would reverberate in Prime Minister al-Maliki's temper tantrums, and usually catch Petraeus and Crocker broadside. Other than in Sadr City, JSOC launched raids based on its own authority and secret criteria.

The F3EA (find, fix, and finish, exploit, and analyze) model of operations had also kicked into a higher gear as the result of an unexpected technological breakthrough. For months Army General Keith Alexander, director of the National Security Agency (NSA), had been periodically visiting Baghdad trying to determine why the results of the agency's communications intercepts and electronic snooping in Iraq were so underwhelming. The problem, he discovered, was a ponderous NSA collection and analysis cycle that was too slow for the manhunts so critical to counterterrorism and counterinsurgency operations.

On average, sixteen hours elapsed from the moment when a voice or e-mail communication by cell phone or computer intercepted somewhere in Iraq was transmitted for analysis back to the NSA's 5,000-acre headquarters campus at Fort Meade, Maryland, and then inserted into a regular intelligence document that was sent back to the front lines. Data streams from various signals intercept platforms—be they ISR (intelligence, surveillance, and reconnaissance) aircraft snooping overhead, spy satellites in geosynchronous orbit, or ground antennas—were also segregated and stove-piped. Commanders in Iraq were asking the NSA to map out a target's entire digital footprint and network of contacts in intelligence packets called Klieg Lights, a time-consuming exercise that was often stymied by insufficient data.

Meanwhile, the cell phones becoming ubiquitous in Iraq were both the insurgents' most powerful communication tool and chief vulnerability. NSA trackers had developed a number of ingenious methods to track and intercept cell phone calls, including devices called virtual base-tower transceivers, which, when outfitted on Predator or manned aircraft, could mimic a cell phone tower and essentially force targeted cell phones to lock on to the NSA's airborne receiver.

After speaking to operators and analysts in Iraq, Alexander zeroed in on how all of that information from communications intercepts was processed and handled. He was increasingly convinced that frontline analysts at the tactical level of war had become overly mesmerized by all the possibilities that lay dormant in the mountains of data they were collecting, when what they really needed to know was the enemy's location. His determination to streamline NSA operations to deliver that single data point in real time would prove a game changer, one that profoundly impacted the United States' global war against terrorists.

Alexander had been chosen to lead the NSA in 2005 as a change agent, and he brought an unusual combination of technical expertise and military acumen at a time when the country confronted two failing wars and a global terrorist manhunt. Rumsfeld's choice of Alexander as the nation's preeminent eavesdropper would eventually be seconded by three successive defense secretaries who would keep him at the helm of the NSA for eight long years, and Alexander would later be given a second hat as the first leader of a new US Cyber Command.

With master's degrees in electronic warfare, physics, and national security to go with his hands-on experience in the field, Alexander was already a leading proponent of maximizing information-age technologies to better target enemies of the state. As the former head of the Army's Intelligence and Security Command in the 1990s, he had done pioneering work on battlefield visualization systems that allowed soldiers to see the relative positions of enemy and friendly forces on detailed terrain maps on the screens of their laptop computers. In those days, the Internet was still relatively new and mostly reliant on scratchy phone connections, and the US military still lacked the satellite bandwidth and computational power to create digital mobile environments that could connect frontline forces to the United States' vast intelligence gathering and analysis apparatus. By 2006 the NSA no longer had that excuse. The problem was that the agency's processes and software were unable to leverage rapid advances in computational power and communications bandwidth, and the world of big data manipulation was still in its relative infancy.

NSA directors bring their own background and instincts to the job, which naturally inform their priorities. As a West Pointer who took the helm of the agency at a time when many of his friends and former classmates were engaged in a desperate fight, and scores of American troops were being killed and wounded every month, Alexander believed that the agency's single most important mission was to help win the war in Iraq.

His answer to that imperative was a prototype called the Real Time Regional Gateway, an intelligence fusion system that his NSA team and private contractors developed in roughly three months, working virtually around the clock. The system was based on a new digital data model designed to rapidly fuse large volumes of metadata from disparate intelligence collection platforms, and integrate those signals for the singular purpose of geolocation. Essentially the system collected and analyzed all of the digital exhaust that emanates from a particular human being and used it to pinpoint his or her exact location whenever the subject appeared in cyberspace. To put all of that data in a format that frontline operators could readily digest, the gateway included a cutting-edge visual data model that displayed its output on computer maps for easier spatial orientation and for perceiving "patterns of life." Theoretically, all a US commander in Iraq had to do was enter the phone numbers, e-mail addresses, or computer signatures of potential targets, and whenever those targets popped up on the grid, the Real Time Regional Gateway would display their exact location on a video map.

Initially there was significant resistance to Real Time Regional Gateway. Intelligence shops throughout Iraq had become comfortable with the more detailed but ponderous Klieg Light intelligence packages, and they had no intention of giving them up. Finally, Keith Alexander sat down in Baghdad with his old West Point classmate David Petraeus to present his case. The intelligence community thought it needed Klieg Lights, Alexander argued, but it's asking the wrong questions. What it really needs to know is where the bad actors who are laying improvised explosive devices or plotting suicide bombing attacks are located. So, rather than stop sending Klieg Lights, and suffer the screams of outrage, Alexander asked for authority to just field test Real Time Regional Gateway. If the system worked, he was convinced, everyone would recognize it as a game changer.

In its first week in use, Real Time Regional Gateway sputtered and crashed. There was considerable sniping from the intelligence community, but Alexander was undeterred, certain that the problem was not the system, he was convinced, but policy issues and firebreaks inserted into the system to regulate what intelligence could be shared, with whom, and how fast. Within a week he had ironed those kinks out, and the system started cranking out geolocation "hits" on suspected terrorists and insurgents.

Initially, even JSOC's Task Force 16 was reluctant to surrender its most sensitive targeting data to a system outside of its direct control. On one of his frequent trips to Baghdad, Alexander called McChrystal, someone who had been a few classes behind him at West Point, and someone he knew and respected, and asked for a meeting in Baghdad.

"Hey, I want to show you what this thing can do," Alexander told Mc-Chrystal, indicating the Real Time Regional Gateway system. "Tell me the names of some of the guys you are interested in."

McChrystal recited some names and Alexander entered them. Rather than take the normal sixteen hours of analysis and distillation, the Gateway kicked out the phone numbers and displayed the exact current location of one of the targeted individuals in roughly one minute. The man was apparently on his cell phone and nearby at that very moment. "There he is, Stan, right there," Alexander pointed, and then turned to an incredulous McChrystal. "Now all I need is for you to share your data with us."

From that moment onward, McChrystal's Task Force 714 in Iraq and Afghanistan became the most prolific and enthusiastic users of Real Time Regional Gateway. The speed and precision of its targeting information threw the F3EA operations cycle into a new gear, greatly accelerating their turnaround times and reducing the decision-making loop by often completing the "find" and "fix" phases in a matter of minutes. Before long, US brigade commanders in Iraq had also embraced the Gateway, using it to inform their own operations and greatly expand their understanding of insurgent networks. In just its first year of operation, the Gateway was credited with the successful targeting of nearly four thousand insurgents and terrorists. The technological breakthrough couldn't have come at a more auspicious time, with the surge of thousands of extra US troops to Iraq underway in a last attempt to salvage the war.

The success of the Gateway was a key inflexion point for both Alexander and the National Security Agency. For the agency it heralded a renewed and dramatic commitment to the multiagency war effort in Iraq and Afghanistan. Before the system was introduced, the NSA had only roughly 30 people forward deployed in Iraq, and far fewer in Afghanistan. At the high-water mark, the NSA would have 6,000 people deployed to the war zones, and the lessons they learned there would inform the NSA's worldwide operations in support of the "global war on terrorism."

For Keith Alexander, the project's reliance on large amounts of metadata and novel ways to rapidly query it was a revelation. If the NSA could not only intercept the electronic communications of the terrorists, but also tell where they were located, it would go a long way toward connecting the dots that went unconnected in the long run-up to the September 11, 2001, terrorist attacks.

For Stan McChrystal and Task Force 714, Real Time Regional Gateway radically compressed the cycle of intelligence-gathering, analysis, and follow-up raids that would have taken months to complete at the start of the war. By the summer of 2007, task force operators sometimes completed three such cycles in a single night at locations hundreds of miles apart, and launched hundreds of raids each month, capturing or killing thousands of al-Qaeda in Iraq terrorists and Shiite death squad leaders in Iraq.

Sitting in the operations center at the task force headquarters in Balad one night, McChrystal marveled at the pace and effectiveness of its operations. Whereas the other senior commanders, such as Petraeus and Dempsey had deployed back to Iraq, McChrystal had never really left. He had spent nearly five years building a counterterrorism network centered in Iraq and Afghanistan but spanning much of the globe, with nodes in scores of countries. The network was flat, consisting of cells of people empowered to act independently in service of an organic whole, so much so that at its command center McChrystal rarely had to make big decisions any more. The network responded to the collective wisdom of the crowd. It learned. That was the biggest epiphany in this new kind of warfare, thought McChrystal. The network *knows what to do*!

BY THE END of the summer, violence in Anbar had dropped dramatically, with insurgent attacks falling from 1,350 in October of 2006 to just over 200 in August 2007. Because Anbar was the staging base for many of AQI's attacks in Baghdad, violence also began tapering off in the capital by the fall of 2007. Equally as important, the relationships at the core of the Awakening movement became the basis for the reconciliation campaign designed to further isolate al-Qaeda in Iraq, and slowly bring the Sunni tribes back under the government tent.

In September Petraeus and Crocker testified together before Congress in the most anticipated wartime hearings since Vietnam, billed as a major review of the Iraq strategy. By that time the US Army general and American diplomat had spent so many months bonding in the crucible of Iraq that they could complete each other's answers, not that they had to. If a lawmaker asked a question that was not specifically directed at either one, Petraeus and Crocker knew instinctively which one of them should answer. They never talked over each other. So as not to look scripted or rehearsed, they had not even read each other's prepared testimony, nor did they clear their statements in advance with their bosses at the Pentagon and State Department. Their relationship was unique in the brotherhood that revolutionized the American style of war, and it proved what could be accomplished when the country's civil-military nexus operated as one.

The narrative of their remarkable turnaround of a losing war in Iraq would become part of accepted lore, with US war colleges and doctrinal centers teaching the need for comprehensive and manpower-intensive counterinsurgency campaigns to pull societies back from the abyss once terrorists and extremists gained the upper hand. That narrative would soon come into conflict with the views of a new president and commander in chief who was elected in large part on his opposition to the Iraq conflict and his determination to end the nation's post-9/11 wars.

# PART II

# EIGHT

# Al-Qaeda Pandemic
## 2008–2010

IN 2008 AMERICANS WERE TRANSFIXED BY THE DRAMA OF AN IRAQ war that seemed perpetually balanced on the precipice of disaster. The long conflicts in Iraq and Afghanistan had conditioned the public to think of the Bush administration's "global war on terrorism" as a fight with discernible borders, where progress could be charted in regimes toppled, territory cleared and held, and enemy leaders killed.

Yet US counterterrorism experts had come to understand the networks of global Islamic terrorism as more akin to living organisms, comprised of cells that formed, linked, split, were destroyed, and then reformed in a process of constant mutation and regeneration. Each new terrorist attack or plot was thus put under a microscope in a search for clues to how that organism continued to grow, transmitting impulses from the likes of Osama bin Laden and other terror masters into acts of wanton bloodshed sometimes half a world away.

Tracing just a few threads of connective tissue, US counterterrorism investigators could thus tie al-Qaeda and its chief affiliates to individuals at the center of a plot to bomb hotels in Jordan during millennium celebrations in 2000; to the 9/11 attacks in the United States in 2001; to multiple suicide bombings in Casablanca in 2003; to the bombings of Madrid's commuter rail system in 2004; to the suicide attacks on the London transport system in 2005; to a foiled plot in Britain to destroy as many as ten US-bound airliners over the Atlantic in 2006; and to the terrorist attacks that paralyzed Mumbai, India, in 2008.

Those plots highlighted the intersection between terrorism and crime, and the key role that prisons often played in radicalizing vulnerable youth. They additionally revealed the global jihadi movement's increasingly effective exploitation of cyberspace for communications, recruitment, and radicalization. Investigations into those plots discerned the centrality of radical imams and theologians in constantly exciting the neural networks of extremism with violent rhetoric. That microscopic view also revealed the pathologies that gave rise to local Islamic extremist groups, and how over time these groups became more ambitious and grew into al-Qaeda affiliates, adhering to the core al-Qaeda leadership through bonds of ideology and branding.

From a macro point of view, al-Qaeda and its chief affiliate in Iraq were on the defensive by 2008, and that country was finally beginning to stabilize. On closer inspection, however, the virus of Islamic terrorism was in the process of mutating and regenerating once again, and there was no better laboratory for understanding the dangers of a renewed terrorism pandemic than the land of its genesis: Afghanistan.


BRIAN MCCAULEY TYPICALLY worked late in his office at the US Embassy, continuing a routine of round-the-clock days fueled by coffee and adrenaline that was slowly wearing him down. In January 2008 he passed the two-year mark in Afghanistan with only one brief trip home in the past year to visit his wife, Audrey, and son Brian Jr. In recent phone conversations, Audrey worried that nine-year-old Brian Jr. was showing signs of "separation anxiety" from being so long without his father, and McCauley knew that he needed to wind up his extended tour. His was already well past the length of the typical overseas deployment, let alone one to a combat zone. And yet there are tours and missions that can define a career, and

McCauley already sensed that his time in Afghanistan would constitute the most important work of his life.

Wartime Kabul turned out to be an ideal if unforgiving incubator for the FBI's post-9/11 transformation from a criminal investigative organization into primarily an intelligence-gathering counterterrorism outfit focused on trying to disrupt terrorist plots and attacks before they happen. Working on the front lines of the "global war on terrorism" in Afghanistan gave the bureau important insights into the inner workings and motivations of various terrorist networks, and forged close relationships within the US intelligence and military communities. Both would prove invaluable in the FBI's effort to keep the terrorist threat from again reaching US shores.

What none of the US forces and officials deployed to Afghanistan could yet foresee was anything approximating victory. After investing more than six years and roughly $120 billion in the country, the United States and its allies had at best fought the Taliban to a draw. Increasingly as much a terrorist organization as an insurgent group or a government in exile, the Taliban continued to enjoy sanctuary in Pakistan. The insurgents had made territorial gains in the more rural parts of Afghanistan, and regularly launched "human missiles" at targets in Kabul. For its part, a weak and notoriously corrupt Afghan government had been slow to reform, or to extend its control far outside of Kabul. The international relief and reconstruction effort still lacked high-profile leadership. The bifurcated US and NATO military command was still constrained by insufficient troops and skittishness on the part of many European military forces to actually engage the enemy, instead opting out of combat operations with national caveats. Meanwhile, the opium trade that financed warlords, insurgents, and criminals alike continued apace.

A recent report on Afghanistan by the prestigious Atlantic Council think tank in Washington, DC, more closely captured the essence of the place. "Make no mistake, NATO is not winning in Afghanistan," concluded the report, which was led by former NATO supreme allied commander and national security adviser General Jim Jones, who characterized the situation as a "strategic stalemate" and counseled "urgent action" to overhaul and reinvigorate the alliance strategy. "Afghanistan remains a failing state," the report concluded. "It could become a failed state." McCauley and other

US leaders on the ground in Afghanistan understood they were still fighting a rear-guard action until the situation in Iraq stabilized and US military and intelligence resources were redirected back to the former home of al-Qaeda and its Taliban allies.

In the meantime, McCauley took solace in the fact that his team had helped buy critical time, insuring that hundreds of US and International Security Assistance Force (ISAF) troops, and probably thousands of Afghan civilians, had been spared from the Taliban's bombing campaign. In the case of the Kabul Counter-IED Initiative that McCauley launched back in 2006, hard necessity had forged the first ever extended joint operation between the FBI and the US military, in the form of the US Special Forces Tenth Group. By early 2008 the task force behind the Counter-IED Initiative had inflicted serious damage to the three major IED (improvised explosive device) cells operating in Kabul. It had prevented forty-three separate attacks targeting coalition forces in and around the capital, and Tenth Special Forces had "neutralized" more than 150 known IED bombers and facilitators in capture or kill raids. Brian McCauley and his FBI team, along with the Green Berets of the Tenth Special Forces Group, would later receive the FBI Director's Award, the bureau's highest honor, for the Counter-IED Initiative.

Their investigation had also exposed the unseen hands manipulating the IED cells and suicide bombers from afar, making them more vulnerable. A chief mastermind behind the murder and mayhem remained the elusive Mullah Dadullah, who had built a cultlike following. He even made regular appearances in regional media outlets, where he boasted of leading an army of "hundreds" of eager suicide bombers. The markets in Peshawar and Quetta were choked with DVDs produced by the Taliban media operation, showing Dadullah beheading "spies," another al-Zarqawi tactic honed in Iraq and embraced by his Afghan brothers. In referring to the Taliban's adoption of "martyrdom" tactics, Dadullah issued an apocalyptic warning to US forces in Afghanistan. "The Americans have sown a seed. They will reap the crop for quite a long time."

Unbeknownst to Dadullah, with the death of al-Zarqawi in Iraq in 2006, Joint Special Operations Command (JSOC) commander Lieutenant General Stan McChrystal had turned more of his attention to the clearly worsening situation in Afghanistan. Whereas Task Force 714 had previously focused its efforts on hunting al-Qaeda leaders in Afghanistan and Pakistan, McChrystal now directed it to also start targeting senior Taliban leaders. And barring only Mullah Omar, none was more dangerous than Dadullah.

Unlike Omar, Dadullah was known to make periodic trips into Afghanistan to rally the foot soldiers and dispense strategic guidance, adding to his legend as a fearless warrior. Unfortunately, Task Force 714 generally learned of these trips only after the fact. But in March 2007, Dadullah orchestrated a controversial prisoner swap, demanding the release of four Taliban commanders held by Kabul authorities in exchange for kidnapped Italian journalist Daniele Mastrogiacomo. The prisoner exchange was criticized as capitulation to terrorists, but the US task force's electronic surveillance unit put a hard stare on one of the released Taliban prisoners, Mullah Shah Mansoor, figuring that his brother Mullah Dadullah would eventually reach out. Dadullah was known to use a satellite phone to communicate with journalists and field commanders, but by then Task Force 714 was also experimenting with a host of clever tracking devices and surveillance techniques, to include nearly round-the-clock tracking by unmanned drones. And when Mullah Dadullah crossed the border into Afghanistan on May 12, 2007, Task Force 714 was tracking his movement, following him to a walled compound in southern Helmand Province.

Two Royal Air Force Chinook helicopters were quickly launched, carrying a squadron of British Special Forces commandos that was working with Task Force 714. The British commandos and US-trained Afghan special forces surrounded the compound and fought a furious, four-hour firefight with Dadullah and roughly twenty fanatical Taliban fighters. When the smoke cleared, Dadullah's body was recovered, shot twice in the torso and once in the head, a typical "double tap" favored by Special Forces commandos.

ON THE NIGHT of January 14, 2008, Brian McCauley was ruminating over the snowfall blanketing Kabul. Outside his window wet flakes steadily fell, wrapping the capital in a shimmering veil of white that masked her many imperfections. Gone were the honking traffic and chaotic crowds, the dirt and sludge underfoot, the thick layer of smog that clung to the city. Practically the only thing the snow couldn't cover was the acrid smell from the thousands of dung fires, and the hacking cough it induced, which they all called the "Kabul crud." Some of the other Westerners who had poured into the country as part of the international relief and reconstruction effort were probably still shopping for deals on oriental rugs and semiprecious stones in the markets and shops of "Chicken Street." Remarkably, large majorities of Afghans still supported that international presence and the US-backed Karzai government it enabled, with 67 percent saying in a recent ABC/BBC poll that they still approved of the presence of NATO military forces. If you squinted your eyes just so, the snow-blanketed Kabul seemed like just another capital in winter repose.

McCauley felt as much as heard the blast wave that began as a rattle in the diaphragm and then blossomed into a bone-jarring concussion, and he knew even before the rumbling echo subsided that his phone was about to start chirping, and that the first reports to pour in would be exaggerated and unreliable. From the noise of the first blasts and subsequent explosions, he also knew that the attack was somewhere nearby in the most heavily guarded section of the capital that included the US Embassy, the headquarters for ISAF, and the Afghan Presidential Palace complex. Winter traditionally spelled a break between fighting seasons in Afghanistan, and the fact that the Taliban had chosen to go after a hard target in January in the center of Kabul was portentous.

Soon enough he had a phone to his ear. The news was bad. The target was the five-star Serena Hotel, one of the few places in Kabul where foreigners and the Afghan elite mingled in luxury. Opened in 2006, the Serena had a swimming pool, 24-hour electricity, a spa, and a bar popular with Western diplomats, journalists, and dignitaries. It also boasted tight security, with a barrier and checkpoint outside with armed guards, and multiple steel gates and metal detectors and X-ray machines in the entryway. The Taliban had never attacked a Kabul hotel before, and McCauley told his people to try to get a roster of guests even as he dispatched an on-call emergency response team to the hotel.

He soon learned that the Norwegian foreign minister and his entire entourage were staying at the Serena, as were apparently more than thirty Americans. Soon enough, the phone McCauley used to talk with headquarters in Washington, DC, buzzed, and now he had a phone at each ear. The South Korean Embassy had called FBI headquarters in a panic, asking for help to rescue the South Korean chief of intelligence who was staying at the hotel. McCauley assured headquarters that they were on it, and then reached out with his other phone to FBI special agent Mike Dupler, head of the emergency response team, with a simple message: you guys had better hurry.

The Taliban shooters were no village yokels brainwashed into martyrdom. Wearing suicide vests beneath their Afghan National Police uniforms, the four-man team had calmly approached the main gate of the Serena Hotel and shot the security guard dead. A firefight had then erupted, and one of the insurgents detonated his suicide vest, killing himself and one of his team members, and seriously injuring three Afghan security guards. After lobbing hand grenades at the hotel entrance, another of the attackers apparently detonated his suicide vest. In the ensuing chaos, the fourth attacker slipped into the hotel and walked through the lobby toward the gym, methodically shooting hotel guests along the way with his high-powered rifle.

Norwegian foreign minister Jonas Gahr Støre was spared, but journalist Carsten Thomassen, a correspondent for the Norwegian paper *Dagbladet*, was shot dead along with six other people killed in the attack. By the time Dupler and the FBI emergency response team arrived, the scene was chaotic and the shooter was still on the loose. Dupler called McCauley and asked for the room number where the Korean intelligence chief was barricaded. He could hear him talking on the other line back to Washington.

"Hey, Mike, he's in Room 208."

As it happened, one of the FBI fly team members was Special Agent Haejun Park, a Korean American. When they pounded on Room 208 and identified themselves as FBI agents, a voice inside shouted back in Korean: "How do I know you are not Taliban?"

"Because I'm speaking to you in fucking Korean," said Park. "Now open up!"

The FBI agents didn't know it, but the Taliban shooter was lurking in a nearby doorway on the second floor. Rather than engage the FBI agents and possibly take them out with his suicide vest, the shooter did a strange thing: he took off his vest and his police uniform, and laid down his AK-47. The mass murderer had apparently reached his tolerance for carnage, and he was later captured outside the hotel, trying to blend in with the panicked guests.

As SOON As FBI profilers Scott Stanley and Tom Neer explained who they were, the shooter lunged at them, screaming and spitting. By their second exploratory interview, he had calmed down, and Stanley was immediately struck by his intelligence and logical thought processes. He had a very linear way of thinking, and was articulate and expressive in rationalizing his murders based on his religion and Afghan culture. Once again Stanley felt the presence of an unseen hand, sensing that the shooter was exactly the type of capable person that someone would choose to independently conduct a complex attack against a well-guarded target. As they quickly learned, in the case of the Serena Hotel attack, the master manipulator was Siraj Haqqani, a warlord whose network had close ties both to the Taliban and the Pakistani ISI intelligence service.

By repeatedly provoking the Serena shooter and then calming him down, Stanley and Neer learned that he didn't like talking about the victims he murdered. Entering the hotel, the attacker had expected to encounter only Westerners. And yet eight of the eleven people he shot were Afghan nationals. Three of the five who died from their wounds were his countrymen.

He tried to rationalize this: "If Muslims are protecting Americans, they have brought American soil into their house," the shooter insisted. "You are not true Muslims if you protect Americans. You deserve to die."

Based on their earlier interviews with suicide bombers, the two behavioral science experts had crafted an interview strategy that centered on the Islamic understanding of the afterlife. The Afghan government and even some local religious scholars, they pointed out, insisted that because the shooter killed Afghans, he was not a true martyr. He was just a murderer who killed fellow Muslims, and he was likely to be executed for it.

"I had the motive. I planned the attack. And I killed the infidels," the man replied. "So, even if the Afghan government kills me, I am still a martyr."

By making the prisoner justify his actions, the FBI profilers learned that he was both proud of the attack and yet disappointed that he had not detonated his suicide vest at the moment of truth. The man was also clearly disturbed by the actual killing. That almost certainly explained why he had suddenly stopped and laid down his weapons. They had seen the same phenomenon in other mass killings: seeing people shot up close is so visceral and disturbing, with brains splattered onto walls and bowels spilling onto blood-slick floors, that at some point shooters can lapse into a mental paralysis. At that point they're done.

During weeks of interviews the FBI profilers also learned that the shooter never told his family about the suicide operation. The man was clearly bothered by the fact that he never got to say good-bye. He expected that his family would never know what happened to him.

"You obviously care about your family. We can get word to them about your whereabouts and what you did," said Stanley.

"No, I won't tell you where they are. You will only kill my family," the shooter responded.

"You said if you die, it will be God's will," said Stanley. "Isn't what happens to your family God's will as well?"

In the end the Serena shooter wrote a long letter to his family trying to justify what he'd done—using the word *ghazi*, which in Arabic means a warrior who participates in religious warfare. He admitted to his actions, told his family that the government was going to hang him, and said good-bye. And when he handed the letter over to the FBI profilers, having found some internal resolution, the man began to pour forth the contents of a dark heart. The same terrorist and mass murderer who had spit at them on first meeting revealed accomplices, safe houses, networks, and the identity of the unseen hand.

Unfortunately, the FBI profilers weren't the only ones who learned from the mayhem and propaganda bonanza of the Serena Hotel attack. Later the same year, Lashkar-e-Taiba, another Islamic extremist group based in Pakistan that also had close ties to Pakistani intelligence, used similar commando tactics on a grander scale in an attack in Mumbai, India, that paralyzed the city, killed 164 people, and wounded more than 300. The unseen hand that would orchestrate that attack, a militant commander named Zaki-ur-Rehman Lakhvi, would later be granted bail by a Pakistani court. Tragically, the Taliban would return to the scene of the Serena atrocity in 2014, once again sending four shooters to the hotel, where on the eve of important Afghan elections they would shoot and kill nine civilians, including the noted Afghan journalist Sardar Ahmad, his wife, Humaira; and his young children, six-year-old Nelofar and five-year-old Omar. The self-proclaimed Islamic warriors also shot Ahmad's youngest son multiple times, but somehow two-year-old Abuzar would survive his wounds.

MORE THAN TWO years in Kabul also taught Brian McCauley that corruption is the handmaiden of extremism. A certain level of pay-to-play was endemic in the Afghan culture after decades of conflict, but at some point the injustice and constant shake-downs by officials in uniform hardened the hearts of the Afghan people against the government, and made the appeals of a more "pure" and incorruptible Taliban "justice" more appealing. For McCauley, it was a constant challenge just determining which senior Afghan officials were in the pockets of various foreign intelligence services, or of the Taliban themselves.

The scene of another suicide bombing in the spring of 2008 raised McCauley's suspicions that a senior Afghan security official he dealt with frequently was actually in league with the bombing networks. McCauley arrived just after the smoke had cleared, the FBI's rapid reaction team in tow, and walked up to a young U.S. soldier who was staggering through the wreckage, clearly in shock.

"It's okay, I'm with the FBI. We've got this," McCauley told him.

The young soldier looked at him without comprehension, as if an alien had dropped from the sky. "You're the FBI?"

Surveying the scene of the bombing, McCauley noted with disgust the same Afghan security official that he always found rummaging through bomb sites in the immediate aftermath of an attack. The man was omnipresent at practically every major crime scene in the crime-riddled capital.

Along with much of the US intelligence community in Kabul, Brian McCauley strongly suspected the man was very possibly the most corrupt security official in the world, and he was intent on trying to prove it. At some point the rampant corruption, double-dealing, and back-stabbing that typified life in wartime Kabul got to even the most hardened and cynical U.S. officials, and in McCauley's case it manifested itself in an Ahab-like determination to see the senior Afghan security official brought to justice. He had become McCauley's "white whale."

McCauley's suspicions first spiked when he constantly found the Afghan official already on the scene at virtually every suicide bombing, but never rendering any real assistance. Curious, McCauley had his investigators look into how many times the Afghan official had beaten them to the scene of a suicide bombing and gone through this Kabuki dance. The tally stood at twenty-six times that the man had somewhat miraculously beaten everyone else in Kabul to the scene of a bombing.

The FBI began peering deeper into the Afghan security official's activities. Sources reported that he was in league with Afghan president Hamid Karzai's half-brother Ahmed Wali Karzai, a suspected major figure in Afghanistan's booming opium trade who had denied those links. The Afghan official they were investigating reportedly controlled the ramp at the Kabul Airport where Afghanistan's cash crop of opium was exported out of country. There was also evidence that he had staged a suicide attack by arranging for a drug addict to bring a suicide vest onto a city bus, and then arresting and manhandling the perp before reporters. The FBI seized the suicide vest as evidence in the attack before the Afghan official could confiscate it, and discovered that it lacked even a detonator. U.S. intelligence officials also had surveillance photographs of the Afghan security official meeting with senior members of Pakistan's ISI intelligence service, which continued to maintain close ties to the Haqqani network and some other Afghan Taliban groups that were behind many of the Kabul bombings.

The Afghan security official was also suspected of links to criminal gangs that were behind a rash of more than one hundred kidnappings in Kabul, driving businessmen and much needed capital out of the country. It was certainly no secret that the kidnappers often wore police or security force uniforms, flashed official identification, and drove official cars.

Convinced that they were closing in on the corrupt Afghan official, McCauley and his counterparts at the Afghan National Security Director-ate coordinated to put a two-man surveillance stakeout on his house. The surveillance agents were mysteriously shot dead in their car. The murders went unsolved, but the NSD suspected some of the goons that the Afghan official surrounded himself with as a personal security detachment.

The case of a kidnapped American of Afghani descent further stoked McCauley's suspicions. The kidnappers sent the victim's U.S.-based family a videotape of them their cutting off one of the man's ears, and demanded a ransom. After the ransom was paid, the victim was brought to the U.S. embassy in Kabul. McCauley debriefed the man and arranged for him to be flown home to New York's JFK Airport the next day with an FBI escort. He had never seen a man more traumatized. Before the debriefing was even completed, the victim's family back in the United States received a call from the kidnappers, informing them that the criminals knew the vic-tim was flying out on the next day's Emirates flight through Dubai to JFK Airport. If the family wanted the man to arrive alive, they were told, they had better not cooperate with the FBI. As it happened, the FBI was moni-toring the family's phone back in the United States, and immediately put a trace on the call. Special Agent Rich Frankel called McCauley with the disturbing results of the trace.

"Brian, the kidnappers' call came from a phone registered at the U.S. Embassy!" There was apparently a mole for the kidnappers inside the United States' innermost sanctum in Afghanistan.

McCauley immediately called the State Department's regional secu-rity officer (RSO), the top security official at the embassy. Once again McCauley's magic Rolodex and penchant for networking paid off. The RSO immediately went to work and soon traced the call to a cell phone issued to the embassy's travel office, where he discovered a possible source of the leak: an Afghan national recently hired by the embassy's travel office, who had booked the victim and his FBI escort on the Emir-ates flight, was the brother of the senior Afghan security official under investigation.

McCauley's "white whale" remained an elusive and dangerous adver-sary. His personal connections stretched all the way to the top echelons of the Afghan government, insulating him. Occasionally at official functions where senior ISAF and Afghan government officials mingled, McCauley would run into the man, who always offered an enigmatic smile in recognition. Given his strong suspicions that the Afghan official had the blood of many Americans on his hands, McCauley could barely resist the temptation to slap a pair of handcuffs on him. After each of those functions, McCauley would have the NSA monitor the Afghan official's cell phone just to make sure he didn't order a hit on the FBI legal attaché.

In late May 2008, McCauley found himself on a charter flight lifting off from Kabul International Airport, heading home. After the plane climbed to altitude he ordered a drink, felt his whole body uncoil, and reflected on the intrigues of Kabul that he was finally leaving behind. His time in Afghanistan had run out and he failed to harpoon his "white whale." No charges were brought against the senior Afghan security official. The corruption that seeped into the highest reaches of the Afghan government was now someone else's problem.

The extensive interviews with failed suicide bombers that Scott Stanley and Tom Neer conducted would shape future FBI interrogations in the long, twilight war with Islamic extremists. The interview strategies they developed would later prove instrumental in the successful interrogations of other suspected Islamic terrorists.

McCauley had no illusion that dismantling the IED cells and exacting a measure of justice from those with American blood on their hands would amount to a permanent victory. None of the soldiers, spies, and special agents deployed to Afghanistan did. This was a different kind of war, and it figured to outlast them all. He also knew with certainty that there were hundreds of US soldiers and Afghan civilians who would return home to their own families in one piece because of the Counter-IED Initiative, and that was enough. The US Special Forces, law enforcement, and intelligence community had also forged a bond in Afghanistan that would endure. They had seen the world as the enemy imagined it, and that vision inspired them to fight together with everything they had, in defense of everything they held dear. What Brian McCauley couldn't have guessed at the time was how quickly the jihad that he had fought so hard to contain in Afghanistan would follow him home to America.

DOMESTICALLY THE FBI was well into its transformation from simply a criminal investigative agency into primarily an intelligence-gathering organization focused on counterterrorism. Like Special Agent Brian McCauley and his Counter-IED Initiative, bureau officials were trying to "get to the left of the boom" by preventing terrorist plots before they could quite literally blow. That mission had driven the FBI to put the dynamics of Islamic radicalization under the investigative microscope, from indoctrination and mobilization ultimately to violence. The challenge was to somehow find firebreaks between millions of sparks of incendiary rhetoric and the human fuses that ignited actual lethal terrorist action. And by the time of his arrest in Yemen in October 2008, FBI agents had every reason to suspect that Carlos Bledsoe, a young African American man from Tennessee, was a potential live wire.

When Yemeni authorities alerted US counterterrorism officials in Washington that they had arrested Bledsoe, details of the case were initially puzzling. At first the US embassy in Yemen was not even informed that an American citizen had been detained, which was a break in diplomatic protocol. Apparently Bledsoe had been stopped at a highway checkpoint and arrested for overstaying his student visa. At that point he would normally have been deported, but Yemeni authorities found out that he was carrying a fake Somali passport.

US and Yemeni counterterrorism officials knew that terrorist training camps in Somalia run by the al-Qaeda affiliate al-Shabab were a magnet for would-be Islamist militants looking to complete their education in violent jihad. A Congressional Research Service report would later reveal that of a total of sixty-three homegrown jihadist attacks and plots between 2001 and 2013, more than half involved intent or actual travel abroad for terrorist training and plotting. At the time of his arrest, Carlos Bledsoe was also carrying a computer thumb drive containing the names of connections he had made in Yemen, as well as bomb-making instructions. In the words of one US official, the information on the thumb drive caused their "hair to stand on end." Certainly the profile that Bledsoe presented caused alarms to sound loudly enough to reach US counterterrorism officials in Washington, DC, and an FBI agent was dispatched to interview him in the Yemeni jail.

Like many Islamist converts who resort to jihad, Bledsoe had early run-ins with the law. While attending Tennessee State University (TSU), he was pulled over by police and eventually charged with drug possession and unlawful possession of a weapon. Staring at a possible fourteen-year sentence, he accepted a plea deal of a year's probation, contingent on his staying out of trouble. The plea deal seemed to have the intended result of scaring Bledsoe straight. Knowing that he had to fundamentally change his life and circle of friends, he set out on a spiritual quest.

Students at TSU were offered the free course "Introduction to Islam," taught by founders of the Olive Tree Education Foundation, the proselytizing arm of the local Islamic Center of Nashville (ICN). Promoting itself as a moderate outreach group embracing a tolerant version of Islam, Olive Tree provided hundreds of hours of instruction to TSU students.

According to Bledsoe's family, signs soon began mounting that Carlos was embracing a very doctrinaire and insular form of Islam. He mostly stopped coming home to Memphis on weekends and holidays, and one time when he did return, he insisted on taking down a photo of Martin Luther King Jr. that had hung in the Bledsoe home for decades. As a practicing Muslim, Bledsoe said he was not allowed to sleep in an abode where photos of "idols" were honored, nor were pictures of anything with a soul permitted. Then he took his beloved dog into the woods and abandoned him because of religious strictures suggesting that dogs do not dwell in the houses of the holy.

The interpretation of Islam that Carlos Bledsoe embraced at the Islamic Center of Nashville is known as Salafism. Salafis believe the only true Islam is that version practiced by the Prophet Muhammad and the first three generations of Muslims that followed him in the seventh and eighth centuries. These fundamentalists read the Koran literally, and reject any separation of church and state in favor of a strict interpretation of Islamic Sharia law. They oppose more secular or progressive strains of Islam that have evolved outside of the religion's birthplace on the Arabian peninsula. The chief guardians and exporters of that ultraconservative strain of Islam are the Wahhabis of Saudi Arabia, home to the holiest sites in Islam and the place where Wahhabi teachings are considered the official form of Sunni Islam, and are sponsored by the state and the ruling House of Saud.

In the Salafi view, anyone who rejects the imposition of religious or Sharia law is not considered a devotee of true Islam. That the imposition of Islamic religious law runs counter to Western norms of religious tolerance, human rights, equality for women, and a separation between church and state, was certainly not lost on Bledsoe's religious instructors. The imam of the Islamic Center of Nashville during Carlos Bledsoe's time there was Abdulhakim Ali Mohamed, an American of Yemeni descent. Mohamed is a fine orator, with a smiling countenance and mesmerizing delivery reminiscent of an Arabian Joel Osteen. He was formerly the imam of Brooklyn's Al Farooq mosque in the 1990s, but apparently after the period when it was linked by federal prosecutors to the 1993 World Trade Center bombing and the assassination of Rabbi Meir Kahane in 1990.

Politics and hate were very much part of the imam's sermons, which reveal the Salafist intolerance of other religions such as Christianity and Judaism. "Tomorrow they'll celebrate Christmas, assuming that Christ is God, or the son of God," he says in one sermon. "There is no greater lie than this! The greatest lie of all time!" About Judaism he also refused to extend an olive branch. "The Jews believe that everyone that is created on the face of the earth was only created for their service. They became more vicious than the Pharaoh, throughout history until today."

When Carlos Bledsoe converted to Islam, he assumed the name Abdulhakim Mujahid Muhammad, apparently taking inspiration from the imam of the Islamic Center of Nashville, and adding the "Mujahid," meaning a person engaged in jihad. There is no doubt that he already considered himself devoted to the ultraconservative Salafi strain of Sunni Islam. A letter of recommendation written on his behalf by an "Imam Abdulhaziz," who was associated with a Somali mosque in Nashville, asks that Bledsoe—a.k.a. Abdulhakim Mujahid Muhammad—be admitted to an Islamist seminary in Yemen to further his studies and teach English. The letter details that Bledsoe "seeks knowledge" of Islam and is a practicing Salafi. "He follows the Quran and Sunnah according to the understanding of the Salafis Salih.

He is Salafi and seeks to increase his knowledge of Quran and Sunna, and the Arabic language."

On his personal journey of jihad, Carlos Bledsoe had taken the critical first step of indoctrination at the Islamic Center of Nashville. As with so many Americans and other Westerners who would later follow a similar path, this led to the Middle East and the epicenter of the faith. There the embers of ideology that were lit inside the mind of a troubled Memphis teenager would be stoked in the forges of a radical theology into a burning rage. At the time no one in the Bledsoe family made note of the date Carlos chose to embark on his new adventure in Yemen: September 11, 2007.

THE YEMEN THAT Carlos Bledsoe visited was impoverished and lightly governed, and the writ of the government in the capital of Sanaa barely extended into hinterlands where deeply conservative tribes still held sway. Money from rich oil sheikhs next door in Saudi Arabia poured into Sunni mosques in Yemeni towns and villages to spread the Wahhabi creed, with its message of intolerance not only of other religions, but also of the Shiite strain of Islam. The satellite dishes sprouting throughout Yemen and other countries in the Middle East carried newly ascendant Arab television stations, such as Al Arabiya and Al Jazeera, with their steady diet of atrocities allegedly committed by US soldiers on Muslims in Iraq and Afghanistan. Conflict between US forces and Islamist terrorist groups, such as al-Qaeda, and the US invasion of two Muslim-majority countries, fed into the Salafi narrative of a conflict between Islam and the West.

US counterterrorism officials were also increasingly concerned by the ascendance of the al-Qaeda franchises in both Yemen and Somalia—al-Qaeda in the Arabian Peninsula (AQAP) and al-Shabab, respectively. Al-Shabab had achieved near dominance of the failed state of Somalia and was running terrorist training camps that were attracting increasing numbers of Somali Americans and other Westerners. For its part, AQAP, almost uniquely among the al-Qaeda franchises, had begun to embrace Osama bin Laden's strategy of striking at the "far enemy," meaning the United States. As fate would have it, Carlos Bledsoe's journey of jihad would intersect with both of those spiking trend lines in international terrorism.

The paths of the most committed Islamist pilgrims, those deemed especially worthy in the constellation of satellite mosques and Sunni Islamic schools scattered throughout the country, often converge in northern Yemen at the remote mountain village of Dammaj. The town of adobe dwellings and vineyards clinging to picturesque hillsides is home to the Dar al-Hadith mosque and Islamic academy, revered as one of the wellsprings of Sunni religious thought and an incubator of the pure and uncompromising form of Islam practiced in the days of the Prophet Muhammad. Dar al-Hadith was started by one of the ringleaders of the fundamentalist militants who seized the Great Mosque in Mecca in 1979. Determined to purge the Muslim world of the impurities brought on by Westernization, the militants took 100,000 fellow Muslims hostage during the annual Hajj pilgrimage to Mecca. More than 1,000 people were reportedly killed in the siege and ensuing battle to retake the Great Mosque, and most of the conspirators were beheaded in town squares throughout Saudi Arabia.

The Saudi Arabian royal family's response to the crisis was to grant even more influence to conservative Wahhabi religious leaders in the country, who apparently won leniency for Muqbil bin Hadi al-Wadi'i, considered a spiritual guide to the militants. Al-Wadi'i was jailed for a time, and then allowed to return to his native village of Dammaj. Soon after, he established Dar al-Hadith, though it was unclear where he received the financial backing for the mosque.

Carlos Bledsoe found his way to Dar al-Hadith along with hundreds of others Westerners from Europe and America. In Dammaj, he truly transformed himself into Abdulhakim Mujahid Muhammad, spending his days there memorizing the Koran and discussing what he learned with a small clique of fellow Westerners, mainly other African Americans. As one student at Dar al-Hadith described the academy, students lived in dorms and learned in tightknit "cells" where they spent long hours discussing and debating the Koran. The idea behind the instruction was that such cells would eventually attach to networks bound by a unifying ideology and spread throughout the world.

Just down the hallway from Bledsoe in the student dorm of Dar al-Hadith lived another American named Theo Padnos. Bledsoe was taciturn and distrustful toward Padnos, as if he suspected the truth: Padnos was an imposter, a journalist who had feigned conversion to Islam so as to peer behind Dar al-Hadith's veil of religious sanctity. There he found what he described as akin to a school for lost boys, many of them second- and third-generation Muslim immigrants to the West who felt suspended in a purgatory between conflicting cultures, neither fully Western nor accepted in their former homelands. Some of the most zealous were converts like Carlos Bledsoe who wholly rejected their former lives but had yet to fully form new identities. And the job of the imam at Dar al-Hadith was to help ground the lost boys in the dogma of a fundamentalist ideology, beginning with unquestioning submission and the surrender of free will.

"I'll tell you how it works and what Carlos Bledsoe and the others were taught," Padnos said in an interview about his experiences at Dar al-Hadith, which he mined for the book *Undercover Muslim*. "They are told that you are the holy and good ones, the true inheritors of Islam, and all others are corrupt and the enemies of God. Your destiny as prophesied in the Quran is to oppose the enemies of God. You are the virtuous and the others are sinners. You are honest and the others are hypocritical. You are sincere and the others are liars. Heaven, Hell. Good, Evil. Arab, Jew. Islam, West. They simplify the world, make it black and white, bring the students 95 percent of the way and then leave it to them to decide how to confront and oppose the 'other.'"

An overwhelming majority of the students even at one of the most stringent Salafi Islamic academies in the world do not make the leap from religious indoctrination to violent jihad. Some might embrace what experts call quiet Salifism, a more pacifistic strain that eschews politics. Others become political Salifists and join a movement that holds that religious principles should be incorporated into and take precedence over the laws of the state. Salifi jihadism holds that violence is legitimate and an important means of achieving that end and changing political systems by force. The strain of Salafism students took away from the instruction at Dar al-Hadith depended on the psychological underpinnings they brought to their education.

THE CHALLENGE THAT bedeviled the FBI agent who interviewed Carlos Bledsoe in a Yemeni jail was becoming increasingly familiar: how do you gauge the threat posed by suspected Islamic militants and extremists before they act on their extremist beliefs and actually commit a crime? In Bledsoe's case, his only offense at the time of his FBI interview was overstaying a visa and acquiring fraudulent documents. Although he was clearly on the FBI's radar, so were thousands of others.

"The answer to the question of whether Carlos Bledsoe was radicalized toward violence in Yemen is that quite possibly he was, but we may never be sure," said Brian McCauley. "We didn't have electronic surveillance on him before he was arrested by the Yemenis. The fact that he was using the same kind of throwaway phones routinely used by terrorists and drug dealers is suggestive. If you have nothing to hide, why would you go to the hassle of constantly changing phones?"

Bledsoe spent the four months between his arrest by Yemeni authorities and his deportation in early 2009 in a political prison with hard-core jihadists. The prison proved an ideal finishing school for violent Islamic extremism, bringing into clear alignment the rage in Bledsoe's heart, the perceived persecution of his Muslim brothers and sisters, and his desperate need to belong to a cause greater than himself. There is some form of personal ruin in the narratives of many who wind up in prison, and prison preachers of every stripe find that captive audience eager to fill the void with spiritual illumination.

In terms of radical Islamic conversions, the critical role that prisons were playing as way stations on the path to violent jihad was already well documented. Al-Qaeda leader and longtime chief ideologue Ayman al-Zawahiri was arrested in the wake of the 1981 assassination of Egyptian president Anwar el-Sadat, and he spent three formative years in an Egyptian prison where he was tortured and further radicalized. Abu Musab al-Zarqawi, the archterrorist and founder of al-Qaeda in Iraq, spent many years in a Jordanian prison where he more fully embraced radical Islam and fomented his jihadist ambitions.

As it happened, FBI agents had been to Yemen only months before Bledsoe was interviewed, to visit another imprisoned American, Anwar al-Awlaki. After being arrested for his links to a plot to kidnap a US military officer in Yemen, al-Awlaki had been held for eighteen months with the encouragement of US officials. After the September 11, 2001, terrorist attacks, he had marketed himself as a moderate and a "bridge between Americans and one billion Muslims worldwide." The FBI had long been suspicious of his shadowy connections to two of the 9/11 hijackers who had prayed at al-Awlaki's San Diego mosque, and who had been seen in long conversations with the imam. The hijackers followed him to a new mosque in northern Virginia. Investigators for the bipartisan 9/11 Commission—which Congress and the Bush administration established to investigate the September 11, 2001, terrorist attacks, and recommend government reforms needed to avoid future attacks—even referred to Anwar al-Awlaki as the "spiritual adviser" for 9/11 hijacker Nawaf al-Hazmi. Yet after interviewing the imam four times in the days after the 9/11 attacks, the FBI had concluded that the connections were probably random.

Angry at that persistent attention from US authorities and with America's wars in Afghanistan and Iraq, al-Awlaki used increasingly strident rhetoric when speaking before youthful audiences of mostly English-speaking Muslims. As with prominent terrorist leaders before him, he found prison an ideal incubator for violent jihad, using his own time behind bars in Yemen for contemplation and to immerse himself deeper in radical Islamist theology. Kept mostly in solitary confinement, he poured over the writings of Sayyid Qutb, an influential theologian and prolific writer and leader of the Egyptian Muslim Brotherhood in the 1950s and 1960s. Qutb had spent significant time in the United States and came away disgusted by what he saw as a culture obsessed with materialism and sexual pleasure. The influence of Qutb's works led some to refer to him as the father of the jihadist movement in modern Islam.

"Because of the flowing style of Sayyid I would read between 100 and 150 pages a day," al-Awlaki would later write on a blog of his imprisonment. "I was so immersed with the author I would feel Sayyid was with me in my cell speaking to me directly."

The problem the FBI agents had in interviewing al-Awlaki in a Yemeni jail and trying to discern his intentions was not unlike the conundrum they faced months later in talking with Carlos Bledsoe: radicalism of thought is not a crime, nor is inspiring others to choose the path of jihad, however they interpret the word. The agents knew in the past al-Awlaki had been visited by al-Qaeda operatives and a close associate of Omar Abdel Rahman, the "blind sheikh" who had preached in several New Jersey mosques and was serving a life sentence for links to the 1993 World Trade Center attack and for plotting to blow up New York landmarks. Unlike Rahman, al-Awlaki had yet to cross the line and become "operational" in helping plot terrorist attacks himself.

By the end of 2007, US officials, concerned about the jailing of an American citizen without formal charges, reportedly signaled to the Yemenis that they no longer supported al-Awlaki's continued imprisonment. They didn't yet know that he would leave prison an even more committed extremist, determined to harness his considerable rhetorical skills to the mission of furthering a global jihad against the West, and to translate Osama bin Laden's vision and message into a more accessible American vernacular. "I eventually came to the conclusion that jihad against America is binding upon myself, just as it is binding on every other able Muslim," he would later say. "Jihad is becoming as American as apple pie, and as British as afternoon tea!"

Carlos Bledsoe would later confirm that he formulated his own plan to carry out violent jihad during his imprisonment in Yemen, and he claimed to have had contact with al-Awlaki. There's no doubt that he emerged from the prison a self-actualized jihadi with the fully formed worldview of a violent Islamist extremist. "Like I said, there's an all-out war against Islam and the Muslims in Afghanistan, Pakistan, Waziristan, Chechnya, Somalia, Palestine, Yemen, etc.," he would later write from a US prison. "We believe in an eye for an eye, not turn the other cheek. Now it's an all-out war on America, and I'm on the other side. The side of the Muslims, Yes! The side of Al Qaeda, Yes! Taliban, Yes! Al Shabab, Yes! We are all brothers under the same banner. Fighting for the same cause, which is to rid the Islamic world of Infidel and Apostate Hypocrite Regimes and Crusader Invaders, and reestablish the Caliphate, the Islamic Empire and Islamic Law. . . . "

ON THE LAST weekend of May 2009, Carlos Bledsoe loaded his black Ford Explorer at his apartment in Little Rock for the final leg of his journey. He felt a sense of urgency. The same FBI agent who interviewed him in Yemen had recently called him into the bureau's Nashville field office and tried to turn him into an informer. Bledsoe had no intension of betraying his Muslim brothers and sisters to the enemy, but he was worried that his plot would be discovered.

Using money from a job with his father's tour company, Bledsoe had purchased an SKS rifle, a Mossberg International 702 rifle with a scope and laser sight, a Lorcin L-380 semiautomatic handgun, a .22 caliber handgun, and over 550 rounds of ammunition. Into a red duffel bag, he stuffed some extra clothes along with two homemade silencers and a set of binoculars. Bledsoe also had maps to his intended targets of military recruiting centers and Jewish organizations.

Almost immediately the lack of the training he had hoped to receive in Somalia betrayed him. The 350-mile drive from Little Rock to Nashville took five hours. He found the address on Mockingbird Lane where one target, an Orthodox Jewish rabbi, was supposed to live. Bledsoe crept up and attempted to throw a Molotov cocktail through the window to firebomb the house, but it bounced harmlessly off the window and he fled back to his car. The ride to the US Army recruiting center in Florence, Kentucky, was another 250-plus miles, and when he finally arrived, the recruiting office was closed. He had failed to check its hours.

By the time he got back to Little Rock on the morning of June 1, 2009, Bledsoe was feeling tired and dejected. He had covered more than 1,100 miles, and at $4 a gallon for gas, that added up to a lot of money with nothing to show for it. As he drove down Rodney Parham Road on the way home, he noticed two soldiers in uniform smoking cigarettes outside an Army-Navy recruiting center, and saw an opportunity to redeem his mission. He pulled into a parking lot next to the recruiting center and approached his unsuspecting targets from around a blind corner.

Privates William Long, twenty-three, and Quinton Ezeagwula, nineteen, were Arkansas natives who had only recently joined the Army. They were at the recruiting station as part of a program that used soldiers recently out of basic training to help recruit in their home regions. In fact, Long's mother, Janet, was watching her son from a car parked nearby, having stopped by to say hello. She heard the unexpected bursts of gunfire from

Bledsoe's SKS assault rifle, and watched in shock as her son and his friend crumpled to the sidewalk. Badly wounded, Ezeagwula crawled back into the recruiting station, leaving a trail of blood. After the black SUV drove off, other soldiers poured out of the recruiting station and tried to administer CPR, but William Long would be pronounced dead by the time he reached a hospital less than an hour later.

Melvin Bledsoe and his wife were in their car and already on the outskirts of Little Rock when his cell phone beeped. All weekend the father had tried to reach Carlos without success, and by Monday morning he was worried enough to call a co-worker and ask him to stop by Carlos's apartment to see whether his son was okay. The parents had hopped in the car and set out from Memphis to Little Rock with a growing premonition that something was wrong. The FBI agent on the phone told Melvin that he needed to come by the Little Rock field office, that something really bad had happened and someone had been killed, and that the authorities thought his son was involved. Melvin had to pull to the side of the road and stop the car before telling his wife the news about their beloved son.

"Every day I wake up in the morning and hear about how radical Islamists have killed somebody else or blown something up, but in 2008 my family and I were ignorant and totally alone in dealing with what was happening," he later recalled in an interview with the author. "It never even occurred to me that my son could be ripped out of his own culture, and brainwashed and programmed to become someone else. I've told Mr. Long that he lost his son to a jihadist, and I lost my son to radical Islamists. There's tragedy and a crime on both sides of that deal, and the world needs to understand it."

Years later, the US Army finally gave Purple Heart Medals to Quinton Ezeagwula and to the family of William Long. The award was enabled by a provision inserted into a defense authorization bill that for the first time authorized the Purple Heart for service members killed or wounded anywhere in an attack that specifically targets them as soldiers, or is carried out by an individual inspired or directed by a foreign terrorist organization. As Long's grieving father said after the attack that killed his son, "They weren't on the battlefield; but apparently, the battlefield's here."

THE FIRST LETHAL attack on US soil by an Islamic extremist since 9/11 was a bellwether, signaling a dangerous new phase in the conflict that would see homegrown extremists and lone-wolf terrorists increasingly bring violent jihad home to America. In September 2009, just a few months after Carlos Bledsoe's attack on the recruiting center, a Denver airport shuttle-bus driver named Najibullah Zazi was arrested for a well-developed plot to bomb the New York City subway system. An Afghan native and permanent US resident who had traveled to Pakistan to receive al-Qaeda training, Zazi closely fit the profile of three Pakistani British terrorists who launched the coordinated suicide bombings on London's public transport system that killed fifty-two people during rush hour in 2005. In November 2009, months after Zazi's arrest, US Army Major Nidal Hasan murdered thirteen people and wounded more than thirty others in a shooting spree on Fort Hood, Texas, in the deadliest terrorist attack on US soil since 9/11. Considered a lone wolf without the direct backing of a known terrorist organization, Hasan nevertheless sought "spiritual guidance" from Anwar al-Awlaki, with whom he corresponded over the Internet. Al-Awlaki called his act of mass murder "wonderful." Before the attack, the FBI had accepted Hasan's explanation that his communication with the archterrorist was part of his professional research as a US Army psychiatrist.

The hand of al-Awlaki and AQAP was also detected when a Nigerian youth named Umar Farouk Abdulmutallab attempted to blow up a North-west Airlines flight carrying more than 280 people on Christmas Day 2009. Like Carlos Bledsoe, Abdulmutallab had apparently been radicalized while attending Islamist institutes in Yemen. His father reported his son's extreme religious views to CIA officers in the US Embassy in Nigeria, and that led to his name being placed on the National Counterterrorism Center's database—called the Terrorist Identities Datamart Environment—which included the names of 550,000 suspected extremists. Because of a lack of collaborating evidence, however, his name was not added to the FBI's Terrorist Screening Database, which fed the US No-Fly List. After AQAP bomb makers outfitted Abdulmutallab in Yemen with explosives hidden in his underwear, a seat was procured for him directly over the aircraft's fuel tanks. Luckily, the bomb failed to ignite.

US counterterrorism officials got lucky again months later with Faisal Shahzad, a US citizen and Connecticut resident. Shahzad had family and tribal ties in Pakistan's tribal regions, which he used to make contact with the Pakistan Taliban, which had previously focused on operations targeting the central government in Islamabad. The group gave Shahzad five days of bomb-making training and introduced him to its leader, Hakimullah Mehsud. On May 2, Shahzad drove a car loaded with explosives into Times Square and attempted to detonate it during rush hour. A mass-casualty terrorist spectacular in the heart of Manhattan was averted only because the bomb failed to explode.

For the better part of a decade, US counterterrorism officials had improbably averted another deadly terrorist attack on US soil. By 2010, just 156 individuals had been arrested or indicted in the United States in connection with jihadi terrorism, out of a Muslim American population of more than 3 million. Only 14 Americans had been killed on US soil by jihadist terrorists. But the spate of plots and attacks on the homeland by lone wolves and homegrown extremists that began with Carlos Bledsoe represented an alarming escalation, convincing many experts that the nation's luck was bound to change.

Their fears were eventually realized with the 2013 Boston Marathon bombings and a follow-on shootout by the Chechen brothers and immigrants Dzhokhar and Tamerlan Tsarnaev that killed 4 people and wounded more than 250 others. An attack eerily similar to Bledsoe's was launched in 2015 against two US military facilities in Chattanooga, Tennessee, when Kuwaiti-born US citizen Muhammad Youssef Abdulazeez killed four Marines and wounded two other service members and a police officer. Another instance of homegrown terrorism linked to foreign terrorist organizations occurred in December 2015, when Syed Rizwan Farook, an American-born citizen of Pakistani descent, and his Pakistani-born wife, Tashfeen Malik, who grew up in Saudi Arabia, killed 14 civilians and seriously wounded 22 others in a mass shooting in San Bernardino, California. Malik professed support for the Islamic State of Iraq and Syria in an online post.

As it became more decentralized under US pressure, al-Qaeda relied more on franchises and affiliates that were growing in strength and proving adept at inspiring online jihadists. In the 2010 report "Would-Be Warriors: Incidents of Jihadist Terrorist Radicalization in the U.S. Since September 11, 2001," RAND Corporation terrorism analyst Brian Michael Jenkins noted that 2009–2010 saw a bigger increase in the number of terrorist plots and individuals involved in them than any similar period since 9/11. Counterterrorism experts Bruce Hoffman and Peter Bergen concluded in the 2010 paper "Assessing the Terrorist Threat" that "an embryonic terrorist radicalization and recruitment infrastructure had [possibly] been established in the U.S. homeland," something the report called previously "unthinkable." In 2010 Michael Leiter, director of the National Counterterrorism Center, the intelligence community's counterterrorism nerve center, called the spate of attacks and plots on the homeland in 2009–2010 "the most significant developments in the terrorist threat to the homeland since 9/11."

That watershed ushered in a new era that would come to define counterterrorism operations. Counterterrorism officials adapted by doubling down on aggressive tactics and intelligence collection techniques, to include the National Security Agency's collection and querying of massive amounts of metadata on the communications of average Americans; closer surveillance of radical imams and mosques by federal and state police forces; elaborate FBI stings to flush out would-be terrorists; and a dramatic expansion of the targeted killing operations by the CIA and Joint Special Operations Command far outside the war zones in Iraq and Afghanistan, and against different targets than just core al-Qaeda leaders. Groups targeted with lethal force included the Pakistan Taliban, al-Shabab in Somalia, and especially al-Qaeda in the Arabian Peninsula. The number of US drone and cruise missile airstrikes in Yemen skyrocketed from just 1 before 2009–2010, to 56 in 2012 alone, according to figures compiled by the New America Foundation in Washington, DC.

The shift in intensity and the widening focus of counterterrorism operations was greatly encouraged by President Barack Obama, who since taking office showed a determination to end the wars in Iraq and Afghanistan, and rely more heavily on discrete, targeted counterterrorism operations to keep the country safe. Nor was a new template for such operations required. The vast US intelligence, law enforcement, and Special Operations Forces communities were now seasoned with veterans of JSOC's joint task forces in Iraq and Afghanistan, and they were rising through the ranks and imparting the lessons of a new style of network-centric, intelligence-driven warfare. Well before the post-9/11 wars ended, the contours of a long twilight struggle against jihadi terrorists that would likely span generations were already visible.

# NINE

# The Ghosts in the Network
## 2009–2010

B ILLIONS OF CALLS AND MESSAGES RICOCHET THROUGH THE global communications grid on any given day, tiny particles crashing through cyberspace seeking the magnetic bond of connectivity. A single e-mail passes through massive servers, hurtles at the speed of light through fiber-optic cables in the murky depths of the ocean, and vanishes into digital infinity. Or a cell phone call hits a tower in Karachi, routes through the circuits of Bharti Airtel or Saudi Telecom, bounces off a communications satellite in space, and disappears into the digital ether halfway around the world. Only these tiny electrons of human discourse don't just disappear. At many nodes in their split-second journey, National Security Agency (NSA) computers filter, tag, and sort them, recording their faint numeric imprints in massive metadata storage banks that are later queried by algorithms designed to recognize telltale patterns. And sometimes two of these digital particles collide in a way that sets off alarms.

On September 6, 2009, an e-mail sent to an Internet Protocol (IP) address in Pakistan that the NSA's eavesdropping system had flagged as a rarely used al-Qaeda mail drop prompted a warning signal at the agency's sprawling headquarters complex at Fort Meade, Maryland. That IP address was linked to Rashid Rauf, a British citizen of Pakistani descent and master al-Qaeda bomb-maker. He was tied to the deadly 2005 attack on the London transport system, and to the failed plot to down as many as ten civilian airliners originating at Heathrow Airport in the summer of 2006.

Rauf had used a similar e-mail drop as al-Qaeda's point of contact for the London bombers who killed 52 civilians and injured more than 700 others. He had a long pedigree in Pakistani jihadist circles: his father-in-law and sister-in-law ran the Darul Uloom Madina, a radical Islamist seminary in Pakistan; Rauf was a relative of Maulana Masood Azhar, who led the Pakistani terrorist group Jaish-e-Mohammad that focused its operations in Indian Kashmir. In al-Qaeda's concentric rings of networks, Rauf had risen to the elite inner circle.

The NSA's PRISM surveillance system flagged the e-mail sent to Pakistan under Section 702 of the Foreign Intelligence Surveillance Act, which allows for surveillance of foreign nationals suspected of terrorism. The content of the e-mail revealed that the sender was asking one of al-Qaeda's chief bomb makers about explosives ingredients. It was bad enough that someone was seeking bomb-making instruction from Rauf, but NSA analysts were especially concerned by the origins of the message: the person making the inquiries sent the e-mail from Aurora, Colorado.

By mid-2009, NSA director Keith Alexander was already well on his way to expanding the signals intelligence system pioneered with the Real Time Regional Gateway in Iraq to a global scale. In the process, he had become one of the most influential military leaders whom almost no one knew about, at least outside close-knit intelligence community circles. NSA operations in Iraq had increased dramatically in effectiveness after the agency began scooping up, storing, and querying massive amounts of communications meta-data via increasingly sophisticated software algorithms, and using that data to map terrorist and insurgent networks. The agency's advanced geolocation technologies employed to find and fix those targets once identified was equally groundbreaking.

Since its introduction in Iraq, Real Time Regional Gateway had been continuously product-improved by the high-tech wizards of the Defense Advanced Research Projects Agency, or DARPA. The software that the

NSA developed to run the system borrowed from the same search technology that powered Google, which was able to field 100 billion user queries each month. General Alexander liked to tell his subordinates that the NSA was becoming the information agency for the information age, and he reckoned that the average citizen now had greater access to information than the president of the United States enjoyed just a few decades earlier. He was determined to harness that knowledge to the task of rooting out terrorists before they could strike.

The alert sounded by that e-mail sent from Colorado reminded Alexander of the case of 9/11 hijacker Khalid al-Mihdhar. The NSA had intercepted calls from al-Mihdhar to known al-Qaeda operatives in Yemen before the September 11, 2001, terrorist attacks on the United States. At that time the NSA was unable to track the call to its origin, and it was assumed that al-Mihdhar was calling from somewhere in the Middle East. As it turned out, he had called his Yemeni connection from San Diego. Had the agency been able to connect those dots between a foreign terrorist and a likely coconspirator inside the United States, it might have been able to alert the FBI to the looming danger.

The NSA is technically barred from spying on the communications of American citizens, but in Section 215 of the USA PATRIOT Act, the agency's lawyers had identified a loophole you could drive millions of domestic communications through each day: it authorized the US government to compel such private telecommunications companies as AT&T and Verizon to produce records that might assist in a terrorist investigation. The section included a gag rule barring those companies from publicly acknowledging the government request for records, lest they jeopardize the investigation. Such Section 215 orders for records are cleared by a judge enforcing the Foreign Intelligence Surveillance Act, and periodically briefed to the House and Senate Intelligence Committees.

In 2005 the George W. Bush administration had been put on the defensive when the *New York Times* revealed for the first time that it had interpreted the PATRIOT Act to allow the NSA to intercept, without warrants, data on the private communications of millions of Americans. The FISA Amendment Act of 2008 added some mild civil liberties protections, but legalized and expanded the NSA's warrantless wiretapping program. It immunized telecom companies for their cooperation in the program and made it easier for the agency to quickly compel telephone companies to surrender records that listed the date, time, and duration of communications—but not the content—made from inside the United States to numbers or addresses overseas.

As a senator, Barack Obama had opposed the FISA Amendment Act, but as president and commander in chief he had reversed course, not only supporting the act, but also fighting a lawsuit by the American Civil Liberties Union that challenged the expanded FISA authorities. Civil libertarians criticized Obama for adopting some of the same surveillance programs over which he once took George W. Bush to task, but Keith Alexander wasn't surprised. Whether you're a Democrat or a Republican, once you are in the Oval Office and personally responsible for defending the country against a dizzying array of threats, you start to look decidedly hawkish on security issues.

The NSA tracked the e-mail to an al-Qaeda bomb maker to a cell phone in Colorado, and passed that information to the FBI. Soon the FBI came back with a name: Najibullah Zazi, an Afghan American who drove a shuttle van at Denver International Airport. The bureau wanted to know who else Zazi was talking to, but finding out would have required the bureau to seek another administrative subpoena called a National Security Letter, and that required time they might not have. Because Zazi was now the subject of a terrorism investigation, the NSA was not similarly constrained. By going out a couple of hops in his circle of contacts, the agency discovered a Bosnian immigrant named Adis Medunjanin, and another Afghan American called Zarein Ahmedzay.

An FBI records search revealed that all three had attended the same high school, and in 2008 they had traveled together from New York to Peshawar, a city just east of Pakistan's lightly governed tribal areas where many core al-Qaeda operatives were based. Suddenly the warning alarms in the counterterrorism community were sounding off. These men didn't appear to be radicalized but poorly trained lone wolves like Carlos Bledsoe or Nadal Hassan, but something that US counterterrorism officials had feared most since 9/11: an American-based al-Qaeda sleeper cell intent on executing a terrorist spectacular.

As HE DROVE cross-country from Denver to New York in a rental car beginning on September 9, 2009, Najibullah Zazi ran the plan through his mind. What he and his al-Qaeda handlers Rashid Rauf and Saleh al-Somali had in mind as a model were the successful terrorist attacks on the transport systems of Madrid and London, attacks that had collectively killed nearly 250 people and wounded more than 2,500 others. The new plan called for three simultaneous suicide attacks on New York City subway trains just as they entered the city's two busiest subway stations at rush hour—Grand Central and Times Square. Everything had been planned to exact maximum carnage.

Zazi and his two high school friends had trained for months in explosives and weapons at an al-Qaeda training camp in Miranshah, Pakistan. During their training, a convoy of vehicles had driven into the camp. Out stepped Rauf and al-Somali, al-Qaeda's head of external operations, and approached them. In impeccable English, Rauf told them that "they would be presented with a serious decision," and he wanted to know if they were willing to become suicide bombers. Eventually all three had agreed.

Zazi had taken copious notes at the al-Qaeda camp. He e-mailed the notes on bomb-making to himself to access them back in the United States. But he required additional advice from Rauf, and this resulted in the intercepted e-mail. Before setting off on his drive to New York, Zazi experimented with mixing the hydrogen peroxide and acetone in a hotel room sink, and he successfully produced the same acetone peroxide–based explosive used in the 2005 London subway bombings. They were ready to execute the plot.

As Zazi drove his rental car over the George Washington Bridge to Manhattan, he was pulled over by New York Port Authority Police. He was suspicious of the police explanation of a random drug search. The next day his father called him. New York police had approached Imam Ahmad Wais Afzali, a Muslim cleric whose mosque Zazi once attended, and had shown the imam a photograph of him. The same day, Zazi's rental car was towed, supposedly because of a parking violation. He realized his laptop computer was still in the car, and that it contained the notes on bomb making.

Spooked, Zazi flew back to Denver on September 12, 2009. In the Queens home where he had stayed, the FBI found an electronic scale, batteries, and a dozen backpacks of the type used in the Madrid and London bombings. When Zazi voluntarily appeared for an interview at the FBI's Denver field office, its interrogators used techniques developed by the bureau's Behavioral Science Unit from interviews of violent Islamist extremists and would-be suicide bombers in Afghanistan. Eventually, Zazi admitted receiving explosives training from al-Qaeda. After authorities charged his Afghan-born father with complicity in the plot and threatened to charge his mother with immigration offenses, Zazi pleaded guilty to conspiring to use weapons of mass destruction, conspiring to commit murder, and providing material support to a terrorist organization. Responding to the guilty plea, US attorney general Eric Holder would call the Zazi plot one of the most serious threats to the United States homeland since September 11, 2001, and he promised that the US government "will not rest until everyone responsible is held accountable."

A SHADOW WAR was raging inside the vast US counterterrorism network. For those in the belly of the machine, it was often disorienting to step outside its confines and listen to the tenor of the debate about the nature of the terrorist threat. When driving through the streets of Washington, DC, Keith Alexander often marveled at the scenes of domestic tranquility that passed by his windows. For a decade after 9/11, the United States had been free from a follow-on terrorist spectacular, and the people on the sidewalks and at outdoor cafés seemed blissfully oblivious to the lurking dangers that shadowed most of his waking hours. It was a sentiment common among the community of counterterrorism officials, especially those who had been to the front lines and witnessed the trauma inflicted on societies once the extremists gained a beachhead. Alexander had been to the Middle East enough to know that the belief system of the jihadists would never let them leave the West alone.

There were times when he worried that the NSA was a victim of its own success, and of a code of secrecy that stifled any response to misleading reporting in the media. Articles often depicted the agency as an "all-seeing, all-knowing" Big Brother. In truth, the NSA was engaged in a deadly game of cat-and-mouse, constantly developing new tools to try to stay a few steps ahead of an utterly determined, equally secretive enemy. Media reports often cited the intelligence community's $75 billion annual budget as evidence of overreach, but the government had spent billions of dollars mapping the human genome, and had still failed to find the cure for cancer because the disease kept mutating and evolving. So it was with the terrorist threat.

Like any four-star officer, Alexander was well read, and one bit of history that naturally intrigued him was the breaking of the German's Enigma code machine by the British during World War II. That signature success by the cryptologists turned the tide of the naval war in the Atlantic. Whether they were dubbed Real Time Regional Gateway, or Nexus 7, or Accumulus, Alexander saw these NSA programs as tools similarly designed to crack the communications code of growing and increasingly sophisticated networks of radical jihadists. Critics might scoff at the comparison, but before they gained the powerful levers of a state, what were the Nazis but a band of slightly absurd, goose-stepping thugs? At their core the ideologies were similarly tyrannical, expansionist, and at least in their most fundamentalist interpretation, genocidal. The difference was chiefly in power, and how much the extremists were allowed to accumulate before the West awoke to its peril.

DURING THE INITIAL days of Operation Enduring Freedom in Afghanistan, Air Force air operations commander Major General David Deptula had glimpsed how such new technologies as advanced sensors and unmanned aircraft—and such operational concepts as remote split operations, which enabled frontline warfighters to reach back instantaneously to a globe-spanning surveillance and intelligence network—might revolutionize military operations. By 2010, Lieutenant General Deptula was the Air Force's very first deputy chief of staff for intelligence, surveillance, and reconnaissance (ISR), and the 480th ISR wing was the embodiment of his original vision.

The 480th wing at Langley Air Force Base, in the scenic tidewater area of coastal Virginia, was unlike any warfighting unit in US military history. The unit's roughly six thousand personnel were globally distributed, working at six major hubs, including three overseas. Like the drone pilots at Creech Air Force Base in Nevada with whom they partnered on missions conducted largely in cyberspace, the analysts and targeting experts in the 480th fought from their home stations. Because of the insatiable demand for their services, 480th analysts worked twelve-hour shifts, six days a week — routinely 220 hours a month. There was a new kind of war being fought at their workstations, and in that darkened incubus they exhibited the heightened physiological stresses associated with a fight-or-flight response. Only at the end of the shift, they went home to their families and made small talk over dinner, and then when the lights were out, some of these new-age warriors lay awake in the dark, eyes wide open.

Inside the expansive command and intelligence fusion center where they worked and fought, a central node in the vast US counterterrorism apparatus called the Sentinel, the network was chill and dark and eerily quiet. The refrigerated air cooled massive banks of computers, and the perpetual gloom lessened the strain on eyes peering into hundreds of screens surveying the globe from the vantage point of satellites and thousands of manned and unmanned aircraft, portals rendering the world in every spectrum known to science. The unblinking eye.

Shadowy figures sat at three-person workstations strewn throughout the cavernous command center, distilling the crush of raw data into usable intelligence. At one station a geospatial intelligence analyst peered into a greenish screen monitoring the video feed from a Predator drone tracking the progress of a car as it wound its way through the dusty streets of a town in Pakistan's tribal region. Because of the level of detail and constant vigilance required, analysts find these "pattern of life" missions tracking the movements of individuals over long periods of time the most stressful. Learn enough about people's daily habits — when they leave for work, if they drop the kids at school, how many extended family members live in the house where they reside — and it can almost feel as if you know them. Inside the network, it's best to maintain several degrees of detachment from someone whose "pattern of life" is likely to end violently.

At the same workstation, an intelligence product analyst took photographic "snaps" that captured every stop the car made, for collection into a detailed intelligence update. Between them a "screener" constantly described the mission's progress in multiple classified chat rooms monitored on his split computer screen, making sure the National Counterterrorism Center in Washington, the Predator aircrew in Nevada, and the Special Operations Task Force in Afghanistan that had tasked the mission through the Joint Staff at the Pentagon were all updated and kept in the loop. Occasionally a civilian analyst who had been watching the same patch of hardscrabble land in North Waziristan for going on a decade might stop by and tell the enlisted airmen at the workstation that it was unusual for the building where the car stopped to be so crowded at that time of day. The best and most experienced analysts inside the Sentinel offered answers to questions that operators in the field hadn't even thought to ask yet.

At numerous other workstations inside the darkened command center, similar dramas were quietly playing out before portals trained on different parts of the world. Unmanned drones acted as robotic avatars, perched unseen over the shoulder of targets the Sentinel's operators were tracking through bazaars in East Africa, in the crowds at mosques for Friday prayers in Yemen, and in the rugged mountain villages of the Hindu Kush.

David Deptula constantly reminded his commanders not to concentrate on the public's obsession with the shiny object, the little pieces of fiberglass flying around, called drones. The Air Force's preferred terminology was remotely piloted aircraft (RPA), a nod to the fact that it could require an air, analytic, and logistics crew of more than one hundred persons to complete a single Predator flight. Whatever you called the aircraft, there was no denying the RPAs were a superstar platform in the vast ISR network. From just 167 unmanned drones in the US arsenal in 2002, the number had grown to nearly 6,000 by 2010, representing a 3,500 percent increase in the length of time the network could put "eyes over target." Drone flights routinely lasted more than twenty hours, and were typically piloted by rotating Air Force crews that worked around the clock, representing an unprecedented degree of persistence in the tracking of targets. Outfitted with new wide-area surveillance cameras, infrared sensors, facial-recognition software, and GPS-guided missiles, RPAs could track targets in an area equivalent to a small city, identify individuals from unseen heights, and target them precisely with Hellfire missiles. They were the entire "find, fix, and finish" cycle of operations resident on a single air platform, and a game changer in counterterrorism and surveillance operations.

Yet the drones were optimized for surveillance, and only roughly 1 percent of their missions involved lethal force. Nearly as groundbreaking as armed Predators was the Air Force's new Gorgon Stare, named after the Gorgons of Greek mythology who could turn men to stone with a hard glance. Gorgon Stare was a wide-area surveillance system mounted on a larger MQ-9 Reaper remotely piloted aircraft, and equipped with electro-optical cameras for daylight operations, and infrared cameras for nighttime. The modern-day Gorgon could track enemy movements in an area measuring roughly 2.5 miles in diameter, and it initially created such a data crush that 480th analysts had to deploy to Afghanistan because the system choked even the massive bandwidth at Langley Air Force Base. But the US Special Operations Task Force in Afghanistan quickly became enthralled with the wide-area surveillance technology and its manhunting attributes.

Remotely piloted aircraft were just the most renowned ISR tool in the 480th's crowded surveillance toolbox, which also included secret spy satellites; venerable, high-flying U-2 spy aircraft; E-8 Joint STARS (Joint Surveillance Target Attack Radar System) ground surveillance and command-and-control aircraft; RC-135 Rivet Joint surveillance and electronic signals intercept aircraft; and smaller, converted Beechcraft MC-12W intelligence, surveillance, and reconnaissance (ISR) aircraft, fielded for operations in Iraq and Afghanistan. The advanced synthetic aperture radars and forward-looking infrared cameras on US fighter aircraft were also excellent ISR sensors, and in Iraq and Afghanistan dirigibles carrying various ISR sensors had become fixtures floating over US bases and protected areas.

Amateurs talked drones, but Air Force ISR experts knew that the real craft was tying all of that disparate data together rapidly and fusing it with other intelligence sources, and then sharing it instantaneously with warfighters or terrorist trackers on the front lines. That network-centric, intelligence-driven style of operations had supercharged their metabolism, shrinking mission planning cycles to the point that by 2010, the Air Force routinely tasked aircraft already in the air with new missions.

"Everyone focuses on the drone, but it was by tapping into the power of the network and developing this concept of remote operations that we increased their effectiveness by an order of magnitude," said Major General James Poss, the Air Force's assistant deputy chief of staff for ISR in 2010.

"We've gone from Desert Storm in 1991—when reconnaissance missions required days to deliver pictures of an enemy with often questionable accuracy—to being able to get thirty frames per second of imagery, with GPS accuracy, to anywhere on earth within seconds. That's the power of the network."

The backbone of that revolution in network-centric operations was the 480th ISR wing and the Sentinel. Originally a convoy of deployable vans designed to analyze and distill surveillance data from U-2 spy planes, by 2009–2010 the Distributed Common Ground System had grown into the US military's premier intelligence fusion and distribution center. On any given day thousands of gigabytes of information flow through its modern brick headquarters building. The Distributed Common Ground System is linked to forty-five intelligence fusion and relay sites worldwide, and connected by a global communication grid that acts as the network's central nervous system, transmitting huge amounts of data at such fiber-optic speeds that can translate a joystick waggle at Creech Air Force Base in Nevada into wing rock in a drone flying over Yemen or Pakistan.

The essence of the secretive craft practiced at the 480th Wing is fusing that electronic data with other streams of intelligence. Because the 480th Wing operates primarily in cyberspace and is constantly engaged in surveillance operations around the world, it can also pivot the network's focus so quickly that people inside the Sentinel describe it almost as a sentient being. Anyone on the top-tier list of terrorists in the US database had only to log onto the grid somewhere—send an e-mail, check flight schedules online, use an ATM card, browse a social-networking site, dial a cell phone, enter an electronically secured building, search for online porn, walk by a security camera, contact a known accomplice—and the network's increasingly sophisticated trackers at the 480th wing might pick up the scent of digital exhaust. At that point the network could direct a hard stare at the new target, turning the unblinking eye in his or her direction and rapidly synthesizing enormous amounts of all-source intelligence so as to discern "patterns of life," the better to anticipate the target's next move and initiate a strike. For all the exquisite technology and human ingenuity involved in an enterprise that spanned the globe and stretched into space, the ghost in the network remained the primal urges of the hunt: Find. Fix. Finish.

ON SEPTEMBER 14, 2009, Saleh Ali Saleh Nabhan was traveling in a convoy of cars in southern Somalia. A Kenyan and top al-Qaeda operative in Africa, Nabhan was wanted by the FBI for his involvement in an attack on a hotel and an attempt to shoot down an Israeli airliner in Kenya in 2002. He had also been linked to al-Qaeda's 1998 bombing of the US embassies in Kenya and Tanzania. As his convoy drove through an isolated track of land, US Special Forces helicopters swarmed in with .50 caliber machine guns blazing. When the shooting stopped, Navy SEAL commandos collected the bodies of Nabhan and another suspected terrorist for identification purposes, and then flew back to US warships patrolling off the Somalia coast.

On December 8, 2009, a car carrying Saleh al-Somali was tracked near the city of Miramshah, in Pakistan's tribal region. The area was controlled by the Haqqani network, the deadliest of the Taliban factions. Saleh al-Somali was chief of al-Qaeda's external operations, and along with Rashid Rauf he had been instrumental in devising the plot for Najibullah Zazi and his cohorts to bomb the New York subway system. Somewhere from overhead the loud shriek of two Hellfire missiles was heard before converging on al-Somali's car. Tribal sources reported that his car disintegrated, scattering body parts in all directions. Rauf had already been reported killed by an earlier drone strike, a death that his family would later confirm.

Al-Somali and Rauf were among a number of top al-Qaeda's commanders to be killed in a targeted killing campaign that shifted into a higher gear beginning in 2009–2010, and would in just two years eliminate fourteen senior al-Qaeda leaders, more than half of the CIA's most-wanted high-value terrorist targets. Those already targeted and killed in Pakistan included another al-Qaeda bomb-maker, Abu Khabab al-Masri; senior leader and spokesman Abu Laith al-Libi; and senior trainer and explosives expert Abu Sulayman Jazairi. The roll call of deaths by drone also included Baitullah Mehsud, the ferocious head of the Pakistani Taliban, who had formed increasingly close ties to al-Qaeda. The Pakistan Taliban was connected to Connecticut resident Faisal Shahzad's plot to detonate a car bomb in New York's Time Square. In Pakistan, Mehsud was already public enemy number one, implicated in a host of terrorist attacks to include the 2008 bombing of the Marriott Hotel in Islamabad that killed fifty people, and the assassination of former prime minister Benazir Bhutto in 2007.

In a single 48-hour period on December 17 and 18, 2009, a barrage of Predator drone strikes killed twenty-two suspected al-Qaeda terrorists and allied militants in North Waziristan, heralding the controversial new tactic of "signature strikes," with unidentified persons targeted because they exhibit suspicious behavior associated with militants. Signature strikes had begun in 2008 under President George W. Bush, but like other aspects of the targeted killing campaign they were expanded under the new Obama administration. According to the *Long War Journal*, a respected website that reports on counterterrorism operations and tracks the US targeted killing program, of the 99 drone attacks carried out inside Pakistan between 2004 and 2010, 89 occurred after Barack Obama's January 2008 inauguration.

Observing that intensifying cycle of lethal targeting, David Deptula was struck by how far their operations model had come in the decade since he had commanded air forces during 2001's Operation Enduring Freedom. He listened as an ISR analyst in Beale Air Force Base, California, supplied signals intelligence to the Sentinel command center in Langley, Virginia, that was immediately fused with other sources of intelligence and shared in real time with a Predator air crew operating out of Creech Air Force Base in Nevada, and a Joint Special Operations Command task force directing the action from Afghanistan. For roughly the first one hundred years of flight, airpower experts had struggled to accomplish the "finish" part of the F3EA equation. Now that they could do that with global precision, the US counterterrorism network writ large was making a quantum leap in "finding" and "fixing" an elusive enemy. Deptula understood that deadly drone attacks were controversial, with the United Nations raising valid concerns about the number of civilians killed. The critics never answered the question of how many more civilians would have died, however, if the enemy in this war was being targeted by dumb bombs, indirect artillery, or a scared nineteen-year-old soldier on the ground with an M-16 rifle. Watching the targeting operations, Deptula noted that every weapon delivered off an airborne platform—manned or unmanned—was recorded in minute detail until the moment of impact for later analysis and bomb damage assessments, something you certainly couldn't say for an artillery shell or a bullet. Killing would forever be an ugly business, and the fog of war and human error still obscured the view, but he believed the new style of operations he was helping pioneer was the most precise and deliberate form of warfare in history.


THE MOTHER NODE and chief command center in the United States' globe-spanning counterterrorism network is the National Counterterrorism Center (NCTC), headquartered on the nondescript campus of modern buildings called Liberty Crossing in the leafy Virginia suburbs of Washington, DC. The NCTC is the most tangible embodiment of the federal government's response to the September 11, 2001, terrorist attacks, and its answer to the 9/11 Commission's criticism that the intelligence community had failed to "connect the dots" on al-Qaeda's long-gestating plot. Along with creation of the position of director of national intelligence, who works out of the same Liberty Crossing headquarters, the NCTC was designed to ensure that terrorists would never again catch the United States unawares with a terrorist spectacular.

Early in 2010 NCTC officials were trying to determine how they failed to connect the dots on al-Qaeda in the Arabian Peninsula's plot to down the airliner over Detroit. Despite being alerted by the bomber's father, the intelligence community had not sufficiently flagged Abdulmutallab. Each day the roughly five hundred civilians and military analysts at the NCTC had to comb through 8,000 to 10,000 reports on potential terrorist activity from more than one hundred databases, cross-checking them against its own database of more than 500,000 known or suspected terrorists. And if one name slipped through, as did Abudulmutallab's, then the fidelity of the entire system came under question.

"Before the Christmas Day bombing attempt, nearly a hundred percent of the complaints we received from Congress were about constituents who were upset at being placed on the terrorist watch list," said a senior NCTC official. "And the next day a hundred percent of the complaints were about why we idiots at NCTC didn't connect the dots on the Abdulmutallab plot. That was a tough time to be a terrorist analyst."

No one was under more pressure than NCTC director Michael Leiter, a former Supreme Court law clerk, US district attorney, and Navy fighter pilot. He was responsible for the terrorist threat matrix that the NCTC compiled and prioritized each day from the databases of the alphabet soup of intelligence and law enforcement agencies

In the institutional soul-searching at the NCTC following the first lethal Islamist terrorist strikes on US soil since 9/11, in the 2009 attacks by Carlos Bledsoe and Fort Hood shooter Nidal Hassan, and in the near misses in the plots by Najibullah Zazi and Umar Farouk Abdulmutallab, Leiter concluded that the terrorist threat had evolved in a number of distinct phases that had made the calculations of counterterrorism officials far more complicated.

First was the continued threat posed by the core al-Qaeda organization led by Osama bin Laden, which was centered in the wild tribal areas of Pakistan. The al-Qaeda core was still focused on launching complex terrorist spectaculars in the West, such as the unsuccessful 2006 plot to destroy as many as ten civilian airliners flying across the Atlantic, which might have proven even more deadly than the September 11, 2001, attacks. And of course the Zazi plot to bomb the New York subway in 2009. But it was under great pressure as a result of the United States' intensifying targeted killing campaign in Pakistan.

A few years earlier, NCTC analysts had noticed a change in the evolution of the Islamist extremist threat with the rise of the al-Qaeda affiliates. These groups responded to Osama bin Laden's call to jihad, but their operational linkages to al-Qaeda's senior leadership were sometimes difficult to establish and often seemed tenuous. Such groups as al-Qaeda in Iraq, al-Shabab in Somalia, the Pakistan Taliban, and al-Qaeda in the Arabian Peninsula (AQAP) were originally localized threats. Increasingly, those affiliates had shown more independence and staying power, and especially in the case of AQAP, under the leadership of the charismatic Anwar al-Awlaki, were heeding bin Laden's call for direct attacks on the US homeland and Western interests.

Al-Awlaki was also connected to the most recent phase in the evolution of the terrorist threat in the decade since 9/11: the increasing appearance of homegrown terrorists and "lone-wolves," many of them radicalized over the Internet and inspired by jihadist propaganda, such as AQAP's online magazine *Inspire*. Al-Awlaki was central to al-Qaeda's strategy to recruit

English-speaking operatives, and doing so on social media, such as You-Tube and Facebook.

In the evolution of terrorism, Leiter was worried that these distinct phases were overlapping. Despite all of the efforts of US counterterrorism forces, none of the threats had disappeared from the threat matrix. They all simply accrued, one on top of the other. Although dramatically weakened, al-Qaeda's core was still plotting attacks on the West, with intelligence indicating that it was focused on a more vulnerable Europe. Al-Qaeda in Iraq was seriously weakened by the death of al-Zarqawi and the Anbar Awakening, but other affiliates, such as AQAP, al-Shabab, al-Qaeda in the Islamic Maghreb, and Boca Haram, were stepping up their deadly game. Intelligence clearly indicated that jihadist propaganda on the Internet was attracting new recruits inside the United States. A decade into this war, the threat from jihadist terrorism was growing. Some of Leiter's colleagues had begun referring to it as a Hydra—cut off one of its many heads and it seemed to grow two more.

The conclusion he and many other counterterrorism officials reached was that US counterterrorism officials had to up their own game in every phase: offensive strike operations against terrorist targets; greater intelligence sharing within the intelligence community and with international allies; tighter perimeter defense; and more aggressive investigations inside the United States designed to thwart lone wolves.

In terms of offensive strike operations in Pakistan to keep the al-Qaeda core on its heels, the Obama administration had made an auspicious start. CIA director Leon Panetta reached a secret deal with the government in Islamabad to greatly increase the intensity of the Predator strikes in exchange for giving Pakistani president Asif Ali Zardari greater say on the target list. That deal helped explain the fifteen strikes that were aimed at Baitullah Mehsud. For domestic political consumption, Pakistan's leaders railed against the drone strikes. But in fact, Predators took off from a secret base in Baluchistan province inside Pakistan, where US contractors working for the US government loaded them with Hellfire missiles and provided logistics support. President Obama was clearly determined to end the wars in Iraq and Afghanistan, but he had campaigned on his willingness to reach into Pakistan unilaterally if that was required to strike bin Laden and his top lieutenants. Obama's doubling down on the targeted killing campaign in Pakistan suggested that he was serious.

Because al-Qaeda's core and its affiliates increasingly had to spend their time and energies on self-preservation, always suspicious of informants and constantly looking over their shoulders, Leiter believed they were less likely to launch another successful terrorist spectacular. The hasty training and slapdash plots of would-be bombers, such as Shahzad and Abdulmutallab, at least suggested that those groups no longer felt that their sanctuaries were safe enough for meticulous plotting and training.

As a direct result of the Christmas Day bombing fiasco linked to AQAP and subsequent soul-searching, the NCTC adopted a number of reforms. Linkages between intelligence community databases maintained by the CIA, FBI, and other agencies and the NCTC's central clearinghouse for suspected terrorists called the Terrorist Identities Datamart Environment, or TIDE, were tightened. The bar for inclusion on the list was lowered in terms of how much specific "derogatory information" was required. As a result, the TIDE database would swell from 540,000 names in 2009 to 875,000 five years later.

More important, the NCTC redoubled its efforts at tracking and targeting terrorists. Fully 40 percent of the center's personnel were on temporary loan from other civilian and military intelligence agencies, and by 2010 many of them had served together in combat in Iraq and Afghanistan as part of Joint Special Operations Command multiagency task forces. For those men and women, the strong emotional bonds of combat endured. A new generation of national security operators had been weaned on the collaborative intelligence-sharing and intense operational ethos of General Stan McChrystal and Admiral Bill McRaven's hunter-killer teams, and they were rising through the ranks.

To tap into that expertise and instinct for collaboration, the NCTC formed pursuit teams of analysts from multiple agencies, whose sole task was to find the connections in the intelligence clutter—to discover that this e-mail or that phone call linked two individuals—and set off an alarm. The pursuit teams had access to every US database. An FBI agent could search the bureau's records of terrorist interrogations and prosecutions. The CIA representative brought the tradecraft and the agency's unmatched trove of human intelligence. The NSA delegate acted as conduit to the agency's global communications intercept apparatus. The Drug Enforcement Administration expert brought information from a global web of informants in the criminal underworld, who often intersect with transnational terrorist groups. Air Force ISR experts provided the perspective of the "unblinking eye." Experts from Joint Special Operations Command (JSOC) brought tactical expertise and the ability to turn intelligence into action.

These NCTC "pursuit groups" borrowed a page from JSOC's groundbreaking joint exploitation teams created by Mike Flynn, and they essentially took the art of establishing "patterns of life" to the doctorate level. They also helped elevate the relentless ethos of JSOC's tactical manhunting teams to the global counterterrorism campaign, supplying the critical "exploit" and "analyze" functions for the strategic F3EA counterterrorism operations. The success of that model of multi-discipline teams and fusion centers oriented on specific missions and regions would later lead to major reorganizations of both the Defense Intelligence Agency and the Central Intelligence Agency, and it solidified the NCTC's position as command central for the emerging new style of counterterrorism warfare.

In deciding that the United States' "global war on terrorism" did not end on a map but, rather, was bordered only by an ideology and pledges of allegiance among loosely defined networks of jihadi terrorists, both the Bush and Obama administrations took an expansive view of their authority to wage a nearly limitless war, one that civil libertarians found breathtaking. Even as the Obama administration sought to shut down the Guantánamo Bay detention center and end the wars in Iraq and Afghanistan, it thus elevated F3EA counterterrorism operations to a strategic warfighting model. The increased body count raised the question of whether a program of such profound impact and breadth could be indefinitely cloaked in a veil of secrecy. Senior Obama administration officials declined to even publicly acknowledge key aspects of the program, including how targets were chosen and prioritized, what evidentiary bar had to be met to land someone's name on the targeted killing list, and what oversight existed for a program that was run entirely out of the executive branch of the US government and acted as judge, jury, and executioner.

As long as Pakistan's lawless tribal regions remained what President Obama called in 2009 the "epicenter of violent extremism," and as long as al-Qaeda and its affiliates continued to gravitate to the dark, ungoverned corners of the world beyond the reach of any law, the Obama administration was determined to send hard men or lethal force after them.

Ironically, even as the network-centric, F3EA model of operations was coming to define a new American style of warfare, the alpha-hunters who pioneered it were struggling with its limitations. General Stanley McChrystal and much of his original Task Force 714 team were back trudging through the dense, tribal thickets of Afghanistan where the hunt for al-Qaeda and the Taliban had begun a decade earlier, and coming to the realization that in its laserlike focus in targeting terrorists and insurgents the United States had missed the forest for the trees.

# TEN

# The Forgotten War
## 2009–2010

PERHAPS IT WAS INEVITABLE THAT THE TWO ALPHA-COMMANDERS IN an age of war, the preeminent generals of their generation of officers, would eventually growl at each other when forced into too close territorial proximity. The video teleconference in the fall of 2009 between Generals David Petraeus and Stanley McChrystal was tense precisely because so much was at stake.

Earlier that spring McChrystal had been named the commander of US and allied forces in Afghanistan, and everyone in military circles understood his burden was to try to turn around a losing war in much the same fashion as Petraeus had managed with his counterinsurgency campaign in Iraq two years earlier. In terms of military reversals of fortune, that piece of generalship by Petraeus ranked with General Douglas MacArthur's bold counteroffensive and amphibious landing at Inchon in South Korea. By rewriting the losing narrative of the Iraq war, Petraeus had become the most celebrated military commander of the modern era.

As the commander of US Central Command (CENTCOM) in 2009, Petraeus was now responsible for a theater that included the wars in both

Iraq and Afghanistan, and he stood directly in the chain of command that stretched from Defense Secretary Robert Gates at the Pentagon, through CENTCOM headquarters in Tampa, Florida, all the way to Kabul, Afghanistan. And as far as McChrystal was concerned, Petraeus needed to surrender the reins of command and operational control in the Afghan campaign.

There was no lack of respect or friendship between the two West Point graduates, with Petraeus being the senior by two years. During the Iraq surge, then JSOC commander McChrystal had willingly subordinated himself to Petraeus, even though technically JSOC's operational chain of command at the time had run directly to CENTCOM. The situation had been dire, and he understood that Petraeus needed unity of command and direct authority over every aspect of operations in Iraq.

Nor was there any disagreement between them over the strategy that was needed to turn a losing Afghan campaign around. The campaign plan that McChrystal and his staff had given to the Defense Department and White House for review was modeled after Petraeus's holistic counterinsurgency campaign in Iraq of clearing ground, holding it, and building governance as the only means to protect the population and win it to the government's side. Both generals had seen in Iraq that at some point JSOC's counterterrorism campaign of targeted strikes on terrorist and insurgent leaders was unable to counter a determined and dug-in insurgency, and check Iraq's slide toward all-out civil war. Petraeus thus supported McChrystal's request for forty thousand additional US troops as part of an Afghan surge, a proposal generating considerable resistance in the White House.

Yet achieving unity of command in Afghanistan, where the United States led an International Security Assistance Force (ISAF) composed of the troops of some forty nations, was nearly impossible on the best of days. McChrystal wanted full operational control of US Marine Corps troops and Special Forces inside the country. For months his staff had chafed under the perceived micro-management of the current command arrangement, with tensions rising in his Kabul headquarters over CENTCOM's interference. A common refrain heard when the subject arose was, "Hey, this is bullshit!"

On the video teleconference with Petraeus and McChrystal was Defense Secretary Robert Gates and his chief military adviser, Joint Chiefs of Staff chair Admiral Mike Mullen. After a tense discussion, it became clear that neither Petraeus nor McChrystal was going to back down from his stated positions. Finally, an exasperated Gates stepped in as the final referee:

"Stan, tell me exactly what you need."

"I'm either in charge, or I'm not," McChrystal replied, letting the words sink in. "I need control of the Marines and Special Forces."

In the brief silence you could almost hear the tension crackle over the connection.

"Okay, Stan," Gates said. "You're in charge."

The McChrystal brain trust in Kabul was relieved by Gates's decision, but the episode was indicative of rising tensions and controversies surrounding the classified strategic assessment calling for a troop surge and counterinsurgency campaign in Afghanistan that the general had recently submitted to the Pentagon and White House. The Obama administration continued to expand and thicken the network that McChrystal and JSOC had created, adopting the targeted killing of terrorists as its preferred counterterrorism strategy. The success of the program had apparently convinced Vice President Joe Biden and others in the White House that another manpower-intensive counterinsurgency campaign in Afghanistan was unnecessary. In that sense McChrystal felt like a victim of his own success. America's preeminent manhunter in uniform was left having to explain to his superiors that the United States simply couldn't kill its way out of the insurgency it faced in Afghanistan. The tensions between his staff and that of the White House revealed a fundamental clash of views about the capabilities of the new model of counterterrorism operations, and the evolving and still potent threat of jihadi terrorism. Both sides would later have reason to profoundly regret that disconnect.

Just a few days later McChrystal was having breakfast with Admiral Mullen in Lisbon, Portugal, where they both were attending a NATO military conference. "The strategic assessment has leaked. Bob Woodward is reporting that he has it, and the *Washington Post* is going to print a version of it," Mullen said, before either of them realized that the White House would suspect McChrystal and his team of leaking the report to put pressure on the president to approve his full troop request. "I'm not happy about it, but it's out there."

Looking back much later, McChrystal would identify the leak as the moment the politics and personality clashes began to eat away at the already razor-thin margins of error of his campaign to turn around the Afghan war. After that breakfast, he would never again feel that he was executing the president's preferred strategy, or that the White House was really behind his effort. McChrystal repeatedly asked to meet with President Obama one-on-one to explain his reasoning. They didn't have to become close, but the commander in chief needed to look his top field general in the eye and determine whether he trusted him to execute the campaign. McChrystal was never sure whether the Pentagon brass objected to his briefing the president as a circumvention of the chain of command, or the White House staff wanted to keep arm's distance from the general who was commanding an unpopular war in a faraway land. McChrystal kept running up against multiple filters that were distorting the messages he tried to convey to the one person whose backing and trust was essential.

BY THE END of 2009, Major General Mike Flynn was on his third "listening tour" across the breadth and depth of Afghanistan, taking the full measure of a war that was soon to enter its ninth year. For someone who spent much of the previous decade hunting terrorists within the cloistered confines of Task Force 714, it was both a disorienting and disheartening experience.

Acting as McChrystal's intelligence chief and eyes on the ground, Flynn visited firebases in the southern deserts that were little more than an encirclement of concrete barriers and concertina wire, where Marines sought refuge from the 120-degree heat in the shade of their lean-tos, and sporadically traded fire with Taliban insurgents who were using rocket-propelled grenades and massed infantry in increasingly bold attacks on US and NATO outposts. Isolated US firebases in the remote mountains and deep valleys of northeast Afghanistan were generally accessible only by helicopter and in constant danger of being overrun, as had very nearly happened on October 3, 2009, when a Taliban force estimated at 350 fighters attacked Combat Outpost (COP) Keating in the Kamdesh Valley. The twelve-hour battle that ensued between the insurgents and roughly sixty defenders from the

Sixty-first Cavalry Regiment of the Fourth Infantry Division was desperate. The base was breached in three places and close air support had to be called in on Taliban insurgents inside the original perimeter. Eight US soldiers were killed in the battle for COP Keating, as were an estimated 150 to 200 Taliban fighters.

The Keating battle closely resembled an attack the year before on another isolated US outpost in northeast Afghanistan defended by the 503rd Infantry Regiment, which lost nine paratroopers killed and many more wounded when an estimated two hundred Taliban fighters nearly overran their base. To the south and east lay Camp Salerno in Khost Province, near the border with Pakistan and not far from the Tora Bora mountain redoubt where Osama bin Laden and his top lieutenants had escaped into Pakistan in 2001. Nearly every fighting season the Taliban launched a mass attack on Camp Salerno, the most recent involving as many as ten suicide bombers backed by infantry who attempted to breach the base's defenses. On the same day Taliban insurgents ambushed an elite French-led reconnaissance patrol, killing ten paratroopers in the deadliest day for French troops in a quarter-century. From their sanctuaries inside Pakistan, Taliban insurgents had long ago regrouped, and they seized the initiative in fighting in Afghanistan. The United States was in danger of losing the Afghan war in 2010 every bit as much as it had been of losing the Iraq war in 2007.

At the Khyber Pass in the shadow of the Hindu Kush, American troops occupied a joint command center in an ancient mud fort that demarcated the Durand Line, a 1,640-mile border drawn on a map in 1893 by Henry Mortimer Durand to delineate British India and Afghanistan, a border never recognized by the Pashtun and Baloch tribes that straddled the line. The journey from Kabul to the Khyber Border Coordination Center passed through Jalalabad, and was similar to the path of retreat that British general William Elphinstone and his force of sixteen thousand troops, civilians, and camp followers chose in 1842, before a gauntlet of ambushes by the wild Afghan tribes and brutal winter weather reduced his force to a single army surgeon who alone lived to tell of the massacre. As a reminder of the potential cost of such miscalculation, Flynn's boss, Stanley McChrystal, kept under Plexiglas on his dining room table an 1800s-era map that traced the route of General Elphinstone's doomed retreat from Kabul.

At each stop in his listening tour, Mike Flynn met with tribal elders
and local political leaders, as well as shopkeepers and customers in open-
air markets. Over countless cups of hot tea he heard the same complaints
of a weak and corrupt government, deteriorating security, and a resurgent
Taliban. And each time he returned to the headquarters of the US-led
ISAF in Kabul and compared notes with its intelligence briefers, Flynn
became even more convinced that although the ISAF could accurately
trace networks of more than twenty insurgent groups operating as part of
the loosely organized Taliban syndicate, by focusing so intently on the
Taliban insurgency, its US commanders had become blind to the bigger
picture in Afghanistan that existed outside the periphery of a targeting
scope.

Now it was America's turn to try and get it right in the "graveyard of empires." At roughly the decade mark in what would become by far the longest foreign conflict in the nation's history, US and allied forces were still
woefully ignorant of the human terrain they were transversing. Flynn had
stood on a little-used bridge built with US reconstruction funds, and asked
a tribal elder why the local villagers were still walking across the shallow
river below. Because that's the way they've done it going back centuries,
the elder told him, and they saw no reason to change. At another stop on
his tour, another tribal elder had pointed out a little-used well the international community had dug despite the tribes' actually having wanted
shovels to dig wells in places of their own choosing. Elsewhere, Flynn saw
gleaming new schools built with US taxpayer dollars, which stood empty
and abandoned. He received intelligence indicating that US reconstruction funds were going to corrupt provincial governors deeply involved in
drug trafficking and supportive of local Taliban groups that were killing
allied soldiers.

When Flynn raised his growing sense of alarm that after nearly a decade
of war, the United States and its NATO allies remained fundamentally ignorant of the human landscape in which they were operating, the response
from the ISAF intelligence briefers and the greater intelligence community
was deafening silence. They fell back on their charts of Taliban networks
and data on enemy killed as a talisman of success.

WHEN IT WAS first announced back in the spring of 2009 that General Stanley McChrystal would become the top US commander in Afghanistan, replacing General David McKiernan, it was understood in military circles that 2010 was to be the pivotal year in the long Afghanistan campaign. McKiernan, who had distinguished himself as the commander of US ground forces during the 2003 invasion of Iraq, had been agitating for more than a year for more forces to turn back a resurgent Taliban. But he was an armored officer from the conventional side of the US Army, and Defense Secretary Gates had decided that McKiernan lacked the background for a counterinsurgency campaign in a time of terror. As President Obama would later comment at the replacement of McChrystal himself, the war was bigger than any one man or woman, whether a private or a general.

Obama had run for president calling Afghanistan the "right battlefield" and promising to "finish the job" there, and soon after entering the White House he approved the deployment of an additional seventeen thousand troops, increasing US forces in Afghanistan by roughly 50 percent. The choice of McChrystal, one of the military's most celebrated unconventional warriors, known for JSOC's campaign to destroy al-Qaeda in Iraq, gave hope to those who favored a similar, more limited counterterrorism campaign in Afghanistan. A war-weary country had lost patience with nation building in such countries as Iraq and especially Afghanistan, where corruption was widespread and endemic. There were those in the White House, to include Vice President Biden, the former chairman of the Senate Foreign Relations Committee, who hoped that McChrystal would embrace a counterterrorism strategy of pinpoint strikes and night raids against Taliban insurgents and al-Qaeda operatives, an approach that would require far fewer US forces and avoid the kind of manpower-intensive "clear, hold, and build" operations that had characterized Petraeus's counterinsurgency campaign in Iraq.

In reassembling his JSOC brain trust, McChrystal had reached out first to Mike Flynn, whom he had personally promoted no less than three times. He viewed Flynn as a chief architect of Task Force 714's transformation and its intelligence-driven, F3EA (find, fix, and finish, exploit, and analyze) style of operations. McChrystal chose as his executive assistant and right-hand man Mike's brother, Colonel Charlie Flynn. For the Flynn brothers it was a welcome opportunity to work together, having seen little of each other in a near constant cycle of combat deployments over the past decade.

Other members of the McChrystal brain trust chosen to form the core of the Afghan leadership team included Brigadier General Scott Miller, the gifted former Delta Force commander. McChrystal's successor as JSOC commander, Navy SEAL admiral Bill McRaven, had at McChrystal's request moved the primary command team of Task Force 714 from Iraq back to Afghanistan, and had similarly repositioned the bulk of its strike assets of helicopters and surveillance drones to Bagram Air Base in Afghanistan. As in Iraq, JSOC's intelligence-driven strike raids, now targeting the Taliban leadership, would be a key element in the campaign McChrystal was crafting. Each member of the close team had signed on for three years—there would be no revolving door at the command level requiring new people to constantly get up to speed, a repeat of the Vietnam War, when the US military was said to have fought not one ten-year war, but ten one-year wars.

When he returned to Afghanistan in the summer of 2009 to help lead McChrystal's strategic assessment, Flynn was astonished to discover the paucity of ISAF's intelligence architecture and assets. There was a sum total of one surveillance aerostat, the radar and camera-carrying blimps that Task Force 714 had found so useful in Iraq. There was not even a single multiagency intelligence fusion center of the type that had proven so critical to their operations in Iraq and that were spreading elsewhere throughout the global US counterterrorism network.

For the McChrystal team, the opportunity costs of the Iraq war were on clear display in Afghanistan, where the situation had been allowed to deteriorate for years to the point where the Taliban had mounted a major comeback. Joint Chiefs chairman Mike Mullen had conceded back in 2007 that "in Afghanistan, we do what we can. In Iraq, we do what we must." Not until they prepared to assume command in Afghanistan did the McChrystal team realize just how little that had amounted to. The Afghan campaign, which the United States had largely transferred to the NATO alliance as a peacekeeping mission so as to concentrate on Iraq, was grossly underresourced and undermanned.

As part of a strategic assessment and campaign plan that the McChrystal team developed, Flynn set about building an intelligence architecture modeled on the network-centric template honed to such effectiveness in Iraq. Within a year he would increase the number of aerostats keeping watch over critical areas and routes from a single one to 150. To create a common intelligence picture for the ISAF coalition, Flynn built five intelligence fusion centers and placed them in each of the major regional commands that were led by such coalition partners as the French, Germans, Italians, and Turks. It was a microcosm of the global network of counterterrorism fusion centers that JSOC had helped build. There were still rules in the US intelligence community against sharing critical information with allies, without a lengthy roll call of people back in Washington, DC, signing off on it first. Flynn broke those rules willfully in mixing a daily intelligence omelet that was shared by all the allies in Afghanistan. US and allied soldiers were being killed almost daily in Afghanistan, and they didn't have time to play by Washington rules. Flynn was considered one of the most innovative minds in the entire US intelligence community, but that kind of creativity came with a maverick streak, and it was on full display in Afghanistan.

Somewhat unexpectedly to many of his cohorts in the intelligence community, the one epiphany that stood out above all others from Flynn's listening tours was how overly focused ISAF had become on simply targeting insurgents. This went beyond the Western "improvements" that confounded local residents; it affected how the very war was being fought. The kinds of manhunting operations they had pioneered at JSOC were now the accepted norm. Every tactical operations center in-country had the link-chain schematic of Taliban networks proudly displayed front and center, but they largely omitted the operational context that made sense of the ongoing conflict. We know who the enemy is, Flynn would stress, but who are ISAF's natural friends in this fight? What are the prices of commodities on local markets, how many children are in schools, who is responsible for mitigating local land disputes, and how do all of those data points affect the thinking of the average Afghan in terms of his or her continuing support for international forces or, conversely, for the Taliban? The lesson Mike Flynn most wanted to stress was that intelligence-driven operations were not limited to hunting terrorists and insurgents. Every conventional foot patrol, logistics movement, and decision-making cycle should be shaped by, and contribute to, a common all-source intelligence picture.

The US military's information dominance on conventional battlefields was so complete that it created a sense of hubris when it came to understanding local cultures and the human terrain. Flynn believed conventional, force-on-force operations, such as Desert Storm in 1991 and the three-week "shock and awe" Iraq invasion of 2003, were the anomalies. The US military had spent far more time operating in complex, unconventional battlefields in Central America, the Caribbean, the Balkans, Iraq, Africa, and now Afghanistan—dirty little wars against insurgencies and terrorists that typically took a decade or more to defeat. Prior to 9/11, no one in the US military wanted to talk about that fact, because it reminded them of Vietnam and defeat. After three "listening tours" in 2009, what he was learning about Afghanistan also called to mind the very real potential for defeat, and he was determined to start an uncomfortable conversation on the topic.

Later, in early 2010, a report that Flynn coauthored about his impressions of intelligence gathering in Afghanistan would be published by the centrist think tank Center for a New American Security (CNAS). In what amounted to a howl of frustration from the Afghan wilderness by a senior official, Flynn, deputy chief of staff for intelligence for ISAF, wrote: "Eight years into the war in Afghanistan, the U.S. intelligence community is only marginally relevant to the overall strategy. Having focused the overwhelming majority of its collection efforts and analytical brain-power on insurgent groups, the vast intelligence apparatus is unable to answer fundamental questions about the environment in which U.S. and allied forces operate." Intelligence officers, he went on, were "ignorant of local economics," "hazy about who the powerbrokers are," "incurious about the correlations between development aid and local influence," and "disengaged from people in the best position to find answers."

After the CNAS report was published, Flynn's inbox would light up with hate e-mail from the heads of the various US intelligence agencies. He had purposely failed to have the report vetted through the normal channels, and he broke protocol by having it published by an independent think tank instead of one of the military's own official publications, where it would undoubtedly have gathered dust in the basements of war college libraries. To each of the hate mails wondering why he had not raised the issue directly with the intelligence agency heads, Flynn would offer a simple reply: I have been trying to tell you about this problem for months. Go check your e-mail inbox.

Despite the bravado, Flynn knew publishing his criticisms might well have sabotaged a promising career. For days after the report was published, he would wait for a call from Stan McChrystal relieving him of duty, but it never came. Given the controversy that the report kicked up for his bosses back in the Pentagon, Flynn didn't feel at ease until Defense Secretary Gates was asked about it by a reporter, and curtly replied that he thought it was brilliant; next question? Soon afterward, Flynn heard that military units scheduled to deploy to Afghanistan in 2010 as part of the surge had expanded their training beyond insurgent sweeps and capture-or-kill counterterrorism missions, to include more instruction on local culture and language. The maverick in Mike Flynn never looked back.

IN WASHINGTON, DC, in the fall of 2009, CENTCOM commander General David Petraeus was fighting a rear-guard action on behalf of General McChrystal's counterinsurgency strategy in Afghanistan, and there were times when the effort very nearly caused him to blow a fuse. Even in internal Pentagon deliberations some of the arguments and counterproposals bordered on ludicrous.

General James "Hoss" Cartwright, the vice chairman of the Joint Chiefs of Staff and a Marine Corps pilot who had spent most of the past decade commanding strategic nuclear forces, was reportedly favored by the White House as the next chairman of the Joint Chiefs. In one meeting, Cartwright proposed to Petraeus that they adopt a strictly counterterrorism strategy in Afghanistan with the addition of an extra ten thousand Special Forces manhunters. Even if that would work in halting the Taliban's momentum and rolling the insurgency back, Petraeus shot back, which it most certainly would not, there weren't ten thousand extra Special Forces troops waiting around to join the fight. Every SEAL, Delta Force, and Green Beret unit was already 100 percent committed to the fight, as were such key enablers as Special Forces aviation and ISR. Many Special Forces troopers had already logged twelve or thirteen four-month combat deployments.

Petraeus finally became uncharacteristically exercised during a meeting at the White House of the National Security Council, where the senior national security team was once again debating the Afghan strategy. Sitting at the large conference table and listening to all the proposals for a limited counterterrorism strategy, he looked around and recognized the essential problem. Even after nearly a decade of conflict, the officials atop the national security pyramid had no personal experience with the wars they were fighting. Joint Chiefs chairman Admiral Mike Mullen had as his frame of personal reference operating a ship during Vietnam. Deputy National Security adviser Lieutenant General Douglas Lute, the "war czar," had served on Central Command's staff, but his personal frame of reference for warfare was the 1991 Persian Gulf War. So it went around the table. Petraeus thought to himself, nobody else in the room has actually experienced this war — that's why the debate made no sense to him.

"Look, the underlying mission in Afghanistan is to insure that it never again becomes sanctuary for al-Qaeda or other transitional terrorist groups," he recalled interjecting. "That means halting the Taliban's momentum, accelerating training of Afghan security forces, and setting the conditions for them to take responsibility for their own security. And you can't do that with a counterterrorism strategy of manhunting alone! You can hunt men all day long, but if you don't clear territory and hold it, then the enemy is just going to keep regenerating. So, anyone who believes we can win in Afghanistan with counterterrorism operations alone is mistaken. There is no foundation for that idea whatsoever."

STANLEY MCCHRYSTAL WAS well aware that the months-long review of his strategy for a way forward in Afghanistan had badly strained the relationship between his team and a White House suspicious that the US military was trying to maneuver a new president already burdened by a historic economic crisis into a Vietnam-like quagmire. When he had first assumed command in the spring of 2009, he had actually believed that no additional forces would be needed. But the mission, as he came to understand it, was to defeat the Taliban and protect the Afghan population so as to give the Afghan government and security forces breathing room to grow and assert their authority. That was the clear implication of Obama's public statements that Afghanistan was a "war of necessity" and the Taliban, if left unchecked, would provide an "an even larger safe haven from which al-Qaeda would plot to kill more Americans." And if the mission was to check the Taliban, then McChrystal realized that the troop numbers didn't add up. Counterinsurgency doctrine called for twenty security force troops—army and police—for every thousand residents in a given area. For a country with an approximate population of 24 million people, Afghanistan by that calculus would need at least 400,000 security force personnel, far more than the 176,000 it currently had. His team thus recommended growing Afghan security forces by 230,000 troops and police, a years-long enterprise. In the interim he had requested deployment of an additional 40,000 US or coalition forces as a bridge to provide security.

The first sign of real trouble with the White House had come when his strategic assessment laying out those numbers was leaked to the press in September. Just as he had feared, the White House staff assumed that McChrystal's team leaked the assessment to put pressure on President Obama, and to limit his options to the ones preferred by the military. Of course, that was possible, but the review had been passed up the Pentagon hierarchy all the way to the Office of the Secretary of Defense. The guilty party could be anyone of scores of people who were familiar with the assessment. As far as McChrystal personally knew, the White House was wrong about his staff's leaking the report, but the damage was done.

Trouble had mounted in October when he gave a speech at a London think tank. In that instance, his many years in "black operations" at the helm of JSOC, sheltered away from the limelight and the prying eyes of the press, may have cost him. When asked by a reporter whether a more limited counterterrorism campaign might be viable for Afghanistan, McChrystal replied honestly that he thought a campaign focused on capture-or-kill strikes would be insufficient to stabilize the country. But it was naive to offer a public opinion on a matter that was still under debate within the administration, and to think there would not be repercussions. Although he never mentioned Joe Biden by name, the comments were interpreted as a swipe at the vice president's preferred option of a limited counterterrorism strategy.

The Obama administration's internal deliberations on the way forward in Afghanistan were further complicated when a United Nations–backed monitor declared a September election won by Afghan president Hamid Karzai so fraudulent that a runoff election was necessary. The pronouncement infuriated Karzai, who blamed Western interference in internal Afghan affairs. This strained a relationship between US officials and Karzai that McChrystal believed was essential to his counterinsurgency campaign.

Karzai's bitter indignation was stoked further by a series of classified diplomatic cables from US Ambassador to Afghanistan Karl Eikenberry, a former Army lieutenant general who had commanded US forces in that country. In the cables, which were released to the press by the antisecrecy group WikiLeaks, Eikenberry described Karzai as "not an adequate strategic partner," and said he very much doubted the Afghan government had the institutional capacity to provide governance in any areas cleared by US or NATO forces. He thus questioned not only the efficacy of more US troops, but also McChrystal's proposed counterinsurgency campaign writ large. Clearly, the tight civil-military coordination forged by US ambassador Ryan Crocker and General Petraeus during the Iraq surge would not be replicated in Afghanistan.

Despite obvious misgiving in many quarters, to include the White House staff, the US military chain had eventually coalesced behind the McChrystal counterinsurgency strategy. Given the dominant narrative that only Petraeus's counterinsurgency campaign had reversed the tide of the Iraq war just a few years earlier, and Petraeus's continued advocacy for McChrystal's strategy, the surprise would have been if US military leaders had concluded otherwise.

After the months-long tug-of-war between the White House and his team, McChrystal finally received his marching orders on December 1, 2009. On that day President Obama traveled to West Point to announce his surge strategy for Afghanistan. Eschewing a limited counterterrorism strategy or a rapid transfer of security responsibilities to unprepared Afghan security forces as "muddle through" options, Obama announced the deployment of an additional 30,000 US troops—10,000 less than the 40,000 troops McChrystal's team had requested—and gave a deadline for withdrawing them of July 2011. McChrystal would have roughly eighteen months to salvage the Afghan war, and the mission would be the integrated counterinsurgency campaign he had advocated.

"We will pursue the following objectives within Afghanistan," the president told the American public. "We must deny al-Qaeda a safe haven. We must reverse the Taliban's momentum and deny it the ability to overthrow the government. And we must strengthen the capacity of Afghanistan's security forces and government so that they can take lead responsibility for Afghanistan's future."

McChrystal was gratified that his campaign strategy had finally won the day, and he could live with the eighteen-month deadline and reduction in his troop request by ten thousand, though that would make an already Herculean job that much riskier. But he would never feel entirely comfortable with the process that produced the decision, which left in its wake a lot of bruised feelings and distrust.

McChrystal tapped his former Delta Force leader to serve as the commander of Coalition Forces Special Operations Component Command–Afghanistan (CFSOCC-A). It was a relatively newly created billet, and the fact that Scott Miller was only the second one-star general to fill it was controversial. Within the Special Forces community there was still residual tension between the traditional Green Berets, or "white" Special Forces, and the direct-action "black" Special Operations commandos from Delta Force. The Green Berets needn't have worried about Scott Miller, though. After spending his career in hyperintense direct operations, Miller was determined to see what lay beyond those narrow fields of fire.

As commander of all Special Forces in Afghanistan, Miller's prime focus was on a pilot program called Village Stability Operations (VSO), begun just the previous fall. Much of ISAF was focused on a top-down campaign of securing major cities and population centers as part of a classic counterinsurgency "ink spot" strategy, where coalition forces "clear, hold, and build" zones of security and normalcy that slowly expand and interlink, like inkblots seeping on a page, extending the reach and legitimacy of the Afghan government. The VSO campaign was a bottom-up approach that embedded Special Forces units in villages, where they helped organize, arm, and train local defense militias to protect their villages from Taliban intimidation. The goal was to help fill in the major gaps and seams between slowly expanding governance at the federal, provincial, and district levels and the thousands of remote rural villages where the majority of Afghans lived.

There was a tradition of such local protective forces in Afghanistan, where they were called by such terms as *arbakai, chalweshtai,* and *mahali satoonkay.* The Musa Hiban dynasty that ruled Afghanistan for much of the twentieth century used them to achieve one of the country's most stable periods, roughly between 1929 and the communist takeover and Soviet invasion in 1979. As opposed to large militias at the command of warlords, the village defense forces answered to local councils called *shura* or *jirga,* and they were traditionally disbanded once dangers passed.

Under Scott Miller's leadership the VSO program was expanded into seventeen Afghan districts, supporting more than three thousand local defenders. One of the earliest deployments was in Khakrez, a village in Kandahar Province that the Taliban used as a sanctuary for staging attacks on nearby Kandahar City. The Taliban employed typically brutal methods of executions and abductions to intimidate the local population, and they made the village a hub for moving weapons and equipment to their local operators. They also replaced the local *shuras* and *jirgas* and established a shadow government that effectively ruled the town. That is, until the arrival of a US Special Forces detachment that quickly expelled the Taliban and, with the consent of local elders, established a village defense force.

The Special Operations Forces (SOF) detachment in Kharez began by establishing a neighborhood watch program to act as an early-warning network in the event of any Taliban infiltration or nearby activity. Because the SOF detachment lived in the village and among the population at the invitation of the local elders, they were able to quickly mount a response alongside local Afghan police and village defenders. The detachment conducted dozens of *shuras* with local leaders, who empowered them to establish a reaction force of men from local villages.

By early 2010 positive results were visible. According to surveys conducted by the US Agency for International Development, the VSO team's efforts led to a reduction in insurgent attacks, the return of many displaced families who had fled Taliban intimidation, and a reopening of a formerly shuttered local bazaar that now boasted more than forty shops and stores. The increased security also led to a surge in tourism at the local Shah Agha Maqsud Shrine, where an estimated twenty thousand pilgrims came during the most recent New Year celebrations. Perhaps most impressive to the SOF detachment, local children would warn them of the Taliban's presence. The willingness of village children to openly interact with US Special Forces troops was a hopeful sign that coalition forces had won the trust of the locals. The grip of the Taliban's shadow government had been broken.

In early 2010, Scott Miller also began to see early sprouts from a seed that he, Mike Flynn, and Stanley McChrystal had planted in the Pentagon back in the spring of 2009. They had been frustrated that the US military, after so many years of fighting, still lacked a basic understanding of the complex human terrain in Afghanistan. Their answer was an Afghan Hands program modeled after the China Hands program of the 1930s and 1940s that had produced a cadre of military officers steeped in local culture, history, and language. McChrystal convinced Joint Chiefs chairman Mullen to create a cadre of several hundred similarly expert Afghan Hands, who were inculcated in the complex cultural and sociological dynamics of Afghanistan and Pakistan, and who would deploy and redeploy to the same regions of Afghanistan so as to build lasting relationships with the locals. The armed services had predictably resisted and slow-rolled the idea as an interference in the career tracking of their personnel, but by early 2010 the first Afghan Hands were finally arriving in theater and being dispersed throughout the country.

After he began his own study of the human terrain on his deployment to Afghanistan, Miller realized it was an exercise in anthropology of infinite complexity, with uncharted depths and dangers that would claim the lives of many US and coalition soldiers. But after desperate fighting in some of the world's dark corners, from Mogadishu, Somalia, to the hardscrabble towns along Iraq's Western Euphrates, just once Scott Miller yearned to end a combat rotation convinced that he had won. That would mean understanding the people you were fighting for.

ON THE NIGHT of June 21, 2010, Mike Flynn was getting settled in the back of the command's Gulfstream IV aircraft, contemplating a stack of briefing books assembled for his long flight back to the United States to brief the next US Army unit scheduled to deploy to Afghanistan as part of the 2010 surge. The bulk of the three thousand extra troops were nearly in place, and the intelligence laydown he was going over was in many ways more hopeful than the previous year. The US-led coalition was finally poised to go on the offensive in Afghanistan, and at long last he felt good about their chances.

As his boss, Stan McChrystal, put it, over the past year they had managed to throw a wet blanket over a raging fire, and reverse the perception among ISAF commanders and Afghan leadership that the country was going down in flames. After dispatching extra US Marines and Special Forces to Helmand Province in the spring of 2010 as part of the initial increase of troops, ISAF had reported a classic counterinsurgency response where security improvements led local leaders and civilians to provide more intelligence on the whereabouts of the Taliban, beginning the virtuous cycle of counterinsurgency that had helped turn around the Iraq campaign.

In the first half of 2010, ISAF and Afghan forces had also inadvertently killed or wounded fewer Afghan civilians than during a similar period in 2009, though the number was still far too high. Incidents of errant allied air strikes tragically wiping out a wedding party, or killing civilians gathered around stalled fuel trucks, recalled the Soviet Army's old carpet-bombing techniques in the minds of the Afghans, and undermined ISAF's argument that the coalition was focused on protecting the population. McChrystal had thus issued a tactical directive asking US and coalition troops to show "courageous restraint" in calling in air strikes and artillery when civilian casualties were possible. If the lives of coalition troops were threatened, then the rules of engagement had not changed. But if it came to a choice between killing insurgents and risking civilian casualties, or letting the enemy escape to fight another day, McChrystal wanted his forces to err on the side of caution. He had also directed all units to stop reporting on the number of insurgents killed, believing that was a false metric in a population-centric counterinsurgency campaign. The McChrystal team had also begun to instill more of the warrior culture in NATO's notoriously laid-back headquarters in Kabul—banning alcohol, closing down the Burger King, and spurring headquarters staff to a breakneck pace of operations.

When Mike Flynn thought about what they had accomplished in the past year, it was his boss's empathy and unmatched relationship-building skills that stood out. People forgot that the man who had built the most fearsome manhunting network in history accomplished the feat only by breaking down the walls of mistrust and suspicion that traditionally separated military, intelligence, and law enforcement agencies, both domestic and international. Every rung in that ladder was a relationship that McChrystal had formed out of candor and follow-through. Not transactional relationships of "you scratch my back, I'll scratch yours," but sturdier ones built on trust and hard promises kept.

Nowhere were McChrystal's relationship-building talents on clearer display than in the close bond he formed with the mercurial Afghan president. Hamid Karzai had confounded and at times infuriated five US ambassadors, eleven previous ISAF commanders, and any number of Western envoys, but therein lay part of the problem. With a constantly rotating and confusing cast of Western supporters, Karzai confronted the challenge of ruling a poor and overwhelmingly illiterate country beset by warlords, drug mafias, and ethnic and tribal clashes among its Pashtun, Hazara, Tajik, and Uzbek peoples. Not to mention a determined Islamist extremist insurgency in the Taliban that enjoyed sanctuary across the border in Pakistan, and some degree of support from Pakistan's opaque Inter-Service Intelligence agency. McChrystal had established a close bond with President Karzai primarily by showing respect for the office and empathy for a man who had one of the hardest jobs on earth, one that included semiregular assassination attempts on Karzai's life.

Similarly, McChrystal had made it a priority to establish a relationship of candor and trust with General Ashfaq Kayani, Pakistan's army chief, trying to shed light on a US-Pakistan relationship that was shrouded in double-dealing and deep distrust. In the spring of 2010, both Kayani and Karzai made high-profile trips to Washington, DC, where they met with top US officials, signaling progress in two relationships that McChrystal and his team believed were critical to their counterinsurgency campaign.

The Gulfstream carrying Mike Flynn back to the United States was only about an hour out of Kabul when he received an e-mail from his brother Charlie over the aircraft's secure Wi-Fi system. "The Rolling Stone article is out, and it's really bad," the message said. As part of the command's media outreach, they had allowed *Rolling Stone* reporter Michael Hastings access to the command team over the previous few months, including during an April trip to Europe for a NATO conference. For the life of him, Flynn could not imagine how the story could be such a problem.

Minutes later the Gulfstream pilot approached Flynn's seat. "Sir, we've been asked to return to Kabul. I'm told General McChrystal may have to travel back to the United States."

When he arrived back at ISAF headquarters and entered a quiet and nearly deserted operation center just before three a.m., Flynn saw his brother and Stan McChrystal, both in their gym gear of shorts and T-shirts. McChrystal looked grim, having just gotten off the telephone offering an apology to Vice President Biden. McChrystal handed Flynn a copy of the article, headlined "Runaway General." As he sat down to read the feature, Flynn's initial reaction was, "Holy shit!"

The idea to embed journalists within military commands in wartime actually started with the 2003 invasion of Iraq and former defense secretary Donald Rumsfeld, whose press shop figured giving the national press a look under the classified curtain of military operations would help counter the propaganda machine of Iraqi dictator Saddam Hussein, which predictably sought to depict the entire operation as a war crime. The experiment worked well enough that the practice of journalistic embeds continued, though it carried risks and tensions for both sides. For journalists who naturally bonded with American soldiers during combat operations, the greatest challenge was to maintain enough distance to report fairly and objectively, and separate the truly meaningful from the merely sensational. Military commanders had to trust that journalists would honor an agreement not to reveal classified information that might jeopardize lives and the mission, and generally not to engage in "gotcha" journalism that sought to make controversies out of comments made in the heat of battle, or in the testosterone-fueled fraternity of a military command in wartime.

McChrystal had somewhat reluctantly agreed to all the media engagements because he felt acutely that no one else was selling his Afghan campaign. The sense he got from Washington was that most people would just
as soon forget the war. He even heard the refrain "McChrystal's War" ban-
died about, as if somehow he were personally to blame for a mismanaged
conflict that would soon pass the decade mark. So, his team reached out to
the media to try to build support for the war effort. When the McChrystal
team allowed Hastings to embed in their inner sanctum, those combustible
tensions and risks ignited in a five-alarm controversy. In "Runaway General," the journalist characterized the McChrystal team as a collection of
loose cannons led by a strutting alpha-male whose "slate-blue eyes have the
unsettling ability to drill down when they lock on you. If you've fucked up
or disappointed him, they can destroy your soul without the need for him
to raise his voice."

As Hastings reported, McChrystal's aides jokingly referred to themselves
as 'Team America,' after a raunchy movie send-up of the time, *Team America: World Police*, which depicts an elite, and clueless, US counterterrorism
organization. In the article, McChrystal's aides are quoted anonymously as
firing scattershot volleys of contempt at much of the civilian chain of command, up to and including President Obama, who is supposedly "intimi-
dated" by the military. Vice President Joe Biden is nicknamed by an aide as
"Bite Me"; National Security Adviser Jim Jones is referred to as a "clown";
Special Afghan-Pakistan Envoy Richard Holbrooke is a "wounded animal"
terrified of being fired; and the US ambassador to Afghanistan, Karl Eikenberry is a betrayer who covers his backside "for the history books." NATO
allies, such as the French, also come in for derision during a visit to Paris
by the McChrystal team, with McChrystal's dining with a senior French
minister characterized by an aide as "fucking gay."

"Who the hell is saying all this crap?" Flynn wondered out loud after
reading the article, feeling a growing sense of dread. He knew the comments didn't come from McChrystal or his brother Charlie, and they
sure didn't come from Flynn. Whoever said them had come awfully close
to running afoul of Article 88 of the Uniform Code of Military Justice,
which prescribes a court-martial for "any commissioned officer who uses

contemptuous words against the President, the Vice President, Congress, [or] the Secretary of Defense."

Feeling himself in a waking nightmare, McChrystal decided to go for a run to try to clear his head. He remembered that his wife had had misgivings about the *Rolling Stone* reporter after reading his earlier book and some articles, which she felt stabbed the US military in the back. It was too late now. Whatever his objections to the fairness or accuracy of the article, he understood right away the potential repercussions. When word came that he was being recalled immediately to Washington, his inner circle conjured the same dismal image: President Harry Truman recalling from the Korean War General Douglas MacArthur, the hero of World War II and the Inchon landing never to return again to the field of command.


IN THE END, McChrystal, despite his unmatched relationship-building skills, could not overcome a White House staff and Pentagon chain of command determined to keep him at arm's length from his commander in chief. The circumstances of a new administration's trying to cope with a historic financial meltdown and not one, but two unpopular wars, sowed distrust between the staffs of the president and his wartime field general, dooming the one relationship that mattered the most.

"Runaway General" predictably ignited a firestorm of controversy in the media, where it was depicted as fresh evidence of a dysfunctional civil-military relationship between the commander in chief and his civilian team and a military chain of command accustomed to getting its way after nearly a decade of war. NATO secretary general Anders Fogh Rasmussen stepped into the controversy with a ringing endorsement of McChrystal as the right commander to lead the alliance effort at a critical moment in the Afghan war, and Afghan president Hamid Karzai lobbied personally against his dismissal. The support gave hope to McChrystal's team, which figured that President Obama might simply dress down the general before the public, and then send him back to Afghanistan to lead the offensive counterinsurgency campaign they had spent more than a year preparing.

The ISAF operations center was standing room only on June 23, the big video screen in the center tuned to BBC television cameras waiting in the Rose Garden. The previous forty hours had been a roller coaster at the Kabul headquarters, as McChrystal's team awaited the verdict from Washington. Mike Flynn had identified the junior staff guys who had mouthed off to the *Rolling Stone* reporter, thinking they were off the clock and thus off the record, and blowing off soldier steam. They had been stupid, but everyone felt legitimately burned by a reporter who would use intemperate comments by junior staff to paint a picture of McChrystal's senior team and the command culture that no one on the inside recognized.

They all watched as a grim-faced President Obama walked to the microphone, flanked by Vice President Biden, Defense Secretary Gates, JCS Chairman Mullen, and CENTCOM commander Petraeus. McChrystal was nowhere to be seen.

The president said he had accepted the resignation of McChrystal as the top US commander in Afghanistan, and he named General Petraeus as his replacement. Although he offered praise for McChrystal's "remarkable career in uniform" and expressed regret, Obama concluded that "the conduct represented in the recently published article does not meet the standard that should be set by a commanding general. It undermines the civilian control of the military that is at the core of our democratic system, and it erodes the trust that's necessary for our team to work to achieve our objectives in Afghanistan."

The Rose Garden announcement was met with stunned silence in the ISAF operations center in Kabul. Many of the officers there were veterans of Task Force 714 and had fought together for many years, and most would echo Scott Miller's sentiment that in Stanley McChrystal they had found that rare combat leader they were willing to follow anywhere. No one was more stunned than the Flynn brothers, and as he looked around the ops center Mike Flynn read in the astonished faces a mirror reaction of his own. "Oh my God," he thought. "What just happened?"

Looking back at that moment much later, McChrystal voiced regret that he never had the chance to build a relationship of trust with a new commander in chief and his staff at the White House. When his classified strategic assessment was leaked to the press, and when his comments at a London think tank endorsing a counterinsurgency strategy were not cleared by the White House, they interpreted it as just short of insubordination.

"If I could do anything different, I would have worked even harder to build trust and respect in that relationship [with the White House], so we had a foundation of personal connections between the key players as we tackled this very hard and complex task," McChrystal told me later. There is always an initial cultural gap between a new administration and the US military to overcome, he noted, and it takes time to build trust between people of very different backgrounds even during the best of times. "In this case, you had a new administration that was dealing with a historic financial meltdown and already committed to fighting a 'war of necessity' that was going much worse than they realized, and suddenly military leaders are asking for even more troops, and the whole dynamic starts to feel like Vietnam to them. There were good people on both sides trying to get to a good outcome, but we needed time to build mutual trust. And there just wasn't any time."

The fact that the torch of command in Afghanistan was passed from McChrystal to Petraeus was rife with ironies. Uniquely among their generation of officers, the two generals stood in the public mind for different approaches to fighting the threat that reached US shores on September 11, 2001: McChrystal, the hard-charging Special Forces commander who built a global counterterrorism network driven by the instincts of the manhunt, and Petraeus, the professor of counterinsurgency who retaught the US military how to drain the swamps that fed extremism in Iraq and Afghanistan. By replacing McChrystal with Petraeus, Obama was essentially doubling down on a counterinsurgency strategy that the country and his own administration had lost patience in. The president's own instincts going forward were to rely ever more heavily on the counterterrorism model once personified by McChrystal. That both these seminal military figures of the post-9/11 era would ultimately resign under clouds of controversy also foreshadowed the wages of duty that would come due for so many leaders of America's longest wars.

# ELEVEN

# American Jihad

## 2010–2011

B Y 2010 THE FACE OF JIHADI TERRORISM WAS CHANGING ONCE again. With an embattled al-Qaeda core in Pakistan unable to launch meticulously planned terrorist spectaculars, its affiliates were increasingly looking for softer targets in the seams of US counterterrorism defenses. They were also adopting an American vernacular and online sophistication that set off alarms in counterterrorism circles. The English-language sermons of Anwar al-Awlaki were increasingly popular on YouTube, and under his direction al-Qaeda in the Arabian Peninsula (AQAP) had that summer published the first issue of its online, English-language magazine, *Inspire*.

Besides al-Awlaki, there was also Adam Gadahn, a Californian who had become a key spokesman for the core of al-Qaeda; and Omar Hammami, a US citizen and former resident of Alabama who had joined al-Shabab and produced jihadist recruiting videos in English from Somalia. This new generation of Islamist extremists were far more adept than Osama bin Laden and his senior lieutenants in exploiting social media to form intimate connections online. FBI officials were increasingly seeing the fingerprints of al-Qaeda and other extremist groups on YouTube, Facebook, and a host of other social media.

The number of would-be jihadists who responded to terrorist recruiting efforts was still small. Since 9/11, only fourteen Americans had been killed on US soil by jihadist terrorists: one by Carlos Bledsoe and the others by Nidal Hassan. Yet al-Qaeda and its affiliates had undoubtedly adopted a strategy of recruiting English-speaking operatives, primarily Americans, and every indication was that the outreach was having the desired effect. That was the message behind the failed plots of Najibullah Zazi, the Denver shuttle-bus driver and permanent US resident who had planned to bomb the New York subway system; Umar Farouk Abdulmutallab, the al-Awlaki acolyte who attempted to down an airliner over Detroit; and Faisal Shahzad, the Connecticut resident who very nearly triggered a car bomb in New York's Time Square. Jihad was coming to America.

The question was whether US counterterrorism agencies were keeping pace with a rapidly evolving threat. After a decade of war, the expansive network of operatives who served together in Iraq and Afghanistan certainly constituted a unique fraternity scattered throughout the intelligence, law enforcement, and military communities. To a person they instinctively grasped that every minute spent on intramural bickering was time lost in the hunt for the enemy. The members of that fraternity were also discovering that there was an inverse relationship between interagency cooperation and dysfunctional bureaucratic competition. The former declined the farther you traveled from a war zone, and the latter increased the closer you came to the Washington, DC, beltway.

That realization occurred to Brian McCauley almost every day he reported for duty at CIA headquarters in Langley, Virginia. His office was bigger than any he had occupied at FBI headquarters. There were the familiar photographs on the wall, some of them of his team in Afghanistan decked out in camo and automatic weapons, a not so subtle reminder to anyone who stopped by that the country was still at war. His title was impressive enough: FBI assistant deputy director for human intelligence, and senior FBI representative to the CIA from the bureau's National Security Branch. And yet when he came to work, McCauley often felt a rumbling in his guts that had nothing to do with the three double espressos it typically took to get through the day, or the parasite he had picked up in Afghanistan that was eating a hole in his stomach. There was a reason his predecessors had nicknamed the CIA-FBI liaison swap a "hostage exchange program."

After working so long in a tightknit multiagency task force in Afghanistan, McCauley was astonished that there were still holdouts in the US intelligence community who had a pre-9/11 mind-set, and came to work each day eager to stiff arm other agencies in order to take credit for some golden nugget of intelligence. Yet he dealt with them more times than he cared to count. An FBI legal attaché overseas would share intelligence on a suspected car bomb plot that the CIA analysts in Washington dismissed out of hand. A State Department regional security officer would complain that the FBI or CIA had shared intelligence with a foreign intelligence agency without going through him first. Or some prima donna analyst would fail to share at all, convinced that a piece of intelligence was beyond anyone else's "need to know." After a day spent mediating such squabbles and turf wars, McCauley felt like the marriage counselor for the US intelligence community.

When the internal arguments became too heated, McCauley would reach out to his network of contacts from Afghanistan to cut through bureaucratic cultures that in some cases valued form over function, members of that wartime fraternity sealed deals with a handshake or a single phone call. Cooperation was instinctive, not transactional. "Victor," the former CIA station chief in Kabul that McCauley had become close to during his Counter-IED (Improvised Explosive Device) investigation, essentially replied to any request from him with two words: Anytime. Anywhere. "Peter," another CIA operative in Afghanistan and a former Green Beret, had also been at the US embassy on the day of the bombing that inspired the Counter-IED project. He was the CIA official who contributed funds to the always cash-strapped FBI to help pay McCauley's sources as part of the investigation.

Peter would sometimes stop by McCauley's Langley office and regale him with stories of strained relations between senior CIA leadership and Joint Special Operations Command (JSOC). After one particularly condescending CIA briefing by a senior agency official at JSOC headquarters in Fort Bragg, North Carolina, complete with a bunch of hand-drawn charts stressing the patently obvious, JSOC commander Admiral William McRaven had become positively frosty toward the agency. A JSOC official stormed out of two subsequent interagency meetings.

Because they were the twin hammers of the counterterrorism program, there was an inherent tension and the potential for an unhealthy competition between the CIA's Counterterrorism Center and Special Activities Division and Joint Special Operations Command. Peter had been worried enough about the strains between the two that he reached out to his former boss in Afghanistan, Lieutenant General John Mulholland Jr., commander of US Army Special Operations Command. With one phone call the problem was smoothed over, and Peter was vouched for as part of the fraternity. And the next time he briefed at Fort Bragg, Admiral McRaven and his staff were friendly and accommodating. Only Peter caught a bunch of flack back at Langley for not taking a more senior agency official along to conduct the briefing.

McCauley recalled how different the spirit of cooperation had been back in Afghanistan. He told the story of the Afghan general who wanted him dead, and how he had enlisted the help of the National Security Agency (NSA) in tapping the man's cell phone. Every time McCauley would meet with the general, the NSA would listen in on his phone calls afterward just to make sure he wasn't putting out a hit on McCauley. Yet recently he reached out to an NSA counterpart to try to arrange a lunch meeting. "True story, I swear to God," McCauley said. "This guy I know at the NSA, he's always looking down at his damn shoes when he talks to you. Never looks you in the eye, like he's afraid he might give away a secret with a direct glance. So I e-mail this guy asking if he wants to do lunch, and he replies, 'Yes. TS.' Top secret! True story, I swear!"

As they rose to the top of their respective agencies, members of the unique wartime fraternity found themselves frequently butting heads against bureaucratic inertia and the interagency tribalism that bred distrust in the nation's capital. They had witnessed firsthand how the enemy exploited those disconnects, and it nurtured in each of them an instinct not traditionally found among Washington bureaucracies: Sure, I have your back. Certainly the intelligence picture they saw each day left no doubt that the terrorists they had fought on faraway battlefields continued to probe relentlessly for gaps in the nation's defenses.

ON NOVEMBER 4, 2010, Mohamed Osman Mohamud, a nineteen-year-old naturalized US citizen from Somalia and a former student at Oregon State University, was driving home in Portland, Oregon, after detonating a backpack bomb as a trial run for mass slaughter. During the drive, Mohamud's handler began to express doubts. The men were preparing to blow up a Christmas tree lighting ceremony at Pioneer Courthouse Square in Portland, Oregon, and now Mohamud's accomplice questioned whether his charge was capable of looking at all of the mangled bodies, including those of women and children.

Mohamud was undeterred. "Do you remember when 9/11 happened, when those people were jumping from the skyscrapers? I thought that was awesome," he replied. "I want whoever is attending [the lighting celebration] to leave either dead or injured."

He soon matched his chilling words with actions. After returning home from the trial run, he donned a white robe and recorded a video in which he claimed responsibility for the upcoming terrorist spectacular. Looking into the camera, he asked, "Did you think you could invade a Muslim land, and we would not invade you?"

On November 26 Mohamud parked his van on the outskirts of a crowd gathered for the tree-lighting ceremony. Walking a safe distance away, he attempted to detonate the explosives packed inside the van by calling a cell phone that had been modified as a triggering device. At that moment Mohamud's terrorist handler, who was actually an undercover FBI agent, arrested him.

Mohamed Osman Mohamud's arrest was among a host of elaborate FBI sting operations designed to ensnare would-be jihadists in fake plots of their own fevered imaginings. It followed closely on the heels of a similar sting that ensnared Antonio Martinez, a twenty-one-year-old convert to Islam who was indicted on charges of scheming with an undercover agent to blow up a military recruiting station in Maryland. In October 2010, four

Muslim converts in the Bronx were convicted of planning, with another FBI informant, to bomb synagogues and shoot down military transports with antiaircraft missiles. Those Potemkin plots were becoming part of the new normal in homeland security, as al-Awlaki and other English-speaking extremists continued to recruit terrorists over the Internet, inspiring them to launch attacks on the homeland.

In response the FBI shifted its focus to preventive investigations that employed confidential informants and undercover agents in elaborate stings—a tactic the bureau had used to infiltrate the Mafia and other organized crime groups. The stings were controversial on a number of fronts. Civil libertarians viewed them as tantamount to entrapment. The technique of ensnaring young radicals, recent Muslim converts, and petty criminals in fantastical terrorist conspiracies also set the American Muslim community on edge, potentially putting at risk a key source of intelligence on actual terrorist plots. In 2010 the Muslim Public Affairs Council documented sixteen terrorist schemes that were disrupted with the Muslim community's assistance—nine of which involved homegrown jihadists. Yet American Muslim leaders drew a distinction between those cases and FBI stings based on the hapless delusions of grandeur harbored by alienated and radicalized youth. They accused the FBI of overhyping the terrorist threat to justify spying on mosques without evidence of criminality, infiltrating Muslim congregations using unreliable informants and agents provocateurs, and threatening to deport religious leaders who refused to spy on fellow Muslims.

Certainly the case of Craig Monteilh proved that the use of informants to infiltrate terrorist plots was a tricky business. In 2007 the FBI reportedly paid Monteilh, a felon and convicted forger, $177,000 to infiltrate mosques in Southern California, home to the nation's largest concentration of Muslim Americans. His incendiary jihadist rhetoric so alarmed congregants at an Irvine mosque that the local chapter of the Council on American-Islamic Relations reported Monteilh to police and obtained a restraining order against him. Ultimately, Monteilh sued the FBI for instructing him to conduct random surveillance on mosques and entrap Muslims.

In another case, Imam Foad Farahi of the Shamsuddin Islamic Center in North Miami Beach said that the FBI tried to recruit him secretly in

2004 to inform on the local Muslim community. An Iranian citizen who had lived in the United States for more than a decade, Farahi alleged that the FBI threatened to have him deported for links to terrorism and immigration violations when he refused to act as an informant. Critics charged that the Monteilh and Farahi incidents indicated that the bureau was crossing the line into domestic spying on religious gatherings, strong-arm tactics in turning informants, and outright entrapment. Some imams even began instructing their congregations not to cooperate with the FBI or other law enforcement agencies investigating the recruiting of young men in their mosques as jihadists.

FBI officials argued that the tactics that so alarmed civil libertarians and American Muslim advocates were a direct result of the hard lessons learned from nearly a decade of the "global war on terrorism." They pointed to the part that extremist Salafi imams had played in the radicalization of such terrorists as Carlos Bledsoe, Nidal Hassan, and many others as justification for monitoring some radical mosques. They had little choice but to explore the elusive seam between radicalization and terrorist mobilization. It was in that seam that FBI investigators discovered Mohamed Osman Mohamud.

Mohamud might have lacked the know-how to pull off a terrorist spectacular on his own, but according to the Justice Department affidavit in his case, he was searching for an experienced enabler by reaching out to a suspected terrorist in Pakistan who was under US surveillance. The plot to bomb a crowded square during a Christmas tree-lighting ceremony may have been grandiose, but as was the case with other FBI stings, it was a plot the target personally concocted. Mohamud might have had second thoughts, recoiling from the mental image of all those mangled bodies of women and children, yet every time undercover agents offered him that off-ramp, he drove on with the plot. Mohamud may have been just another hotheaded young man willing to trigger the bomb, but that profile matched a lot of successful terrorists.

What truly worried FBI officials was the appetite for destruction and carnage that a new generation of Islamist extremists were revealing. Terrorist plots that ended in arrests in FBI stings by 2011 included plans for mass-casualty bombings in Baltimore, Portland, Columbus, New York City, and Washington, DC; a Mumbai-style suicide shooting attack on an Illinois shopping mall; the toppling of the Sears Tower in Chicago and an office building in Dallas; the rupturing of the Trans-Alaska Oil Pipeline; attacks on John F. Kennedy International Airport and Los Angeles International Airport; and the destruction of the Brooklyn Bridge.

In its "Terrorist Trial Report Card," the Center for Law and Security at New York University compiled evidence from the fifty most serious terrorist cases since 9/11. The report found that informants were used in 62 percent of the cases, and federal prosecutors won convictions in 92 percent of them. Even though defendants claimed they were entrapped in 28 percent of the cases, an entrapment defense has never been successfully used in a federal terrorism trial since 9/11.

In trying to strike a balance between security and civil liberties, FBI officials insisted that they never launched investigations or surveillance without some indication of wrongdoing, and they denied engaging in religious profiling. "But we are focused on identifying and preempting the threats we see on the horizon," said a senior FBI official. "That means our special agents in charge have to reach out and interact with all the communities we are supposed to protect, and to see in the seams between cases. There's no question that we have adopted a zero-tolerance attitude in terms of terrorism, because we think that's what the American public expects of us."

THE "SOMALI TRAVELERS" disappeared into one of those seams. In a case the FBI used as a model for its counterterrorism and counter-radicalization campaigns, Ralph Boelter, the FBI's special agent in charge in Minneapolis, learned in 2008 that six Somali American youths had vanished from their homes in the Minneapolis–St. Paul area. When word reached relatives that they had resurfaced in Somalia, no one in the tightknit community of Somali immigrants could explain how the young men were able to afford the $2,000 airline tickets. Suspicion in the counterterrorism community immediately focused on the al-Qaeda affiliate in Somalia, al-Shabab ("the Youth").

Boelter had needed answers quick, but the special agent also sensed the investigation needed to proceed delicately. If the bureau rushed the investigation, he worried they would alienate the Somali community and exacerbate the threat. The FBI's new mission of discerning threats on the horizon before they manifest themselves in acts of terrorism required opening good channels of communication with affected communities. "So, we developed a strategy to investigate the case in a way that drew the Somali community closer to us, and that meant overcoming a number of obstacles to mutual trust and understanding, chief among them the investigation itself," Boelter told me.

The strategy of community outreach developed by Boelter and B. Todd Jones, the US attorney for Minnesota, required overcoming deep suspicion of government agents among the clannish Somali immigrant population. Boelter and Jones established regular consultations with local elders and religious leaders. Both men made themselves available to Somali newspapers and television stations in the region. They formed a council of Somali American youth, where they learned of the frustrations and sense of split identity among the young men that made them such inviting targets for terrorist recruiters—alienated young men like Mohamed Osman Mohamud.

The FBI established a two-way cultural exchange. "We basically provided the Somali American community with a 'Civics 101' lesson, explaining how our criminal justice system works, telling them what was and was not a federal crime, and answering their concerns about the immigration system, and suspicions that they were being profiled," Jones recalled. "At the same time we learned a lot about the Somali community, about their clan structure and approach to Islam. In the process of developing those personal relationships and trust, we also hit on an important point of commonality. We are all parents, and all parents are worried about bad things happening to their kids."

In the case of the Somali travelers, the concerns were justified. The investigation revealed that nineteen Somali-American youths had initially traveled to Somalia and joined forces with al-Shabab. Some were recruited by "jihadi rapper" Omar Hammami, who was already under indictment for providing "material support" to terrorists. The Somali Americans were most likely trained by Saleh Ali Saleh Nabhan, a longtime al-Qaeda commander known to work at al-Shabab terror training camps. Two of the Somali youths later became the first known Americans to carry out suicide bombing attacks.

The FBI's engagement with the Somali diaspora in Minneapolis would become the template for its counterradicalization strategy nationally. The outreach borrowed techniques used by local police departments to counter gang activity, and often required ceding the lead to other influence leaders who could better connect with young men at risk, whether it was religious leaders, coaches, teachers, or other mentors. It wasn't sexy work and some radicalized extremists would always slip through the cracks, but every young man diverted from the path of jihad represented a military recruiting station not attacked, an airliner not downed, or a crowded marathon not bombed.

# TWELVE

# Retribution
## May–December 2011

Director of National Intelligence (DNI) James Clapper sat in the White House Situation Room the entire day of May 2, 2011, with the rest of the Obama administration's national security team. If there had been space to pace in the cramped room they called the "Woodshed," they would have all worn holes in the floor to relieve the tension. Instead they stayed mostly glued to their seats around an oblong conference table, or in chairs that lined the walls, consumed with their own thoughts and the drama that periodically unfolded on the video screen at the front of the room.

In ways obvious and not, nearly all the elements of the post-9/11 transformation in the American style of war were coming together in Operation Neptune Spear, the culmination of the decade-long hunt for Osama bin Laden. Clapper owed the creation of his position atop the pyramid of seventeen US intelligence agencies to the 9/11 Commission, for instance, and since becoming only the fourth DNI the previous August, he had assumed the responsibility of briefing the president on intelligence matters each day. Most of those briefings over a span of nearly nine months had centered on the intelligence trail that led to Abbottabad, Pakistan, culminating on this day that none of them would ever forget. During the course of those intelligence briefings, an unlikely rapport had developed between Obama, the former Ivy League lawyer and community activist, and the older and sometimes gruff Clapper, who started his career as a rifleman in the Marine Corps reserves, flew combat support missions over Laos and Cambodia as an Air Force pilot during the Vietnam War, and had risen to the rank of an Air Force lieutenant general specializing in intelligence, before retiring from the military.

Osama bin Laden's trail had gone cold years earlier, but CIA trackers had recently picked up a faint sign in their investigation of the courier network that he used to release more than thirty videos and audiotapes since 9/11. They spent countless man hours trying to stitch together the critical chain of custody for those tapes, and for eight long years the final link in that chain had eluded them. Then analysts learned that a former trusted bin Laden aide and courier who went by the pseudonym Abu Ahmed al-Kuwaiti was actually a Pakistani named Ibrahim Saeed Ahmed. Wiretaps eventually captured a call between Ahmed and an old al-Qaeda acquaintance, who asked what Ahmed had been up to. "I'm back with the people I was with before," he replied. The friend's reply was succinct: "May God facilitate." That short exchange began the endgame to the largest manhunt in history.

Armed with that exchange and the cell phone number, US intelligence agencies traced Ahmed from the teaming streets of Peshawar to a walled compound in the city of Abbottabad, where he and his brother Abrar lived with their families. Their compound became the focal point of a hard stare using the full complement of US surveillance assets: satellite imagery from the National Geospatial-Intelligence Agency that Clapper had once commanded, NSA communications intercepts, Air Force stealth drones with infrared cameras, and an on-scene CIA surveillance team equipped with sophisticated video equipment and powerful telescopes. In a controversial move, the agency even sent a faux "vaccination team" to the compound in an unsuccessful attempt to collect DNA samples that might identify the occupants as bin Laden family members. The ruse led Taliban commanders to later ban polio vaccination teams in Pakistan's tribal areas. The surveillance confirmed that the compound housed a third, large family whose patriarch never ventured outside. His frequent walks in the garden earned the man the nickname "the Pacer."

Clapper was in the White House Situation Room because the 9/11 Commission had recommended separating the functions of what was then a dual-hatted CIA director and director of national intelligence. Under the reorganization, the DNI alone would be responsible for oversight of the entire intelligence community. The reorganization was controversial, with some CIA officials in particular being convinced that it only added an unnecessary layer to an already overly bureaucratic intelligence apparatus. As he observed the mission to capture or kill Osama bin Laden unfold over a matter of many months, Clapper felt it more than validated that initial vision of the 9/11 Commission of an intelligence director separate and above the day-to-day operations of the CIA.

To grasp how intermingled the US military and intelligence communities were becoming, you had only to consider that Defense Secretary Robert Gates was a former CIA director, and CIA director Leon Panetta would eventually replace him as defense secretary. Clapper himself was a former Air Force general officer. General David Petraeus, who executed the counterinsurgency campaigns in Iraq and later Afghanistan, would eventually replace Panetta as CIA director.

There was no doubt in Clapper's mind that the CIA's bin Laden team deserved the credit for developing the initial lead long after bin Laden's trail had gone cold. But watching the globe-spanning intelligence and counterterrorism network then swing into action to run that lead to its source had truly opened his eyes. He also credited General Stanley McChrystal, and the five years he had spent transforming Joint Special Operations Command and infusing it with an operational ethos of F3EA (find, fix, finish, exploit, and analyze). McChrystal had drawn every intelligence and military agency under his big tent and opened the intelligence-sharing architecture to allow them all to plug in to his expanding network. Along the way he helped mentor an entire generation of young operators steeped in mission-focused collaboration, a sociological by-product that was having a profound impact on the entire intelligence community. McChrystal's successor as JSOC commander, Admiral Bill McRaven, was building on that legacy.

What Clapper found most remarkable about that new style of operations was the intermingling and synthesizing of all sources of intelligence into a dramatically compressed time cycle, which was a capability the US government never had in the past. As a Vietnam-era Air Force officer, he remembered when *intelligence* mostly referred to historical information, and the phrase *intelligence integration* never passed anyone's lips. Even signals intelligence and communications intercepts in those days took so long to be absorbed into the intelligence bloodstream that it was rarely actionable in terms of impacting decision-making or operations.

By contrast, when the CIA developed the initial lead on Ahmed that pointed toward the chief perpetrator of the 9/11 attacks, the wider intelligence community had swung into motion to help "fix" his exact location and identity. The fact that JSOC was even then in the process of executing the "finish" and "exploit" phases of the operation, with analysis of intelligence gathered on-scene hopefully soon to come, also spoke to the trust now placed in JSOC and its operational culture of F3EA. McChrystal himself thought that in the old days the CIA would have been reluctant to even share a "golden nugget" of intelligence such as bin Laden's suspected lair. Instead, early proposals for a CIA paramilitary team to execute the operation, or for bin Laden's compound to be bombed from the air, were put aside once Admiral McRaven briefed his plan, and stressed that JSOC and its Special Operations counterterrorism teams of Delta Force and SEAL Team Six had been executing such capture-or-kill night raids for a decade, sometimes a dozen in a single night.

The tension in the White House Situation Room spiked when one of the radar-evading Black Hawk helicopters carrying SEAL Team Six experienced a sudden loss of lift while descending into bin Laden's compound. The helicopter pitched suddenly and careened into one of the compound's high walls, its tail clipping the top in a controlled crash landing. Many of the officials in the Situation Room shared the same mental image: the crash between a Chinook helicopter and a C-130 aircraft at the Desert One staging area in 1980, capping Delta Force's failed mission to rescue the US hostages in Iran with tragedy and dooming the reelection chances of an earlier Democratic president. Defense Secretary Gates had been in that same Situation Room as a CIA analyst in 1980 when the Desert One debacle occurred. That awful memory helped explain why he had initially advised against the raid on bin Laden's suspected compound, before changing his mind and backing the operation.

When the helicopter crashed, President Obama abandoned a video teleconference link with CIA director Leon Panetta, and entered the Situation Room with chief foreign policy speechwriter Ben Rhodes to monitor a video feed. Obama indicated that everyone should stay in their seats, telling his team, "I need to watch this."

OPERATION NEPTUNE SPEAR showed just how far Special Operations Forces had come since 1980. Back then, the first pioneering Delta Force commander, Colonel Charlie Beckwith, and his hostage-rescue team were ferried to Desert One by Marine Corps helicopter pilots with whom they had never worked before, or even rehearsed. Two of the Marine pilots aborted the mission before reaching Desert One because of an unexpected sandstorm. Once there, a third Marine Corps pilot refused to continue due to a mechanical failure. On the ground, the sacrosanct principle of unity of command was broken by a bifurcated command arrangement that split responsibilities between Beckwith and an Air Force colonel he had never met, who was in charge of the C-130 transport on-scene. The Marine Corps helicopter pilot and the Air Force C-130 pilot who ultimately crashed their aircraft into each other, killing eight service members, had likewise never worked or trained together. The senior officers in the chain of command were not from the Special Operations community that planned the mission. When Murphy's law threw a sandstorm and mechanical failure at the operation, the hostage rescue team lacked the experience, adaptability, and margin of error needed to overcome the ever present "unknown unknowns."

In effect, Operation Neptune Spear to capture or kill Osama bin Laden was ten years in the making. After a decade of the war against radical Islamic terrorists, some of the commandos involved had many hundreds of raids under their webbed belts, far exceeding the experience level achieved by their counterparts during the Vietnam War or World War II. Notably, the same SEAL Team Six commander and unit had two years earlier successfully

rescued American merchant marine captain Richard Phillips, who was being held at sea by Somali pirates, three of whom were killed during an operation that included a tricky high altitude–low opening (HALO) parachute
jump over open ocean at night. In the pilots and helicopters of the Army's
160th Special Operations Aviation Regiment, the famed "Night Stalkers,"
the SEAL commandos had their own dedicated air force that had fought
alongside them for a decade. The SEAL Team Six commander reported directly to JSOC commander Admiral Bill McRaven, himself a Navy SEAL,
at his task force headquarters in Bagram Air Base, Afghanistan. JSOC and
its higher headquarters US Special Operations Command in Tampa, Florida, were both the direct result of post–Desert One reforms. The SEAL
team had carefully rehearsed the assault on the bin Laden compound, even
to include contingency planning for a possible downed helicopter.

In those rehearsals the SEALs and Night Stalker pilots had practiced as-
saulting a mock compound with chain-link fences representing the walls of
bin Laden's complex. Only the air inside the thick compound walls turned
out to be warmer and less dense, causing the heavily loaded stealth helicopter to founder. The expert reactions of the Night Stalker pilot in bringing
it to a controlled crash inside the compound walls likely saved the lives of
the SEAL commandos inside, who poured out of the crippled aircraft and
proceeded with the mission. Seeing what had occurred, the second Black
Hawk immediately aborted the plan to drop an assault team on the compound's rooftop, landing it instead to the north side of the compound near
the main gate. McRaven immediately ordered another helicopter staged as
part of a rapid reaction backup force to move forward. Meanwhile, SEAL
Team Six continued almost as if nothing had gone awry.

As a translator and a police dog kept curious onlookers at bay outside the
compound, roughly a score of SEAL commandos swarmed over the complex, blowing doors and reacting by instinct and years of practice to whatever they discovered inside. The commandos anticipated that the house was
wired with explosives, and its inhabitants likely outfitted with suicide vests.
The trusted courier Ibrahim Saeed Ahmed—a.k.a. al-Kuwaiti—responded
with a burst from an AK-47 automatic rifle, signaling that the compound's
inhabitants were not surrendering. He was killed by return fire from the
SEALs that also wounded his wife. Ahmed's brother Abrar and his wife were

shot and killed in the bottom floor of the main house, as the commandos moved methodically to secure all the rooms and gather up terrified children and women.

At the back of the ground floor hallway two operators used C-4 explosives to blow a reinforced door, and quickly a line of commandos formed on the staircase, peering up through night-vision goggles and protecting one another's blind spots with raised weapons. A CIA analyst had already alerted them that bin Laden's twenty-three-year-old son Khalid was likely on the second floor and represented the last line of defense. Halfway up the staircase, the lead SEAL stopped and did something his own team hadn't expected: He quietly called out, "Khalid!" "Khalid!" When a slight, bearded man dressed in white peered around the top of the staircase, he was shot dead.

The lead commandos spread out to secure the second floor, bringing up from the rear two SEALs who continued the assault up the third-floor staircase. At the top of the staircase, the lead SEAL snatched back a curtain obscuring a doorway and immediately tackled two women in robes that he assumed were wired with suicide vests, clearing the way for his teammate.

At that moment Navy SEAL Robert O'Neill turned to his right and looked down the barrel of his weapon at Osama bin Laden. Tall and with a bushy beard, bin Laden had his hand on the shoulder of his wife, Amal, pushing her forward, not surrendering. Either of them could have been wearing a suicide vest. O'Neill shot Osama bin Laden in the face, and then administered two more killing shots to make sure. Other SEAL teammates rushed into the room, administering to a wounded Amal and a young boy on the bed. Someone began taking photographs of bin Laden's body.

"What do we do now?" asked O'Neill, obviously in a daze.

His teammate just smiled at the man who shot Osama bin Laden. "Now we go find the computers."

THE SITUATION ROOM was quiet as the national security team waited for word from inside the compound. In Bagram, Admiral McRaven was closely monitoring the communications net and the grainy, infrared video feed from a drone overhead. His SEAL team was clearly visible as human heat signatures in a pool of green, swarming around the compound. Bright flashes from explosions and automatic weapons fire punctuated the silent video, indicating the human drama playing out.

The intensity of that moment was captured by a White House photographer in an iconic photo that showed the team staring at a video screen at the head of the conference table: Barack Obama, Vice President Joe Biden, White House chief of staff Bill Daley, National Security Adviser Tom Donilon, Secretary of State Hillary Clinton, White House counterterrorism adviser John Brennan, Defense Secretary Robert Gates, Joint Chiefs chairman Admiral Mike Mullen, and DNI James Clapper. Endless minutes passed and the fate of the mission hung in the balance until JSOC commander McRaven, his signature Texas accent unmistakable, radioed back the single code word they had all hoped to hear: "Geronimo." Osama bin Laden had been positively identified.

Watching Operation Neptune Spear unfold, Clapper had marveled at how the norm had become decentralized joint task forces operating largely independently, connected by a globe-spanning network that pulsed with intelligence, surveillance, reconnaissance, and analytic data. Over a decade of conflict, the ethos and techniques of that model of operations had become second nature to a new generation of operators who didn't know anything else. Everyone involved in the hunt for bin Laden had worked as a team, combining the capabilities of their discrete agencies and organizations into a whole that was greater than the sum of its parts. In that sense the raid did represent a high-watermark in the "global war on terrorism," and a model of operations that would increasingly come to define twenty-first-century warfare.

The prominent role that intelligence exploitation and analysis played in that operational model was revealed in the precious time that SEAL Team Six remained at the Abbottabad compound collecting intelligence, even with bin Laden dead and the Pakistani air force potentially bearing down on the site. Computers and logs gathered at the compound would reveal that a decade of hiding and self-imposed isolation had not quelled bin Laden's desire to strike again at the United States. The aging terrorist had written reams of memos to his lieutenants, exhorting them to reclaim the glory of 9/11 by launching another major terrorist attack aimed at America. He had suggested assassinating President Obama and General David Petraeus, then the top US commander in Afghanistan. Bin Laden had urged his deputy to "nominate one of the qualified brothers to be responsible for a large operation in the United States." His correspondence also revealed a deep paranoia brought about by the US targeted killing program. In the year leading up to his death, the CIA had launched a record 118 drone strikes into Pakistan's tribal regions, killing many of those closest to bin Laden. In a forty-eight-page memo written to his deputy, he urged his followers and his own son Hamza to abandon Pakistan's tribal regions for more remote mountain redoubts where thick forests offered cover from prying American satellites and the despised drones.

In death, as in life, Osama bin Laden unified the United States. The administration's national security team followed President Obama from the Situation Room to the East Room, where he would officially confirm that America had at last meted out justice to its old nemesis. Even before the president made the official announcement that bin Laden was dead, word had leaked and crowds were gathering in Lafayette Park outside the gates of the White House. Chants of "USA! USA! USA!" rang out in the night as the national security team followed Obama to the East Room of the White House.

They had been cloistered in the tense confines of the Situation Room all day, and the exuberant sounds of the chants hit James Clapper like a cold wave. He knew that the death of one terrorist was not going to end the threat of terrorism. By the time you are seeking to identify, track, and kill someone, you are probably responding late to the problem. The ideologies and conditions that create people for whom mass murder is a creed were the root cause, but bringing the chief ideologue of violent Islamist extremism to justice at last sent an important message about America's long reach and stubborn memory.

The sense of euphoria that Clapper and the others felt matched and perhaps even exceeded those outside the gates, because it carried a measure of personal redemption. "When I heard those chants of 'USA, USA,' that's when it hit me," Clapper recalled in an interview. "Bin Laden's death was emotional for everyone, but particularly for those of us in the intelligence community, because it provided a sense of closure. We felt like we were closing the circle after a monumental failure."


IN THE JOYOUS faces of young celebrants hugging and singing "The Star-Spangled Banner" outside the White House on the night of bin Laden's death, it was certainly easy to read the emotional and psychological trauma that attended the 9/11 era. The demise of the archterrorist was obviously cathartic for a nation that for years was transfixed by the terrorist threat, and members of Barack Obama's inner circle saw an opportunity to use it as a means to heal the wounds that terrorism had inflicted on the American psyche, and move beyond an era when terrorism was not only a national preoccupation, but the central organizing principle of US foreign and national security policy.

In their view, Obama had been elected president to end the post-9/11 wars in Iraq and eventually Afghanistan, and to turn a page from George W. Bush's "global war on terrorism." They had been sharply criticized by Republicans for abolishing "enhanced interrogation techniques" that amounted to torture, and for four years Congress had blocked the administration from fulfilling its promise to close the Guantánamo Bay detention center that the rest of the world equated with extrajudicial imprisonment and the persecution of Muslims. All of that resistance spoke to the grip that 9/11 and terrorism continued to have on the national consciousness.

In launching the "global war on terrorism" after the 9/11 attacks, President Bush had famously warned the public that "there will be no surrender on the deck of a battleship." But what if the spontaneous celebrations by revelers who heard the news of his death and flocked unbidden to the White House and Ground Zero in New York, followed by bin Laden's burial at sea from the deck of the aircraft carrier USS *Carl Vinson*, represented something like a "Victory Day" in the war against jihadi terrorists?

As the deputy national security adviser for strategic communications, Ben Rhodes had been at Obama's side virtually the entire day of May 2, 2011. "It was only after bin Laden was killed that it sunk in how essential it was for this to happen for us to accomplish our broader goals," he said in an interview with the author. "His death doesn't finish this chapter altogether, but after seeing him brought to justice, Americans can now envision the ultimate defeat of al-Qaeda. And that needed to happen for America to move on to the next chapter."

The narrative of closing the chapter on the war on al-Qaeda and jihadi terrorism, and turning the page to the "new normal" envisioned by the Obama administration, received an unexpected boost by events in the months after bin Laden's death. On September 20, 2011, CIA drones launched from a secret base in Saudi Arabia locked onto firebrand American cleric Anwar al-Awlaki inside Yemen, killing him and members of his entourage, to include the American Samir Khan, the creative director of al-Qaeda in the Arabian Peninsula's online jihadist magazine *Inspire*. The deaths of bin Laden and al-Awlaki only a few months apart—along with roughly half of al-Qaeda's top twenty leaders having been killed in the space of a little over a year between 2010 and 2011—suggested that the administration could lean ever more heavily on discrete, targeted counterterrorism operations to keep America safe.

White House officials also saw serendipity in the fact that bin Laden and al-Awlaki's deaths came while the Arab Spring revolutions were offering an alternative model for empowerment in the Arab and Muslim worlds. In toppling autocratic Arab regimes in Tunisia and Egypt initially through largely peaceful demonstrations, Arab Spring protesters directly refuted al-Qaeda's argument that only violence and terror could redeem Arab dignity.

When Libyan strongman Muammar el-Qaddafi prepared to massacre opposition groups in the spring of 2011, threatening to turn back the tide of democratic revolutions sweeping through the Middle East, the United States joined NATO's Operation Odyssey Dawn in Libya, while insisting that France and Germany take the lead as the allies most eager to intervene. The administration was later criticized when an unnamed White House official referred to this model as "leading from behind," but the Libyan operation that toppled el-Qaddafi suggested a new form of burden sharing, one in which the United States contributed technologies and warfighting techniques associated with the network—long-range precision strike, advanced ISR (intelligence, reconnaissance, and surveillance), unmanned drones—but let partners or proxies do the dirty work on the ground.

The last seismic shift of 2011 was the White House's decision, taken against the advice of its top military and defense officials, to abandon negotiations with the Iraqi government for a continued US troop presence past a December 2011 deadline agreed upon earlier by the Bush administration. The increasingly difficult Iraqi prime minister Nouri al-Maliki had balked at exempting US military personnel from prosecution in Iraqi courts as part of the proposed Status of Forces Agreement, a standard requirement. Al-Maliki knew that his refusal of such an exemption was a likely deal breaker for the United States. Frustrated by al-Maliki's stubbornness and seeing an opportunity to fulfill Obama's pledge to decisively end the Iraq war, the administration washed its hands of the negotiations and decided to pull all US military forces out of Iraq as scheduled. As the last US troops prepared to leave Iraq in December, President Obama declared that the United States was leaving behind a "sovereign, stable and self-reliant Iraq, with a representative government."

With a presidential election year approaching, Obama could run as the leader who killed Osama bin Laden, ended the Iraq war, and began bringing the troops home from Afghanistan, and the White House team liked his chances. His doctrine of sustained diplomatic engagement, military retrenchment, and discretely targeted counterterrorism operations had reached its zenith. From that vantage point, the White House envisioned a return to normalcy for America, one that was more sustainable for a nation wearied by more than a decade of unsatisfactory wars and preoccupied by the threat of terrorism.

The White House team argued that the post-9/11 wars were largely over, and the "global war on terrorism" needed to end as a national preoccupation, and in ways subtle and not the Executive Branch adjusted itself to that narrative. That left many members of the brotherhood of soldiers, spies, and special agents who had fought in the trenches for much the decade—or were still manning the front lines against the forces of anarchy and terror—as increasingly lonely dissenters. From their vantage point, the administration had confused walking away from a fight with ending one.

# PART III

# THIRTEEN

# Retrenchment

## 2011–2012

O<small>N</small> D<small>ECEMBER</small> 15, 2011, J<small>OINT</small> C<small>HIEFS</small> <small>OF</small> S<small>TAFF</small> <small>CHAIRMAN</small> G<small>EN</small>-eral Martin Dempsey found himself back in Baghdad under a clear blue sky, presiding at an understated ceremony at the international airport to lower the flag of command and bring the last US troops home. As younger men in what already seemed like a lifetime ago, the US military commanders had come into that land boasting of "shock and awe" and bursting with confidence that they would leave democracy where they had found only tyranny. Now that the moment had come at last, it was a proud but somewhat chastened Dempsey who willed himself to believe that the progress was enduring.

"We've paid a great price here, and it's a price worth paying," he told the crowd, ever mindful that nearly 4,500 US troops who came to liberate Iraq returned in flag-draped coffins, and that 30,000 more bore the permanent scars of wounds suffered there. The United States had spent nearly $1 trillion trying to build and secure the institutions of governance in Iraq. As many as 150,000 Iraqis may have died in the birthing of a free Iraq, though the exact number will never be known.

Dempsey could not admit it publicly, but he feared the United States was leaving too soon. Of all the decisions that his civilian bosses had made in his first year as chairman of the Joint Chiefs, the decision—made largely by default—not to leave a residual US force in Iraq struck him as one of the riskiest.

All of the Joint Chiefs had recommended to the White House that they leave a residual force of US troops in Iraq after the December 2011 deadline for the withdrawal of all troops, a deadline agreed to by the Bush administration back in 2008. They debated the size of that force, with a consensus military view being that it should probably stand at roughly ten thousand troops. No one understood better than Dempsey, the former head of the Multi-National Security Transition Command tasked with building Iraqi security forces, that those Iraqi forces remained severely deficient in key areas, including logistics, advanced ISR (intelligence, surveillance, and reconnaissance), and airpower.

Most important, the presence of US troops to train and mentor their Iraqi counterparts was critical in ensuring the development of a professional Iraqi officer corps. The Americans had used their leverage to resist frequent attempts by Iraqi prime minister Nouri al-Maliki and other Iraqi politicians to place cronies and yes-men in senior military ranks, a favored tactic of Arab autocrats to secure the personal loyalty of their militaries.

The role was little understood in Washington, but the US military had also served as the connective tissue between the Shiite-dominated government in Baghdad and the Sunni provinces in western Iraq that had risen up against al-Qaeda in Iraq as part of the Anbar Awakening movement. Since regaining power as a result of mostly backroom maneuvers following 2010 elections, al-Maliki had revealed an increasingly sectarian and authoritarian streak, persecuting Sunni politicians he viewed as a threat, reneging on agreements to put Sunni Awakening fighters on the government's payroll, and turning increasingly toward Shiite Iran for support.

In negotiations with the US government over a Status of Forces Agreement to allow for a residual US force, al-Maliki had pushed back against granting immunity to US soldiers from Iraqi law. Yet the US government still retained significant leverage in Iraq to try and get its way, including a generous Foreign Military Sales program that would be critical to equipping Iraqi security forces for years to come.

The White House did not explicitly overrule the Pentagon on its preference for leaving a troop presence in Iraq to secure its continued development. But neither did Dempsey ever sense any enthusiasm for the idea from the West Wing. There was an attitude at the White House that since the United States didn't have an enthusiastic partner in al-Maliki, why even bother? Dempsey argued that the United States still had significant national security interests in Iraq and the immediate region, and those equities could not be adequately secured without a continued US troop presence in Iraq. But that advice was largely ignored.

Already by the end of 2011, a hopeful Arab Spring of democratic revolutions was turning into a long winter of instability and unrest in Arab lands. In line with American values, the Obama administration had chosen to side with democratic, bottom-up revolutions that swept through the region. The Bush administration did the same thing in promoting an earlier Arab Spring of democracy reforms in hopes of capitalizing on free elections in Iraq in 2005. And then Iraq had devolved into sectarian civil war, Egyptian autocrat Hosni Mubarak abandoned liberalizing reforms that resulted in the 2005 election to Parliament of members of the Islamist Muslim Brotherhood, and in 2006 the Sunni terrorist group Hamas won elections in the Palestinian territories and the Shiite terrorist group Hezbollah had started a war with Israel—upon which the Bush administration abandoned its "freedom agenda" and went back to the venerable US policy of supporting Middle East autocrats who could deliver stability.

In calling for Egypt's Mubarak to step down, in using force to oust Libyan strongman el-Qaddafi, and in declaring that Syrian tyrant Bashar al-Assad had to go, the Obama administration was once again trying to align US interests with democracy movements in the region. And once again the same revanchist and undemocratic forces that conspired to suffocate the earlier democratic reforms in their cradle had their pillows figuratively poised over the Arab Spring movements: namely, dictators who tie their militaries close in a Gordian knot, so that the survival of the tyrant and his uniformed henchmen becomes one and the same; and Islamists who form the most organized and popular nongovernmental groups in most Middle Eastern countries, and whose devotion to an undemocratic version of Sharia law tends to make them believers in "one man, one vote, one time."

In Egypt, the most populous Arab nation and thus a bellwether, the Muslim Brotherhood was poised to capture the most seats in elections scheduled for 2012, that country's first democratic elections in living memory. That prospect was alarming to an Egyptian military that saw US support for Mubarak's ouster in 2011 as a gross betrayal of its longtime ally. Since the overthrow of el-Qaddafi in Libya in October 2011, the most powerful military leader to emerge in that country was Abdel Hakim Belhaj, the former leader of a hardline jihadi group once linked to al-Qaeda. In Syria Bashar al-Assad and a military led by handpicked officers from his extended family and minority Alawite sect were indiscriminately bombarding civilian neighborhoods in rebel-held areas, turning what began as peaceful demonstrations into a civil war that inflamed the larger region's Sunni versus Shiite divide. Sunni Saudi Arabia, Turkey, and the Persian Gulf Emirates were lavishing money and weapons on Islamist proxies in Syria, even as Shiite Iran, Lebanese Hezbollah, and Russia supported the al-Assad regime with money, men, and weapons.

At the height of Iraq's own civil war between the Sunni terrorists of al-Qaeda in Iraq and Shiite death squads, many of them supported by Iran, it had taken 170,000 US troops to quell the burning sectarian fires. As he stood at a podium in Baghdad and watched the colors of US Forces Iraq being lowered and cased for a final time, Martin Dempsey could be forgiven for worrying that the United States was letting its fire insurance lapse in Iraq even as alarms were sounding throughout the region.

Departing from his prepared text, he noted the different circumstances of his return to a country where he had fought and toiled for so many years. "The next time I come here, I'm going to have to be invited by the Iraqi government, and I kind of like that," said Dempsey, who couldn't help but notice that the seat at the front row reserved for al-Maliki sat empty throughout the ceremony. At that moment neither the US general nor the Iraqi prime minister could yet imagine the circumstances that would lead to that invitation being sent.

THERE IS A truism that wars are harder to end than to start, and there are few tasks more daunting than trying to manage the vast US military bureaucracy during a time of postwar retrenchment, bringing the troops home as you try to wind down two ongoing conflicts and steer a course through the tricky transition between war and whatever comes after. Over the course of a decade of conflict Martin Dempsey and other top commanders had witnessed a new model of US warfighting evolve, but no one knew whether the doctrines, technologies, and especially the spirit of collaboration at its core could be preserved in a time of severe cuts to defense and intelligence budgets, when all the various agencies and military services involved would be competing against each other for scarce resources. Already in 2011 the Pentagon was set to cut 100,000 ground forces and $487 billion out of its budget over the next decade if all went as planned, and in the hyperpartisan dysfunction of Washington, DC, nothing ever went as planned.

There were reasons Dempsey never aspired to become the nation's top military officer. He had already pinned on a fourth star as commander of the US Army Training and Doctrine Command (TRADOC) back in 2008. His lack of ego among officers of that top rank, where the baggage of ambition and arrogance often weighs heavily, was widely recognized. He was also recovering from throat cancer, and feeling blessed to even be alive. Then in early 2011 the Senate had confirmed him as Army chief of staff by unanimous consent, an honor he could scarcely have imagined as a young man, and he was sworn in on April 11, 2011. Within days Defense Secretary Robert Gates had sent word that he wanted to see Dempsey in his Pentagon office, presumably to give marching orders to the new Army chief.

"I'm going to make you really mad," Gates told him as soon as Dempsey sat down.

"Sir, I owe you so much, there's nothing you could ever do to make me angry with you," Dempsey told Gates, who had already recommended his promotion to acting commander of US Central Command, TRADOC commander, and now Army chief of staff.

"I want you to be the next chairman of the Joint Chiefs," Gates said, recognizing in the selfless and dedicated general something of himself.

An awkward silence hung in the room.

"Sir, there's nothing you could do to make me angry *except* that," Dempsey finally replied.

"You really don't want to be chairman?"

"No, sir, I really don't," Dempsey told his boss.

"Good," concluded Gates. "That's exactly why I want you to take the job."

Dempsey's reticence was informed by a deep understanding of military history. Almost without exception, the United States botched postwar transitions. After every "war to end all wars," a weary American public demanded a "peace dividend" that cut too deep for too long, gutting military readiness and tempting opportunistic foes. When the bugles sounded once again, brave but unprepared American troops were badly bloodied in early battles of the next war, whether at Kasserine Pass in North Africa at the outset of World War II, with Task Force Smith at the beginning of the Korean War, or in the Ia Drang Valley in Vietnam in 1965, a blood-letting made famous in the book *We Were Soldiers Once . . . and Young*. Military historians had a name for these postconflict epochs of military retrenchment: they called them the interwar years. Dempsey could not yet see how short his own interwar interlude would last.

As a young officer fresh out of West Point, he had personally lived through the desultory drawdown of the post-Vietnam 1970s, an experience that scarred the officers of his generation. Racial tensions ran high throughout the force in those days, and the military faced an acute manpower crisis as a result of the transition from a draft army to a new and untested all-volunteer force. The lessons of counterinsurgency warfare in Vietnam were forgotten in the US military's determination to leave that defeat behind and focus on conventional warfare against the Soviet Union.

The pillar of military capability that almost always suffered first was readiness, which encompassed day-to-day operations, the training necessary to keep troops prepared and motivated, and equipment maintenance. Unlike investments in weapons programs that were often funded for over a decade and enriched home-state congressional districts, readiness funding was like cut flowers: it was spent in the year it was authorized, making it a favored target of budget cutters.

After the post-Vietnam drawdown of the 1970s, Army chief of staff General Edward "Shy" Meyer had publicly informed the country that the

United States had a "hollow army," a rare public admission of vulnerability by a senior officer that caused headlines at the time. The reality underlying that warning certainly wasn't lost on adversaries, who sensed a moment of strategic weakness for the United States: in November 1979, Iranian revolutionaries deposed the shah of Iran, the United States' chief ally in the region, and stormed the US Embassy in Tehran and took fifty-two Americans hostage. A month later, an emboldened Soviet Union invaded Afghanistan. The US military's failed operation to rescue the hostages held by Iran put a tragic exclamation point on the botched 1970s military drawdown. The reverberations of those seismic events could still be felt three decades later.

Even after a much more hopeful victory in the Cold War and the 1991 Persian Gulf War, the United States arguably repeated the cycle in the 1990s drawdown. Once again Americans wanted a "peace dividend," and the Clinton administration responded by shrinking the Cold War military by roughly one third. The Clinton administration reasonably concluded that the nation could take a "strategic pause" from great-power competition, and safely defer modernization for much of a 1990s "procurement holiday." By the end of the decade, US military leaders were thus confronted with a rapidly aging arsenal. On average in 2000, Air Force fighters were fourteen years old, the tanker and airlift fleet was twenty-five years old, and 1960s-era B-52 bombers constituted one third of the long-range bomber fleet.

Only the "strategic pause" never materialized, and the hopeful post–Cold War "New World Order" turned out to be, in the words of former Army chief of staff General Dennis Reimer, "long on 'new' and short on 'order.'" Throughout the 1990s, the US military was engaged almost continually in peacemaking, nation-building, and stability operations in Somalia, Haiti, and Bosnia, as well as in limited air wars in Kosovo and in the no-fly zones inside Iraq, which US aircraft patrolled throughout the decade. As a midcareer officer in the 1990s, Dempsey had watched with concern as military planners wiped the "lesson learned" slate clean after each operation, preferring to focus on high-intensity conventional operations rather than unsatisfying "operations other than war."

As he learned personally in Iraq—and planned never to forget—that cycle left US forces wholly unprepared for the counterinsurgency fight they confronted in Iraq and Afghanistan. The Army had eventually adapted, elevating his West Point classmate David Petraeus to the doctrinal ivory tower of its Combined Arms Center, where Petraeus crafted the counter-insurgency doctrine he executed in Iraq. But it had been a very near thing. Had al-Qaeda in Iraq successfully fomented an all-out civil war that drove US forces out of Iraq, Operation Iraqi Freedom might have gone down in the history books as the worst US military defeat since Vietnam.

What most concerned Dempsey and the other Joint Chiefs by late 2011 were signs that the aftermath of the post-9/11 wars in Iraq and Afghanistan would prove even more challenging. After the Great Recession following the 2008 financial meltdown, the United States was saddled with far more debt than during previous postwar drawdowns, raising the temptation for the government to cut defense spending too steeply, for too long. The sovereign debt and financial crises caused the United States' closest allies in the NATO alliance to dangerously slash their own defense spending, to the point where the strongest among them—Great Britain and France—were contemplating having to share a single aircraft carrier between them.

A decade of constant combat had also placed burdens on the relatively small volunteer force that its architects had never anticipated—they had originally shaped the force as a core around which the country would mobilize with a draft in the case of a prolonged conflict. Instead, the US government had treated it as a modern-day American Foreign Legion, sending its volunteer warriors off to three, four, or five combat deployments, and the resultant pathologies and stress fractures were becoming impossible to ignore, and difficult to mend.

Just keeping faith with and adequately treating the cohort of wounded warriors was a major and expensive challenge. Pentagon figures indicated that 168,000 service members wounded or injured in Iraq and Afghanistan were graded "60 percent disabled" or higher, and the Veterans Administration faced a 492,000-case backlog of disability claims. The Congressional Budget Office estimated that the medical costs associated with veterans of Iraq and Afghanistan could come to $40 billion to $55 billion over the next decade.

Improvised explosive devices—the enemy's weapon of choice in both conflicts—had created more than 1,300 amputees, numerous burn victims, and unknown numbers who suffer from traumatic brain injury. According to the advocacy group Veterans for Common Sense, more than 190,000 troops had suffered a concussion or brain injury. There was also growing evidence of links between traumatic brain injury (TBI) and post-traumatic stress disorder (PTSD). According to a 2008 RAND organization survey, one in five veterans of these wars—some 300,000 people—were suffering either from major depression or PTSD, while 320,000 had suffered concussions or TBI.

The military suicide rate would spike to 22 percent between 2011 and 2012, with more service members killing themselves in some months than were dying in combat. Military sociologists and clinicians worried that the rising suicide rate was just a leading indicator in a tide of mental and physical suffering. Other indicators included unacceptably high rates of substance abuse, a military divorce rate that had risen 38 percent between 2001 and 2010, and what Defense Secretary Leon Panetta called a "silent epidemic" of "military sexual trauma," a catchall category that included everything from sexual harassment to rape, and which the Veterans Administration said afflicted one in five female veterans, or 20 percent.

Prolonged exposure to combat triggered such intense emotions—fear, revulsion, regret, sadness, grief, survivor's guilt—that some military psychiatrists had coined a new name for the resultant malady: "moral injury." Signs that moral corrosion had reached even to the top ranks of the military were evident in a rash of scandals involving senior officers in 2011–2012, to include General William Ward, the four-star head of Africa Command, who took his wife and a large entourage on lavish government-paid trips before he was stripped of a star and ordered to repay the US Treasury $82,000; and Brigadier General Jeffrey Sinclair, the married former deputy brigade commander of the Eighty-second Airborne who became involved with five separate women and was charged with adultery and sexual misconduct with a subordinate. At least sixty senior Navy officers were relieved of command in the three-year stretch leading up to 2012, representing a 40 percent rise over the previous three-year period, and twenty-five instructors at the Air Force's basic training center at Lackland Air Base, Texas, were under investigation for the systematic sexual abuse of female cadets. Wars create a culture where mission accomplishment is everything, and there was growing evidence suggesting that it had fostered a "rules don't apply" attitude even among the top ranks.

Perhaps hardest for Dempsey and the other Joint Chiefs was trying to render a "peace dividend" demanded by the administration and Congress, when there was so little peace to be kept. Major power competition had not abated while the United States fought a decade-long war on terrorism. China had used America's lost decade of war to accelerate its economic and military ascendancy, and it was bullying neighbors in the South and East China Seas. A nuclear-armed and totalitarian North Korea was building multistage missiles that one day would be able to reach the United States, and it was going through an unpredictable leadership transition. A revanchist Russia under the leadership of former KGB officer Vladimir Putin had sent its army to occupy breakaway regions of Georgia in 2008 in response to that country's ambition to join NATO, and was asserting dominance of its "near abroad" through intimidation.

Islamist extremist groups of various stripes continued to torment Afghanistan and Pakistan, and were gaining a greater foothold in North Africa and the Middle East. After destabilizing Egypt and then Libya, the instability sparked by the Arab Spring revolutions now showed signs of igniting an all-out civil war in Syria. Powerful nonstate actors such as the narco-mafias of Latin America continued to destabilize other regions. In the eyes of many experts, cyberwarfare could result in the next Pearl Harbor or 9/11-like strategic surprise.

When the Joint Chiefs and senior military leadership gathered to discuss those challenges and the coming drawdown, another issue was often raised. "I constantly have to remind people around here that the war is not over and we are still training and equipping soldiers and sending them to fight in Afghanistan," said Lieutenant General John Campbell, the Army's head of strategic plans and future vice chief, who had recently returned from a tough deployment in Afghanistan as the commander of the 101st Airborne Division. Like Dempsey's own children, John Campbell's son John Jr. had followed him into the Army. John Campbell Jr. would himself soon deploy to Afghanistan.


INSIDE HIS EXPANSIVE office in the Pentagon's E-Ring, General Dempsey conducted his work behind the same desk once used by General Douglas

MacArthur. Although he couldn't have been more different in temperament from the imperious and self-centered MacArthur, the desk reminded
Dempsey of the leaders who had come before, and had faced down whatever doubts and perils had darkened the councils of their day. That long
view helped keep him grounded.

On the desk, Dempsey kept a small wooden box engraved with the words
"Make It Matter." The box was a memento from his command of the First
Armored Division, which had adopted the motto to help make sense of the
sacrifices required during its fifteen-month deployment to Iraq. Inside the
box were cards containing the photos and brief biographies of the more
than 130 soldiers that Dempsey had lost in Iraq. Many of them were buried
under white crosses on the green hillsides visible from his house at nearby
Fort Myer, which sat on a bluff overlooking Arlington National Cemetery.
Dempsey missed being with the troops, but even on his bad days in Washington, all the inspiration he needed could be found inside that box. Leave
this a better place than you found it. Have the courage to do the right thing
no matter the potential personal cost. *Make It Matter.*

Certainly those memories of Iraq spoke loudly to Dempsey's ideas
about the efficacy and limitations of military power, and what he called
the lurking "black swans"—unpleasant surprises and unanticipated, often
third-order consequences of deciding to point a gun or pull a trigger. His
experiences in war also shaped his convictions on what ends justified putting the lives of American troops at risk, knowing that some would pay the
ultimate sacrifice.

That wellspring of experience also helped Dempsey define the agenda
that he would pursue as chairman. Like many senior leaders, he believed
that new technologies fueling the information age revolution and globalization would continue to enable terrorists and malevolent nonstate actors.
He pointed to the example of the terrorist attack in Mumbai, India, in 2008.
That operation was controlled by an operations and intelligence fusion
center in Pakistan that used commercial, off-the-shelf technology, such as
Google Earth's real-time mapping, satellite communications, GPS, smart
phone texting, social media, and rapid Internet searches. Thus equipped,
just ten terrorists were able to kill roughly 200 people and wound another
300 in an operation that took the security forces of the largest democracy

in the world three days to end. One malcontent with a laptop could potentially rob 100,000 people of their wealth and intellectual property in an era
of cyber vulnerability.

"So, the ability to commit violence and do harm is proliferating along
with technology, and I want to be very clear about that growing threat,"
Dempsey told the author early in his tenure as chairman. "The world we
are entering is one that feels safer on some level, but it is actually much
more dangerous."

As chairman of the Joint Chiefs, Dempsey was responsible for shaping
the military force that would defend the nation roughly a decade hence
in 2020, and 80 percent of that force was preordained due to decisions
already made by his predecessors. That freed him to focus on the 20 percent he could change, and he looked first at the new, intelligence driven,
network-centric style of warfare that Joint Special Operations Command
(JSOC) had helped pioneer and that increasingly influenced all US military operations. General Stanley McChrystal was one of the most innovative military leaders to emerge from a long era of conflict, and Dempsey
intended to expand on the capabilities that were central to the F3EA
(find, fix, and finish, exploit, and analyze) style of operations. The areas
he chose for special attention were advanced ISR (intelligence, surveillance, and reconnaissance), Special Operations Forces, and increased
cyber capabilities. Whereas current Pentagon plans called for cutting
100,000 US ground forces, Dempsey's plan was to boost the arsenal of
unmanned aerial vehicles by 30 percent, and to continue growing Special Operations Forces from 48,000 in fiscal 2007, to 61,000 in 2011, and
to 70,000 by 2015.

As the United States military wound down operations in Iraq and
Afghanistan and "pivoted" east to confront an ascendant China and an
increasingly revanchist Russia, the Pentagon would have to refocus the
attention of a generation of midlevel officers who had known only counterinsurgency on more conventional operations. But as chairman of the
Joint Chiefs, Dempsey was determined that the US military not repeat
the Vietnam-era mistake of expunging the lessons of counterinsurgency
warfare. He commissioned a study by the Joint Staff, "Enduring Lessons
from the Past Decade of War." A brutally honest assessment of mistakes

made and lessons learned, its very first takeaway went to the "black swan" Dempsey and other senior commanders encountered in Iraq: "In operations in Iraq and Afghanistan, a failure to recognize, acknowledge and accurately define the operational environment led to a mismatch between forces, capabilities, missions and goals." Lesson number two was equally unsparing: "Conventional warfare approaches often were ineffective when applied to operations other than combat."

In trying to reshape a smaller military in ways that reflected those lessons, Dempsey had a willing and eager partner in Army chief of staff Ray Odierno, his close colleague and fellow division commander in Iraq. Under Odierno's guidance, the Army was aligning its conventional combat brigades with certain geographic areas to build higher levels of regional and cultural expertise in the ranks, borrowing a page from the Special Operations handbook. Similarly, he had launched a "Mission Command" initiative that decentralized decision-making and pushed it down to junior officers on the front lines, another part of the Special Forces ethos that was migrating to combat-seasoned conventional forces. In Army doctrine, Odierno had made joint operations that exploited the synergy between conventional and Special Operations Forces the seventh, core warfighting function. He embedded Army officers with the FBI, CIA, and State Department to capture the synergy created in joint task forces in Iraq and Afghanistan. Odierno was determined to further strengthen the tight bonds that had developed between conventional Army units and Special Operations Forces forged over a decade of counterinsurgency warfare, by integrating them together in every training exercise.

"We have a whole generation of officers from generals down to majors in both conventional and Special Operations Forces who have collaborated together on the battlefield for more than a decade, and I cannot overstate how much those relationships and the mutual trust they have built have broken down barriers," he said. "No one wants to go back to their separate corners now."

Above all, both Dempsey and Odierno, Army officers who cut their teeth during the drawdown of the 1970s, were determined during the drawdown to avoid the kind of cuts in readiness that led to the "hollow force" of their youth. Confronting a world of crises, both generals believed that maintaining a battle-ready force was essential to retaining arguably the most combat-seasoned and experienced US military force in history.

Unfortunately, the Joint Chiefs' plans for an orderly drawdown were already threatened in 2011 by the Budget Control Act, which was passed in order to avoid a sovereign debt default resulting from partisan gridlock. A poison pill specifically designed to be so distasteful that it would force compromise in a city that had lost the habit, the act included a "sequester" trigger that imposed compulsory caps on domestic and defense spending if the White House and Congress were unable to agree on a compromise on taxes and spending. In 2011, the institutions on either end of Pennsylvania Avenue couldn't reach compromise or muster bipartisan support to rename a post office.

In some of the sternest warnings ever issued by top military leaders, members of the Joint Chiefs publicly warned that budget cuts of the magnitude imposed by sequester would be "catastrophic" to the military. The civilian leadership seemed not to hear.

MARTIN DEMPSEY WAS an optimist by nature, and generally he took the long view that eventually the American people would get it right. His moral compass required that he provide elected officials in the White House and Congress with an honest assessment of how their actions were impacting the health of the US military, and the security of the nation. Early on in his tenure he pledged to himself that he would not shrink from explaining the real harm that could flow from their decisions, up to and including unnecessarily costing the lives of American troops on some future battlefield. He hoped to be persuasive, but the White House's premature withdrawal of all US troops from Iraq in 2011 against the recommendations of the Joint Chiefs, and Congress's decision to impose catastrophic defense budget cuts during a time of great global instability, suggested that he was failing. At the end of the day, Dempsey reasoned that the United States was a democracy, and elected officials would ultimately decide.

# FOURTEEN

# Shadow War

## 2013

DESPITE ENDURING CORRUPTION AND POVERTY THAT HAD MOST Africans subsisting on less than $2 a day, seven of the ten fastest-growing countries in the world in 2013 were on the African continent. Foreign investment had soared tenfold over the past decade. Mobile phone use exceeded that in Europe and the United States. According to the International Monetary Fund, Africa's average annual economic growth was already about the same as Asia's, at nearly 6 percent. Democracy was also taking root and spreading on the continent. Two cover stories on Africa in the *Economist* magazine told the story: The first was from 2000, entitled "The Hopeless Continent"; the second cover story was from 2011, "Africa Rising."

Under intense pressure in Pakistan's tribal areas and drawn to the lightly governed spaces, restless Muslim populations and sectarian conflict on the continent, al-Qaeda and its affiliated groups were also gaining strength throughout Africa and much of the Middle East. The al-Qaeda affiliate al-Nusra Front was emerging as one of the most brutal and successful of the rebel factions battling the regime of Bashar al-Assad in Syria. Even without

Anwar al-Awlaki at the helm, al-Qaeda in the Arabian Peninsula (AQAP) had made gains the previous year by capturing swaths of territory in Yemen in the chaos that followed the resignation of President Ali Abdullah Saleh, a corrupt autocrat who had been a willing partner in the United States' fight against AQAP, but who was forced out of office by Arab Spring unrest. Al-Qaeda in the Islamic Maghreb (AQIM), a Salafi jihadi group that emerged from Algeria's civil war in the 1990s, was linked to the attack on the US consulate in Benghazi, Libya, in 2012 that killed US ambassador Christopher Stevens and three other Americans, and the seizure of Northern Mali by a loose confederation of AQIM extremists, Tuareg mercenaries, and assorted criminal groups. Nearly half of Nigeria's territory lived in the shadow of the al-Qaeda–linked Boca Haram terrorist group, whose calling card was the massacre of whole villages down to the last man, woman, and child, and the kidnapping and sexual enslavement of young girls. Al-Shabab, or "the Youth," in Somalia had formally pledged allegiance to al-Qaeda a few years earlier, and the group was arguably further along than any other affiliate in turning a failed state into a caliphate run by Islamist extremists. Even with al-Qaeda's core in disarray and its figurehead dead, Osama bin Laden's vision of a global Islamist insurgency bent on conquest was very much alive.

After withdrawing from Iraq and beginning the pullout from Afghanistan, the US military needed a new, sustainable model of operations that built on the counterterrorism and counterinsurgency lessons of those conflicts, yet was tailored to the coming period of postwar austerity. The fundamental strategy was to leverage unique US capabilities, such as advanced ISR (intelligence, surveillance, and reconnaissance), precision strike airpower, and Special Operations Forces' "train and assist" and "capture or kill" operations to empower local or regional partners willing to put their own boots on the ground. To a large degree that model reflected the transition that had occurred in Iraq and Afghanistan after a decade of direct action and nation-building, as US commanders gradually shifted governing and security responsibilities to local actors. With the dark corners of Africa increasingly alight with the bonfires of jihadis, the Pentagon chose to fully field test the model on a large scale at US Africa Command (AFRICOM).

ON A JANUARY morning in 2013, Major General Rob Baker, commander of Combined Joint Task Force–Horn of Africa (CJTF-HOA), sat inside his joint operations center at Camp Lemonnier to receive a daily staff brief on his East Africa Campaign Plan. After his three tours in Iraq, Baker had finished a tour on the Joint Staff at the Pentagon, and it felt good to be back in the field with troops. Field command was what he did best. The frenetic pace of an operational command even kept his mind off the fact that his frequent deployments to Iraq had wrecked his marriage. CJTF-HOA had the feel of a wartime command, which was not accidental. Nor was it happenstance that the Pentagon leadership had selected a combat-seasoned commander like Baker to lead the task force and intensify its counterterrorism focus.

A former French Foreign Legion outpost in the tiny East African country of Djibouti, Camp Lemonnier is the US military's primary toehold on the vast African continent. The base sits atop a low hill guarded by blast walls and the kind of mazelike vehicle security checkpoints you find in war zones. US Marines first arrived at Camp Lemonnier shortly after the 9/11 terrorist attacks to secure the Bab el-Mandeb, or "Gate of Tears," one of the most trafficked waterways in the world and a strategic shipping choke point along the maritime supply route to Afghanistan. At that time, they had to form hunting parties to track down packs of wild hyenas that roamed the sprawling base. On hot nights, the stench of burning camel carcasses from an adjacent dump still forces camp dwellers to seek refuge inside. Camp Lemonnier seemed like an odd spot to field test a new model of twenty-first-century warfare, but that's what US forces were doing in 2013, in what many intelligence analysts predicted was the next major front in the war on jihadi terrorists. Major General Baker and the Combined Joint Task Force–Horn of Africa organized and enabled the counterterrorism campaign from the shadows, mostly in support of the military and police forces of other nations.

A "link chart" diagram on a video screen in CJTF-HOA's operations center traced the connections between the various Islamist extremist groups in Africa and their leaders, with al-Shabab at the center of the web. The video map revealed why Camp Lemonnier was considered one of the most strategically important US bases in the world: it sat right between and in close proximity to both Yemen and Somalia, two of the world's most unstable countries, and hosts to the two major al-Qaeda affiliates, al-Shabab and al-Qaeda in the Arabian Peninsula (AQAP).

The primary focus of Baker's East Africa Campaign Plan was the perilous situation next door in Somalia. A few years earlier, al-Shabab beat back Ethiopian forces sent into the country to support the UN-backed transitional government, and boxed African Union peacekeepers into a few square blocks in downtown Mogadishu. US officials feared that thousands of African Union troops would need evacuation from Mogadishu—a dismal reminder of the 1993 US evacuation after the *Black Hawk Down* debacle.

For years US intelligence officials also had under surveillance two al-Shabab training camps in Somalia. Roughly 50 percent of the two hundred or so trainees who studied bomb making and weapons each "semester" were Caucasian foreigners. US intelligence officials had surveillance video of "graduation ceremonies" conducted at both camps, but so many women and children were present that approval had never come to destroy the camps. Scores of Somali Americans had trained there, raising fears that the trainees would return home to launch attacks on the US homeland. A Somali American named Shirwa Ahmed joined up with al-Shabab back in 2008 and became the first known American suicide bomber. Al-Qaeda's then number two, Ayman al-Zawahiri, trumpeted al-Shabab's gains as "a step on the path of victory for Islam."

With al-Shabab poised to turn a failed state into a caliphate run by Islamist extremists, Assistant Secretary of State for African Affiars Johnnie Carson and Secretary of State Hillary Clinton had met personally with the president of the transitional, UN-backed Somali government, Sharif Sheik Ahmed, in Nairobi, Kenya, in 2009. After the meeting, Clinton gave Carson two marching orders: do not let the transitional government in Mogadishu fail, and do not let al-Shabab win. Carson would later recall not sleeping easily that night.

To stave off an al-Shabab takeover, Carson and the rest of the "Africa hands" at the State Department began an unusually close collaboration with US Africa Command. Congress had only established AFRICOM in 2007, giving the Pentagon's newest geographic command responsibility for the entire African continent except Egypt. State Department officials were initially resistant to the idea, noting that anticolonial sentiments still ran deep on the continent, and at Foggy Bottom the "Africa hands" worried that a big US military headquarters would exacerbate those tensions and militarize US foreign policy on the continent. The Pentagon responded to those concerns by locating the headquarters in Stuttgart, Germany, keeping a light footprint in Africa and focusing its operations on relatively benign "confidence building" operations, such as civil affairs projects and joint military exercises.

To roll back al-Shabab and transform the CJTF-HOA into a counterterrorism command, AFRICOM commander General Carter Ham embraced the East Africa Campaign Plan. Under the plan, Baker had responsibility for coordinating all military activities in East Africa. The task force was made a "supported command," meaning that the individual armed forces represented in Djibouti answered to Baker, and not to their "mother" commands back in Germany.

Baker and his staff devised a program with two major pillars: training African Union troops to a combat-ready standard, and developing cutting-edge ISR capabilities to gain a more granular understanding of the battle space. AFRICOM's constellation of drone bases already included Djibouti, Arba Minch in Ethiopia, and the Seychelles in the Indian Ocean, and it was building a new drone base in Niger to support French troops who had deployed to counter AQIM's incursion into Mali. AFRICOM was also secretly building a new base for its Predator drones in Djibouti to relieve traffic at the low-tech international airport, where the wasplike aircraft could be easily seen squatting on the tarmac on the military side of the airfield. In written testimony for his Senate confirmation hearing in February 2013, incoming AFRICOM commander General David Rodriguez, fresh from commanding US and allied combat forces in Afghanistan, declared that the US military needed to increase its ISR and intelligence-gathering capabilities in Africa fifteenfold to counter the growing terrorist threat on the vast continent.

By early 2013 the results of the East Africa Campaign Plan were already evident inside the task force's operations center as Major General Baker's staff briefed ongoing operations. To share vital overhead images and other intelligence gathered by a fleet of sixteen Predator drones stationed in Djibouti, Baker's director of C-4 (command, control, computer, and communications) systems, Air Force Colonel James Clark, helped create the innovative Africa Data Sharing Network. Using outdated and surplus computers donated by the Defense Reutilization and Marketing Service, they equipped African Union units in Somalia with a secure data network that could access US surveillance imagery already "scrubbed" to avoid compromising sensitive sources and methods. Task force intelligence analysts become so expert in the craft that they could tell the strength and position of al-Shabab units by counting the numbers of fires in their camps at night, information that they shared with African Union units in the area via the Data Sharing Network. Essentially, they plugged African Union troops into the United States' globe-spanning intelligence and surveillance network.

"It was like turning on a lightbulb in a dark room, because suddenly AMISOM [African Union Mission in Somalia] forces were aware of who and what was moving all around them," Colonel Clark explained in an interview with the author. "At that point operations against al-Shabab improved by a whole order of magnitude."

In terms of training, Baker's task force conducted an assessment of every African country that contributed forces to AMISOM, including Burundi, Djibouti, Kenya, and Uganda. State Department officials used that information to customize a training program called ACOTA, military-speak for African Contingency Operations Training and Assistance. ACOTA drew on the services of US Special Operations Forces as well as private contractors operating at clandestine bases in East Africa, to identify weaknesses and tailor their training and mentorship programs to specific vulnerabilities. Military-to-military engagements with African Union countries shot from just 15 in 2008 to 140 by 2012.

Unlike in Iraq and Afghanistan, the US military was not in the lead, and thus had to work through the State Department and African governments that were not interested in taking orders from those in uniform, or engaging in a leader-follower relationship. "That requires a peer-to-peer relationship that doesn't always come naturally to the US military," noted Navy Captain Peter Haynes, director of strategy and plans for CJTF-HOA. "It takes a humble mind-set." To instill that humility, Baker and other CJTF-HOA officials adopted a motto: "African solutions to African problems."

A third pillar of the East Africa Campaign Plan was direct targeting of terrorist leaders. Those missions were carried out by a Joint Special Operations Command (JSOC) task force that operated in a secure facility on Camp Lemonnier, flying drones from the Djibouti airport into both Yemen and Somalia. Signs of their handiwork were evident in the May 2008 air strike that killed Sheikh Aden Hashi Ayro, the former military commander of al-Shabab; a helicopter-borne Special Operations Forces raid in September 2009 that killed Saleh Ali Saleh Nabhan, an architect of al-Shabab's merger with al-Qaeda; a 2011 Predator strike on an al-Shabab training camp outside of Kismayo; and a 2012 Predator strike that killed Bilal al-Berjawi, a British citizen who served as a senior al-Qaeda and al-Shabab leader.

By early 2013 the results of those efforts were promising. AMISOM had pushed al-Shabab out of the major Somali cities and urban centers, and AFRICOM's support of French troops in Mali with surveillance drones, air transport, and midair refueling had helped them check AQIM's advance in Mali after it nearly split the country. In an interview in CJTF-HOA's command center, Baker argued that teaching the counterterrorism and counterinsurgency lessons learned in Iraq and Afghanistan to foreign partners, and empowering them with advanced US capabilities, such as intelligence gathering and surveillance, would allow African militaries to police their own backyards.

"That doesn't mean the United States will never again intervene militarily in another country with boots on the ground," he said. "But the more proactive we are in engaging with foreign partners, and the more predictive we are in identifying common threats, the less likely a future US intervention will be necessary."

Drawing on the lessons of the counterinsurgency campaign in Iraq, Baker closely coordinated CJTF-HOA's East Africa Campaign with the "Africa hands" at the State Department. Their corresponding diplomatic counteroffensive included securing funding and aid for troop contributing countries taking part in the AMISOM mission. They reached out to the various political factions inside Somalia to ensure that AMISOM's battlefield momentum was matched by progress toward a functioning government. By early 2013, the Somalis had formed a constituent assembly, chosen a parliament, and elected a president. They had also begun writing a constitution.

Major General Baker would become the first US officer in uniform to return to Somalia since the 1993 Battle of Mogadishu, and while he was visiting its neighbors in January 2013, newly elected Somali president Hassan Sheikh Mohamud was receiving a state welcome in Washington, DC. It was the first time since 1991 that the United States had recognized a government in Somalia.

Assistant Secretary of State for Africa Johnnie Carson offered the "Somalia model" as a template for dealing with other African countries beset by conflict and radical Islamist terrorism. "Today, African peacekeepers and Somali security forces have rolled al-Shabab out of every major Somali city, and for the first time in two decades Somalia has a representative government," he told an audience at the Woodrow Wilson Center in Washington, DC. The United States' behind-the-scenes strategy had "turned one of Africa's most enduring conflicts into a major success story."

VAST EXPANSES OF African savannah stretched out beneath the wings of the small Beechcraft C-12 Huron aircraft carrying Rob Baker and his CJTF-HOA team, its shadow racing herds of wild animals across sunlit tundra and skipping across rivers bright as liquid mercury. The sheer amount of time it took to fly across the task force's area of operations in East Africa spoke to the tyranny of distance that factored into every operational calculus on the continent.

At the end of the journey the twin-engine turboprop banked hard and dropped through a break in thick cloud cover, and suddenly Kenya's pristine Lamu Archipelago stretched out below like an undiscovered country. Emerald green waters and cuticles of virgin white beach mingled at the edge of tangled jungle, and in the distance were grasslands and plains stretching back toward the endless Serengeti, hunting ground of the earth's most fearsome natural predators. And yet it was the secret destination of the aircraft, never previously visited by a journalist or opened to the outside world, which represented something new in the pecking order of hunters and the hunted.

At the lower altitude, a vast alluvial plain filled the cockpit windows, its contours dissected by rivers running inland through thick mangrove swamps. Banking again, the pilot spotted a short airstrip cut out of the dense foliage below, and nearby, fenced-in rows of rectangular buildings gleamed white in a ray of sunlight. Not on any official map of worldwide US military bases, the small camp was one of the most remote outposts in the network of secretive US forward staging pads in Africa that was expanding rapidly. When the clouds closed and the rainy season arrived in mid-March, "Camp Simba" could go for weeks, even months, without so much as a mail drop.

On the ground the C-12 taxied down a single airstrip without lights or a control tower, stopping by a squat one-story building. Just behind, a transport aircraft landed on the airstrip, its flat gray fuselage devoid of any official markings. Unbeknownst even to the African military forces it was supplying in nearby Somalia, the aircraft was specially outfitted with state-of-the-art communications intercept radios and multispectrum cameras, one more sensor feeding the United States' rapidly expanding, global surveillance network. The pilots and aircrew who flew the nondescript aircraft for JSOC were just returning from a bucket run to Mogadishu.

Baker and his team were met by the Navy captain in charge of Camp Simba. They clasped hands and smiled, standing in the hot backwash of the turboprops. Back home in Washington, politicians were debating how fast to pull the last US combat troops out of Afghanistan after more than twelve years, and the talk was of an end to war, and good riddance from a war and recession-weary America. The two officers standing on the tarmac in a remote airstrip in Africa knew better. They understood that it takes two to end a war. And the enemy that brought them together that day had voted to fight on.

Everywhere around them were signs of a new front opening in the global war against terrorists. On the tarmac, a detachment of Navy Seabee engineers worked round-the-clock shifts to finish a runway extension that, once completed, would allow larger aircraft, such as C-130 transports, to land and supply US and African Union troops stationed at Camp Simba and Kenya's Manda Bay military base. The job was a throwback to the Seabees' original mission of building airfields in the far-flung Pacific theater during the island-hopping campaigns of World War II. Given the conflicts on the continent that were drawing extremists like moths to a flame, Africa figured to offer the Seabees constructive work for years to come.

After completing predeployment training at Manda Bay and similar outposts in Africa, AMISOM troops fly into Somalia aboard US-contracted aircraft, and once on the ground they are equipped with US-supplied armored personnel carriers, body armor, and night-vision equipment. The mission's commanders use US-provided intelligence, including reconnaissance from Predator and Raven unmanned drones. Once in-country, they fight alongside Somali National Army troops that draw a salary from the United States. If wounded, African Union troops are typically evacuated aboard US-funded medevac flights. Yet almost nowhere were US fingerprints visible on AMISOM's fight with al-Shabab, a shadow war that the United States led from remote outposts like Camp Simba.

Baker's team and their hosts climbed into a pair of SUVs for the short ride to Camp Simba, passing down a long asphalt road lined by a fence that barely held the encroaching jungle at bay. In the shade of umbrella-like acacia trees, baboons the size of teenagers picked lazily at themselves. A video went viral within CTFJ-HOA's communications network of two US Marines playfully trying to put a "USMC" T-shirt on one of the baboons, the kind of hijinks that passed for entertainment at Camp Simba. Both Marines ended up in the hospital. Baker noted that in Africa close encounters with the wildlife was a top cause of injury to his troops.

After passing a Kenyan security checkpoint, the SUVs drove by black-clad Kenyan antiterrorism commandos mustering in the sun. Their disciplined ranks and proud bearing showed the effects of many months of training with US Army Special Operations Forces in Kenya's Great Rift Valley, a spine of volcanoes and ancient caldera lakes that spilled down steep mountain streams into valley floors ranged by rhinoceros and lion prides.

Stopping at a dock that accessed the nearby Indian Ocean, Baker met with US Navy Special Warfare boat crews who were training Kenyan Special Boat Forces how to operate inflatable, rigid-hull boats armed with sophisticated radars and machine guns fore and aft. They gave him a ride, and in the hands of the Navy commandos the inflatables were as nimble as Jet Skis. Just the summer before, Kenyan commandos operating out of Manda Bay, and armed with operational doctrine and training right out of the US Special Operations Forces handbook, had launched an amphibious landing at the Somali port city of Kismayo, quickly routing al-Shabab insurgents from one of their most important urban strongholds in Somalia. The operation denied the terrorist group control of a key bazaar they ran through shakedowns and extortion, and their primary resupply route to the Arabian Peninsula and the rich Arab sheikhs in Saudi Arabia and the Persian Gulf monarchies who supported their jihad.

The Special Warfare crews also inserted and extracted SEAL commando teams on their occasional capture-or-kill night raids into Somalia. "Ralph," a crew chief on one of the teams, was asked whether the craft could keep up with the streamlined "go-fast" boats that coastal smugglers were increasingly using. "Sir, we may only be able to do forty knots, but I've yet to see a 'go-fast' boat that can outrun a 7.62 or .50 caliber machine gun bullet," Ralph said. "We're all about shooting on the water."

In the pitch darkness of the African nights, with the yowling and caterwauling of the wildlife closing in all around, Camp Simba could seem like the most forsaken spot on earth. Baker was visiting one of his foremost operating bases precisely because al-Shabab had been rocked back on its heels, and they all knew from bitter experience that a wounded and cornered enemy was often the most dangerous. Inside a low-slung building bristling with large satellite dishes and flanked by antennae towers, he took a seat at the center of a tactical operations center and was briefed on operations inside Somalia. Members of a multiagency task force that included representatives of the major US intelligence and law enforcement agencies, along with JSOC operators and troops from the various armed services, sat before laptop computers in concentric semicircles before large, flat-screen video displays.

One flat-screen video map displayed the disposition of "friendly" African Union forces in Somalia, as well as the "foes" in known insurgent clusters. In the center of the semicircle of computer terminals a screen displayed full-motion video captured the previous evening by an unmanned MQ-1 Predator drone that was circling unseen above a compound of rough cement dwellings inside Somalia. Another screen displayed a link chart schematic of al-Shabab leadership.

Under pressure from AMISOM troops and lethal US drone strikes, the terrorist group was beginning to fracture, creating a leadership crisis. A nationalist faction wanted to continue the fight to subjugate Somalia, and a more radical faction advocated conducting splashy terrorist attacks in neighboring countries that contributed troops to AMISOM. At the top of the more radical faction was al-Shabab leader Ahmed Abdi Godane, a.k.a. Abu Zubair, a self-styled poet with a $7 million US bounty on his head. Godane's brutal vindictiveness and penchant for beheadings, amputations, and murders of even his partners in terrorism was already splintering al-Shabab. He assumed the helm of al-Shabab in 2008 after his predecessor Aden Hashi Ayro was killed by a US air strike. Godane had a resume that set off alarms in US counterterrorism circles. He was clever, ambitious, and a good orator whose speeches were sprinkled with the poetry of Mohammed Abdullah Hassan, the "Mad Mullah" and Somali hero who had fought against British colonial rule.

As a young man Godane had won scholarships to study Islam in Sudan and Pakistan, where like so many others he was radicalized by jihadi ideology in madrassas funded by rich Gulf sheikhs. He eventually crossed into Afghanistan in the early 1990s to receive military training from al-Qaeda. A year after taking the helm of al-Shabab, he pledged allegiance to al-Qaeda and adopted Osama bin Laden's strategy of launching terrorist attacks regionally and against the international community. Under his tutelage, al-Shabab terrorists bombed the United Nations compound and the Ethiopian embassy in Somaliland in 2008, and in 2010 they killed nearly eighty civilians watching a screening of a World Cup soccer match in the Ugandan capital of Kampala.

Leaders in Godane's more radical faction of al-Shabab included Abdikadir Mohamed Abdikadir, a Kenyan of Somali origin also known as Ikrima. He served as the head of "external operations" for the group. Ikrima was among the hardliners eager to strike out regionally as a way for al-Shabab to regain lost credibility and cache in the terrorist pantheon.

Al-Shabab's leadership also included Omar Hammami, better known as Abu Mansour al-Amriki, or "the American." The so-called jihadist rapper

from Alabama was under indictment in the United States on charges of pro-
viding "material support" to terrorists. Hammami successfully recruited the
Somali American travelers from the large Somali diaspora in Minneapolis.
The United States had a $5 million reward on his head.

The US commander and operators sitting in the tactical operations center at Camp Simba were all veterans of multiple combat tours. They intently watched the Predator video feed of the building containing senior
al-Shabab leaders taken the night before. They had all wanted very much
to send them a message about America's long reach and memory, which is
why they were reviewing the Predator video.

"How many unknowns were there in the house?" Baker asked.

He was given an estimate in double-digits. The al-Shabab leaders were
on the Pentagon's classified Joint Integrated Prioritized Target List—the
"capture or kill" list central to the United States' targeted killing program—
but the rules governing drone strikes had recently been tightened. If the
number of civilians or unknown persons in the vicinity exceeded a classified number, they were not allowed to launch the Hellfire missile that
could put an end to terrorists with the blood of hundreds on their hands,
and murder in their hearts. Yet it was a near thing, and the estimate could
be wrong. They could have taken the shot and let Allah sort it out, as the
al-Shabab extremists surely would have if their roles were reversed. Instead
the AFRICOM commander who had the final execute authority had declined to fire.

"Given the potential harm to locals that was the right call. We'll get him
another time," Baker said, standing up to leave, not fully believing his own
words. They all learned the hard way that letting the big prey out of your
sights could come back to haunt you. Al-Shabab's leaders found themselves
in the US crosshairs precisely because they were among the new lords of
anarchy, and the coin of the realm and price for advancement in their king-
dom was bloodshed. To see their work up close was to know them.

# FIFTEEN

# The Enemy Votes
## September–December 2013

THE SPRAWLING WESTGATE SHOPPING MALL SAT ATOP A LEAFY knoll known as High Ridge, above the traffic and smog-clogged streets of sprawling Nairobi, a gleaming retail oasis of upscale shops and restaurants favored by wealthy foreigners and the country's burgeoning upper class. In an art store near the entrance, the same one where Major General Rob Baker had purchased African prints on a visit to Kenya months before, customers browsed through woodcarvings, handmade jewelry, and brightly colored surrealistic paintings of African wildlife. Midday on Saturday, September 21, 2013, there was already a crowd at the trendy Artcaffe, a popular eatery that displayed its fresh-baked breads and signature pastries on a long counter looking out on the mall's main concourse. The back of the mall was dominated by a sprawling grocery store spread out on two floors and boasting an escalator, a rare luxury in Kenya. Its neatly spaced aisles formed a maze of conspicuous abundance.

On the rooftop under a long tent, a white-clad woman in a chef's hat worked behind a cooking station with a brightly colored sign designating her "superchef," and she showed the seated audience of mostly women and children how to prepare apple pudding. Weekend shopping at the bustling Westgate was a favorite pastime of Western diplomats, visiting officials, and tourists in Nairobi, and there were many Americans and Europeans looking for souvenirs to send home among the crowd strolling through the mall.

Emerging from the traffic, a silver Japanese compact car with four doors and a rear spoiler drove up the road that ran to the mall's entrance, pulled sideways, and braked hard, blocking the traffic behind. Four young men piled out, calmly adjusting their backpacks and the slings that sluiced their assault rifles easily into firing position. Two of them walked down the line of cars toward the entrance, looking into the open windows of each car and firing point-blank into the surprised faces of the occupants. As they walked away, songs still blared from some of the open car windows, the music mocked by the sudden stillness.

At the entrance the first two gunmen threw grenades. Deafening explosions echoed through the corridors of the mall and sent shards of shrapnel hurtling through the crowd enjoying lunch on the patio of Urban Burger. Among the bodies on the ground, a wounded man dragged his wife back into the restaurant seeking cover, their passage eased by a greasy slick of blood. Inside the mall, panic took hold as people ran screaming in every direction. Young children separated from their mothers froze in fear and confusion. Two al-Shabab militants, one in light pants with a black, long-sleeved shirt, the other in dark pants and a blue shirt, shouldered their rifles and took aim. The tracer rounds from the high-powered rifles helped them find their targets.

The other two gunmen headed for the rooftop tent in the rear of the mall where the cooking lesson had been held. A crowd of women and children huddled just inside the mall's rear entrance; with sounds of gunfire and explosions echoing up the stairwell, they were unsure in which direction to flee. Mothers tried to shield their children from the gaze of the gunmen.

"Please, just let the children go," an Indian woman pleaded.

"You have killed our women and children in Somalia, and we are here to take revenge," one of the gunmen answered. "We are here to kill."

They opened fire on the huddled group of Saturday shoppers, children and mothers dying in each other's arms, the sickening sound of high-powered rounds ripping into soft flesh filling the close quarters. The few survivors who recalled that sound would remember it for the rest of their lives. After the gunmen walked away in search of other prey, a young boy who had been shot started screaming in agony. "They killed my mother! They killed my sister! Why? Why?" A woman who had herself been shot tried to calm the boy, but he would not stop screaming. Other survivors tried to shush the child, afraid he would cause the gunmen to return. But the wounded bled out and their protests died down, and the boy was left to scream into a gathering silence.

There was no rush; the gunmen and their vengeance would not be hurried. Kenya had dared join the African Union force that was battling al-Shabab for supremacy in Somalia, and they had come to exact payment. Stepping calmly around bodies in the main corridor, one of the first two gunmen came upon a man trying to hide his head under a counter, his feet and part of his body sticking out into the walking space for anyone to see. The gunman shot him and moved on, returning later to finish the job with two additional rounds when it became clear that the man yet lived.

The gunmen came upon another cowering group. A portly, middle-aged man and his wife were praying, "There is no God but Allah, and Mohammed is his messenger," the man intoned.

"Are you a Muslim?" the gunman asked.

"Yes, I am."

"Go!" the gunman barked, before swinging his rifle toward an older African woman.

"Please, I am old, and I am in a lot of pain. Please let me go."

"Are you a Muslim?" he asked.

The woman hesitated as she grasped for the answer that might save her life. The gunman executed her with a single gunshot.

A few hours into the massacre, the lights went out inside the mall. In the darkness the moans and wailing of the wounded and dying gave voice to a collective despair, families and couples out for a day of Saturday shopping unexpectedly finding themselves trapped in a human slaughterhouse. But at least for a time the sound of gunfire ceased. A group of roughly twenty shoppers who had taken refuge behind the meat counter in the back of the grocery store cowered in the darkness, whispering to each other that perhaps the danger had finally passed. Then the lights came back on and they looked up to see two of the gunmen approaching, deliberate and unhurried.

"Now is your time," the lead gunman told them. "We have come for you."

BY THE END of the second day of the siege, the FBI Rapid Deployment Team that Brian McCauley dispatched to Kenya was already in place. Special Agent in Charge Richard Frankel stood behind a barricade outside the smoldering wreckage of Westgate, listening to sporadic gunfire and waiting for the okay to send in his team of more than eighty special investigators. The agents were familiar with al-Shabab's handiwork, many of them having investigated the group's bombing of the Kyadondo Rugby Club in Uganda during the World Cup final in 2010. In that attack, explosive devices had been placed among a large crowd gathered before a giant video screen to watch the match. More than seventy people were killed in the attack in Kampala that night. Standing outside the Westgate in Nairobi, and looking at a makeshift morgue that already contained scores of hastily wrapped corpses, many of them clearly young children, Frankel worried that the body count could exceed that number. He would later learn that the occasional gunshots were fired by the Kenyan security forces inside to keep prying eyes away while they looted the mall.

That four Americans were among the hundreds seriously wounded in the attack partially explained Frankel's presence in Kenya. The tactical command post set up on the perimeter of Westgate was a reflection of the multiagency Joint Terrorism Task Forces spread across the United States, or the joint task forces that Joint Special Operations Command (JSOC) had run in Iraq and operated still in Afghanistan. It was crawling with special agents and operators from the major US intelligence, law enforcement, and military agencies. With only hours of notice and a green light from the chain of command, they could now deploy a major new node in the counterterrorism network involving hundreds of operators nearly any place on earth as circumstances dictated. In Kenya, personnel fell in on and expanded the multiagency "country team" at the large US embassy in Nairobi, a replacement for the one badly damaged in the 1998 al-Qaeda attack.

The primary job of the eighty-agent FBI "fly team" was to conduct "sensitive site exploitation," a bureau specialty. Already Frankel and his investigators were helping interview eyewitnesses, and processing the assailants' car for fingerprints and other evidence. Later they would review videotape from the surveillance cameras and conduct a methodical search of what was left of the collapsed mall. His forensics experts would categorize each piece of evidence, from shell casings to cell phones, noting exactly where they were found and which terrorist they were most likely connected to.

Frankel and his team were finally given the all-clear, the Kenyan security personnel waving them through without so much as checking their weapons. Numerous men in civilian clothes were carrying away cardboard boxes stuffed with merchandise. Inside, the building was a smoldering ruin, shattered glass crunching underfoot and blood splattered everywhere. The Kenyan army's preferred method for clearing a shop of a suspected al-Shabab terrorist was simply to fire a rocket-propelled grenade into it. The Kenyans didn't lose any soldiers with that technique, but it was almost certainly responsible for the collapsing infrastructure of the mall, and for some of the friendly fire victims who were lying in local hospitals, or outside in the makeshift morgue.

Frankel and the FBI Rapid Deployment Team were focused on identifying the people responsible for the massacre, and collecting enough evidence to either put them behind bars or in the crosshairs of a US drone or direct action team. They already knew that media reports of a dozen or more al-Shabab fighters were way off the mark. The FBI had tracked four shooters and perhaps a fifth facilitator. By matching surveillance videos with evidence on the ground, they could tell where the shooters killed certain victims, where they stopped to rest, and most important, where they bedded down inside the mall the first night. That was the spot where FBI forensic experts found a trove of evidence that Frankel was certain would lead them to positively identify at least two of the terrorists.

That information was passed to onsite analysts from the CIA and the NSA's Counterterrorism Mission Aligned Cell, or CT MAC, which matched the names to known accomplices and phone records and fed that information into the massive database of the National Counterterrorism Center (NCTC) at Liberty Crossing, Virginia. There special multiagency pursuit groups would synthesize the data with other all-source intelligence to establish "patterns of life" for someone whose mosaic of terror would hopefully soon end.

INSIDE LIBERTY ONE, a nondescript, modern edifice, hundreds of counterterrorism analysts from more than twenty intelligence, national security, and law-enforcement agencies sifted through the initial raw intelligence from Westgate. They ran the forensic evidence against terrorism-related information from more than one hundred databases, and cross-checked the names of the suspects against the NCTC's own Terrorism Identification Datamark Environment watch list of more than 740,000 suspected terrorists or persons of interest.

Because of the horrific nature of the Westgate attack, al-Shabab was elevated near the top of the thirty to forty most credible ongoing threats. Through an analytic process that is as much art as science, the group was also added to the top handful of threats that made it into the Situation Report sent out twice a day, seven days a week to the intelligence community and top levels of the US government. The Westgate attack quickly became a chief subject of the secure video teleconferences that the NCTC conducted three times a day with the other twenty-odd agencies, a confab that also included the National Security Council staff. The attack also figured prominently in the Presidential Daily Briefing delivered at the White House each morning. Al-Shabab had officially made it onto the top-forty hit list the NCTC staff called the threat matrix, and they were rising with a bullet. Near a round conference table in his expansive office at Liberty One, NCTC director Matthew Olsen kept a carved plaque given to him on one of his frequent visits to Joint Special Operations Command at Fort Bragg, North Carolina. On one side of the plaque was JSOC's emblem of crossed swords spanning the globe, signifying that no place was beyond the reach of the hard edge of US military power. The other side displayed the NCTC emblem, the American eagle beneath a globe circled by a ring of stars, the all-seeing constellation. Olsen's memento signified that the two agencies were different sides of the same counterterrorism coin, critical nodes in an increasingly seamless "network of networks" whose genesis was the joint hunter-killer teams that General Stanley McChrystal had evolved in Iraq and Afghanistan. Unless Olsen misread the intelligence that reached his desk in October 2013, the reach and rapid response of that network was soon to be tested far from any declared war zone.

In many ways Olsen was an unlikely choice to run the world's premier counterterrorism clearinghouse. A still boyish-looking fifty-one and going to gray, Olsen was a Harvard Law School graduate who had worked as an attorney for the Justice Department's Civil Rights Division in the 1990s. That was followed by stints as a federal prosecutor, acting director of the Justice Department's National Security Division, and general counsel of the National Security Agency. He also led the Obama administration's Guantánamo Review Task Force that looked into legal avenues for closing the Guantánamo Bay detention center.

Throughout his career Olsen had shown a penchant for management and a lawyer's grasp of complexity and nuance, useful attributes in trying to understand the mutations of Islamist terrorism as it continued to go viral more than a decade after 9/11. In those years he believed the NCTC had moved much closer to fulfilling the original vision of the 9/11 Commission of a single, central clearinghouse for counterterrorism intelligence, a mother node in the network of networks where the dots of disparate terrorism plots could be connected. Unique within the intelligence community, NCTC had the ability to fuse all-source intelligence from both foreign and domestic intelligence sources.

The NCTC's maturation into the premier counterterrorism fusion center had not been without growing pains. The original vision of the 9/11 Commission of a central counterterrorism headquarters had been more aspirational than actual in the early years, as the twenty-plus agencies operating under the NCTC's roof learned to share and play nice. Initially, intelligence operatives trained to guard their secrets jealously had resisted even operating on a common computer network. Olsen never forgot seeing, inside his directorate of intelligence, desks with four separate computer terminals on them, each stove-piped to a different intelligence agency's database. By 2013, they were all networked into a single, common database.

As it happened, two major streams of counterterrorism intelligence intersected at the top of the NCTC's threat matrix in October 2013, and thus featured prominently in Olsen's briefing book: one from al-Shabab's Westgate Mall attack, and the other involving a longtime al-Qaeda operative named Nazih Abdul-Hamed al-Ruqai, a.k.a. Anas al-Libi. Al-Libi was under indictment and flying just beneath the radar of US intelligence agencies for his role in the 1998 bombing of the US embassies in Kenya and Tanzania. Recently he had been spotted by a reliable source in his hometown of Tripoli, Libya. Of greater concern to Olsen, there was intelligence indicating that core al-Qaeda leaders in Pakistan had sent al-Libi home to establish a new cell in the chaotic landscape of Libya. After the fall of Muammar el-Qaddafi, Libya had descended into ungovernable chaos, a failed state in the making ruled by competing militias, some of them Islamist extremists who were behind the ransacking of the US consulate in Benghazi.

Olsen generally briefed the president every other week on the counterterrorism threat. Although the NCTC was not an operational command in terms of executing counterterrorism missions, he was a key player in the highly classified decision-making process by which terrorists are targeted for capture or death. While that machinery operated in utmost secrecy, it drew on legal authorities to use lethal force against al-Qaeda and associated groups bestowed by Congress after the 9/11 attacks. The list of terrorists to be targeted passed through an elaborate, multiagency vetting process that culminated at the level of the National Security Council, and often required presidential approval.

Whenever major counterterrorism operations were discussed, Matthew Olsen attended those cabinet-level "Principals" meetings with his boss, Director of National Intelligence James Clapper. The intelligence streams on the Westgate Mall attack and the high-value target Anas al-Libi were placed on the agenda of a Principals meeting. Depending on the final targets, the intelligence on their whereabouts, and the potential legal authorities involved at the likely point of contact, the NCTC would develop and coordinate a strategic level plan and hand it off either to the CIA's Special Activities Division or to JSOC to execute the mission.

In the early post-9/11 days, that kind of elaborate planning and decision-making process had taken months, but out of long repetition and years of working closely together the cycle had been compressed dramatically.

The ethos of joint, network-centric operations that JSOC had pioneered in Iraq and Afghanistan now "rippled through the government's entire counterterrorism apparatus," according to a top White House counterterrorism official. In the case of the Westgate and al-Libi intelligence, the Obama administration quickly decided to launch two nearly simultaneous operations thousands of miles apart, involving JSOC's two elite counterterrorism strike forces—Navy SEAL Team Six and the Army's Delta Force. The date chosen for the commando raids was October 5, 2013. Ironically, on the day US counterterrorism forces launched the operations, the rest of the US government was shut down by political paralysis in Washington.

THE DRAMATICALLY COMPRESSED intelligence-gathering and decision-making cycle in the F3EA (find, fix, and finish, exploit, and analyze) model of counterterrorism operations was evident in the fact that just two weeks after the Westgate Mall attack, US Navy SEAL commandos listened to a muezzin's call to predawn prayers as it echoed down the crooked alleys and side streets of the ramshackle Somali seaside town of Barawe. The time was two hours before sunrise, and the mournful lament was picked up by other mosques and in nearby towns along the coast until the land itself seemed to stir to the summons.

A lone figure stepped out of a two-story villa a few hundred yards from the water's edge, and into the darkness of a walled compound to smoke a cigarette. His face was rhythmically illuminated in the glow of the ash, an effect heightened by the night-vision goggles trained on him. The moment he stepped back inside, the commander of SEAL Team Six, his own face hidden under black grease, motioned with his hands for his commandos to take up their positions and prepare to storm the villa. Inside they expected to find Abdikadir Mohamed Abdikadir, a.k.a. Ikrima—the Kenyan in charge of al-Shabab's "external operations" who was suspected of masterminding the gruesome massacre at the Westgate Mall.

Before the SEAL team could reposition, the al-Shabab fighter came back out of the door, firing an AK-47, and quickly was cut down by the SEAL team's return fire. Soon the entire compound erupted in automatic weapons fire, and the SEAL commandos quickly lost the all-important element of surprise. They blasted down a side door and fought their way into the villa, killing an Ikrima bodyguard but encountering heavy fire and resistance. There were also more women and children inside the villa, scrambling for cover in the darkness, than intelligence had led them to believe. SEAL commandos securing the perimeter reported taking fire from reinforcements who were threatening to cut off their exfiltration route to the sea, and their commander ordered his raiding team back to the inflatable boats waiting on the beach. The commandos suffered no casualties, but it undoubtedly irked them that they had to break contact with a high-value target with a $5 million bounty on his head, a terrorist whom they reportedly glimpsed through one of the villa's windows and was very nearly in their gunsights. At the very least, they had sent an important message to al-Shabab leaders about their ability to stay hidden from the long reach of US counterterrorism forces.

Two hours after SEAL Team Six assaulted Ikrima's seaside villa, and nearly 3,000 miles away, Anas al-Libi was returning from dawn prayers as the sun rose over Tripoli, Libya. An al-Qaeda operative whose tenure traced back to the 1990s and the original core group led by Osama bin Laden, he had returned to Libya in 2011. Like so many Islamist militants, al-Libi was drawn to the chaos and weak governance left in the wake of Arab Spring revolutions. US intelligence officials believed he was in Libya to establish an al-Qaeda cell, providing the connective tissue between a new Libyan affiliate and Ayman al-Zawahiri and other leaders of al-Qaeda's core still thought to be hiding in Pakistan.

As he pulled up in front of a comfortable house in an upscale suburb of Tripoli, al-Libi's car was suddenly boxed in from the side and the front by two white vans with darkened windows. Commandos from the Army's elite Delta Force counterterrorism unit leaped out, one training his gun on al-Libi from the front as another broke the car's window, pulling the terrorism suspect out of the car and bundling him into one of the vans before both vans and a third trailing vehicle that had been providing overwatch sped off. Next door, al-Libi's brother Nabih witnessed the abduction, but it was over before he could raise the alarm. The entire operation had taken sixty seconds. Alerted to the raid, angry Islamist militiamen detained Libyan prime minister Ali Zeidan, who denied any knowledge of the operation. By that time al-Libi had already been moved to the USS *San Antonio*, a warship operating in international waters in the nearby Mediterranean.

In a remarkable indication of the synergy between law enforcement and Special Operations Forces engaged in counterterrorism operations, specially trained members of the FBI's elite Hostage Rescue Team had accompanied both SEAL Team Six and Delta Force on the nearly simultaneous raids in Somalia and Libya. When asked about the twin commando raids executed just hours apart in different countries with whom the United States was not at war, Secretary of State John Kerry was unapologetic. Speaking from Bali, Indonesia, where he was attending an Asia-Pacific conference, Kerry said the raids signaled the United States' long memory and determination to bring terrorists to justice: "This sends the message that members of al-Qaeda and other terrorist organizations can literally run, but they cannot hide."

Kerry's message was underscored a few days later, when an armed Predator drone operated by the JSOC team attached to US Africa Command's Combined Joint Task Force–Horn of Africa (CJTF-HOA) in Djibouti established visuals with a car known to be carrying two top al-Shabab commanders, including the group's chief bomb maker named Anta. The two men and the car disappeared in the blast cloud of a Hellfire missile. Alabama native Omar Hammami—who was on the FBI's most wanted list—had fallen out with al-Shabab's mercurial leader Ahmed Abdi Godane, who had Hammami killed in September in an ambush. Before another year passed, another US airstrike inside Somalia would kill Godane, whose determination to export the group's terror to the wider region pushed his name to the top tier of the US threat matrix.

A WEEK AFTER the commando raids in Somalia and Libya, an FBI agent was sitting in a spare interrogation room below decks on the USS *San Antonio*, reading al-Libi his Miranda rights. He now had the right to remain silent, and anything the Libyan said would certainly be used against him in a court of law. If he could not afford an attorney, a lawyer in New York would surely jump at the chance to argue one of the most high-profile terrorist cases tried on US soil since 9/11. With the recitation of those magic words, al-Libi was transformed from an "enemy combatant" in America's war with al-Qaeda to just another criminal in the US justice system, with all the rights so accorded. Even for those involved in that delicate alchemy, the transformation was dizzying.

The FBI agent was part of the US government's High-Value Detainee Interrogation Group (HIG), another multiagency hybrid peopled by senior military, intelligence, and law enforcement officials, created specifically for the "global war on terrorism" and partly in response to the CIA's disastrous early foray into the interrogations of terrorism suspects. The US warship was operating in international waters, and the interrogators had broad wartime authorities bestowed by Congress's post-9/11 Authorization for the Use of Military Force. They could question al-Libi at length before reading him his rights, but they no longer used long since banned "enhanced interrogation techniques," such as waterboarding. They didn't hit al-Libi or even threaten to harm him, and what they learned could not be used in a court of law. But the FBI-led interrogators kept at it with patience and maddening persistence, and a psychological manipulation that appealed to the terrorist's preening sense of self-importance and to his professed religious convictions. That was another lesson the FBI had drawn from more than a decade of interrogating Islamist extremists, expertise that was informed by the FBI's Behavioral Science Unit's interviews of would-be suicide bombers in Afghanistan.

At first al-Libi cooperated with the interrogators, but he suffered from hepatitis C, and after days of questioning his mood soured and he stopped eating or drinking. At that point he invoked the Miranda rights that had already been offered and explained to him. The FBI agent halted the interrogation and made arrangements to have him flown to New York. The gravely ill terrorism suspect would later die at a hospital while in US custody.

The Miranda episode underscored the duality at the center of a shadow war that was part military, part criminal, and endless by the enemy's own definition of the struggle. The Obama administration had not placed any newly captured terrorist suspects in the Guantánamo Bay detention center since 2008, and after questioning, captured terrorists were given their Miranda rights and charged under criminal statutes in federal courts. Other terrorist suspects, including at least three American citizens, were blown apart far from any acknowledged battlefield under the laws of warfare.

With US troops having withdrawn from Iraq and in the process of leaving Afghanistan by 2013, the public seemed to believe that the country's longest war was finally ending. It felt different to those sprinting along the battlements to fill holes in the defenses or interrogating prisoners in their keep. This was another kind of war, and such traditional concepts as victory or surrender seemed not to apply. There was the thrill of the hunt, and the adrenaline rush of the contest, and always the nagging feeling of trouble coming that there was no holding off.

SIXTEEN

# Reflection in a Broken Mirror
## 2013

A S THE STACCATO IMPACT OF HIS FOOTFALLS BEAT TIME, MIKE
Flynn's scattershot thoughts ordered themselves to the steady cadence
and his own deep breathing. The early morning runs around sprawling
Joint Base Anacostia-Bolling always helped clear his head, and settling into
an easy gait Flynn relished spending a precious hour unmolested by the
burning inbox he knew awaited back in his office. The route took him
through streets of carefully manicured lawns and tidy houses, and along
the banks of the Potomac River where dawn mists still lay in pools on the
ground.

As the director of the Defense Intelligence Agency (DIA), Lieutenant
General Flynn had more than seventeen thousand intelligence officers reporting to him, spread out in more than 140 nations—a lot of fingers on the
wildly beating pulse of a world in a state of profound upheaval. Flynn was
at odds with what passed for conventional wisdom in Washington, DC, in
2013. He sensed that his analysis of increased global instability and a growing threat of Islamic terrorism was also increasingly at odds with the White
House and his commander in chief, and that made Flynn not a little uneasy.

Following the successful raid that killed Osama bin Laden in 2011, President Barack Obama was determined to decisively turn the page away from George W. Bush's "global war on terrorism." Obama understandably wanted to widen the aperture of American foreign policy once again, and to shrink the fear that terrorism had imposed on the national consciousness.

In May 2013 President Obama delivered a seminal counterterrorism speech at the National Defense University (NDU), located just across the Anacostia River from Flynn's DIA headquarters. The speech was a marker breaking decisively with the post-9/11 past. The core of al-Qaeda that struck America that day was on the path to defeat, Obama declared, and it was time to finally close the military detention center at Guantánamo Bay, Cuba, a stain on the national reputation and a constant reminder of an America that flouted the rule of international law. Obama also suggested it was time to begin rolling back the legal authorities that underpinned the war on terrorism.

"Today, Osama bin Laden is dead, and so are most of his top lieutenants. There have been no large-scale attacks on the United States, and our homeland is more secure. Fewer of our troops are in harm's way, and over the next nineteen months they will continue to come home. Our alliances are strong, and so is our standing in the world. In sum, we are safer because of our efforts," Obama told the audience at NDU. The nation was still threatened by terrorists, the president conceded, a fact driven home by the Boston Marathon bombings just the month before in April 2013 that killed three people and injured more than 250 others. But Obama plausibly argued that it was time to distinguish the current, more manageable threat from the existential menace that came to US shores on September 11, 2001.

"So, America is at a crossroads. We must define the nature and scope of this struggle, or else it will define us," he said. "We have to be mindful of James Madison's warning that 'No nation could preserve its freedom in the midst of continual warfare.'"

Obama's obvious concern about the impact of the nation's longest wars on civil liberties was understandable. He seemed to sense that what made this period of conflict almost uniquely dangerous was its hybrid nature — part criminal and part military—and its endless horizon. His attempt to move beyond the "global war on terrorism" mind-set was thus understandable and laudable as far as it went. In the NDU speech he never suggested that the threat from terrorism had passed altogether. Given the administration's successful raid that killed Osama bin Laden, and the withdrawal of US troops first from Iraq in 2011, and its stated goal of withdrawing the last combat troops from Afghanistan by the end of 2014, it was hardly surprising that President Obama would want to capitalize on that momentum in order to focus on his oft-stated priority of "nation-building here at home."

Only Washington doesn't do nuance, and the vast executive branch bureaucracy had begun to realign itself to the White House message that the threat from al-Qaeda and its ilk had largely passed. In 2012, the National Intelligence Council had even reportedly crafted a draft National Intelligence Estimate that was supposed to represent the consensus view of the US intelligence community, and which concluded that al-Qaeda was no longer a threat to the United States. A number of senior intelligence officials had pushed back hard against that conclusion as grossly premature, with Flynn essentially signaling that such an assessment would gain DIA approval over his dead body. Eventually he prevailed and the judgment that al-Qaeda no longer posed a threat to the homeland was expunged from the classified document. Ever since then, however, Flynn and like-minded intelligence officials felt like increasingly lonely voices in internal counterterrorism debates.

Like many senior military officers, Flynn was surprised by the speed with which the nation was turning its back on the unpopular wars in Iraq and Afghanistan, and seemingly anything associated with them. That was another hard lesson about the danger of wars that drag on indefinitely in a democracy.

That was the clear message behind Congress's willingness to gut military readiness with the so-called Budget Control Act known as sequester, even with troops still fighting and dying on a foreign battlefield. Moreover, the public backlash against the National Security Agency resulting from the revelations of former NSA contractor Edward Snowden, who gave to selected journalists documents detailing the techniques and procedures the agency used in its global wiretapping and eavesdropping operations, were putting critical counterterrorism surveillance programs at risk. In his

NDU speech President Obama even talked about rescinding the wartime authorities put in place after 9/11 that permitted the close intermingling of military, intelligence, and law enforcement capabilities, a synergy that was at the core of the new warfighting and counterterrorism model of operations that Flynn had helped create, and which represented one of the most important takeaways from a decade of war.

Mike Flynn thought about the intelligence reporting he read for hours, and the briefings he prepared each day. There were the familiar threats and challenges, ones he had studied closely at the Naval War College while earning his masters in national security and strategic studies: a rising and increasingly assertive China claiming disputed islands in the South China Sea, an increasingly belligerent Russia determined to carve out a sphere of privileged influence around its borders, a nuclear-armed North Korea ruled by a communist cult frozen in a Cold War mind-set, a hegemonic and aggrieved Iran ruled by mullahs who secretly hungered for the prestige and power that nuclear weapons bestow.

Yet for Flynn and the other mandarins of US intelligence, it was not the familiar ambitions of nation-states, but rather their failure that was of chief concern. To a degree not witnessed in their professional lives, whole regions of the world were gripped by societal upheaval and the failing of national governments. The entire system of nation-states with unchallenged sovereignty over their own territory, which traced back to the mid-seventeenth century, was shaking, rocked by increasingly powerful nonstate and transnational actors, such as terrorist groups, insurgents, criminal cartels, or simply social media–inspired flash mobs. The essence of globalization and the Information Age—the ability to move people and products long distances with little regard for national borders, instant communications over the Internet that allowed for global recruitment and incitement, the rapid flow of money electronically that could shift fantastic wealth quickly into the hands of a relative few—all of it had empowered individuals and groups to a degree never seen before in recorded history. Groups driven by motivations as ancient as religion, ideology, and a hunger for power.

Flynn believed that the threat from these nonstate actors was growing, not receding, and anyone who disagreed had better come armed with some facts. Because right before their eyes national governments were faltering

and nation-states were disintegrating, and boundaries on the map were being redrawn in ways and by groups that directly threatened US interests and
allies. Look at Libya, or Mali, or Somalia, or Nigeria. Dare to look closely
at what was happening inside of Syria.

The overflowing inbox that awaited him back at DIA headquarters
dominated his thoughts. Pakistan remained a wilderness of mirrors, with its
Inter-Services Intelligence agency double-dealing with numerous Islamic
extremist groups that had the blood of hundreds of American troops on
their hands. US intelligence officials worried that those Islamist extremists
could one day threaten the viability of that nuclear-armed state. For all the
talk of NATO leaving Afghanistan, the Taliban remained a potent insurgency, and the government in Kabul was still weak and riven by sectarian
intrigue and corruption. Al-Qaeda's core leadership had been decimated
in Pakistan, but its close affiliates were drawing strength from instability
spreading across the Middle East and Africa in the wake of the Arab Spring
upheavals that began in 2011. That dynamic had worrisome parallels to the
conditions in Afghanistan in the 1990s that originally spawned al-Qaeda.

MIKE FLYNN WAS especially concerned about the wanton murderers and
expert bomb makers of al-Qaeda in Iraq (AQI) that he had hunted for
years as the former intelligence chief of Joint Special Operations Command (JSOC). Revitalized by Syria's brutal civil war, al-Qaeda in Iraq
had morphed into the Islamic State of Iraq and Syria, or ISIS. Along
with the al-Qaeda franchise the al-Nusra Front, the two Islamist extremist
groups emerged as the strongest of the rebel factions fighting against Syrian strongman Bashar al-Assad's murderous regime. The terrorist groups
had even captured territory in northern Syria, where they were imposing
strict Sharia law with frequent amputations, beheadings, and executions
by stoning—a dream fulfilled for the fundamentalist jihadists. Intelligence intercepts indicated that ISIS was attracting hundreds, and possibly
thousands, of Western fighters to its black banners, and already planning
"external operations" in the wider region.

ISIS had also turned its attention back to Iraq. Over the past year it
launched bold prison breaks in Baghdad and elsewhere in the country,

freeing hundreds of the hardened fighters whom Flynn had helped capture in his years with JSOC. They in turn killed more than five thousand Iraqis in a merciless bombing campaign, putting 2013 on track to become the worst year of violence there since the US troop surge in Iraq in 2007. The carnage threatened to reignite Iraq's own civil war between Sunnis and Shiites, and spread to the wider region the violence that had already claimed more than 100,000 lives in a Syrian conflict that was increasingly sectarian in nature.

Thinking about ISIS brought back a flood of memories for Flynn, including the long nights he had spent interrogating the men who formed the corporate board for al-Qaeda in Iraq. He remembered how those men defied terrorist stereotypes. One had been a doctor, another an engineer, and yet another a professor. They were college educated, and some had earned advanced degrees. By rights, they should have been leading the effort to rebuild their country and make better the lives of their children. Instead those savvy, sophisticated men had pledged their lives and considerable talents to visiting the most horrific violence on Iraq, most of it directed at fellow Muslims. All in hopes of cleansing the country in the purifying fires of civil war so that an ancient caliphate based on a seventh-century interpretation of Sharia law might rise from the ashes.

Flynn recalled the captured AQI PowerPoint briefing that laid it all out in surprising detail, including command-and-control link charts, mission statements, organizational charts, financing structures, and established infiltration networks between Syria and Iraq—AQI's whole grand vision broken down into its component parts in a campaign plan nearly as sophisticated and detailed as the US military's "Iraqi Freedom" invasion plan.

One of the masterminds of the campaign for a Greater Caliphate had been AQI's second-in-command, Abu Ayyub al-Masri, an Egyptian with long ties to al-Qaeda leader Ayman al-Zawahiri, the former head of the Egyptian Islamic Jihad terrorist group. As the leader of AQI's daily operations and the emir of its foreign-fighter network, al-Masri had been responsible for establishing and maintaining the intricate network that funneled foreign jihadists from Syria through the Euphrates valley and down into the villages and towns that formed the suburban belts surrounding Baghdad. After Task Force 714 finally tracked down and killed al-Zarqawi in 2006, al-Masri was named his replacement within days. Although al-Masri was killed during a raid on his house in April 2010, the news did little to alter Flynn's calculation of a growing threat from the group.

The White House was apparently convinced that killing Osama bin Laden had sounded the death knell for al-Qaeda. Everyone wanted to believe that, no one more than Mike Flynn. But in his time in the field in Iraq and Afghanistan, Task Force 714 had killed no less than seven al-Qaeda "number threes," making the chief operating officer for the group the world's most hazardous job. Another true believer always appeared from the ranks to take their place. Decapitation of leadership was an important tactic for keeping these groups back on their heels, but Flynn learned the hard way that as a war-winning strategy, it was a proven failure.

Flynn was troubled by a flow chart of al-Qaeda in Iraq's foreign fighter pipeline that they had captured during the hunt for al-Zarqawi and al-Masri. It identified the latter's top lieutenant in charge of the foreign fighter operations inside Iraq. That man personally managed the network of safe houses and infiltration routes. He knew all the key players in the terrorist networks working both sides of the Iraq-Syria border. After the al-Qaeda lieutenant was captured in a US raid, Flynn had largely forgotten about him. But his name had recently resurfaced.

According to the Defense Department, Abu Bakr al-Baghdadi had been released in 2004 from the US military detention center at Camp Bucca, Iraq, named after Ronald Paul Bucca, the only fire marshal in the history of the New York City Fire Department to die in the line of duty when he was killed in the September 11, 2001, terrorist attacks. On his release from prison and US custody, al-Baghdadi rose rapidly through the ranks of al-Qaeda in Iraq. After the 2011 Arab Spring protests and Bashar al-Assad's iron-fisted response ignited a sectarian civil war in Syria, al-Baghdadi instinctively grasped that the same ratlines that had long funneled foreign fighters from Syria into Iraq during the long US occupation could be reversed, sending AQI's Sunni jihadists the other way to carve a sanctuary out of the rotting corpse of Syria.

By the fall of 2013, ISIS had captured large swaths of territory in Syria and was causing havoc in Iraq. Flynn grew uneasy thinking about the familiar menace of Abu Bakr al-Baghdadi, a swarthy, powerfully built man with eyes as dark and opaque as the bottom of an ocean, now leading a vanguard of thousands of seasoned al-Qaeda in Iraq operatives and former senior Baathist military officers in Saddam Hussein's army that he had freed from Iraqi prisons. In 2006–2007 AQI and its Sunni insurgent allies had very nearly defeated the US military, the world's most powerful military force. Now a new generation of Islamic and Sunni tribal leaders had returned to the battlefield in Iraq and Syria, and every dispatch that came across his desk convinced Flynn that they were smarter and more capable for apply-ing the lessons learned from fighting US forces. They were better armed and funded than in the past, and more experienced in manipulating weak governments and societies in the Muslim world, through fear and intimida-tion. Just between 2012 and 2013, worldwide terrorist attacks had increased by a shocking 43 percent, and through its burgeoning affiliates al-Qaeda had a bigger footprint in 2013 than it did prior to September 11, 2001.

Al-Qaeda's far-flung network of affiliates and associated jihadists were also communicating more with one another, and with core al-Qaeda leader Ayman al-Zawahiri, thought still to be hiding in Pakistan's tribal regions. If al-Zawahiri or al-Baghdadi could unite them under a single black banner of Islamic extremism, forging a cohesive and coherent terrorist collective, then they would be tantalizingly close to Osama bin Laden's original vi-sion of a global Islamist insurgency intent on waging endless war, locally, regionally, and against the West. They weren't there yet, but every instinct Flynn had honed in tracking these men for much of his professional life suggested that they were getting closer.

Thinking back on those AQI leaders during his jog around Joint Base Anacostia-Bolling, remembering those long nights of interrogation simply trying to understand what made the enemy tick, Flynn felt a stab of recogni-tion that worried him these long years later: The al-Qaeda and ISIS leaders were true believers, equally as committed to their cause and skewed moral universe as Flynn was to his own. In that sense the men sitting on opposite sides of an interrogation table years ago were reflections in a broken mirror, men with unrecognizable belief systems and ideologies, yet utterly familiar in their shared sense of devotion.

Flynn's morning runs always helped clear his head, and by the time his jogging route looped back to DIA headquarters, the sun was up and the flags that lined the street in a long row in front of the building were fluttering in a strong breeze. He had agreed to conduct an on-the-record interview with the author. Flynn knew the questions he would likely be asked, and he knew his answers would run counter to the narrative preferred by the White House and even in some corridors in the Pentagon. Are the terrorists on the run? No, they are not. Is the al-Qaeda brand of Islamist extremism close to being defeated? No, it is not. Anyone who answered yes to those questions was either misinformed, didn't know what they were talking about, or else they were flat out lying.

You couldn't sit where Mike Flynn did every day, knowing what he knew about the enemy and reading the classified and unclassified intelligence dispatches from around the world, and not realize that al-Qaeda's core was not crippled when Osama bin Laden's body slipped over the side of an aircraft carrier at sea in 2011. Al-Qaeda's core was an extremist ideology rooted in intolerance, violence, and hatred, and the unholy warriors who took it to heart. And that ideological movement and its legions of followers were growing.

From his corner office on the top floor of DIA headquarters Flynn had an unobstructed view of Ronald Reagan National Airport just across the Potomac, and in contemplative moments he sometimes watched the commercial airliners bank on their final approach down the river and pass low above the Pentagon before touching down in a swirling burst of landing gear smoke. There was a time when such a view invoked only the stunning beauty of the nation's capital, but for Mike Flynn and the other members of the brotherhood, that more innocent time was a distant and receding memory.

# SEVENTEEN

# Twilight Warriors

## 2013–2014

THE ORWELLIAN J. EDGAR HOOVER BUILDING LOOMS OVER PENN-
sylvania Avenue, its totalitarian vibe and imposing facade towering
over pedestrians like an implied threat. The building's controversial name-
sake would probably have loved it. Yet from Brian McCauley's upper-floor
office fronting Pennsylvania, the building offered a view of the National
Archives across the wide boulevard and beyond, to the green expanse of
the National Mall. Given the work that consumed him as the FBI's deputy
assistant director for international operations, the tranquility of that scene
usually offered comfort. Only January 16, 2013, was not one of those days.

Overseas reporting by the BBC and Al Jazeera described an apparent
terrorist attack on the remote Amenas gas plant in Algeria, a sprawling facility spread across nearly 40 acres that was operated by British Petroleum
(BP), Norway's Statoil, and the Algerian state oil company. The natural gas
production plant was located in the Sahara desert some 800 miles from the
Algerian capital of Algiers. Early reporting suggested that more than eight
hundred people worked at the Amenas facility, including more than one
hundred foreigners and an unspecified number of Americans. Many were

being held hostage by a marauding band of gunmen who attacked the facility at first light with explosives and automatic weapons.

FBI suspicions quickly fell on al-Qaeda in the Islamic Maghreb (AQIM). A toxic byproduct of Algeria's bloody civil war of the 1990s between the Algerian military and Islamists, AQIM was a Salafist group that had previously focused mainly on local operations, amassing a fortune from smuggling and kidnappings for ransom across the broad expanse of Africa's remote Sahel region. The previous year AQIM had taken advantage of regional instability and political chaos in northern Mali by forging an alliance with ethnic Tuaregs, and launching an offensive to capture territory in northern Mali around the towns of Timbuktu and Gao. Only a US-assisted intervention by French troops turned back AQIM's bold offensive.

The group's most effective field commander was a flamboyant, one-eyed jihadist and former Afghan mujahedeen named Mokhtar Belmokhtar. Apparently unsatisfied with AQIM's local focus and modest ambitions, Belmokhtar formed a breakaway militia called the al-Mulathamun Battalion, or "the Masked Battalion." He also allied his militia with a Salafist group in Libya called Ansar al-Sharia, which was linked to the deadly September 11, 2012, terrorist attack on the US consulate in Benghazi. Intelligence indicated that known members of Ansar al-Sharia had called Belmokhtar after the Benghazi attack to offer their congratulations on a successful operation, indicating that he had a hand in planning it.

By 2013, alarms were sounding in US counterterrorism circles over the growing linkages between a loose-knit network of Salafi terrorist groups in North Africa and the Middle East, which included Boca Haram in Nigeria, AQIM in Algeria and Mali, Ansar al-Sharia in Libya and Tunisia, al-Qaeda in the Arabian Peninsula (AQAP) in Yemen, al-Nusra Front in Syria, al-Shabab in Somalia, and the Islamic State of Iraq and Syria (ISIS). Osama bin Laden's vision of a jihadist international sowing instability across an arc of Muslim lands stretching from Africa to Southwest Asia was coming into sharp relief. The question for those twilight warriors who fought in Iraq and Afghanistan, and had risen to the upper echelons of their various agencies, was whether the US counterterrorism network could keep pace with that rapidly evolving threat.

On January 16, 2013, Brian McCauley was concerned that Belmokhtar and AQIM—if they were actually behind the assault on Amenas—had exhibited a willingness to execute their hostages if demands were not met. In 2009 the group had killed US citizen Christopher Leggett in Mauritania, and in 2011 AQIM executed two French hostages during an attempted rescue operation. Another French hostage would be executed later in 2013 in retaliation for France's military intervention in Mali. Now reports indicated the group potentially had eight hundred hostages, including an unknown number of Americans.

McCauley worked his extensive network of contacts. The head of security at British Petroleum was a former CIA official he knew from his days as a liaison at the agency. The BP contact supplied the FBI with the names and contacts of Americans working at Amenas, as well as the frequencies of its radios that the terrorists had captured and were using to communicate across the sprawling complex. That intelligence would prove vital, and serving as a conduit between the private oil and gas industry and the US counterterrorism network planted the germ of an idea in McCauley's head that would later flower into a formal relationship.

McCauley contacted the NSA, which was soon monitoring the conversations on BP radios. He called his friend Mike Flynn at the Defense Intelligence Agency (DIA), which began monitoring the crisis. He reached out to John Mulholland, another close friend and the deputy commander of US Special Operations Command (SOCOM). He connected everyone on a video teleconference and shared what the FBI knew with SOCOM, which might have to mount a hostage rescue operation if the Algerian government requested assistance. Imperceptibly to outside observers, the network adjusted its focus and trained a hard stare on a remote gas plant in the remote Sahara Desert.

As the Amenas hostage drama played out over the space of four days, McCauley and the FBI monitored the text messages between American workers at the complex and their wives back in Houston, Texas. They learned that scores of foreigners were hiding throughout the complex in false ceilings, under beds, and in darkened maintenance rooms, information the FBI kept out of news reports so as not to tip off the terrorists. Reports from those in

hiding indicated that the complex had been attacked by thirty to forty militants armed with guns and explosives, and they had already killed a number
of workers who attempted to flee the facility. Many of the Algerian workers
were reportedly let go, but the terrorists were rounding up foreigners and
strapping explosives around their necks and waists.

Monitoring the texts from husbands telling wives how much they loved
them, both knowing there was a good chance the men would not survive
the night, was heartrending. These were just hard-working men toiling in
some god-forsaken patch of North African desert to be able to feed their
families and send their children to school. The sudden horror of their situation formed a knot in Brian McCauley's gut: they were also Americans,
and in his book that made the FBI ultimately responsible for their safety.

On the third day of the drama, an intercepted radio transmission indicated that the terrorists were gathering the foreign hostages into a particular building, which they intended to level with explosives. The Algerian
military was ordered to move in, and in the ensuing firefight thirty-eight
hostages were killed, many of them while being used as human shields.
When their cause was lost, the terrorists lined up and shot the remaining
foreign hostages execution style with a bullet to the head, including three
Americans. Twenty-nine of the hostage takers also died in the final assault.

After the smoke cleared, McCauley contacted the US ambassador to Algeria and asked that an FBI interrogator be allowed to speak with the three
terrorists who had been captured alive, including a Canadian. If the bureau
could can gain access to the site, he assured the ambassador, it could tell
the Algerians not only who was behind the attack, but which weapon belonged to what terrorist and who they had killed. The FBI was given access
to the site and the captured terrorists.

The FBI soon learned that the Amenas attack was an inside job: the Islamist extremists had a contact inside the facility, which explained how they
knew the layout and where foreign workers were housed. The mastermind
behind the attack was indeed Mokhtar Belmokhtar, the maverick jihadist
whose splinter group was calling themselves "those who sign in blood."
And yet there were others who traveled under that sign, and as a result of
Belmokhtar's rising ambitions a $5 million bounty was placed on his head.
The AQIM field commander rose to the top ranks of the National Counter-

terrorism Center's threat matrix. At that point the network knew what to do. A year and a half later, two US F-15 aircraft would streak across Libyan skies and bomb a facility where Ansar al-Sharia was holding a high-level meeting thought to include Belmokhtar. AQIM confirmed in a statement that an "elite group from among the sincere sons of Libya and its resplendent knights" was killed, but insisted that Belmokhtar was not among them. If the one-eyed jihadi had survived, presumably he had received the message about America's long memory and reach.

THE AMERICANS KILLED in the Amenas terrorist attack were oil and gas workers Victor Lynn Lovelady, Gordon Lee Rowan, and Frederick Buttaccio. For his own reasons, Brian McCauley wasn't willing to just let them go down as another terrorism statistic. Perhaps it was the texts between the men and their families back in Houston that made them so real. The sense of injustice that McCauley felt recalled the US Embassy bombing in Kabul back in 2006, what already seemed a lifetime ago. There were times when the image of fifty-two-year-old Sergeant First Class Merideth Howard still came to him unbidden, helmet still on but her face gone, and missing a leg: the handiwork of fellow jihadi travelers.

McCauley was troubled that the US intelligence community had enough chatter prior to the attack to have reasonably guessed that AQIM was plotting something big, but no method to share that intelligence and warn private oil companies. While discussing the problem with US Special Operations Command, Lieutenant General John Mulholland handed over the business card of an oil company CEO. That led to a number of discussions and meetings with top oil company executives, who impressed on McCauley their vulnerability to terrorist attacks. Not only did their companies operate in some of the most unstable countries in the Middle East and Africa, but they represented conspicuous wealth and prestige in an international order that the jihadists were sworn to destroy. AQIM and Mokhtar Belmokhtar targeted the Amenas gas facility for the same reason that other jihadists had slaughtered tourists at Egypt's Luxor in 1997, and had attacked New York's World Trade Center in 1993 and 2001: to land a blow both symbolic and real on the targeted economy.

The discussions with a growing circle of oil and gas company executives crystalized McCauley's thinking on the need for a formal link between the industry and US counterterrorism officials, but he would need a champion to help sell it to the wider intelligence community and overcome the inevitable institutional resistance to sharing intelligence with civilians. So he called Mike Flynn again, who as the head of the Defense Intelligence Agency had the institutional heft to help get the initiative off the ground.

Flynn immediately liked the out-of-the-box idea of forming an informal, public-private partnership between the intelligence community and an oil industry that had its own significant intelligence-gathering and security capabilities, and globe-spanning operations. It jived with his ideas about broadening and thickening the United States' global intelligence-gathering network by continually adding nodes and additional inputs, while at the same time making it flatter and less hierarchal in order to facilitate the smooth flow of information.

Since taking the helm of DIA in 2012 with orders from then defense secretary Leon Panetta to "shake things up," Flynn had been doing just that and then some, applying ten years' worth of combat "lessons learned" in terms of intelligence integration and collaboration into transforming DIA. Building on JSOC's success with multiagency task forces and intelligence fusion centers, he had created five new DIA Intelligence Integration Centers to support warfighters around the world, and increased critical human intelligence gathering by growing the Defense Clandestine Service of spies even as he shrank headquarters staff in Washington. He also fought a constant rear guard action against DIA's hidebound bureaucracy, reassigning more than one hundred senior civilian managers who had used their bureaucratic power bases to resist his reforms. By 2013 it was already clear that the instincts for collaboration and concepts of truly joint, network-centric warfare honed in Iraq and Afghanistan were at odds with the bureaucratic mind-set so typical of Washington, DC.

The first meeting of the informal public-private partnership between US intelligence and security officials and oil and gas executives was held later in 2013 in Stuttgart, Germany, headquarters for US Africa Command. A follow-on meeting would be held at DIA headquarters in Washington, DC, an attempt by Flynn to institutionalize the innovative process of intelligence sharing. The top executives from the twenty-six global oil companies who attended the Stuttgart meeting were briefed on threats and ways to share sensitive intelligence by Mike Flynn; John Mulholland of US Special Operations Command; Marine Corps Lieutenant General Steven Hummer, deputy commander of US Africa Command; and, of course, McCauley. McCauley articulated the philosophy of the unusual partnership, one which required careful scrubbing of intelligence and a constant back-and-forth within the community to clear the sharing of information: Whenever the intelligence community came across evidence of a credible threat, a way would be found to share that information and warn the innocent civilians whose lives were at risk.

THE UNUSUAL PUBLIC-PRIVATE partnership between the intelligence community and the oil and gas industry was tested soon enough. McCauley was sitting in his favorite lounger in March 2014, recuperating from the latest of six surgeries to try to kill the Afghan parasite that was eating away at his bowels, when the call came in. His doctors speculated that the bug came from insufficiently cooked eggs he had eaten in Kabul, but no one seemed able to get rid of it. The doctors had been forced to remove so much of his intestine that McCauley had come close to dying during his last operation.

On the other end of the telephone call was Jim Snyder, the chief security officer at ConocoPhillips and one of the participants in the informal partnership McCauley had helped form. The news was bad: one of the company's contracted ships carrying more than 1 million barrels of crude oil had been hijacked by armed gunmen in Libya and was heading in the direction of Cyprus. Snyder suspected that the *Morning Glory* was being taken to an area just outside the territorial waters of Cyprus where Libyan black market oil was often traded. The crude oil would likely be stolen via a ship-to-ship transfer with an Iranian or Venezuelan tanker.

McCauley called Mike Flynn at DIA, who raised the issue to the top of the intelligence community agenda. Intelligence analysts who had been monitoring the armed groups operating in Libya raised another, distinctly more threatening scenario: there had been chatter among extremists about possibly hijacking an oil tanker and purposely discharging its contents in the Mediterranean, creating an Exxon *Valdez*–like environmental disaster that could wreck the tourist economies of NATO members Italy, Greece, or Turkey. Flynn alerted his close contacts at Special Operations Command and Africa Command, and his counterpart with Italian intelligence. The State Department had originally resisted the intelligence community partnership with global oil companies as an infringement on its authorities in terms of managing government-to-government relations. Yet recognizing the immediate danger presented by the *Morning Glory*, state officials sent letters of démarche to all the countries in the area, asking for cooperation and for measures to prevent the vessel from discharging its cargo. The US government was responding to the crisis with singular purpose.

On the night of March 16, 2014, the guided missile destroyer USS *Roosevelt* was operating in international waters southeast of Cypress. Part of the George H. W. Bush Carrier Strike Group, the *Roosevelt* was vectored to the area and was acting that night as the command-and-control and helicopter support platform for a team of US Navy SEALs attached to Special Operations Command–Europe. Just after ten p.m. local time, the SEAL team boarded the *Morning Glory* and captured the three armed Libyans aboard without having to fire a shot. US sailors took command of the tanker and returned it to Libya.

The chairman of ConocoPhillips reached out to Secretary of Defense Chuck Hagel to commend the US military for its rapid and successful response to the *Morning Glory* crisis. The operation averted what could have been an environmental disaster of historic proportions. Mike Flynn believed the genesis of the successful operations were the relationships forged in wartime that bound the national security brotherhood together. Luckily, Brian McCauley had organized the FBI's response to the terrorist attack on the Amenas gas plant in Algeria. It reminded McCauley of a pledge made long ago at the scene of another terrorist attack in Afghanistan that killed two American soldiers, which inspired him to reach out to other members of that unique fraternity. The successful response to the *Morning Glory* crisis would likely never have happened otherwise. Flynn also knew that the leaders who came of age in the post-9/11 wars were quickly passing from the scene. He often worried what would happen when the voice on the other end of that three a.m. call for a crisis response was a stranger asking for an inconvenient favor.

The day after the SEAL team captured the *Morning Glory*, the Pentagon held a press briefing on the operation, and the Navy commandos won significant praise. Flynn sent his unheralded friend at the FBI a simple e-mail, knowing McCauley would understand the subtext: "It takes a network to defeat a network!" Flynn wrote. And then, "Happy Saint Paddy's Day!!!" The date was March 17, 2014.

THE GROWING DANGER posed by empowered nonstate actors in an age of weak and faltering governments was also evident much closer to home. Since the 1990s, the United States and its Latin American allies had fought a clandestine war against drug cartels grown rich and powerful on America's voracious appetite for illicit narcotics. The fact that the cartels were driven by greed rather than a nihilistic religious ideology made them more predictable from a strictly business standpoint, but no less ruthless and depraved than radical Islamic terrorists. Between 2007 and 2014, more than 164,000 people were killed in Mexico's fight against the drug-trafficking cartels, outpacing the estimated 103,000 who died by violence in Afghanistan and Iraq during the same seven-year span.

US officials were especially concerned about signs of overlap in the "global war on terrorism" and the drug trade. Since 9/11, the most resilient al-Qaeda franchises and related terrorists groups had survived by constantly adapting to US pressure. In that Darwinian landscape, many extremist groups responded to the US Treasury Department's attempts to dry up their funding sources by turning to drug trafficking and other independent streams of money, to include kidnapping and extortion. According to Drug Enforcement Administration (DEA) statistics, by 2014 nearly 40 percent of the State Department's designated terrorist groups were also involved in drug trafficking.

Arguably, no US official was more alarmed by growing signs of collusion between drug traffickers and terrorists than Marine Corps General John Kelly, who took command of US Southern Command (SOUTHCOM) in 2012. The tall, lanky officer, one of the few ever to rise from the enlisted ranks all the way to four-star general, was a veteran of multiple combat tours. As chief of SOUTHCOM, headquartered in a sprawling complex on the outskirts of Miami with a staff of more than 1,200 people, Kelly was tasked with helping to counter some of the most powerful and violent criminal cartels in the world. That was a shadow war in its own right, being fought on America's doorstep.

Somewhat to his surprise and disappointment, Kelly discovered on assuming the helm of Southern Command that it was one of the most underresourced of the US military's six geographic combatant commands, in large part because its area of responsibility was Latin America. A vast region of thirty-one countries with more than 475 million people, Latin America was nevertheless a strategic afterthought for US officials traditionally preoccupied with higher-priority areas, whether it was an announced "pivot to Asia," trouble with a revanchist Russia in Eastern Europe, or five-alarm crises throughout the Middle East. Part of the official ambivalence about the region, as Kelly also learned, stemmed from the fact that SOUTHCOM's primary missions involved some of the most intractable problems the US government had ever faced, including a long and unsuccessful "war" on drugs and an inability to secure the southern US border from illegal immigrants and smugglers.

Yet as Kelly stressed during his periodic visits to Washington to try to drum up support and resources for his operations, SOUTHCOM dealt with a threat matrix that had a direct impact on the lives of millions of Americans. The evidence could be found in each day's headlines.

Governors and mayors across the United States had recently begun warning of an unanticipated heroin epidemic, with heroin-related deaths jumping by 39 percent from 2012 to 2013. Largely because of gang violence associated with the trade in illegal drugs, tiny El Salvador was on track to replace little Honduras as the world's most murderous country outside a war zone. In just an eight-month span in 2014, more than fifty thousand unaccompanied migrant children had been detained trying to cross the southern US border—an almost 100 percent increase over the previous year—many of them seeking asylum from Central American gang violence.

Ongoing peace talks between Colombia and the hybrid narco-terrorist and insurgent group Revolutionary Armed Forces of Colombia, or FARC, were perennially on the brink of collapse. In Argentina, the country's best-known prosecutor was building a case that Iran's terrorist proxy Hezbollah—still remarkably active in Latin America—was behind the long-ago bombing of a Jewish center in Buenos Aires, and he claimed that the Argentinian government knew about it. Special prosecutor Alberto Nisman would later be found with a bullet to his head under decidedly suspicious circumstances hours before he was expected to publicly accuse then president Cristina Fernández de Kirchner of making a secret deal with Tehran that glossed over Iran's role in the bombing.

Recent years had also seen splashy headlines and media reports detailing operations and arrests targeting Mexican drug kingpins, including the February 2014 arrest of Sinaloa cartel leader "El Chapo" Guzmán, one of Mexico's richest men and a gangster the US Drug Enforcement Administration considered the "godfather of the drug world," who would later escape from prison and be recaptured; and the 2013 arrest of Miguel Treviño Morales, the leader of a hyperviolent cartel of former Mexican special forces commandos who called themselves Los Zetas.

The linkages between those seemingly unrelated stories were easily missed in a frenetic news cycle, but John Kelly and his staff were paid to connect the dots. Because SOUTHCOM was a military command in a region where there was no war in the conventional sense, its operational role was primarily to support law enforcement efforts in the region by monitoring and detecting drug trafficking. The command's operational headquarters for that multiagency mission, Joint Interagency Task Force South located in Key West, was actually an early model and precursor to the multiagency task forces that Joint Special Operations Command honed to such a lethal effect in Afghanistan and Iraq under Stanley McChrystal. The style of joint, networked operations that McChrystal and JSOC had taken to a new level had become the gold standard for US counterterrorism operations by 2014.

SOUTHCOM headquarters represented another node in that network, an analytic hub for US counterdrug and counterterrorism activities in Latin America that included more than 30 representatives from US intelligence and law enforcement agencies, as well as liaisons from their law enforcement counterparts in numerous Latin American countries. Those experts knew the heroin epidemic in the United States was just the latest evidence of the American public's unabated appetite for illegal drugs, which sustained a $650-billion-a-year criminal enterprise. Each year forty thousand Americans died in that epidemic of drug use and addiction, mostly from the "big three" of heroin, cocaine, and methamphetamine, the overwhelming majority of which came from Latin America. The Mexican cartels that fought over that lucrative market were responsible for the deaths of tens of thousands of Mexicans, and the tactical alliances they formed with brutal street gangs, such as Mara Salvatrucha and Barrio 18, along the smuggling pipeline explained why eight of the ten most violent countries in the world were in Latin America.

John Kelly had witnessed firsthand in Iraq the darkness that descends when a government fails and the rule of law breaks down and extremists gain the upper hand. The memory made him sensitive to the wolf he perceived at the country's southern border. Most worrisome from SOUTHCOM's perspective was the nexus of violent drug cartels, transnational smuggling organizations, and terrorist groups. In that shadowy space, such narco-terrorist hybrids as Colombia's FARC and Peru's Shining Path had thrived.

The nexus of terrorism and drug smuggling was not new, nor was it hypothetical. The history was instructive. In the 1990s, US Special Forces had joined in the fight against Pablo Escobar's violent Medellín cartel, which had turned to terrorism in its fight against Colombian authorities, routinely bombing police buildings, assassinating judges and politicians, and even blowing up a civilian airliner in flight. Colombia's successful fracturing of the Medellín and Cali cartels in the 1990s had the unintended consequence of creating a vacuum in the lucrative drug trade. The vacuum was eventually filled by Mexican cartels and Colombia's FARC, which morphed from a Marxist insurgency relying on terrorist tactics into primarily a drug production and trafficking organization with a thin ideological veneer of communism. Under pressure from the Mexican and Colombian governments, those groups were fracturing once again, forming new alliances and seeking sanctuary in weak or more permissive countries, such as Venezuela and Bolivia.

John Donnelly was the DEA's special agent assigned to SOUTHCOM. The Mexican cartels were fragmenting like the Colombian cartels before them, he noted. In that reordering, the DEA was detecting more contact between transnational criminal organizations and terrorist groups, though the overlap was still tenuous. He once asked a CIA counterpart and intelligence analyst about that connection between transnational criminal organizations in the region and terrorist groups like Lebanese Hezbollah. "His reply was, 'Define connection,'" Donnelly recalled. "Both terrorist and smuggling groups swim in the same pool and use some of the same services, such as money laundering. That connection exists, but it's not an ideological connection."

The model that most concerned DEA officials remained the FARC in Colombia. It had evolved from a terrorist insurgency into primarily a sophisticated drug-trafficking organization because, in the words of one senior DEA official, "it's more profitable being a rich drug trafficker than a poor Marxist." That same phenomenon was repeated around the world as terrorist groups and drug smuggling cartels formed partnerships of convenience and shared "best practices." Thus the Afghan Taliban, Somali al-Shabab, al-Qaeda in the Islamic Maghreb, and the Kurdish PKK terrorist group in Iraq all sustained themselves partly through drug smuggling and sales.

SOUTHCOM analysts spent a significant portion of their time studying the connective tissue between terrorists, drug cartels, and smuggling networks. That crossover effect was evident in the case of an Iranian operative named Mansour Arbabsiar, who had dual Iranian and American citizenship. In 2011 he approached an extremely violent Mexican drug cartel with a murder-for-hire proposal. Arbabsiar, who was working for the Iranian military, proposed that a cartel hit man assassinate the Saudi ambassador to the United States by bombing a popular restaurant in Washington, DC, that the ambassador frequented. The risk of being tied to a violent drug cartel and a mass-casualty terrorist attack in the heart of the US capital did not deter Iranian military officials. Luckily, and only by chance, the individual Arbabsiar approached was a DEA informant, and the plot was thwarted.

In another instance the same year, DEA agents in Guatemala intercepted a shipment of cocaine and $20 million tied to the murderous Los Zetas group of former Mexican special forces soldiers. In a wide-ranging conspiracy investigation, the DEA discovered that the drug shipment was part of a smuggling network that moved product from South America to Europe via West Africa. The profits were laundered through the Lebanese Canadian Bank, which "scrubbed" the money clean in part by financing a string of used-car dealerships in the United States. The ultimate benefactor of the proceeds was Hezbollah, which has the blood of hundreds of Americans on its hands going back to the Marine Corps barracks bombing in Lebanon in 1983 that killed 241 US service members. The US Treasury Department ultimately shut down the Lebanese Canadian Bank by exposing its links to Hezbollah and sanctioning it under the Foreign Narcotics Kingpin Designation Act. In many particulars the Los Zetas–Hezbollah connection resembled the DEA's arrest of Afghan heroin kingpins Khan Mohammed and Haji Juma Khan, both of whom shipped heroin to the United States and used the profits to arm the Afghan Taliban who were killing US soldiers in Afghanistan.

The investigation of the Lebanese Canadian Bank was among a number of cases that suggested to SOUTHCOM analysts that Africa was the next front in a shadow war where drug trafficking and terrorism converged. South American drug smugglers discovered the advantage of shipping product through West Africa, where governments were often corrupt and weak, and there was little interference from US law enforcement. Not only was the African route safer, but it led to a more lucrative market in Europe where street prices for drugs were much higher.

The ability of hybrid narco-terrorist groups in Latin America to corrupt and undermine governments as far away as Africa was revealed in a 2012 DEA case involving Guinea-Bissau. One of the world's poorest nations, Guinea-Bissau was already dubbed Africa's first "narco-state," because so many of its top military and civilian leaders were on the payroll of drug cartels. As a hub for transshipment and a marketplace where drug proceeds were traded for arms, the nation attracted representatives of Hezbollah, FARC, and al-Qaeda in the Islamic Maghreb.

In 2012, DEA sources posing as Latin American drug traffickers approached Admiral José Américo Na Tchuto of the Guinea-Bissau navy, who agreed to help store and transship two tons of cocaine. Admiral Na Tchuto also agreed to supply advanced weapons to the FARC narco-terrorists as part of the deal, including surface-to-air missiles that were a threat to civilian air traffic. To spring the trap, the DEA chartered a large yacht and anchored it in international waters just off the coast of Guinea-Bissau, and then sent a motor skiff to shore to bring the admiral and his coconspirators out to the ship to "celebrate" closing the deal. They were met by DEA special operations commandos who trained alongside Delta Force and SEAL Team Six and were a direct outgrowth of joint DEA and JSOC operations in Afghanistan. US warships assigned to AFRICOM backed the operation off the coast of Guinea-Bissau, revealing the close handshake that had developed between law enforcement and military organizations in the post-9/11 era.

The consensus view inside the US intelligence community was that the connections between drug cartels, criminal smuggling organizations, and terrorists groups remained tenuous and transactional, and thus didn't represent a major threat. John Kelly disagreed, and he pushed back on that assessment often. Kelly was paid to worry about worst-case scenarios, and in his mind, if a known terrorist group was doing business with a known illicit smuggling network, it amounted to convergence. And he was increasingly seeing that kind of synergy throughout SOUTHCOM's area of operations.

Terrorists and drug kingpins may not share the same motives or ideology, Kelly reasoned, and trafficking cartels would probably consider it bad for business to smuggle a load of anthrax or some other weapon of mass destruction into the United States. On the other hand, illicit smuggling networks didn't check passports or do baggage checks, and they involved thousands of unscrupulous subcontractors who were primarily interested in money, not motive. Kelly also saw intelligence indicating that Islamist extremist groups in the Middle East recognized the porous US southern border as a major vulnerability, and talked about it often on jihadi websites.

When the wave of immigrant minors from Latin America detained at the southern border neared the seventy thousand mark in 2014—many of them desperate to escape drug-fueled violence and the tens of thousands of ruthless Central American gang members who had been deported by the United States and were veterans of US gang wars—John Kelly had seen enough. He knew the message was potentially unwelcome at the White House as it struggled to cope with the migrant crisis, but his first-hand experience with the wages of anarchy made him impatient with political niceties. So, as commander of US Southern Command, he made headlines by calling the confluence of terrorism, violent drug cartels, collapsing societies, and out-of-control migration an "existential" threat to the United States.

In a later interview in his office, Kelly stood by that stark assessment. "There have been notable successes in Latin America, such as Colombia's fight against a FARC that has really lost strength and influence, but I continue to be concerned about this convergence between known terrorist organizations and illicit smuggling and money-laundering networks," he said. There are those in the intelligence community who disagree and argue that those groups will never find common cause, he conceded. "I think those who take that view are simply trying to rationalize away the problem. Because no one wants to raise another major threat at a time when we face so many around the world."

As they rose to the tops of their respective professions, the wartime brotherhood who came of age together on the battlefields of Afghanistan and Iraq brought a unique perspective to their organizations. Like the FBI's Brian McCauley and Special Operations Command's John Mulholland in their outreach to the oil industry, they were instinctively collaborative, having experienced the synergy of collective action. Like DIA's Mike Flynn and SOUTHCOM's John Kelly, they were also acutely sensitive to the dangers posed by resilient and still evolving enemies, and the tough steps necessary to confront them. To a person they carried home the message that the war they fought was not bounded by lines on a map or withdrawal deadlines, but, rather, was a generational struggle. And by 2014, it was already clear that the members of this wartime fraternity were out of step with the prevailing zeitgeist of Washington, DC.

# EIGHTEEN

# Going Dark

## 2013–2014

J AMES CLAPPER GENERALLY LOOKED FORWARD TO BRIEFING THE president, viewing the regular face time with the commander in chief as critical to his role as director of national intelligence. Yet the responsibility was a double-edged sword when there was bad news to deliver. When the director of national intelligence entered the Oval Office in late May 2013, that blade cut deep. Clapper delivered the news to President Obama that a young National Security Agency (NSA) contractor named Edward Snowden had disappeared from his job at an NSA facility in Hawaii, and it was conceivable the young man had stolen the crown jewels of the US intelligence community. Clapper had rarely seen the man some called "no drama Obama" lose his cool, but on that day the president erupted in a fit of anger, delivering an Oval Office tirade worthy of a drill sergeant. Not that Clapper blamed the man.

A year later, it was clear that Barack Obama had grasped even before intelligence professionals just how profoundly damaging and embarrassing Edward Snowden's revelations would prove.

After taking refuge first in Hong Kong and then in Russia, Snowden had released thousands of classified NSA documents to a handful of selected journalists. Their articles laid bare the most sensitive details of US intelligence collection and the mechanics of secret counterterrorism operations. Articles in the *Washington Post* and Britain's the *Guardian*, and later in a host of media outlets, dribbled out the secrets of the intelligence community in water torture droplets: eavesdropping on the private phone conversations of foreign leaders, including close allies, such as Germany's chancellor Angela Merkel; collection and storage of vast amounts of "telephony metadata" on the communications of millions of American citizens; NSA wiretapping that reached deep into the largest US Internet companies and into the fiber-optic cables, network switches, and computer servers that formed the architecture of global communications; "incidental collection" of the e-mails and text messages of hundreds of thousands of US citizens never actually targeted for surveillance; a heavy reliance on the NSA's "geolocation" of cell phones in the CIA and Joint Special Operations Command (JSOC) targeted killing operations; the locations of secret spying and drone bases overseas, to include a growing constellation throughout Africa; the mechanics of "roving wiretaps" of terrorist suspects.

All of the pioneering work that General Keith Alexander and his team had accomplished before he retired as the NSA director and chief of the new US Cyber Command in 2013 — essentially having expanded the Real Time Regional Gateway concept of communications intercepts and geolocation targeting to a global scale — was exposed to public scrutiny. The backlash in the media and Congress was thunderous and unrelenting.

Both Alexander and Clapper were routinely vilified in the press and depicted as the faces of an intrusive, omnipresent Big Brother. They were publicly called liars, and worse. Alexander publicly scoffed at the idea that the NSA had "millions or hundreds of millions of dossiers on people." Clapper went a step further, denying during congressional testimony in 2013 that the NSA wittingly collected *any type of data* on hundreds of millions of Americans. The Snowden revelations that the NSA kept a "telephony metadata" database that stored the related phone number, time, and duration of hundreds of millions of phone calls called the veracity of that statement into question. Clapper clumsily described the answer as "the least untruthful" he could give in public testimony.

In December 2013 seven Republicans members of the House Judiciary Committee called on Attorney General Eric Holder to launch an investigation of Clapper, arguing that "witnesses cannot be allowed to lie to Congress." In January 2014, six members of the House wrote to President Obama, urging him to fire Clapper for lying to Congress. The White House declined, expressing its "full faith in Director Clapper's leadership."

Looking back, Clapper wished that the intelligence community had been more transparent about its data collection methods in the aftermath of the 9/11 attacks, when memories were still fresh of the result of inadequate intelligence collection. Back then intelligence officials had information that known al-Qaeda terrorists were communicating with people inside the United States, but they lacked the authorities and capabilities to quickly connect those dots. They could have been a little more forthcoming, telling the public that collecting, storing, and occasionally querying the time and duration of telephone calls could help make those connections and reveal crucial "patterns of life" of terrorists and their cells. Clapper doubted the public would have been any more bothered by that program than it was about the FBI routinely collecting and storing fingerprint files. The telephone metadata lacked even names or the content of conversations, and yet the general impression left by the media was of a "mass surveillance" machine. Never mind that no one was actually being observed. In the previous year the intelligence community had queried the database less than two hundred times, in each instance with an authorization from the Foreign Intelligence Surveillance Court.

After being put on the defensive by the string of sensational media revelations based on Snowden's intelligence trove, the intelligence community was fast losing the argument on the correct balance between security and privacy. There were serious proposals in Congress to let the PATRIOT Act—authorizing much of their intelligence collection—expire. This would strip the community of its ability to store telephone metadata, or to execute roving wiretaps that allowed investigators to track individuals who used multiple, disposable cell phones. The phones, called burners, were an increasingly common tool of criminals and terrorists who were studying the Snowden revelations closely and adapting accordingly.

In congressional testimony Clapper was often pressed to explain how many terrorist plots had been foiled by querying the telephone database, which he felt was a false metric. The Obama administration had cited more than fifty, a number that the press generally viewed with skepticism. One of the most valuable aspects of the program was determining whether terrorist plots uncovered overseas had a domestic connection. Just the year before in 2013, the State Department closed more than twenty diplomatic facilities based on credible intelligence of a pending terrorist attack traced to al-Qaeda in the Arabian Peninsula (AQAP). Wiretaps that "hopped" a couple of times from the cell phones at the center of the plot revealed roughly a dozen phone numbers connected to users inside the United States. By querying the telephone metadata, the NSA had been able to tell FBI investigators where to look for possible conspirators inside the United States. Ultimately all of the contacts "washed out," meaning the FBI found no connection to the AQIP plot. Counterterrorism officials breathed a sigh of relief, but it was not the kind of work that made headlines. Normally that was how the NSA preferred it.

Counterterrorism successes were mostly hidden from the media. Much of the reporting on the Boston Marathon bombing in 2013 highlighted the fact that the FBI previously interviewed the Chechen brothers Dzhokhar and Tamerlan Tsarnaev as people of interest, but had let them drop off their threat radar. Investigators ran into the same quandary with the Tsarnaevs as they confronted with Carlos Bledsoe and Anwar al-Awlaki, other suspected extremists whom the FBI interviewed but couldn't charge before they committed a crime. Certainly the bureau didn't have the resources to place under surveillance the more than 700,000 people on the terrorist watch list.

From his vantage point at Liberty Crossing, James Clapper had seen an intelligence collection effort to quickly identify the perpetrators of the Boston bombing that spanned three cabinet departments as well as the CIA. That kind of rapid and relatively seamless collaboration was impossible in the days before 9/11. Practically the entire intelligence community was also involved in amassing intelligence showing that Syrian president

Bashar al-Assad had used chemical weapons against his own people in the summer of 2013. Reporting at the time had focused on President Obama's failure to enforce his own "red line" against Assad's use of chemical weapons. The intelligence collection effort went largely unnoted. The massive US surveillance and intelligence support provided to French troops who successfully pushed back the al-Qaeda in the Islamic Maghreb offensive in Mali was another unheralded success.

Both the nature of the business and the intelligence community's culture of secrecy put them at a disadvantage when it came to defending their practices and publicly touting successes in times of controversy. Edward Snowden's revelations thus provoked the most painful examination of intelligence practices since the 9/11 attacks and the failure to find weapons of mass destruction in Iraq. Congress had cut the intelligence budget for three straight years, and was threatening to strip the intelligence community of key authorities. Lawmakers demanded to know how intelligence officials failed to prevent the Boston Marathon bombing, and to anticipate a strategic surprise, such as the Arab Spring revolutions. There had been numerous intelligence reports of growing instability in the region, but Clapper didn't know many analysts clairvoyant enough to predict that a Tunisian fruit seller setting himself on fire would ignite a firestorm that swept through the Middle East.

Sometimes Clapper joked that in the post-Snowden era, Congress and the public expected the intelligence community to produce high-fidelity intelligence that anticipated and predicted events that had yet to occur, and collect it in such a fashion that no one's privacy was ever compromised, with no risk of embarrassment, or worse, if intelligence operations were exposed to the public—*immaculate collection.*

If Congress wanted to cut the intelligence budget, strip the intelligence community of authority, and permit private phone manufacturers to install encryption software that could not be decoded even with a federal warrant, that was its prerogative. Congress giveth, and Congress taketh away. But in his more than a half-century in the security and intelligence business, he had never seen a more complex array of threats confronting the country. Now, thanks to the Snowden revelations, those threats were gathering at a time when key pixels in the intelligence picture were going dark. If, God forbid, the nation were hit by another terrorist spectacular, Clapper hoped that Congress would shoulder its share of the responsibility, rather than pinning the failure entirely on the intelligence community. But in his heart Clapper knew that would never happen.


"LOOK DOWN THERE on the street, see how quiet it is," Keith Alexander told a visitor in the summer of 2014. The former director of the NSA had recently retired, and he was standing in a sparsely furnished corner office with a 180-degree view of downtown Washington, DC. The midday streets of the nation's capital were busy, with crowds of tourists and office workers filling the sidewalks and going about their workaday lives unconcerned by the threats that clouded the thoughts of counterterrorism officials. "Why do you think that is? It's not because the terrorists have stopped trying to attack us, I can assure you. It's because we've developed great counterterrorism capabilities, and Edward Snowden has now revealed them to the entire world. And if you believe we can just publicly expose our most sensitive intelligence techniques and procedures without the people hoping to attack us noticing and changing their behavior, well, honestly, you're an idiot."

Alexander was more than a little bitter about being painted as Big Brother run amok, a secretive puppet master whose overzealous determination to connect the dots of terrorists plots was somehow un-American. For someone who had devoted his career to the cause of national security, that depiction stung. The worst in his mind were the grandstanders in Congress, the likes of Senator Rand Paul (R-KY), the libertarian whose thirteen-hour filibuster against the NSA and the drone program had made national news. Seemingly, the whole country was enthralled by the image of a dark dystopia that Paul conjured from thin air, a United States in which its future presidents rained down Hellfire missiles on the heads of unsuspecting American citizens in neighborhood cafés. "The Fifth Amendment protects you . . . from a king placing you in the tower, but it should also protect you from a president that might kill you with a drone!" Paul proclaimed from the floor of the US Senate.

Alexander believed the politicians knew better, and the thought grated. Congress was apprised of surveillance programs through the intelligence committees, and lawmakers understood that much of what was being written and said about the NSA regularly listening in on everyone's phone calls and reading their e-mails was simply untrue. After a year of investigations by Congress, the press, and the administration, NSA activities had been wire-brushed, and no one had been accused of serious wrongdoing. The NSA's own internal watchdog found roughly a dozen instances in the past decade involving employees wrongfully misusing their surveillance power, in some cases to spy on their love interests. A dozen miscreants out of a workforce estimated at over thirty thousand people. Each of them had been disciplined. Nevertheless, members of Congress continued to rail against the NSA's alleged misdeeds and privacy violations, and to inflame public reaction. In the United States in 2014 that kind of grandstanding was a sure-fire vote getter, and Keith Alexander had a big problem with that. If playing loose with the truth about something as serious as the terrorism threat was required to win votes, then Alexander wondered what had happened to the country he'd sworn to defend.

He knew that part of the problem was self-inflicted, a result of the intelligence community's culture of absolute secrecy and acute press aversion. They were admittedly terrible at public relations. Their fear of revealing critical capabilities meant they rarely effectively rebutted sensational or inaccurate reporting, or adequately responded to even obvious and legitimate questions. Often the record went uncorrected. He also felt that some reporters took advantage of that reticence by upping the sensationalism quotient in their stories without fear of rebuttal. If that won them a Pulitzer Prize, then Alexander thought they should get another prize when the secrets revealed led to another deadly terrorist attack on American soil. And he believed that day would surely come as a result of Snowden's revelations.

The view from inside the network, where participants took part in the nearly constant parry and thrust between terrorists and their pursuers, tended to harden an individual. In the space of just one year between 2013 and 2014, the number of terrorist attacks worldwide and the resultant body count nearly doubled. Alexander would rather take a beating in the press every day for the rest of his life than have to explain how he failed to prevent another 9/11 attack—they were all that way. So, he made no apologies. Still, sometimes he had to wonder at the depiction in the press of an all-seeing NSA that was omnipotent and omnipresent. Senior intelligence sources confirmed that the volume of intelligence chatter that often tipped off major terrorist plots was being turned down. There had been virtually no advance warning, for instance, of al-Shabab's September 2013 attack on the Westgate Mall in Nairobi. Nor would there be much advance warning the following year before ISIS-linked terrorists massacred nearly 130 civilians in Paris in November 2015. The terrorists they were tracking on their threat radars were disappearing from the screen one by one as they switched to more-difficult-to-trace communications platforms, such as Snapchat and WhatsApp, or to encrypted telephones, such as newer models of the Apple iPhone. The effect was as if someone had told them to turn off a transponder. They were invisible now.

In June 2014 the world was shocked by one of the most improbable offensive campaigns in the annals of military history. Somehow a juggernaut consisting of just a few thousand Islamic State of Iraq and Syria (ISIS) extremists captured major cities in northern Iraq stretching from Mosul to Samara, in the process overrunning four Iraqi Army divisions and putting much of northern Iraq under the control of militants. In just a week the extremists were on the doorstep of Baghdad, threatening the US embassy there as well as a US consulate in the northern city of Irbil in the Kurdish region. For many officials in Washington, DC, where Iraq had long ago been relegated to an unpleasant afterthought, the ISIS offensive seemed to come out of nowhere. Some of those inside the US intelligence community saw it differently.

Bob & Edith's Diner in Arlington, Virginia, near the Pentagon, was packed with a Saturday morning crowd on June 21, 2014, and nobody took notice of the men in a corner booth gesturing with knives and forks. The other patrons might have found the conversation interesting, because they were two of the nation's top national security sentinels. Over plates stacked with ham and eggs-over-medium, they were comparing notes on recent events that would soon accomplish the seemingly impossible, drawing the United States back to war in Iraq.

"I tried to pull our FBI people out of the Baghdad embassy, but the ambassador refused," Brian McCauley said with obvious consternation. "He's afraid a pullout of personnel at this point will start to look like a routed retreat."

"We've been saying all spring that something like this could happen, the reports from Baghdad were there for everyone to see," replied Mike Flynn, referring to classified cables from the military liaison in the US Embassy in Baghdad about the deteriorating conditions in Iraq. The situation had started sliding downhill ever since ISIS fighters captured Fallujah, the capital of Anbar Province, back in January 2014. "But the White House didn't want to hear it. The mind-set from [National Security Adviser Susan] Rice on down was, 'figure out how to get us out of Afghanistan, and how to stay out of Iraq and Syria.' I doubt the warnings on Iraq ever even hit the president's desk."

Flynn knew from experience how that indifference manifested itself. Rice, a longtime Obama confidant and former UN ambassador, was the frequent chair of the Deputies Meetings. Those meetings played a critical gatekeeping function in terms of elevating important issues to the level of the Principals, whose meetings involved the president and his cabinet. The subject of Syria and the growing strength of ISIS rarely even made the agenda of the Deputies Meetings. Flynn sometimes attended and he always read the minutes, so he knew. When the issue did get raised, it was invariably met with a "kick that can down the road" response by the deputies. The previous year, President Obama had received withering criticism for the failure to enforce his own publicly stated "red line" against the al-Assad regime's use of chemical weapons, and everyone understood that the commander in chief had no interest in getting further involved in the Syrian conflict.

The intelligence community responded to the White House's preferences by focusing on other priorities. Flynn was surprised that the CIA station chief in Baghdad had not even bothered to put the right people in the critical places in Iraq to get a clearer picture of ISIS activities. The frustrations Flynn felt were shared by many of the intelligence analysts at US Central Command, more than fifty of whom would later formally complain to the Pentagon's Inspector General that their reports on ISIS were inappropriately watered down by more senior intelligence officials. Some of the analysts felt that their warnings of ISIS's growing strength were down-played to fit President Obama's description in a January 2014 interview that ISIS amounted to terrorism's junior varsity, or "jayvee," team. That same month, ISIS captured Fallujah.

By June 2014, however, the situation in Iraq could no longer be kicked down the road. The vanguard of Islamist extremists gathered under ISIS's black banner amounted to al-Qaeda 3.0—following bin Laden's al-Qaeda 1.0, and Abu Musab Zarqawi's al-Qaeda in Iraq 2.0. The newest iteration had in just a few weeks rolled back much of what the US military had ac-complished in almost a decade of fighting and toil in Iraq. ISIS would soon reveal how the new and improved version of Islamist extremism had distilled and refined the brutality always at the core of the brand, conducting mass executions by machine gun fire of over a thousand captured Iraqi soldiers, engaging in gruesome mass beheadings and the burning alive of prisoners, and with the mass rape and sexual enslavement of non-Muslim women.

The news media was filled with stories of ragtag convoys of lightly armed ISIS militants in pickup trucks rolling over mechanized army divisions and capturing major cities. That improbable terrorist juggernaut was in reality a more general uprising by a coalition that included savvy and ruthless ISIS militants who had honed their craft during the long war against US forces, and more recently during three years of civil war in neighboring Syria. They were joined by senior Baathist military officers schooled in of-fensive military operations involving organized formations, many of them freed by daring ISIS attacks on Iraqi prisons. ISIS leader Abu Bakr al-Bagh-dadi had also reached out to disenchanted and corrupt Iraqi Army officers who knew that Iraqi security force defenses were weak, and who essentially threw open the gates to their garrisons from within in Trojan horse fashion. The ISIS coalition also included a network of armed Sunni tribes and resis-tance groups who found common cause with the Sunni Islamist extremists, just as they had before the Anbar Awakening—all maneuvering in a swamp of Sunni grievance and resentment against the sectarian, Shiite-dominated government of Prime Minister Nouri al-Maliki in Baghdad.

The savvy al-Baghdadi had used the years since his imprisonment con-structively, carefully planning AQI's comeback and building his network of disaffected Sunni militants. In January 2014, ISIS captured the strategic

crossroads city of Fallujah, a Sunni stronghold where US forces had fought
the bloodiest urban battles of the Iraq war. In successfully repelling multiple counteroffensives by Iraqi security forces, al-Baghdadi had learned two
valuable lessons. First, al-Maliki had so corrupted the leadership of Iraqi security forces with cronyism and purges of competent Sunni officers trained
by the United States that even its best units were unable to dislodge ISIS
from Fallujah despite months of bloody fighting. Al-Maliki had even turned
some of the crack Iraqi Special Forces units in Baghdad that had been
mentored by JSOC into a Praetorian Guard for personal self-protection and
for the political intimidation of his rivals. He had them report directly to the
prime minister's office instead of the Ministry of Defense. Al-Baghdadi had
also purposely recruited former Baathist military officers for his offensive,
many of whom formed the midlevel leadership of his forces.

Second, al-Baghdadi discovered on the return of his forces to Iraq that
the Sunni tribes and numerous armed resistance factions who switched
allegiances and found common cause with US forces in 2007 as part of
the Anbar Awakening felt betrayed by al-Maliki's sectarian rule. Once US
troops left in 2011, the Baghdad government largely reneged on promises
to continue paying salaries to Sunni tribal fighters who had turned against
al-Qaeda in Iraq. Mostly peaceful demonstrations against al-Maliki in Anbar the previous year were crushed by Iraqi security forces, who killed a
number of protesters and imprisoned many more. The Sunni vice president, Tariq al-Hashimi, an al-Maliki rival, was convicted of murder in 2012
and sentenced to death in absentia, in a trial most outside observers viewed
as political. As a result of those perceived sectarian slights, many Sunni
tribes were once again willing to reconsider a tactical alliance with the
Islamist extremists. Those who refused were slaughtered in massacres that
eliminated whole tribal bloodlines.

Evidence of the planning and collusion between ISIS and former Iraqi
military officers quickly emerged in Mosul, where in the first week of the
offensive ISIS fighters handed over administration of the city to the General Military Council for Iraq's Revolutionaries (GMCIR), whose spokesman, Muzhir al-Qaisi, was a former Iraqi general. The GMCIR was tasked
with operating government facilities and airports and trying to keep banks,
hospitals, and power stations open in a city of over 1 million inhabitants.

Hundreds more mid- and high-level al-Qaeda commanders and other Sunnis were also released from northern prisons. According to US intelligence sources, many of them joined ISIS ranks that swelled to an estimated twenty-thousand fighters. That allowed the ISIS militants, many of them foreign fighters, to gain strength as they moved from city to city intent on the next conquest.

Initially, many of the people in those Sunni-majority cities embraced ISIS for "liberating" them from the constant humiliations of life under the government of the hated al-Maliki in Baghdad. By the time the brutal tenor of life under the rule of ISIS became clear—with its tyrannical dictates, brutal punishments, and religious laws grafted from the seventh century— it would be too late. At long last, the Islamist extremists had their dreamed of caliphate.

As they finished their breakfast at Bob & Edith's, Flynn and McCauley checked their cell phones and monitored contacts at the US embassy compound in Baghdad, who reported that ISIS forces had already infiltrated into the Sunni belts surrounding the capital on three sides. The FBI chief of international operations and the head of the Defense Intelligence Agency (DIA) also knew what the public did not: namely, that in overrunning the Iraqi Army divisions equipped with modern US armament, the militants had captured howitzers that could accurately range downtown Baghdad from as far away as 15 miles. Neither of them doubted that the US Embassy would be high on ISIS's target list. An Obama administration that had made the withdrawal of all US military forces from Iraq a campaign slogan and article of faith, had weeks or maybe only days to respond and interject US forces into the crisis to prop up a teetering Iraqi government. McCauley and Flynn knew the only alternative, and it was one that neither wanted to contemplate: US military helicopters hovering over the roof of the US Embassy, frantically evacuating Americans and their Iraqi friends as the ISIS noose tightened around the Iraqi capital, signaling another historic, Vietnam-like defeat.


FOR THE BETTER part of a year, Mike Flynn had known that there would be no fourth star in his future, nor would he be allowed to serve the customary three years as director of the Defense Intelligence Agency. He had been hired by former defense secretary Leon Panetta to "shake things up" at DIA, and he had done just that, applying the hard lessons learned in more than ten years of conflict in reorganizing the agency and making it more relevant to the warfighters. Those commanders in the field were always at the center of Flynn's thoughts, not the Machiavellian political intrigues that often consumed Washington.

Flynn's legacy would be the five Intelligence Integration Centers he created at DIA to support warfighters, major new nodes in the globe-spanning intelligence network, and a direct outgrowth of his experiences in Iraq and Afghanistan. Not long after Flynn retired in August 2014, the CIA would announce a similar major reorganization, with the creation of ten centers devoted to different areas of the world or functional missions like counterterrorism. CIA director John Brennan, Obama's former counterterrorism adviser, would insist that the new centers would combine both spies and analysts, and break down the walls that traditionally separated the agency's operational and analytic arms. When the CIA reorganization was announced, Mike Flynn's e-mail account would light up with messages with a common theme: "Wow, the CIA's reorganization sounds like a *really good idea*, Mike! Has kind of a familiar ring, doesn't it?"

Everyone in the community understood the irony, knowing Flynn was being put out to pasture a year early for being too "disruptive." The always politically and turf-conscious CIA didn't care for his expansion of DIA's Clandestine Service, viewing it as encroaching on its own rice bowl. The DIA bureaucracy didn't like a reorganization that would upend comfortable lives in Washington by sending more analysts and managers out into the field. At times it felt as though Flynn was trying to institutionalize lessons from a war that Washington would just as soon forget.

Certainly the White House was miffed by his statements that the nation was actually less safe from terrorism in 2014 than it was before 9/11. But he had charted what everyone in the inner sanctum instinctively knew: in 2004, there were 21 total Islamic terrorist groups spread out in 18 countries. In 2014, the threat had grown to 41 Islamic terrorist groups spread out in 24 countries. A lot of those groups had both the intention and the capability to attack Western interests, even the US homeland. Some were actively seeking chemical and biological weapons. While fighting the US military for a decade, the leaders of such groups as ISIS had created adaptive organizations so as to survive. They constantly wrote about their lessons learned, a trait of self-improvement instilled by bin Laden before he died. The Islamist extremists had a deeply rooted belief system and a core ideology that was spreading, not shrinking.

When Flynn previewed congressional testimony making many of those points, the White House would often send it back with whole sections scratched out and deleted. He would be told that a staffer on the National Security Council had made the cuts. And he would just ignore the edits and give the testimony that he felt most closely comported with the truth. But he was never so naive as to believe that there was no cost to bucking the government's preferred narrative.

The bill was presented by his boss, Undersecretary of Defense for Intelligence Michael Vickers. Vickers had served in US Army Special Forces and in the CIA's Special Activities Division in the 1970s, where he played a major role in arming the Afghan mujahedeen in their fight against the Soviet Army.

Vickers was also a notoriously abrasive man. He constantly tried to micromanage DIA operations, wasting Mike Flynn's time by telling him where to place individual case officers. That was about three levels below the strategic horizon that Flynn tried to keep in focus, so when Vickers had called him into his Pentagon office the previous summer of 2013, Flynn was already predisposed to want to be somewhere else. Vickers had been passed over for the coveted CIA director's job, which Flynn figured would make him even more abrasive than usual.

Vickers told him that the situation was no longer working, and it was time for Flynn to go.

"Are you questioning my leadership?" Flynn asked. "Because I've kept you briefed on my reforms every step of the way."

Vickers told him that it was not a matter of leadership. Flynn suspected that it was all the flak from disgruntled DIA managers who didn't care for reform or a leader with a combat mentality. Both men also understood that if Flynn wanted to push back publicly, Vickers would have hell to pay with Congress for firing a famous war hero.

At that moment Flynn had made a split-second decision, falling back on his soldier's instincts. Vickers was his civilian boss, and he wanted Flynn gone. So, Flynn stepped aside.

"Next summer I'll have three years in grade as a lieutenant general, and I'll retire then," he said, before turning his back and walking out the door. When he got back to his office, Flynn called his friend General John Campbell, who was slated to deploy back to Afghanistan to take charge of the withdrawal of the last US troops. Campbell assured Flynn that he had done the right thing and should be proud of what he had accomplished at DIA, and the two officers fell into a discussion about what it was like to try to fight a war in faraway lands when the country back home had so clearly moved on.

On the night before his official retirement, Flynn received a phone call from Chairman of the Joint Chiefs Martin Dempsey, who was scheduled to preside at the ceremony. The fliers had already been printed for the ceremony featuring Dempsey's photo and biography, but the chairman would be unable to attend after all. The next day, August 7, 2014, President Obama would announce that US combat operations were recommencing in Iraq, even as US aircraft were dropping bombs on ISIS formations and providing humanitarian relief to embattled Kurdish forces. Flynn assured Dempsey that he understood, and wished him luck.

After he hung up the phone, it occurred to Flynn that it was starting all over again. There were other phone calls he could make, messages of "I told you so" he could deliver. But he knew better than most the hard road that lay ahead for his friends and the troops still in this desperate fight, and he realized there would be no satisfaction in it.

# NINETEEN

# A World on Edge
## 2015

A T THE END OF HIS LONG CAREER IN UNIFORM GENERAL MARTIN Dempsey was in a reflective mood in the fall of 2015. As chairman of the Joint Chiefs of Staff he had served as a top military adviser to no fewer than four secretaries of defense, a record unmatched in more than half a century. That spoke to the turmoil of the times they were living through and the desire for some continuity, and to Dempsey's even temperament in adapting to the very different styles of Robert Gates, Leon Panetta, Chuck Hagel, and now Ashton Carter. They were all good Americans and patriots, in his eyes, but they couldn't have been more different as individuals. Learning their quirks and disparate styles while trying to steer the nation through some of the rockiest shoals in its modern history had been a challenge, and one of the great surprises in a job that never lacked for them.

On a crisp September morning in 2015, the convoy carrying Dempsey sliced lights flashing through the streets of Berlin, drawing stares from the crowds of shoppers and tourists on Kurfürstendamm. The line of cars snaked past the bombed-out ruins of the World War II–era Kaiser Wilhelm Memorial Church, and circled the Brandenburg Gate where the Iron Curtain once split East and West, tyranny from freedom. A swarm of military police motorcycles weaved in and out of the moving procession with breathtaking choreography, parting traffic in every direction to ease the passage of the man soon to be awarded the Knight Commander's Cross of the Order of Merit of the Federal Republic of Germany.

The procession of gleaming cars stopped at a parade ground before the Ministry of Defense, and General Dempsey stepped out from behind the dark tinted windows of the lead limousine. He shook hands with his German counterpart, and the two leaders of their respective militaries then walked the length of an honor cordon, returning the soldiers' salutes as the band played "The Star-Spangled Banner" and "Das Deutschlandlied" ("The Song of Germany"). Then Dempsey laid a wreath to the war dead of Germany's modern army next to the same building where Adolf Hitler and his Nazi minions once plotted the conquest of Europe.

On his final overseas trip as chairman, the one reality Marty Dempsey could not escape was just how much war and conflict there still was to be fought, and how many memorials to the fallen had yet to be erected.

He had begun his military career more than forty years earlier in a small German village, a fresh-faced second lieutenant just out of West Point, guarding the border against massed Soviet and Warsaw Pact forces. He and his wife, Deanie, had begun their family in Germany. There were fond memories of watching Chris, Megan, and Caitlin spend part of their childhood in Germany, and recalling the pride he felt when each of them had decided as young adults to follow their father into the Army. Dempsey remembered the moment Chris revealed that he was going to West Point, when there were numerous offers from other prestigious schools. When he asked his son why West Point, Chris's answer was simple: Because I've been following you and mom around the world my whole life, and I really like the people you're always surrounded by. Apparently Megan and Caitlin did, too.

Next stop on this final trip was a NATO conference of defense chiefs in Turkey that would give Dempsey a chance to bid farewell to his alliance counterparts, many of whom he had grown close to during his unusually long four-year tenure as a chairman of the Joint Chiefs. A final stop in Estonia would give Dempsey an opportunity to thank troops from that tiny Baltic nation who had served bravely under him as a division commander in Iraq a decade earlier.

Dempsey never imagined that at each stop along his final official journey, crises would crowd out nostalgia, and the tyranny of the present constantly encroach on memories of the past. The Western alliance he had spent a career defending, and had helped lead in three wars going on four, was confronting multiplying and potentially overwhelming challenges.

During his time in Berlin in September 2015, German leaders opened the country's doors to a tsunami of refugees flooding into Europe from conflict zones in Syria, Iraq, and Afghanistan, only to reverse itself days later by shutting its borders, throwing the European response to the refugee crisis into disarray. The exodus to Europe of people desperate to escape war-ravaged countries that were besieged by radical Islamic groups was the worst the world had witnessed since World War II.

In Istanbul, Dempsey knew that he and the other NATO military chiefs would hear impassioned entreaties from Turkish officials struggling to cope with the instability and terrorism along their southern borders with Syria and Iraq, and with 2 million Syrian refugees. In Estonia, Dempsey would be visiting a NATO ally that lived in the shadow of a revanchist Russia, its leaders ever fearful the Russian Bear would turn on them next after it finished dismembering Georgia, swallowing Crimea, and carving up the borders of Ukraine by force. The entire alliance anxiously awaited a US decision on whether to remove all NATO troops from Afghanistan by the end of 2016 as planned, keeping faith with war-weary publics on both sides of the Atlantic, but risking creating yet another wellspring of instability, mass migration, and terrorism. He couldn't yet reveal it, but just the month before he had presented a plan and a recommendation to President Obama to freeze the withdrawal of US forces from Afghanistan and leave a residual US and NATO force there beyond the president's 2016 deadline. It was a bitter pill for a commander in chief who had staked his legacy on ending the post 9/11 wars, but to his credit Obama had swallowed it. Anyone who needed evidence of what could go wrong with a too-hasty withdrawal from Afghanistan had only to look toward Iraq.

The war that began on that terrible September morning so long ago was not over, and the noxious ideology that fueled it had spread in a world

teetering on the edge of instability. The network-centric model of targeted
operations that the soldiers, spies, and secret agents developed had helped
turn the tide of battle when the situation was most desperate, and had
largely kept their nation safe. But it could not quell the fires of a radical ideology nor deter major powers from exploiting a perceived power vacuum
as America looked inward, and until that happened the US military was
fighting a rear-guard action in defense of a war-weary nation.

Dempsey never thought that his swan song tour would end on such an
alarming note. Visiting Germany vividly recalled the Western alliance's
victory in the Cold War when the Berlin Wall had come down in 1990.
That success had left the United States that most exceptional of all nations,
a lone superpower in a unipolar world. Rapid NATO expansion in the
1990s to secure those gains had very nearly realized the venerable dream
of a Europe whole and free. Yet by Dempsey's own reckoning, the current
array of threats confronted NATO with its greatest challenge since at least
the end of the Cold War.

As recently as four years earlier, most of the strategic white papers and
plans within the alliance began with some version of the following sentence: "Europe is experiencing an age of prosperity and peace unlike any
in its history." At all his private meetings with his NATO counterparts,
Dempsey's challenge to them was simple: "If you can still write that sentence with candor and a straight face, please give me a call. Because I just
don't see it that way."

What he saw were escalating crises and Western capitals slashing defense
budgets and vainly searching for a "peace dividend," when there was little
real peace to be leveraged. The elephant in the room whenever NATO military leaders met was declining resources and rapidly increasing commitments. Dempsey's own struggles to break through the political dysfunction in
Washington had been well documented, and they had left a bitter aftertaste.

Each of his four years as chairman the Joint Chiefs had gone through
the same dispiriting exercise: under pressure from the Office of Management and Budget they would come up with a budget topline that left them
on the ragged edge of readiness, below which they simply could not meet
their international commitments. Key military enablers such as remotely
piloted drones, air refueling tankers, and Special Operations Forces were

already 100 percent committed to ongoing operations. And each year Congress would slash defense spending well below that floor, to stay within "sequester" budget caps. The politicians seemed to think the Pentagon would simply find more "waste" to cut, and "fraud and abuse" to curtail, with no discernable impact on national security. They were wrong.

Dempsey feared the Joint Chiefs had talked themselves into a corner with ever more alarming rhetoric, trying to describe to politicians how Congress's inability to reach a workable consensus on spending was going to come back to haunt the country. They tried to articulate it in terms of inadequate readiness to respond to crises, and unacceptable risks as adversaries closed the gap in military capability. He watched as superpower responsibilities got defined down to match inadequate budgets. Instead of "defeat" the enemy, they would "contain" or "deny" him. And then instead of "deny" the enemy, they would "impose costs" on him. At the current rate of rhetorical deflation their strategic plans would soon call for impressing on the enemy that they were "really, *really* angry," thought Dempsey. Russia and China were not impressed, could smell Washington's lack of will like a faint stench. At the end of Dempsey's career, the US Army general with a master's degree in literature was at a loss for words to convey a simple truth to Washington politicians: the continued subtraction of seemingly abstract numbers in a budget document would one day translate into blood spilt and American lives unnecessarily lost on a future battlefield.

In his private conversations with German military leaders, Dempsey sensed that the refugee crisis of 2015 harkened back to the refugee crisis of 1994 prompted by the breakup of the former Yugoslavia, which finally galvanized the political leadership in Europe to accept that besides treating the symptom of refugees, they also had to address the source of the instability in the Balkans. The current mass exodus of refugees and the toll of human suffering it represented had the potential to change the politics, demographics, and even cultural norms of Europe for generations. Dempsey stressed that point to try to get the Germans and other NATO allies to become more involved in finding a solution to the Syrian conflict, rather than just dealing with its spillover effects.

American and allied publics tended to take US military power for granted, but Dempsey knew that it was a declining resource and one to be husbanded and doled out with extreme care. That meant acting in partnership with allies whenever possible, and even in support of substate groups, such as the Kurds of Iraq and Syria, when necessary. So, he spent much of his time trying to cajole collective action out of reluctant allies, such as the Germans, who for obvious reasons had a large pacifist streak and a constitution that required that the German parliament approve any military deployment to a conflict zone. Dempsey had helped convince the Germans to send troops to northern Iraq to arm and equip Kurdish forces fighting the Islamic State of Iraq and Syria (ISIS). Teasing collective action out of NATO was often like herding cats, all the more so since Washington had announced a "pivot to Asia" a few years back that was interpreted in Europe as abandonment. He saw it as one more example of how a catchy phrase inserted into a speech by a clever speechwriter could be misconstrued as hard policy, and then actually *become* policy as a ponderous bureaucracy in Washington adjusted to the beautiful words. In that sense "pivot to Asia" could join "axis of evil," "no boots on the ground" and "redlines" in the speechwriters' hall of infamy.

Before his plane took off from Berlin, Dempsey was asked by a reporter what the United States intended to do about the Syrian civil war, the epicenter of the conflict that was sending refugees pouring into Europe. In September 2015 it was the one subject that no top official could dodge. Was he satisfied with the US and NATO response to Syria?

It had been a long day, and Dempsey's exasperation showed. "Given the enormous human tragedy and suffering, it would be inconceivable for me to say I'm satisfied with what's happening in Syria," he replied. "I'm General Dempsey, but I'm also Citizen Dempsey. I grew up in an Irish Catholic family of immigrants. That brings with it a sense of humanism that hopefully I've been able to sustain in a world that often tries to beat it out of you. So, no, I'm not satisfied with what's happening in Syria. How could anybody be?"

IN TRUTH, MARTY Dempsey had agonized over the issue of Syria. As a former field commander in Iraq, he sat atop a unique fraternity, the select group of US division and task force commanders who stared into the abyss

in the early days in Iraq, returned during the surge of 2007–2008 in a desperate attempt to snatch an acceptable outcome out of the jaws of almost
certain defeat, and went on to attain four-star status where those lessons
could be institutionalized. They were part of the most influential clique of
officers in modern US history, one that had shaped the wars in Iraq and Afghanistan and the future of their respective services. They had forged a new
American style of war. But they had also shared the same recognition of the
limitations of military power. None would forget the danger inherent in a
military campaign that exceeds national will or is divorced from achievable
political ends, nor the herculean effort required to rescue societies once the
grip of governance and the soft bonds of civilization are decisively broken.
As one of the last of that unique group of officers to retire, Dempsey had
been the keeper of those lessons and memories, which still spoke loudly to
his ideas about the limits of military power, and what ends can justify putting the lives of American troops at risk.

On Syria all of the Joint Chiefs had been reluctant to become entan-
gled in a conflict where the rebel opposition was a hodgepodge of quarrel-
ing groups in competition not only with the murderous Assad regime, but
also with each other. Some of them were Islamic extremist groups, such
as the al-Nusra Front and, of course, ISIS. As a member of the Principals
Committee, Dempsey supported the CIA's outreach and tacit support for
some of those groups as a way to shed light on the operational situation inside Syria. As someone who led when the United States stumbled blindly
into Iraq, however, he was wary of repeating the maneuver. Nor was the
Defense Department ever asked to do anything other than keep a military
option available in Syria, which was not surprising given that President
Obama had emphasized diplomacy over the military instrument of power
since his first day in office. Certainly Dempsey shared with the president
his reluctance to involve US military forces in a conflict before fully understanding the players and environment better.

The turning point for Dempsey and the other chiefs was ISIS's offensive
the previous summer that overran roughly a third of Iraq. Having helped
build the Iraqi security forces as the former commander of the Multi-
National Security Transition Command–Iraq, Dempsey was surprised, along
with the intelligence community, at how rapidly they folded. He suspected

it was due to a combination of an officer corps corrupted by the cronyism of Prime Minister al-Maliki, and some military units having accepted
bribes to disappear from the battlefield. The moment of truth came when
ISIS fighters blew through Mosul and threatened the Kurdish city of Irbil,
where the United States maintained a consulate and the Kurdish Peshmerga forces were in danger of being overrun.

Knowing the Peshmerga couldn't hold for long, Dempsey had traveled
to the White House, advising President Obama that it was time get into the
fight in Iraq once again on behalf of the Peshmerga, and in defense of the
US Consulate in Irbil. "The principals all agreed that ISIS was a threat to
our national security, and we adopted an anti-ISIS strategy that where we
have a credible partner such as a government, we will enable that partner,
and where we don't have a credible partner, we will try and find or create
one," Dempsey said in an interview with the author aboard his aircraft as
it flew from Berlin to Istanbul. "And once a decision was made to act, we
were able to establish a joint task force and deploy it to the region just in a
matter of days, and to use it as a hub to plug in other agencies and coalition
partners. When it comes to establishing another command-and-control
node in the network, we're like Google or Facebook now."

In internal deliberations Dempsey constantly pushed for a similar networked mind-set. Whenever someone asked for a meeting about Syria, Afghanistan, Iraq, or Yemen, he rebelled. Instead of meeting about discrete
crises in isolation, he wanted to talk about the counterterrorism network
they were building, and what additional nodes were needed in North Africa, Iraq and the Levant, or in South Asia. He tried to persuade the Joint
Chiefs, the combatant commanders, and the civilian policymakers that
they should try and think in terms of a trans-regional network designed
to keep pressure on violent extremist groups that stretch from Afghanistan
all the way to Nigeria and that are united by a common ideology that is a
perversion of Islam. There was a sense of historic grievance in the hearts of
20 million Sunnis, he noted, who reside just in the area between Baghdad
and Damascus, and it served as a wellspring of extremism. "So, a strategic
success will require that they reject ISIS's ideology and feel inclusive governance," he said during the interview. "That's why I believe that this will

be a generational struggle. In the meantime, Stan McChrystal had it right: It takes a network to defeat a network."

In Istanbul Dempsey dined with the other NATO military chiefs on the banks of the Bosphorus. Low-hanging clouds obscured the tops of skyscrapers on nearby hillsides, and the slate surface of the waterway disappeared into a gray horizon to form a misty dividing line between Europe and Asia. The haunting cadences of a muezzin's call to prayer sounded from a nearby mosque, reminding everyone at the dinner that they were in the only Muslim-majority country in the alliance. A surprise visit and blunt speech by Turkish prime minister Ahmet Davutoğlu drove home the point that the alliance's southern border was besieged.

Turkey's position was undeniably perilous. As a result of Syria's long civil war, it had absorbed an estimated 2 million refugees since 2011, costing the country roughly $6 billion to house and care for them. Foreign fighters, thousands of them from Europe, continued to travel through Turkey to cross its porous southern border and join the ranks of ISIS, representing an acute terrorist threat on their return to Western homelands. The fighting and instability had also shattered a fragile truce between Turkish military forces and the Kurdish terrorist group the Kurdistan Workers Party (PKK), based in northern Iraq, with a subsequent increase in Turkish air strikes and PKK terrorist attacks along the southeastern border and even in the capital of Ankara. News that Russia had been deploying fighter aircraft and other military forces into Syria in recent weeks to bolster the regime of Bashar al-Assad further clouded an already murky conflict, with myriad competing players working at cross-purposes. Russian fighters and unmanned drones would soon start wandering into Turkish airspace, and in a few months' time Turkish fighters would shoot down a Russian warplane, leading to the death of the pilot and an escalating crisis between a NATO ally and Moscow.

In Istanbul, Dempsey and the other NATO chiefs of defense were forced to concede the reality that the US-led anti-ISIS coalition had achieved only an impasse. Some of the Islamic State's early momentum has been checked by coalition airstrikes, but without fundamentally altering the dynamic of continued sectarian violence, terrorism, and refugee spillover that was spreading well beyond the immediate region. A $500 million US program to train and equip a viable Syrian rebel force had, by the recent admission of US Central Command leader General Lloyd Austin, produced only a literal handful of fighters.

On his last official trip, Dempsey became increasingly blunt in assessing the dangers. "The fight against ISIS has reached a phase that I would call tactically stalemated," he confessed in Istanbul. On the plus side, he argued, coalition airstrikes have been effective in interdicting ISIS's supply chain, interfering with its information operations, striking its command and control, and putting pressure on the group from numerous directions. "On the other side, we've had some leadership changes and logistics challenges with the Iraqi security forces, and some internal disagreements within the Iraqi government about the role of Popular Mobilization Forces, some of which are under the influence and control of Iran," Dempsey told a reporter. "That's a very important debate for the Iraqis to have, and how it turns out will probably determine the future of Iraq."

Privately, Dempsey figured that the United States had taken three swings of the bat at Iraq, and he'd be damned if they would take a fourth swing without adjusting the stance. They had tried taking ownership of Iraq for the better part of a decade, building institutional capacity and imposing security. He remembered all those horrible metaphors about running behind the Iraqi government and security forces as if with a kid on his bicycle without training wheels for the first time, looking for exactly the right moment to take the hand off his shoulder. And for what?

The Iraqis had shown themselves either unwilling or unable to take responsibility for their own affairs, leaving the US military holding the bag. Well, Dempsey figured, never again. He was brutally honest with his Iraqi counterparts that they were the ones facing an existential threat from ISIS, not Washington. The United States was willing to provide a lot of help, but unless the government reconciled the country's sectarian divides, and brought Sunnis, Shiites, and Kurds together in a unity government, then it wouldn't matter. And if the Shiite government in Baghdad turned to Shiite Iran as its chief patron, then Dempsey was equally blunt: the United States did not need to own Iraq again to secure its national security interests in the region.

At the NATO conference Dempsey and other US officials hopefully noted an increased willingness by alliance partners to join the US-led coalition operating in Iraq and Syria with airstrikes and training-and-equipping operations. Both France and Britain had committed to expanding their role in air strikes, for instance, and Turkey had recently made its Incirlik Air Base available to US strike aircraft, including Predator drones. Although the United States had struggled to find reliable partners in Syria, it continued to reach out to substate actors, such as the Syrian Kurds, which successfully pushed ISIS out of some towns along the Syrian-Turkish border in the summer of 2015, and the Syrian Arab Coalition, a group of several thousand fighters.

When pressed by a reporter why the Joint Chiefs have not devised a more decisive strategy for dealing with the Assad regime, Dempsey replied publicly that the White House had not requested one. He also resisted the notion that the military can solve the Syrian conflict unless the US, allied, and regional governments were more fully committed to a holistic effort combining military operations with diplomacy, massive economic and humanitarian assistance, and nation-building.

"My belief is that when the military is used as the sole instrument of power, that never has a good outcome," he said. US or NATO ground forces could quickly defeat ISIS on the battlefield, he noted, and at the same time pave the way for some other extremist group, and help create a failed state such as Libya in the bargain. "If there's no one to take ownership and develop that failed state, human suffering can be even worse than that created by the conflict itself."

If that approach was too cautious for neoconservatives and hawks in Washington who had criticized the administration and top military brass relentlessly for being too tentative in prosecuting the anti-ISIS campaign, Dempsey made no apologies. The nation had followed their advice and gone down that road before, and he vividly recalled the horror show at the end of it. Never again. "As I've said from my first day in the chairman's office, we need to think our way through our security challenges, not bludgeon our way through them," he said. "I hope that's part of my legacy, because the use of the military instrument of power is extraordinarily complex—shame on us if we allow it to be a simple answer to a complex problem."


IN TINY ESTONIA, with its border with Russia and a large Russian-speaking population, Dempsey held high-level talks with the country's leadership that were consumed by the "little green men" with modern Russian weapons and no insignia on their uniforms who had mysteriously appeared in Crimea shortly before Moscow annexed it in 2014. Just as they had materialized suddenly in Georgia's "breakaway republics" of Abkhazia and South Ossetia before Russia occupied them in 2008. Just as they still fought alongside separatist, Russian-backed rebels in Ukraine's eastern Donbass region. In NATO circles, the form of hybrid warfare the Russians specialize in—combining disguised Russian Special Forces, local guerrilla fighters, information warfare, and cyberattacks—even had a name: they called it the Gerasimov Maneuver, for Russian chief of the general staff Valery Gerasimov, one of its architects.

In Estonia Dempsey learned that Estonians simply called the signature form of Russian aggression "history," and by 2015 it had returned with a vengeance. No one in the country had forgotten that Moscow used similar tactics to occupy and then incorporate Estonia in 1939–1940, after which the founding fathers and elite of an independent Estonia were shipped off to gulags in Siberia to rot and die. More recently in 2007, in response to Estonia's decision to relocate a memorial to Soviet troops from the center of the capital of Tallinn, Russia launched a cyberattack that crippled the government and banking sectors for nearly two weeks. The day after a 2014 visit to Estonia and rousing speech by President Obama meant to reassure NATO's eastern allies in the midst of the Ukraine crisis, Russian border guards brazenly crossed into Estonia and kidnapped a member of the country's special police, who was later tried and imprisoned in Russia. The message that the Russian bear next door enjoys the advantage of proximity was not lost on Estonian officials.

In high-level talks with NATO counterparts, Dempsey began dusting off venerable concepts, such as deterrence, containment, and supply line interdiction, which had not darkened alliance counsels in decades. "I'm the oldest chief of defense in the alliance now, and the youngest was probably a teenager at the end of the Cold War, so when we talk about deterrence, I've actually had to reeducate some folks that never had the task of delivering it," said Dempsey. "As an alliance we've taken deterrence for granted for twenty years now, but we can't do that anymore."

The US response to the Ukraine crisis had been to keep a nearly constant rotational presence of US and NATO troops and aircraft in the Baltic countries, conducting joint ground exercises, and flying expanded air patrols. At a remote Estonian army base Dempsey met with a company of US paratroopers from the 173rd Airborne Brigade Combat Team. They represented a minuscule, tripwire force, a sign of the precipitous withdrawal of US forces from Europe over the past decade as the nation fought a war in the Middle East and "pivoted" to Asia. But the US flag on the shoulder of their uniforms still stood for a commitment, and a line that no nation would lightly cross.

Something in the American character makes it easy to forget that geography and history still matter, perhaps because our own have been so provident. And yet the final overseas journey of General Martin Dempsey recalled the grip that contested geography and bloody history still retain on the present. Certainly in the young US lieutenant who commanded a company of the 173rd Airborne, Dempsey couldn't help but see a mirror image of himself as a young officer, guarding the border of West Germany against stiff odds. In the forty-year gulf of memory that was his career, the alliance had managed to push that border nearly a thousand miles east, putting over one hundred million people on the side of freedom. That would have to be enough: Marty Dempsey was hanging up his stars.

# Epilogue

I FLEW BACK ON AN AEROMEDICAL EVACUATION FLIGHT FROM AF-ghanistan once, at the height of the fighting there. The flight began in the dark on a windswept flight line at Bagram Air Base, our bus with the large red cross on it maneuvering behind the open ramp of a C-17 transport aircraft. Those able to walk filed off first, shuffling their way to webbed seats lining the aircraft's cavernous hold. Then came the passengers on stretchers carried off the bus and lashed bunkbed style to metal stanchions running down the center of the cargo bay. The last boarded were three troopers on wheeled gurneys, swathed in bandages and tethered to an emergency room's worth of medical equipment. A three-member Critical Care Transport Team would hover over them as the young men clung to life on the long journey home.

Beside one of the critical care gurneys, a nurse constantly monitored the vital signs of a young Marine covered almost entirely with dressings, multiple tubes perforating his head, chest, and abdomen. Someone had crossed miniature American and Marine Corps flags atop his gurney. The

359

nurse told me she believed the young man would make it, but it broke her heart that in the induced coma he didn't even know yet he'd lost both legs.

Afghanistan was an infantryman's war, and body armor was saving the lives but not the limbs of many foot soldiers caught in the blast of improvised explosive devices. The possibilities made a foot patrol a badge of courage. One doctor told me the orthopedic wards at Walter Reed Army Medical Center near Washington, DC, and other military hospitals were filling up with numbers of amputees not seen since the Civil War. When later I visited Walter Reed, I saw he was right. A nurse on the aeromedical flight told of bringing a trooper back who was already brain dead, and of being met in Germany by the boy's father. The man accompanied his son the rest of the way home and then the family donated his organs to save someone else's children. By the ten-year mark of the war, the Air Force had already flown more than 30,000 aeromedical evacuation missions, bringing more than 150,000 sick, wounded, and in some cases dying service members home from Iraq and Afghanistan.

On the long flight I spoke with a Military Police officer who was accompanying his German shepherd "Alf" back stateside. Alf was a bomb-sniffing dog, and he had come down with post-traumatic stress disorder. I admitted not even knowing that a dog could get PTSD, and the handler looked at me like I was a fool, and then I felt like one.

"Everything in war gets traumatized," the MP told me, matter-of-factly.

No one gets out of this unscathed. Even the ones who seem fine often are not. An Army colonel I met, a decorated commander and the veteran of multiple combat tours who was himself suffering from PTSD, described to me the dizzying sense of alienation that troops feel coming home from war much the way they left—largely invisible to a distracted nation.

Returning units are typically met at an airfield by buses that shuttle them to a gated military base. On the parade ground, a commander reminds the assembled, some of the more than 2.5 million service members deployed during the past decade of war, of all that they accomplished overseas. He recalls the brothers in arms who didn't make it back, and the memories that unite those who did—the shared hardships, the moments of terror and elation, the constant joking that held the awfulness at bay. The unbearable melancholy that will always accompany the playing of "Taps."

When the commander dismisses the formation, the troops realize that the ties that bound their lives so tightly together in war are breaking. The married service members run into the open arms of their families, husbands holding babies they've never met, uniformed women hugging young children they hardly recognize. Even before the smiles and tears subside, some of the spouses sense the vast gulf in experience that separates them, and wonder how they will ever get across. Single troopers head for the barracks, wisecracking but often wishing that they, too, had family nearby to welcome them home. And inevitably, the Army colonel told me, there were the stragglers—young soldiers shuffling and chain-smoking, unsure of where to go or what to do next. Having come of age on distant battlefields, they were suddenly lost in America.

Like the wider fraternity of combat veterans, members of the brotherhood profiled in this book came home burdened by their share of scar tissue, both visible and unseen. There were the obvious physical ailments, the net result of wounds, exotic parasites, too many jumps out of an airplane, or the physical depletion brought about by too many years on antibiotics to stave off sickness. There were broken marriages from too much time spent apart, and those with fracture lines from what transpired in the long absences.

For men of fierce pride, there was undoubtedly pain in the fact that Generals Stanley McChrystal and David Petraeus were both forced to retire early under a cloud of controversy, undone by a journalist reporting offhand remarks of a junior aide and an extramarital affair that led to the release of classified information to a biographer, respectively. As a society we might ask how it reflects on us that the two preeminent field commanders to emerge from their generation of officers, and during this nation's longest wars, are identified as "The Runaway General" and the "Petraeus Scandal" in a Google search. We can demand that our military leaders act as warrior monks, without ill temper or the taint of human frailty, but that standard would have excluded the hard-drinking Ulysses S. Grant, the bombastic George Patton, and the adulterous Dwight Eisenhower. Think how the world might look differently if each of them had been passed over for a lesser but safer alternative at a critical moment in the nation's fortunes. There's little doubt that Stanley McChrystal and David Petraeus will take their place beside those military leaders in future war college text-books, alongside the likes of Colin Powell, Creighton Abrams, Douglas MacArthur, Omar Bradley, Raymond Spruance, and the soldier-statesman father of the modern US military, George C. Marshall.

Certainly there is a measure of "moral injury" associated with too much exposure to the war toxin. The malady doesn't excuse bad behavior, but in some cases it may help explain it. By 2015 the Pentagon was coping with a series of cases involving personal misconduct by senior leaders. A number of general officers lost their jobs for alcohol-related misconduct, including the commander of US Special Operations forces in Latin America who admitted to PTSD; a deputy commander of the Eighty-second Airborne who was cleared of sexual assault charges, but admitted to multiple inappropriate affairs; and Major General Rob Baker, the counterterrorism commander of Combined Joint Task Force–Horn of Africa, who seemed destined for top command. After becoming intoxicated at a diplomatic function in Djibouti, Baker was accused of groping a female State Department official who had also been drinking, while they were both in the back of Baker's government SUV. Baker denied the charges, and his driver and a naval criminal investigator in the front seat at the time could not corroborate that the incident took place, but at a time when rape and sexual assault were considered a "silent epidemic" in military ranks—another clear indication of moral injury—the allegation of sexual misconduct and admitted excessive drinking were enough to end a stellar career.

Less seriously, in 2014 the Defense Department Inspector General (IG) substantiated allegations that Lieutenant General John Mulholland, deputy commander of US Special Operations Command, had acted inappropriately when he subjected his junior staff to a profanity-laced tirade over a subpar briefing. The IG noted that the outburst was not indicative of his normal comportment, and Mulholland later apologized.

I asked the noted military professionalism expert Dr. Don Snider, a senior fellow at West Point's Center for the Army Profession and Ethic, and a Vietnam-era combat veteran, about the rash of misconduct cases by senior leadership. "Moral corrosion has spread throughout the entire profession of arms as a result of a decade of war," he told me. "War creates a culture where cutting corners ethically becomes the norm."

And there was loss, foremost of the invisible wages of war. Navy SEAL Matt Bissonette, a veteran of fourteen combat deployments that included Operation Neptune Spear to find Osama bin Laden, told me he kept the phone numbers of forty fallen comrades on his cell phone, unable to bring himself to delete them yet haunted by their memory. When you carry the baggage of lost brothers home from war, post-traumatic stress and depression is not a disorder, it's the natural response of a broken heart. Michael Kelly, my former editor and good friend at Atlantic Media, and an honorary member of the Irish Brigade for his warrior spirit and journalistic courage, taught me that lesson when he was killed covering the war in Iraq.

Loss BOUGHT MANY of members of the brotherhood together on a chill November day in 2010 at Arlington National Cemetery, America's Valhalla. The crowd of mourners who gathered that day at Section 60, Gravesite Number 9480, was larger than most. The highest ranking US military officer to lose a child in combat in Iraq and Afghanistan was there to bury his youngest son, First Lieutenant Robert Michael Kelly, killed in action in Afghanistan.

John Kelly had spoken with the families of the fallen Marines and soldiers many times at other gravesides in Arlington, and at Dover Air Force Base Port Mortuary, which had accepted the flag-draped caskets and prepared the remains of many of the more than 5,200 Americans killed in action in Iraq and Afghanistan. Many times he had been asked the same question by grieving families—Was it *worth it*? Always he had been struck mute by the immensity of their loss, and his inability to fathom, let alone find the words to dull, their sorrow.

In November 2010 John Kelly heard the knock on his own door, and the Kelly family passed into the realm of stricken comprehension. There was faint resentment in that realm of the able citizens who "decided to sit it out and watch in amazement from the sidelines," he said, but mostly there was love for the small fraction of young men and women who volunteered even in a time of war, the next Greatest Generation that had run to the sound of guns as their fathers and uncles had in Vietnam, and their grandfathers had in Korea and World War II. Sitting at gravesite 9480 next to his son's wife, watching her accept the folded flag with the thanks of a grateful nation, hearing the retort of the rifle salute and the sound of the bugler playing "Taps," John Kelly finally understood that his young son Robert had already given the answer to the question of whether the cause was worth the sacrifice.

"In his mind—and in *his* heart—he had decided somewhere between the day he was born at 2130, 5 September, 1981—and 0719, 9 November 2010—that it was worth it to him to risk everything—even his own life—in the service of his country," Kelly would later tell other Gold Star families. "So, in spite of the terrible emptiness that is in a corner of my heart and I now know will be there until I see him again, and the corners of the hearts of everyone who ever knew him, we are proud. So very proud. Was it worth his life? It's not for me to say. He answered the question for me."

JOHN KELLY TRAVELED to Washington, DC, in July of 2015 to attend Brian McCauley's retirement ceremony. Months earlier McCauley and the Tenth Special Forces Group that worked with him on the FBI's Counter-IED Initiative in Afghanistan—"G-man, meet your SWAT team," as retired General Dan McNeill put it so memorably—had received the FBI's highest honor, the Director's Award for Excellence. At the retirement ceremony Mike Flynn spoke, joking that whenever he mentioned McCauley's name back on their home turf in Rhode Island, someone either bought him a drink or threatened to punch him in the face. "Victor," the former CIA station chief in Kabul, paid the highest compliment he knew how to give: "Brother, *anytime, anywhere.*" Everyone understood that with his humor and bias for action, McCauley was instrumental in forging the tight relationships between law enforcement, the intelligence community, and Special Forces that were at the heart of the new, American style of war.

"Brian's team saved countless lives, and how can you put a price on that? Someone's son or daughter got to come back from Afghanistan alive because of the work they did," said big John Mulholland from Special Operations Command. Every Special Operations unit deployed "down range" has an FBI guy sitting nearby, he noted, because of McCauley. "Brian hides it behind all that Irish charm, but he's a force of nature. If he sees a problem, he brings together all the people and all the tools in the toolbox necessary to fix it in order to protect American citizens. So, on behalf of the Special Operations community, and as a member of the Irish Brigade, brother, I thank you."

As I left McCauley's retirement ceremony, John Kelly was in deep conversation with Brian McCauley Jr., the teenager clearly awestruck with the attention from the four-star general, but you could see the pleasure in the encounter went both ways. Brian McCauley had given his son a poster with signed messages from the top flag officers in the Army, Navy, Air Force, and Marines, each playfully making a pitch recruiting the boy. You could tell from the conversation that Brian McCauley Jr. shared his father's dream that he would one day join the Marines.

Afterward Brian McCauley Sr. took me aside. "Hey, I hear Hollywood is going to make a movie, and Brad Pitt's going to play General McChrystal. You think they could get Jim Belushi to play me?"

WITH ITS CASTLELIKE stone edifices, towering cathedrals, and leafy, tree-shaded avenues, Yale's campus speaks of old money and ivory towers, privilege redeemed by rigorous learning. In the fall of 2015, a campus message board outside a lecture hall on Hillhouse Avenue advertised a Yale chess club workshop, a lecture on "Communicating the Value and Values of Science," and a discussion with the author of "The Coddling of the American Mind."

For someone who spent the better part of a decade in the world's darkest corners, engaged in a life-and-death struggle with some of its most violent people, Yale would seem an ideal setting for serene contemplation, the better to distill the hard truths learned there. That explained the students filing into Luce Lecture Hall in the fall of 2015 to learn about "Future Conflict: The Evolving View of Conflict," taught by Professor Stanley McChrystal.

The subject of the evolution of war was much on McChrystal's mind as he prepared the course. He recalled reading military analyst Daniel Ellsberg's book on the Pentagon Papers while in Iraq, and discovering how current its lessons seemed. As a young man McChrystal considered Ellsberg a traitor for leaking the Pentagon's secret history of the Vietnam War, a war his father had fought in. But Ellsberg had started his research on the Pentagon Papers convinced that somehow the experts had botched the analysis of Vietnam, leading to the disastrous policies that sank the United States ever deeper into a quagmire. In nearly every instance, Ellsberg discovered instead that the analyses were sound, but time and again decision makers in government adopted policies they knew had little chance of success, because it was politically expedient at the time. And McChrystal worried that was still happening.

The man responsible for crafting the greatest manhunting network in history wondered whether the politicians and the policymakers possessed the wisdom to effectively wield it. Targeted killing had its uses, and there were undeniably some enemies who needed killing. But divorced from a workable policy and broader strategy, McChrystal believed that the signature targeting operations were deceptive. They gave the *illusion* of progress when little actually existed. Because of their antiseptic nature, often with no US troops placed in harm's way and the lethal blow landed by a robot, the threshold for approving such operations was also lower than for manned missions, making them all the more tempting from a policymaker's standpoint. In the wrong circumstances targeted killings were like a narcotic, McChrystal felt, lulling decision makers into a false sense of accomplishment where showy gestures were confused with solving root problems.

The network Stan McChrystal helped build was able to synthesize a lot of information focused very narrowly on counterterrorism targeting. That definitely enabled a more elegant model of operations, one that exploits the unique capabilities of each of the military, intelligence, and law enforcement agencies involved through centralized command and decentralized execution. The key elements of that new American style of operations—joint interagency task forces, an extremely high tempo of operations, and cutting-edge advances in ISR (intelligence, surveillance, and reconnaissance) technologies—are revolutionary when combined. In the final analysis that new model helped keep the nation safer, but it represents fighting at the tactical level of conflict, not at the strategic level where wars are truly won.

The next big breakthrough in network-centric operations, McChrystal believed, would come from constructing a much wider network that synthesized greater amounts of information and achieved a higher order of understanding at the level of grand strategy. Not just locating *where* an enemy was on a grid, but understanding *why* he was an enemy in the first place.

In Luce Lecture Hall, McChrystal and his British wartime compatriot Lieutenant General Graeme Lamb walked the Yale students through the morass of the Middle East, explaining how conflicts there were tearing societies apart and encouraging students to embrace the underlying complexity. They had students outline on the blackboard the players, relationships, and issues at play, and possible US strategies for dealing with fighting and unrest in Egypt, Yemen, Somalia, and Syria. Then they had the rest of the class grill the students on their proposed strategies, addressing the cultural, economic, social, and military issues, building "situational understanding" one question at a time.

The most complex puzzle to disassemble was clearly Syria. McChrystal put a PowerPoint slide on the video projector, showing an indecipherable web of relationships between the various players involved in the fighting. The blowback from Syria was likely to last a lifetime, he told his students, beginning with the largest exodus of refugees since World War II. Given Europe's problems in assimilating its current Muslim population, knowing how extremists had planted the seeds of terror in Muslim ghettos in Europe that blossomed darkly into the Madrid train bombings, the London subway bombing, and the *Charlie Hebdo* massacre in Paris, it was impossible not to worry about a refugee crises that was sending millions of displaced Muslims to an unprepared Europe in 2015. Those fears would be realized months later when eight ISIS suicide assailants spread the darkness in their souls over the "city of light," murdering 130 civilians and wounding many hundreds more in Paris in November 2015. Follow-on investigations would reveal that at least two of the assailants had entered Europe through Greece along with the flood of Syrian refugees. The same ISIS terrorist cell behind the Paris attack would strike again four months later in Brussels, killing 32 people and wounding more than 300 in suicide bombing attacks on the airport and a subway station.

Pointing to the slide of a link chart connecting all the players in Syria in a tangled web, McChrystal was blunt: "It's impossible to construct a matrix of relationships this complex that is ruled by logic—it defies logic. This is one of those cases where if you decide to kill your enemy, you're likely to discover he's the brother of your closest ally."

He also raised the issue of belief in a cause, something that originally drew me to these warriors who fought America's longest wars. "When we see the Islamic State put a Jordanian pilot in a cage and burn him alive, and then proudly display that video on YouTube, our reaction is horror and disbelief. But put yourself in the shoes of that Islamic State fighter, and ask why he is willing to do something so horrible. What are the reasons suicide bombers are willing to blow themselves up?" said McChrystal. "You better get inside their heads and try and understand what belief system motivates them, because some of them will sell their souls—and sell your soul—for their cause."

We now know that the FBI profilers were right to get inside the heads of the terrorists with methodical interrogations so that we might know our enemy, and that it was wrong to turn toward torture and detention policies that stained our reputation and served as recruiting posters for the terrorists. We know that as the brotherhood of soldiers, spies, and special agents at the center of this tale disbands, the spirit of cooperation that drove them must endure or gaps will appear in our defenses for the enemy to exploit. As to where America will find young men and women willing to volunteer for this twilight struggle, First Lieutenant Robert Kelly and the thousands of other heroes who paid the ultimate sacrifice—and the hundreds of thousands who answered the call after 9/11—gave us the answer with their own questions: "If not me, who? If not now, when?"

To defeat a global insurgency of true believers, Stanley McChrystal, Mike Flynn, Scott Miller, Bill McRaven, and all the others at JSOC understood that the United States had to build and sustain its own global counterterrorism network. *It takes a network.* David Petraeus was right that where the forces of religious tyranny rule and radical ideology takes root, those dark corners of the world will have to be contested, the fanatics under the black flag cleared, the ground held, and the foundation of civilization rebuilt. *Clear, hold, and build.*

As I watched McChrystal's lecture at Yale, it occurred to me that many of the country's most notable wartime leaders had traded in their uniforms for professor's garb, including David Petraeus at Harvard; Karl Eikenberry, the former US commander and ambassador in Afghanistan, at Princeton; and Marty Dempsey at Duke University. I knew that somewhere in a crowded mosque in Raqqa, or a madrassa in Peshawar, or a dusty cell block in Sanaa, radical imams were spreading the gospel of intolerance and planting the seeds of hatred in the next generation of jihadists. It was heartening to see America's twilight warriors turned gardeners themselves, their orchard of young saplings destined to grow into the nation's leaders. They would need those lessons to prevail in a long, complex struggle.

"In the world I would design we would require our presidential candidates to engage in this kind of blackboard exercise, rather than give bumper sticker answers and catchy sound bites during debates, like 'Bomb the bastards!'" McChrystal was telling his students. "And if we the public let them get away with bumper sticker answers, then we're at fault, too. So, whenever a politician or policymaker comes up with a simplistic answer to a complex problem — 'Bomb them!' — ask them this question: 'And then what?'"

Stanley McChrystal was into it by then, his eyeglasses aglow in the reflection of the auditorium's lights, his hands gesturing in the air in exclamation.

"And ask it again after they answer!" he told the students. "'And then what?' And keep asking it until the answers aren't simple anymore. 'And *then* what?'"

# Acknowledgments

I WOULD LIKE to thank the entire team at Basic Books, and especially publisher Lara Heimert and former editor Alex Littlefield for originally recognizing the worth in this project, and my editor Dan Gerstle for steering it to completion with a steady hand and unflappable professionalism. My agent Andrew Stuart and former colleague Paul Starobin helped convince me this subject was worth exploring for a few years of my life.

I am also very grateful for the support of Maxmillian Angerholzer III, president of the Center for the Study of the Presidency and Congress, and the CSPC team, who offered safe haven during the always turbulent journey of researching and writing a book. My sister Allison Kitfield Cohen, the editor in the family, was instrumental in helping me smooth the final edges, and my wife Lydia was the essential sounding board throughout.

A special thanks to the soldiers, spies, and special agents who were willing to share their stories and insights with me, and all the brave men and women who guard the furthest battlements so that we can sleep peacefully at night.

# Notes

## Prologue: The Brotherhood

The description of Lieutenant General Mike Flynn's retirement ceremony is from the author's firsthand reporting of the event. Flynn's last on-the-record interview with the author, including comments on Defense Intelligence Agency (DIA) reforms and the growing terrorist threat, was published August 7, 2014, and appeared on *Breaking Defense* under the title "Flynn's Last Interview: Iconoclast Departs with a Warning." The author's referenced article quoting Director of National Intelligence James Clapper on a post-9/11 revolution in intelligence fusion was "Patterns of Death," published in *National Journal* on March 10, 2012. The controversy over Clapper's Senate testimony denying that the NSA collected data on hundreds of millions of Americans is recounted by *POLITIFACT* in an article published on March 11, 2014, entitled "Clapper's Testimony One Year Later." The description of General Martin Dempsey's comments to his staff on the Gettysburg Battlefield is from the author's firsthand reporting. Recollections from former National Security Agency (NSA) director General Keith Alexander are from an interview with the author. Quotes from General John Campbell's interview with the author originally appeared in the article "The Interwar Years," *National Journal*, July 28, 2012. The nature of the new model of intelligence-driven, network-centric military operations developed by General Stanley McChrystal, Mike Flynn, and other leaders of Joint Special Operations Command is described in the author's "Patterns of Death," and recounted in great detail in McChrystal's book *My Share of the Task*. The details behind Flynn's early retirement are from an interview with the author. The unpopularity of Flynn's reforms with the DIA bureaucracy were recounted in an interview with a knowledgeable source. As noted in the copy, the rich military tradition of Irish immigrants to America is examined in Terry Golway's excellent book *The Irish in America*, while details of the military tradition of Scots-Irish immigrants came largely from James Webb's book *Born Fighting*. The author was embedded with the forward tactical headquarters of General William "Scott" Wallace, the descendent of William Wallace of *Braveheart* fame, during the 2003 invasion of Iraq. Facts about the makeup of the United States' current all-volunteer military force are from the author's "The Great Draft Dodge," *National Journal*, December 13, 2014.

## PART I

### Chapter One: Where There's Smoke

Biographical information on Brian McCauley is from interviews with the author, as well as reminiscences from friends and family at his 2015 retirement ceremony at FBI headquarters. Details of the Valhalla case and the connection between IRA gun runners and James "Whitey" Bulger were recounted in "Mob Underling's Tale of Guns, Drugs, Fear," *Boston Globe*, February 27, 2000. The role of the Congressional Church and Pike Committees in reforming intelligence practices and correcting abuses in the 1970s, and erecting walls between domestic and foreign intelligence gathering, is explained by the author in "Shining a Light on Spycraft," a chapter in the book *Triumphs and Tragedies of the Modern Congress*, 2014, which was coedited by the author and published by the Center for the Study of the Presidency and Congress. The pre-9/11 disconnects, bureaucratic infighting, and vast culture divide between the FBI and the CIA as they struggled to work together on counterterrorism were detailed in depth in the author's article "CIA, FBI and Pentagon Team to Fight Terrorism," *Government Executive*, September 19, 2000, which included interviews with FBI Counterterrorism Center chief Dale Watson, and CIA director George Tenet. The various threat warnings and bureaucratic disconnects that enabled the 9/11 terrorist plot are taken from "The 9/11 Commission Report: Final Report of the National Commission on Terrorist Attacks Upon the United States." Descriptions of the Pentagon after the 9/11 attacks are from interviews with Brian McCauley and other FBI agents on scene. FBI special agent Steve Gaudin recounted his interrogation of al-Qaeda operative Mohammad Rashed Daoud al-Owhali in an interview with the author. The outline of the CIA's post-9/11 interrogation of terrorist suspects, including President George W. Bush's signing of an executive order to the effect that Common Article 3 of the Geneva Conventions, which prohibits "mutilation, cruel treatment and torture," does not apply to al-Qaeda or Taliban captives, is from "A History of the C.I.A.'s Secret Interrogation Program," *New York Times*, December 9, 2014.

### Chapter Two: Another Kind of War

Lieutenant General John Mulholland's experience leading Fifth Special Forces Group in Afghanistan as a colonel in the fall of 2001 are recounted in an in-depth interview with the Defense Media Network, published on May 25, 2010. The origins of US Special Forces are recounted in "Special Ops: The Hidden World of America's Toughest Warriors," a special edition of *Time*, copyrighted in 2013. President John F. Kennedy's close relationship and identification with Special Forces "Green Berets," and his famous "another type of war" speech at West Point on June 6, 1962, are detailed in the JFK Presidential Library and Museum's online history.

The role of then major general David Deptula in managing the air war portion of Operation Enduring Freedom was recounted in an interview with the author. Many of the details on conduct of the air war, including the critical role of Air Force Joint Terminal Attack Controllers (JTACs) in acting as the conduit to airpower for Special Forces, are from the RAND Corporation's 2005 report "Airpower Against Terror: America's Conduct of Operation Enduring Freedom." That critical role was also examined in the author's firsthand report-ing from Afghanistan that appeared in "With the JTACs," *Air Force Magazine*, April 2012.

The revolutionary capability represented by armed, unmanned drones was explained in an interview the author conducted with retired Air Force Colonel James "Snake" Clark, one of the pioneers of the Air Force's remotely powered aircraft programs, and the director of the Air Force's Intelligence, Surveillance and Reconnaissance Innovation Division. Circumstances surrounding the er-rant Air Force strike that nearly killed future Afghan president Hamid Karzai are recounted in "The U.S. Bomb That Nearly Killed Karzai," *Los Angeles Times*, March 27, 2002. The Fifth Special Forces Group's part in the Battle of Tora Bora are explained by John Mulholland in his interview with the Defense Me-dia Network, and substantiated by other members of the group interviewed by the author. The description of Operation Anaconda and details of the Battle of Robert's Ridge are from the author's article "To the Top of Takur Gar," *Air Force Magazine*, July 2011. John Mulholland recounted to the author his argument with a senior conventional US Army general about the outsized role of Special Forces in the early stages of Operation Enduring Freedom.

## Chapter Three: Descent into Darkness

Details of the CIA's interrogation of al-Qaeda suspects using "enhanced interrogation techniques" at undisclosed "black sites," and events surrounding the interrogation of Abu Zubaydah specifically, are revealed in the Senate Select Committee on Intelligence's 2014 "Committee Study of the Central Intelligence Agency's Detention and Interrogation Program." Events in this chapter were corroborated and recounted by FBI special agent Steve Gaudin in an interview with the author. FBI special agent Ali Soufan recounted his side of this story to *Newsweek* in an April 24, 2009, article entitled "Ali Soufan Breaks His Silence." The role of former Air Force psychologists John "Bruce" Jessen and James Mitchell in designing the CIA's interrogation regime is recounted in numerous media stories, including "Two Psychologists' Role in CIA Torture Program Comes into Focus," *Los Angeles Times*, December 14, 2014.

## Chapter Four: The Crucible

Events surrounding the attack on the Al Rashid Hotel, First Armored Division's Operation Striker Elton to find the perpetrators, and the Ramadan Offensive of 2003 are from the author's firsthand reporting in Iraq, much of it originally appearing in "The Ramadan Offensive," *National Journal*, November 1, 2003. The early successes of the 101st Division in implementing a counterinsurgency campaign in Mosul in 2003 were recounted in an interview with General David Petraeus (Ret.). Major General Stanley McChrystal's early impressions of Iraq as the commander of Joint Special Operations Command (JSOC) are detailed in his book *My Share of the Task*, and were shared with the author in an interview. Evolving counterterrorism operations behind Operation Striker Elton were explored in the author's firsthand reporting in "Building Up, Tearing Down," *National Journal*, March 27, 2004, and from follow-up interviews with General Martin Dempsey and Major General Ralph "Rob" Baker. The mishandling of the postinvasion aftermath in Iraq by the Pentagon and Coalition Provision Authority head L. Paul Bremer, and the dysfunctional relationship between the Defense and State Departments, are also from the author's firsthand reporting, notably in "The Generals' Case Against Donald Rumsfeld," *National Journal*, May 6, 2006. Events surrounding the twin Sunni and Shiite uprisings in Iraq in April of 2004 were described to the author in interviews with Generals Martin Dempsey, David Petraeus, Stanley McChrystal, John Kelly, and Rob Baker.

## Chapter Five: Martyrs' Den

Descriptions and figures of the badly deteriorating situation in Afghanistan in the 2006–2007 timeframe were taken from the author's firsthand reporting, much of it first appearing in "The Neglected Front," February 9, 2008, and "Backsliding," September 13, 2008, both in *National Journal*. Details about the car bombing outside the US Embassy in Kabul are from the Australian *Advertiser*, September 9, 2006, and from interviews with FBI legal attaché Brian McCauley. The relationship between the CIA and FBI in Kabul are from interviews with sources in both agencies. Details of the joint Kabul Counter-Improvised Explosive Device Initiative, the first extended joint Special Forces and FBI collaborative operation, are from interviews with the participants who received in 2015 the FBI Director's Award, the bureau's highest honor. An explanation of the budding operational relationship between the US military and the FBI in Afghanistan are from interviews with FBI special agents involved, and with General Dan McNeill, commander of the International Security Assistance Force (ISAF) in Afghanistan. The precipitous rise in suicide bombing in Afghanistan is detailed in a journal essay of the Middle East Policy Council, vol. 15, no. 4, dated Winter 2008, entitled "Mullah Omar's Missiles: A Field Report on Suicide Bombers in Afghanistan." The FBI's Behavioral Science Unit's groundbreaking work in interviewing and profiling would-be suicide bombers was described in an interview with the author by Special Agent Scott Stanley, one of the initiative's pioneers. The numbers and locations of radical madrassas and terrorist training camps in Pakistan's tribal areas are from Stanley McChrystal's *My Share of the Task*. The final operation taking down the suicide bombing cells run by the Dabazorai brothers was described in an interview with the author by Brian McCauley and his right-hand Afghan agent, "Mohammad," who was on-scene.

## Chapter Six: Five Assassins

The manhunt for Abu Musab al-Zarqawi and the other four assassins of American Nick Berg, including the evolution of Task Force 714's increasingly network-centric operations, was recounted in the author's interviews with former JSOC commander General Stanley McChrystal and JSOC intelligence chief Lieutenant General Mike Flynn, and with other members of the task force. Details are also from McChrystal's *My Share of the Task*. Events and trends pushing Iraq to the verge of all-out civil war were also examined in the author's cover story, "Endgame," *National Journal*, October 21, 2006. The increasingly close relationship between Delta Force and the FBI's Hostage Rescue Team is explored in "Inside the FBI's Secret Relationship with the Military's Special Operations,"

*Washington Post*, April 10, 2014. The collaboration of members of SEAL Team Six and Delta Force in the Western Euphrates campaign in Iraq is detailed in the book *No Easy Day: The Firsthand Account of the Mission That Killed Osama bin Laden*, by SEAL Team Six member Matt Bissonette, writing under the pen name Mark Owen; also from the author's interview with Owen. The transformation of JSOC's interrogation practices and intelligence-gathering focus is from an interview with intelligence head Lieutenant General Mike Flynn.

### Chapter Seven: Prodigal Soldiers

Description of Baghdad during the 2007 troop surge and Dagger Brigade's struggles to stabilize mixed Sunni-Shiite sections of Baghdad are from the author's firsthand reporting, including in "Baghdad Surged," *National Journal*, July 14, 2007. The unique roles of Generals David Petraeus, Martin Dempsey, and Stanley McChrystal in executing the new counterinsurgency strategy are from interviews with the author. The unprecedented civil-military bond developed between Petraeus and Ambassador to Iraq Ryan Crocker was also described in interviews both men conducted with the author. The role of the US Marines of Multi-National Force–West in the "Anbar Awakening" was recounted in the author's interview with General John Kelly (USMC). The role of General Martin Dempsey and the Multi-National Security and Transition Command–Iraq in building Iraqi security forces was explored in the author's firsthand reporting from Iraq, included in "The Thin Iraqi Line," and an interview with Dempsey published under the heading "More Art Than Science," both in the June 9, 2007, issue of *National Journal*. Joint Special Operations Command's role in conducting counterterrorism raids and manhunts as part of Petraeus' more holistic counterinsurgency campaign was recounted in interviews with Generals Petraeus, McChrystal, and Flynn. The key role of the National Security Agency in developing Real Time Regional Gateway to help locate terrorists in Iraq, and how that transformed the NSA's approach to global intelligence gathering, was recounted in the author's interview with former NSA Director General Keith Alexander, and detailed in the article "Advances in Computer, Software Paved Way for Government's Data Dragnet," *Wall Street Journal*, June 9, 2013. The circumstances surrounding the congressional testimony of Petraeus and Crocker is recounted in the author's article "Shifting Strategies," *National Journal*, September 15, 2007, and from interviews with both men.

### PART II

### Chapter Eight: Al-Qaeda Pandemic

The organic nature of terrorist networks as they mutated and evolved under US pressure are from the author's article on the Madrid train system bombing "Al

Qaeda's Pandemic," *National Journal*, September 2, 2006, which also examines the key roles that prisons and radical imams play in Islamic radicalization.

The resurgence of the Taliban, increase in suicide bombing, and rapidly deteriorating situation in Afghanistan in the 2007–2008 time frame are from the author's firsthand reporting, including in "The Neglected Front," *National Journal*, February 9, 2008, and in "Backsliding," *National Journal*, September 13, 2008. Figures on the success of the FBI-led Counter-IED Initiative in Afghanistan are from the FBI Director's Award.

The role of Mullah Dadullah as one of the unseen hands behind the increase in suicide bombing is recounted in *My Share of the Task*, and the manner of his death in a joint Special Forces operation is detailed in "Key Taliban Leader Is Killed in Afghanistan in Joint Operation," *New York Times*, May 14, 2007. The role the Iraq war and al-Qaeda in Iraq played in exporting suicide bombing to Afghanistan is examined by Brian Glyn Williams in the journal essay "Mullah Omar's Missiles: A Field Report on Suicide Bombers in Afghanistan," *Middle East Policy*, vol. 15, no. 4, Winter 2008.

The Taliban's first attack on the Serena Hotel in Kabul is detailed in "Haqqani Network Behind Kabul Hotel Attack," in the *Long War Journal*, January 15, 2008, and the FBI's response was recounted by then FBI legal attaché Brian McCauley in an interview with the author. The Taliban's subsequent attack on the Serena Hotel was reported in the *Guardian*, March 21, 2014, under the heading "Taliban Gunmen Kill Nine Civilians at Kabul's Serena Hotel." The FBI's interrogation of the surviving Serena Hotel attacker in 2008, and the role of the FBI's Behavioral Science Unit's profiling of would-be suicide bombers in future high-profile terrorist interrogations, was recounted by Special Agents Scott Stanley and Brian McCauley in interviews with the author.

The alleged corruption of a senior Afghan official was detailed in "Dirty Ali: The Gene Hunt of the Kabul CID [Criminal Investigative Department]," *Daily Mail*, November 22, 2008, and in interviews with FBI deputy assistant director for international operations Brian McCauley and with other intelligence sources. Ahmed Wali Karzai's suspected role in the drug trade and activities as a CIA informant is recounted in "Brother of Afghan Leader Said to be Paid by CIA," *New York Times*, October 27, 2009.

The case of Carlos Bledsoe, who launched the first deadly attack on US soil by an Islamic extremist after 9/11, draws on the author's firsthand reporting, much of which appeared in the article "Tennessee Is the Capital of American Jihad," *POLITICO Magazine*, July 23, 2015. Major primary sources include "Abdulhakim Mujahid Muhammad (Carlos Bledsoe): A Case Study in Lone Wolf Terrorism," by Daveed Gartenstein-Ross, a counterterrorism analyst and senior fellow at the Foundation for the Defense of Democracies whom the author interviewed; and "A Muslim Son, a Murder Trial and Many Questions,"

*New York Times*, February 16, 2010. The existence of terrorist training camps in Somalia was confirmed by US intelligence sources. The suspected role of the Olive Tree Foundation in Bledsoe's radicalization, and incendiary remarks by Sheikh Abdulhakim Ali Mohammed, are detailed in the documentary *Losing Our Sons*, produced by the Boston-based nonprofit Americans for Peace and Tolerance, and coproduced, directed, and written by A. R. Maezav and Ilya I. Feoktistov.

Details of Carlos Bledsoe's gradual radicalization are from the author's interview with his father and sister, Melvin and Monica Bledsoe. Bledsoe's further radicalization at the Dar al-Hadith Islamic seminary in Yemen was described to the author by Theo Padnos, who met Carlos Bledsoe there and described his experiences impersonating an Islamist in his book *Undercover Muslim*. The growing and increasingly central role of American Anwar al-Awlaki in radicalizing English-speaking extremists and homegrown terrorists is detailed in the author's article "The Enemy Within," *National Journal*, October 16, 2010. Al-Awlaki's connection to the 9/11 hijackers is detailed in "The 9/11 Commission Report." Carlos Bledsoe's letters from jail are cited in "A Case Study in Lone Wolf Terrorism," by Daveed Gartenstein-Ross. Details of Bledsoe's final days before committing an act of terrorism are from interviews with his family members. Figures on the growing threat of domestic radicalization and homegrown terrorists are from "Would-Be Warriors: Incidents of Jihadist Terrorist Radicalization in the United States Since September 11, 2001," RAND Corporation, 2010, by counterterrorism expert Brian Michael Jenkins.

## Chapter Nine: The Ghosts in the Network

The role of the NSA's PRISM program in revealing the plot of would-be New York subway bomber Najibullah Zazi was described in an interview with former NSA director General Keith Alexander, and with other intelligence sources. That role was also examined in "PRISM Stopped Najibullah Zazi from Blowing Up Backpacks in the Subway," *New York Magazine*, June 7, 2013. Al-Qaeda bomb maker Rashid Rauf's long pedigree in jihadi circles is explored in "Al Qaeda Operative Rashid Rauf Reported Killed in North Waziristan Strike," *The Long War Journal*, November 22, 2008, and in Rauf's biography at West Point's Combating Terrorism Center. The NSA's use of Section 215 of the USA PATRIOT Act to compel such private telecommunications companies as AT&T and Verizon to produce telephone metadata records that might assist in a terrorist investigation is examined in "AT&T Helped U.S. Spy on Internet on a Vast Scale," *New York Times*, August 15, 2015. The legal authorities behind the US government's electronic spying operations and Barack Obama's evolving view of those program are examined in the author's chapter "License to Spy: The USA PATRIOT Act," in the anthology *Triumphs & Tragedies of the Modern Congress*, published by the Center for the Study of the Presidency and Congress. Further details of Zazi's plot to bomb New York subways are examined in "Najibullah Zazi Pleads Guilty in New York Terrorism Plot," CNN, February 23, 2010.

General Keith Alexander's comparison of Real Time Regional Gateway and other NSA tools to the Enigma team that cracked the code of Nazi Germany during World War II is from an interview with the author, and from a May 2014 interview with the *New Yorker*. The description of the Air Force's 480th ISR Wing as the mother node in the United States' globe-spanning ISR network from the author's firsthand reporting and interviews with the wing and Air Combat Command commanders and ISR analysts, first appearing in "Airpower Comes of Age," *Air Force Magazine*, September 2015. The revolutionary ISR capability of the United States' rapidly expanding arsenal of unmanned aerial vehicles is from interviews with retired lieutenant general Dave Deptula, the Air Force's first deputy chief of staff for intelligence, surveillance and reconnaissance, and retired colonel James "Snake" Clark, director of Intelligence, Surveillance and Reconnaissance Innovation, headquarters US Air Force, Washington, DC.

The ability of the United States' global communication intercepts and ISR network to detect digital "patterns of life" and direct a hard stare almost anywhere on the globe, and the rapidly increasing body count resulting from the US targeted killing program, is examined in the author's feature articles "Wanted: Dead," January 9, 2010, and "Patterns of Death," March 10, 2012, both in *National Journal*. The precision of those targeted operations relative to other forms of warfare are from an interview with General Deptula. National Counterterrorism Center (NCTC) chief Michael Leiter's belief that the terrorist threat in 2010 was worse than at "any point since 9/11" was articulated in his September 22, 2010, testimony before the Senate Homeland Security and Government Affairs Committee. The NCTC's creation of "pursuit teams" to mimic JSOC's joint task forces was explained to the author by NCTC director Matthew Olsen, and was first reported in "Patterns of Death."

## Chapter Ten: The Forgotten War

The nearly year-long effort of the Obama administration and newly named US commander in Afghanistan General Stanley McChrystal and his team to reach consensus on a troop surge and strategy for the way forward is detailed in the author's firsthand reporting in the feature articles "It's Obama's War Now," October 17, 2009, and "New Lease on a Long War," December 5, 2009, in *National Journal*. The disagreement between McChrystal and General David Petraeus over direct command of Marine Corps and Special Forces in Afghanistan is from sources familiar with the exchange. McChrystal's unease over the controversies that arose from the strategic review were recounted in an interview with the author. The Taliban's resurgence and willingness to take on NATO forces in frontal engagements were detailed in the author's firsthand reporting and in *My Share of the Task*. Mike Flynn reorganization of the NATO intelligence structure in Afghanistan as the director of intelligence, and his conclusion that allied forces had overemphasized man-hunting over stability operations, were recounted in interviews with the author. Those concerns were detailed in a report Major General Flynn coauthored, "Fixing Intel: A Blueprint for Making Intelligence Relevant in Afghanistan," January 2010, Center for a New American Security. General David Petraeus's frustrations with the debate in the White House over McChrystal's counterinsurgency strategy was recounted in an interview with the author. The Village Stability initiative launched by US Special Forces in Afghanistan is detailed in "Village Stability Operations: More Than Village Defense," in the July-September issue of *Special Warfare*, a publication of the US Army's JFK Special Warfare Center. The Afghan Hands program was explained by Mike Flynn in an interview with the author, and mentioned in "My Share of the Task." Circumstances surrounding *Rolling Stone's* publication of "Runaway General," and General Stanley McChrystal's subsequent firing, were detailed in the author's article "A Warrior Undone," *National Journal*, June 26, 2010, and explained in interviews with McChrystal and Flynn.

### Chapter Eleven: American Jihad

The resurgence of bureaucratic infighting as the wars in Iraq and Afghanistan wound down and intelligence and law enforcement agencies in Washington, DC, retreated back to their respective corners in a fight for increasingly scarce resources was recounted in interviews with multiple sources within the Intelligence and Special Forces Communities, to include the FBI, CIA, and JSOC. The growth of homegrown terrorism that accelerated the FBI's transformation from a post facto criminal investigative service to a domestic intelligence agency focused on preempting acts of terrorism was examined in the author's feature article "American Jihad," *National Journal*, January 29, 2011. The FBI's successful use of informants in elaborate "stings" of would-be terrorists that produced a conviction rate of over 90 percent is revealed in the "Terrorist Trial Report Card," New York University Law School's Center on Law and Security.

### Chapter Twelve: Retribution

The successful raid on Osama bin Laden's compound in Abbottabad, Pakistan, is informed by a host of reporting and recollections of the operation, to include

"The Hunt for 'Geronimo,'" by Mark Bowden, *Vanity Fair*, October 12, 2012; Navy SEAL Robert O'Neill, who shot bin Laden, in an interview with Fox Network's Sean Hannity, November 14, 2014; and the book *No Easy Day: The Firsthand Account of the Mission That Killed Osama Bin Laden*, by Navy SEAL Matt Bissonette, writing under the pen name Mark Owen. Bissonette elaborated on the operation in an interview with the author published under the heading "Did the SEALS on the Osama bin Laden Raid Break Their Code of Silence for Fame and Fortune?" *National Journal*, November 13, 2014.

Director of National Intelligence James Clapper's recollections of Operation Neptune Spear, and what it revealed about the successful integration and fusion of multiple streams of intelligence, are from an interview with the author. Historical information about the creation of Delta Force and the botched 1980 raid to rescue American hostages held by Iran are from the author's interview with original Delta Force commander Colonel Charlie Beckwith, for "Third World Wars," *Military Forum*, 1988. Intelligence gathered at Bin Laden's complex indicating the archterrorist never stopped plotting to strike another major blow on the United States was reported by CNN counterterrorism expert Peter Bergen in "Secrets of the Bin Laden Treasure-Trove," May 20, 2015.

The desire of President Barack Obama's inner circle to use bin Laden's death to close the chapter on the "global war on terrorism" as the central organizing principle in US foreign policy, and the interview with Deputy National Security Adviser Ben Rhodes, are examined in the author's feature "The 'War on Terror' Is Over," *National Journal*, May 7, 2011. The Obama administration's determination to decisively turn the page on the "war on terrorism," and the difficulty of doing so, are explored in the author's cover story "Republic of Fear," *National Journal*, April 28, 2012.

## PART III

### Chapter Thirteen: Retrenchment

Chairman of the Joint Chiefs Martin Dempsey's disagreement with the White House over the decision to withdraw all US troops from Iraq in 2011 was recounted in an interview with the author. The critical role that US commanders played as connective tissue between Sunni tribes and the Shiite-dominated government in Baghdad, and as referees in stopping Iraqi politicians from having undue influence over leaders of the Iraqi security forces, are examined in the author's firsthand reporting from Baghdad in "Breaking with History," *National Journal*, March 13, 2010.

The risks of the Obama administration's decision to embrace democratic movements as part of the Arab Spring, as the Bush administration had unsuccessfully tried in 2005, is explored in the author's features "Ghosts of the Arab

Spring," February 12, 2011, and "Dynamic Instability," March 5, 2011, both in *National Journal*. Defense Secretary Robert Gates's surprise decision to promote Dempsey to chairman of the Joint Chiefs was recounted by Dempsey in an interview with the author. The United States' dismal record of managing postwar military drawdowns, and the devastating impact of Washington's partisan political dysfunction on military readiness, are examined in the author's feature "The Interwar Years," *National Journal*, July 28, 2012.

The extraordinary physical and psychological toll that more than a decade of war had exacted on the all-volunteer force is investigated in the author's feature "The Reckoning," *National Journal*, September 10, 2011. The phenomenon of "moral injury" and the part it plays in numerous scandals in the uniformed ranks is described in the author's article "Moral Injury," *National Journal*, December 8, 2012. Army chief of staff General Ray Odierno's determination to build on the close bonds between conventional and Special Forces forged in Iraq and Afghanistan were described in an interview with the author. The United States' perceived retrenchment after a decade of war, and the degree to which adversaries were exploiting the resulting vacuum of power, are examined in the author's feature "Power Down," *National Journal*, November 19, 2011.

### Chapter Fourteen: Shadow War

Observations of US Africa Command's East Africa Campaign against the al-Qaeda affiliate al-Shabab in Somalia are from the author's firsthand reporting in Africa, to include multiple interviews with Major General Ralph "Rob" Baker, commander of Combined Joint Task Force–Horn of Africa, and his senior staff; travels to US training facilities in Tanzania and Kenya; and a rare reporter's visit to Camp Simba in northern Kenya, where US Special Forces train and assist Kenyan military forces before they deploy to Somalia as part of the AMISOM (African Union Mission in Somalia) peacekeeping force. Much of that reporting appeared originally in the feature "Leading from the Shadows," *National Journal*, March 9, 2013. The comments from Johnnie Carson, assistant secretary of state for African affairs, were delivered at the Wilson Center on January 17, 2013. The fracturing of al-Shabab's leadership under relentless US pressure is substantiated in numerous reports, and summarized in "Succession in Somalia: al-Shabaab After Godane," the Atlantic Council, September 4, 2014.

### Chapter Fifteen: The Enemy Votes

Descriptions and eye witness accounts of al-Shabab's massacre at the Westgate shopping mall in Nairobi, Kenya, are included in the excellent 2014 HBO documentary film *Terror at the Mall*, directed by British Emmy Award nominee Dan

Reed. The role of the FBI Rapid Deployment Team in investigating the terrorist attack was explained in interviews with Brian McCauley, deputy assistant director for international operations, and Special Agent Richard Frankel, who headed the deployment team. The process by which that intelligence was integrated into the National Counterterrorism Center's (NCTC) threat matrix and elevated to the Presidential Daily Brief was described in the author's interview with NCTC director Mathew Olsen and his top staff.

Descriptions of JSOC's raid on an al-Shabab leadership compound involving Navy SEALs, including eyewitness accounts, are from the British newspaper the *Guardian*'s article "How the US Raid on al-Shabaab in Somalia Went Wrong," October 9, 2013, and in the Associated Press account, "Navy SEALs fail in assault on Kenya Attack Terrorist," October 6, 2013. Delta Force's capture of al-Qaeda operative Abu Anas al-Libi in Tripoli, Libya, was captured by a security camera and can be viewed on YouTube. The participation of members of the FBI's Hostage Rescue Team in both Special Forces raids was revealed in "Inside the FBI's Secret Relationship with the Military's Special Operations," *Washington Post*, April 10, 2014. How the twin raids revealed the contours of a new model of US counterterrorism operations was examined in the author's cover story "Twilight Warriors," *National Journal*, May 17, 2014, and article "5 Takeaways from the U.S. Special Ops Raids in Somalia and Libya," *Defense One*, October 8, 2013. Details of the interrogation of Abu Anas al-Libi aboard the USS *San Antonio* by a high-value detainee interrogation group (HIG), another multiagency hybrid manned by senior military, intelligence, and law enforcement officials, was described to the author by knowledgeable intelligence sources.

## Chapter Sixteen: Reflection in a Broken Mirror

President Barack Obama's seminal speech on the terrorism threat was given at the National Defense University on May 23, 2013. DIA director Mike Flynn's rejection of a National Security Council assessment that al-Qaeda was no longer a threat to the United States was reported in the article "'Over My Dead Body': Spies Fight Obama Push to Downsize Terror War," *Daily Beast*, May 21, 2014. The assessment of a growing threat from proliferating Islamic extremist groups and other nonstate actors from DIA briefings, and from interviews with DIA director Mike Flynn, including his last official interview in office, given to the author and appearing under the headline "Flynn's Last Interview: Iconoclast Departs DIA with a Warning," *Breaking Defense*, August 7, 2014. The circumstances of ISIS leader Abu Bakr al-Baghdadi's release from a US detention center were investigated in "Setting the Record Straight: When Did U.S. Free Islamic State Leader?" *Punditfact, Tampa Bay Times*, December 31, 2014.

## Chapter Eighteen: Twilight Warriors

Details behind al-Qaeda in the Islamic Maghreb's attack on the Amenas gas plant in Algeria are from various news accounts, notably *The Guardian's* in-depth "The Hostage Crisis: The Full Story of the Kidnapping in the Desert," January 25, 2013, and the PBS documentary *Held Hostage*, first aired on October 22, 2013. The FBI's role as a conduit between the US counter-terrorism network and the private oil and gas industry was gleaned from interviews with FBI International Division chief Brian McCauley. The informal public-private partnership between US intelligence and security officials and oil and gas executives, and its critical role in the response to the hijacking of the *Morning Glory*, were described in interviews with McCauley and DIA director Mike Flynn, and discussions with oil company executives involved in the initiative. Details about the recapture of the ship by a JSOC SEAL team are from an e-mail stream supplied to the author by various participants in the drama, and from various news reports, including "SEAL Team Raids a Tanker and Thwarts a Militia's Bid to Sell Libyan Oil," the *New York Times*, March 17, 2014, and "SEALs Seize Ship from Libyan Rebels," *POLITICO Magazine*, March 17, 2014.

The growing overlap between the "global war on terrorism" and the drug trade, and the growing threat of narcoterrorism, is revealed in the author's first-hand reporting and interviews with General John Kelly, commander of US Southern Command, and his senior staff of military, law enforcement, and intelligence officials, much of it originally appearing in the article "Confronting the Narcoterrorism Nexus," *Yahoo! News*, August 6, 2015. Mexico's costly fight with drug cartels and the rise of hyperviolent groups such as Las Zetas, are examined in the author's article "Fighting the Shadow State," *National Journal*, July 14, 2012. Iran's plot to hire assassins from a Mexican drug cartel to murder Saudi Arabia's ambassador to the United States was detailed in "Man Sentenced in Plot to Kill Saudi Ambassador," the *New York Times*, May 30, 2013. The investigations of cases that reveal the intersection of drug trafficking and terrorism were recounted in the author's interview with Special Agent Derek Maltz, chief of the DEA's Special Operations Division, and detailed in the DEA publication "Combating Transnational Organized Crime," Counter-Narcoterrorism Operations Center, November 21, 2013.

## Chapter Nineteen: Going Dark

President Barack Obama's angry reaction to news that NSA contractor Edward Snowden had stolen and planned to reveal sensitive US intelligence techniques and procedures, and the intelligence community's reaction to those revelations, was recounted by Director of National Intelligence James Clapper in an interview with the author. The phenomenon of US intelligence surveillance and threat radar screens' "going dark" after the Snowden revelations, as targets of surveillance adjusted their field craft and communications protocols, was described in interviews with DNI Clapper, former NSA chief Keith Alexander, DIA chief Mike Flynn, and FBI international division chief Brian McCauley, and other intelligence sources. That phenomenon was reported by the author in "U.S. Flying Blind to Looming Terror Plots," *Breaking Defense*, July 17, 2014. The Institute for Economics and Peace's Global Terrorism Index revealed that the number of people killed by terrorists increased 80 percent in 2014 to 32,658 victims (see "Terrorist Killings up by 80% in 2014, Fueling Flow of refugees, Report Says," *The Guardian*, November 17, 2015). The true nature of the Islamic State's juggernaut offensive in Iraq in June 2014 was first reported by the author in "Iraq's 'Sunni War of Liberation,'" *Yahoo! News*, June 23, 2014. Events surrounding the early retirement of Mike Flynn as director of the Defense Intelligence Agency are from interviews with the author, including "Flynn's Last Interview: Iconoclast Departs DIA with a Warning," *Breaking Defense*, August 7, 2014.

## Chapter 20: A World on Edge

Events surrounding the last official overseas trip of General Martin Dempsey as chairman of the Joint Chiefs of Staff are recounted from the author's firsthand reporting of the trip and interviews with the chairman, some of which appeared in "Martin Dempsey's World Is Falling Apart," *POLITICO Magazine*, September 26, 2015. The Joint Chiefs' great reluctance to commit US forces to fight ISIS on the ground lacking reliable partners in the region or political will in Washington; their disagreements with the White House about pulling all US troops out of Iraq in 2011; and their advice to freeze troop withdrawals from Afghanistan and reintroduce troops to Iraq were recounted by Dempsey in an interview exclusive to this book.

## Epilogue

The aeromedical evacuation of the wounded from Afghanistan and Iraq are detailed in the author's article "Ambulance In the Air," *National Journal*, May 29, 2010. The physical, psychological, and moral toll more than a decade of war exacted on the all-volunteer force is similarly explored in the author's articles "The Reckoning," September 10, 2011, and "Moral Injury," December 8, 2012, in *National Journal.* Navy SEAL Matt Bissonette expressed the sense of loss that kept him from deleting the phone numbers of forty fallen brothers-in-arms in an interview with the author. General John Kelly's moving speech to Gold Star families who have lost loved ones in the wars in Iraq and Afghanistan can be found on YouTube. The description of FBI special agent Brian McCauley's retirement, and Stanley McChrystal's advice to his students at Yale University, are from the author's firsthand reporting.

# Index

Rob Baker

**JAMES KITFIELD** is a senior fellow at the Center for the Study of the Presidency and Congress. He has covered national security issues for more than two decades as a senior correspondent for *National Journal* and is a three-time winner of the Gerald R. Ford Prize for Distinguished Reporting on National Defense. Kitfield lives in Alexandria, Virginia.